THE GOOD
FOOD GUIDE
LONDON

which?

"A man who can dominate a London dinner table can dominate the world."

Oscar Wilde, 1854–1900

Distributed by Littlehampton Book Services Ltd
Faraday Close, Durrington, Worthing, West Sussex BN13 3RB

Base mapping by Cosmographics
Printed and bound by VivaPress

A catalogue record for this book is available from the British Library

ISBN: 978 1 84490 052 7

Consultant Editor: Elizabeth Carter
Senior Project Editor: Caroline Blake

The Good Food Guide makes every effort to be as accurate and up-to-date as
possible. All *Good Food Guide* inspections are anonymous but every main entry
has been contacted separately for details. We have very strict guidelines for fact-
checking information ahead of going to press, so some restaurants were dropped
if they failed to provide the information we required. Readers should still check
details at the time of booking, particularly if they have any special requirements.

Please send updates, queries, menus and wine lists to:
goodfoodguide@which.co.uk or 2 Marylebone Road, London, NW1 4DF.

For a full list of Which? books, please call 01903 828557, access our website at
www.which.co.uk, or write to Littlehampton Book Services. For other
enquiries call 0800 252100.

Arctic Volume White is an elemental chlorine-free paper produced at Arctic
Paper Hafrestroms AB in Asenbruk, Sweden, using timber from sustainably
managed forests. The mill is ISO14001 and EMAS certified, and has PEFC
and FSC certified Chain of Custody.

CONTENTS

Welcome

Welcome to *The Good Food Guide London*. After 56 years as Britain's leading restaurant guide, *The Good Food Guide* is taking the best elements of the redesigned UK Guide to champion the London restaurant scene. What took us so long? Well, this is not the first *Good Food Guide* to London – Raymond Postgate brought out a London edition in 1969. In those days, old-school French and Italian cooking dominated, ethnic food was just a handful of Indian and Chinese places, and the Guide contained reviews of the likes of the Playboy Club and Danny La Rue's nightclub in Hanover Square (under the heading 'Dancing to Pop Music'). Postgate's guide was ahead of its time; reading it today shows how far the London eating out scene has come.

It was another two decades before there was a shift in culinary direction. The then editor of the *Good Food Guide*, Drew Smith, coined the term 'Modern British Cooking', and the Guide effectively launched the movement that has changed the shape of British cooking today. Today, London is buzzing with new ideas, new influences, and an astonishing diversity of cuisines, unmatched by any other capital city.

Indeed, in the past year, we could barely keep up with the many, high-profile London openings. It was also the year that we launched the new-look *Good Food Guide 2008*. Such has been the success of the UK-wide Guide, it was felt timely for the *Good Food Guide* team to explore the full range of London eateries, from ethnic cuisines via gastropubs to the latest openings by world-class chefs. With a useful cuisine and tube index, all of our entries come with the same *Good Food Guide* guarantee: our independence, incisive writing and grading system remain the same. Just to reiterate – unlike other guides, we don't accept sponsorship, advertising or free meals. All entries are based on genuine reader feedback and all of our reviewers conduct their inspections anonymously.

In the end a good restaurant is one where you choose to go back a second time. We hope this London edition leads you to many such places.

Elizabeth Carter

Consultant Editor

Introduction

Raymond Postgate's assertion that, *'You can corrupt one man. You can't bribe an army'* remains as true today as it was in 1951. Although much has changed since he published the first edition of the Guide in 1951 – both in terms of restaurants and publishing – the ethos of the original book remains. *The Good Food Guide* empowers diners, helping readers to find great places to eat, and encouraging restaurants to supply the best possible food, service and experience. And all of the content – every single entry – is based on a completely impartial assessment.

The Good Food Guide London only reports on the top establishments in the capital, from à la carte and fine dining to bistros, pubs and ethnic cuisines. The Guide accepts no advertising or sponsorship. Critically, all of our inspectors are anonymous. And, unlike some other guides, restaurants cannot pay for inclusion in the book.

We encourage all of our readers to submit their reviews using the feedback address below. These reader submissions provide the basic list of restaurants for possible inclusion. We reject hundreds of restaurants before we compile our final inclusion list. To score even 1/10 in the *Good Food Guide* is a real achievement. Every successful entry is based on a mixture of independent, expert inspection and reader feedback. *The Good Food Guide* does not accept any kind of advertising.

If you'd like to make a recommendation for the next edition of the Guide, please log on to: www.which.co.uk/gfgfeedback.

We collect, read and count every bit of feedback – so we may well use some of your recommendations in next year's edition of the Guide.

How to use the Guide

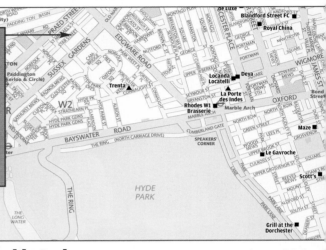

Organised by Central, North, East, South and West London, the Guide is fast and easy to navigate. The header page of each section shows its relevant areas.

▌Marble Arch

Locanda Locatelli

A peerless reputation for seasonal food

8 Seymour Street, W1H 7JZ
Tel no: (020) 7935 9088
www.locandolocatelli.com
⊖ **Marble Arch**
Italian | £56
Cooking score: 6

Locanda Locatelli is smartly swanky, with plenty of wood, leather and spotlights. It can be difficult to book a table here, and with good reason as the Guide receives a steady stream of praise for Giorgio Locatelli's true Italian cuisine and the restaurant's excellent service. Although Locatelli could be described as a celebrity chef, his reputation was built and continues to be maintained in the kitchen (using the finest ingredients) and he delivers a menu that is laid out along traditional Italian lines. After antipasti, start with perfectly cooked, fresh linguine with delicate langoustines, garlic and sweet chilli in a tomato sauce, say, or with pappardelle, broad beans and fresh peppery rocket. At inspection, a main course of chargrilled rolled pork was bursting with fresh herbs and came with meat jus and deep-fried courgettes in batter, while a dish of grilled tuna with rocket salad and tomatoes, simply served with a wedge of lemon, showed off the freshness and quality of the raw materials. A chocolate tasting dessert, including everything from parfait to ice cream, gave Amadei chocolate the attention it deserves, while a perfect vanilla pannacotta with berries, red fruit sauce and stracciatella (chocolate chip) ice cream on a biscuit base also hit the spot. The wine list is all-Italian, apart from champagne. Whites and reds are arranged by region, and feature well-known growers such as Gaia and Antinori. There is a good range of wines by the glass, priced from £3.50 to £18.

Chef: Giorgio Locatelli **Opening hours:** all week 12 to 3 (3.30 Sun), 7 to 11 (11.30 Fri and Sat, 10 Sun) **Closed:** bank hols **Meals:** alc (main courses £12 to £29.50) **Service:** not inc **Details:** Air con. No mobile phones. 70 seats. Wheelchair access. Music. Children's portions. Cards accepted.

Cuisine, price, score and symbols are quick to find

★ NEW ENTRY ★

Rhodes W1 Brasserie
Best-of-British brasserie
Cumberland Hotel
Great Cumberland Place, W1A 4RS
Tel no: (020) 7479 3838
www.garyrhodes.com
⊖ **Marble Arch**
Modern British | £23
Cooking score: 3

V ⓥ₃₀

The Gary Rhodes-accented dishes are exactly what you would expect from this longstanding TV chef. The vibrant, unfussy modern British cooking with a European twist here and there delivering the likes of beautifully presented mackerel rillette on soft potato with dill, spring onion and a radish salad. There's a tempting grill section for mains, offering a variety of fish or steaks, such as the thick slab of hake smothered in Montpellier butter tried at inspection, otherwise there could be calf's liver in a rich gravy with a side of smooth and very moreish mash. A tangy lemon curd tart was flawless; brilliantly matched by a scoop of cocoa sorbet. Friendly, efficient staff lift the experience, although the dimly lit surrounds (plush red velvet banquettes and dark wood tables) give the place a nightclub feel and the music from the adjacent bar can get loud, which might not be to everyone's taste. A surprisingly reasonable and concise wine list starts at £3.50 a glass and £16.00 for a bottle.
Chef: Gary Rhodes **Opening hours:** Daily, L 12 to 2.30, D 6 to 10.30 **Meals:** alc main courses £13 to £22 **Details:** Separate bar. 142 seats. Wheelchair access. Music. Children allowed. Cards accepted.

READERS RECOMMEND

Trenta
Italian
30 Connaught Street, Marble Arch, W2 2AF
Tel no: (020) 7262 9623
'An intimate scene for accomplished cooking'

ALSO RECOMMENDED

▲ La Porte des Indes
32 Bryanston Street
W1H 7EG
Tel no: (020) 7224 0055
⊖ **Leicester Square**
Exotic and evocative, with dark red, wooden floors, spectacular flower arrangements and a cascading waterfall, this is perhaps the grandest setting of all London's Indian restaurants. Conventional dishes such as a classic chicken tandoori (£11.90) and pork vindaloo (£12.90) share the billing with colonial French (Creole) inspired dishes, including a starter of parsee fish (sole fillets encased in a mint and coriander chutney and lightly steamed in banana leaves, £9.50). Good house menus plus global wines from £18. Closed Sat L.

Heston Blumenthal

Why did you become a chef?
Aged 16, my father took us to the restaurant l'Oustau de Baumaniere in Provence. I was captivated by the whole dining experience.

Do you have a favourite local recipe?
Eton Mess, a dessert we serve at the Hinds Head, from our local Eton College tuck shop.

What's your guilty food pleasure?
Tomato ketchup.

If you could only eat one more thing, what would it be?
A menu I discovered recently from the court of King James, comprising of 174 courses.

Scoring

We should begin by saying that a score of 1 is actually a significant achievement. We reject many restaurants during the compilation of the Guide. Obviously, there are always subjective aspects to rating systems, but our inspectors are equipped with extensive scoring guidelines, so that restaurant bench-marking is accurate. We also take into account the reader feedback that we receive for each restaurant, so that any given review is based on several meals.

1/10   Capable cooking, with simple food combinations and clear flavours, but some inconsistencies.

2/10   Decent cooking, displaying good basic technical skills and interesting combinations and flavours. Occasional inconsistencies.

3/10   Good cooking, showing sound technical skills and using quality ingredients.

4/10   Dedicated, focused approach to cooking; good classical skills and high-quality ingredients.

5/10   Exact cooking techniques and a degree of ambition; balance and depth of flavour in dishes, using quality ingredients.

6/10   Exemplary cooking skills, innovative ideas, impeccable ingredients and an element of excitement.

7/10   High level of ambition and individuality, attention to the smallest detail, accurate and vibrant dishes.

8/10   A kitchen cooking close to or at the top of its game – highly individual, showing faultless technique and impressive artistry in dishes that are perfectly balanced for flavour, combination and texture. There is little room for disappointment here.

9/10   At the moment, this is the highest mark in the Guide and it is not given lightly. This mark is for cooking that has reached a pinnacle of achievement, making it a memorable experience for the diner.

10/10   While it is extremely rare that a restaurant can achieve perfect dishes on a consistent basis (chefs are only human, after all), we live in hope.

Symbols

Restaurants that may be given main entry status are contacted ahead of publication and asked to provide key information about their opening hours and facilities. They are also invited to participate in the free glass of wine voucher scheme. The symbols on these entries are therefore based on this feedback from restaurants, and are intended for quick, at-a-glance identification. The wine bottle symbol, however, is an accolade assigned by the Guide's team, based on their judgement of the wine list available.

Accommodation is available.

£30   It is possible to have three courses at the restaurant for less than £30.

V   There are more than five vegetarian dishes available on the menu.

The restaurant is participating in our free-glass-of-wine scheme. (Please see the vouchers at the end of the book for terms and conditions.)

The restaurant has a wine list that our inspector and wine expert have deemed to be exceptional.

£XX   This year, we have aligned the pricing for each restaurant in the book with our online feedback system. The price indicated on each review represents the average price of a three-course dinner, excluding wine.

Vote for your favourite restaurant

THE GOOD
FOOD GUIDE
2009

The best restaurants in the UK reviewed by which

The Good Food Guide Restaurant of the Year award will recognise excellence and good service at restaurants, pubs and cafés throughout the UK.

Members of the public are invited to nominate their favourite, independently owned establishment – preferably one that offers regional dishes and/or uses local produce.

Ten regional award winners will be identified, and will feature in the 2009 edition of *The Good Food Guide*. The overall winner of the Restaurant of the Year Award will be chosen by a panel of experts, led by the editors of the Guide.

All voters will be entered into a prize draw to win a meal for two at the winning restaurant in their region.

Nominations are invited from 3rd March 2008 until 23rd May 2008. We will then reveal our ten regional winners, to be followed by the announcement of an overall national winner at the annual Which? Awards ceremony at the British Museum on 17th June.

How to vote

There are three methods of voting – via text, through our website or by mail.

By text

Text GFG, followed by the name and town/county of the restaurant, to 62233 (standard network rates apply).

Online

Register your vote at www.which.co.uk/gfgfeedback

By post

Send us a postcard, which can be found in restaurants around the UK, or can be downloaded via our website: www.which.co.uk/gfgpostcard.

For terms and conditions of the prize draw, please see: www.which.co.uk

London award winners

Best new restaurant
Sake No Hana, Mayfair

Best set menu
Wild Honey, Mayfair

Best wine list
The Square, Mayfair

Best for breakfast
Roast, London Bridge

Best value for money
Tom Ilic, Battersea

Best vegetarian restaurant
Manna, Primrose Hill

Best up-and-coming chef
Tristan Mason, Orrery, Marylebone

Best fish restaurant
One-O-One, Knightsbridge

Best gastropub
Carpenter's Arms, Hammersmith

Best budget restaurant
Viet Grill, Shoreditch

Top 40 London restaurants

1. Gordon Ramsay, Royal Hospital Road (9)
2. Le Gavroche (8)
3. Pétrus (8)
4. Square (8)
5. Pied à Terre (8)
6. Tom Aikens (8)
7. The Capital (7)
8. Maze (6)
9. Club Gascon (6)
10. The Greenhouse (6)
11. The Ledbury (6)
12. Hakkasan (6)
13. Wild Honey (6)
14. La Trompette (6)
15. Galvin at Windows (6)
16. Arbutus (6)
17. Bacchus (6)
18. Theo Randall at the InterContinental (6)
19. Chez Bruce (6)
20. L'Atelier Joël Robuchon (6)
21. St John (6)
22. Rousillon (6)
23. River Café (6)
24. Lindsay House (6)
25. Zafferano(6)
26. Sketch (6)
27. Locanda Locatelli (6)
28. Bonds (6)
29. Galvin Bistrot de Luxe (5)
30. Sake No Hana (5)
31. Café Anglais (5)
32. L'Autre Pied (5)
33. One-O-One (5)
34. Zuma (5)
35. Gordon Ramsay at Claridges (5)
36. Rasoi Vineet Bhatia (5)
37. Hibiscus (5)
38. Orrery (5)
39. Glasshouse (5)
40. Le Cercle (5)

Notable wine lists

Almeida
Andrew Edmunds
Aubergine
Bacchus
Bentley's
Bibendum
Bleeding Heart
Bonds
Bradleys
Cafè du Jardin
Cambio de Tercio
The Capital
Le Cercle
Chez Bruce
Club Gascon
The Don
Enoteca Turi
Eyre Brothers

Fifth Floor
Le Gavroche
Glasshouse
Gordon Ramsay at
 Claridge's
Gordon Ramsay,
 Royal Hospital Road
Greenhouse
Greyhound
Hakkasan
Kensington Place
Ledbury
L'Etranger
Lindsay House
Locanda Locatelli
Maze
Metrogusto
Odette's

Orrery
Pearl
Pètrus
Pied-á-Terre
Le Pont de la Tour
Ransome's Dock
Rasoi Vineet Bhatia
Restaurant Semplice
Roussillon
RSJ
Square
Tate Britain Restaurant
Tom Aikens
La Trompette
Umu
Wolseley
Zuma

Wine voucher scheme

Al Hamra, Green Park
Angelus, Lancaster Gate
Arancia, Bermondsey
Bacchus, Shoreditch
La Buvette, Richmond
Champor-Champor, London Bridge
Chowki, Soho
Coach and Horses, Clerkenwell
Ebury Wine Bar, Victoria
Eyre Brothers, Shoreditch
Fish Hook, Chiswick
Flâneur, Clerkenwell
Franklins, Dulwich
The Gate, Hammersmith
Harrison's, Balham
Inside, Greenwich

Istanbul Iskembecisi, Stoke Newington
Kiasu, Bayswater
Kiku, Mayfair
Light House, Wimbledon
The Lock Dining Bar, Tottenham Hale
Metrogusto, Islington
Mint Leaf, Piccadilly
La Saveur, East Sheen
Tamarind, Mayfair
Theo Randall at the InterContinental,
Mayfair
Thomas Cubitt, Victoria
Victoria, Richmond
Village East, Bermondsey
Wapping Food, Wapping
Yakitoria, Paddington

Please see back of the book for vouchers. Relevant terms and conditions are printed on the back of each voucher.

Getting about town

Getting to London

From the airport

London has good transport links to five international airports – Heathrow, City, Gatwick, Stansted and Luton. If you're flying into Heathrow there are three rail services you can take. Heathrow Express runs direct from all airport terminals to London Paddington (journey time approx 15 mins), Heathrow Connect is a stopping service from all airport terminals to London Paddington (journey time approx 25 mins) and the Piccadilly line of the London Underground takes approx 1 hour. For drivers, the M4 motorway is the fastest route from Heathrow to London. City airport is served by the Docklands Light Railway which connects directly with Bank station on the Central line (overall journey time into central London approx 35 mins). Gatwick airport is situated to the south of London and the quickest route into the city is the Gatwick Express, from the airport to London Victoria rail station takes around 30 minutes. The fastest routes by road are the M23 and M25 motorways. From Stansted take the Stansted Express rail service into London Liverpool Street (journey time approx 45 mins). Finally, if you're travelling from Luton, the First Capital Connect rail service runs from Luton Airport Parkway station (accessible by shuttle bus from the terminal building) into London St Pancras International.

By train

The Eurostar terminal station London St Pancras International has good Underground links – Victoria, Hammersmith and City, Piccadilly, Circle Metropolitan line and Northern lines all stop at St Pancras.

Getting around London

The tube

Although sometimes crowded, the tube is a relatively cheap and easy way to travel through and around London. However, it's not 24-hour and is usually closed between midnight and 5 am Monday to Saturday.

Tube zones

The tube network is dived into 6 roughly-concentric zones, Zone 1 being central (including the main visitor attractions such as the West End, Oxford and Regent Street, Buckingham Palace and the London Eye). The cost of a single trip within Zone 1 is £4 for adults, £2 for children. However, travelling on an Oyster card, rather than a paper ticket, is much cheaper. The Oyster card is a reusable plastic card that can be credited online or at any London Underground station. You pay a £3 deposit for the card which can then be topped-up for immediate use (a single trip within Zone 1 is £1.50 for adults, 50p for children). Oyster cards can also be used on London buses and the Docklands Light Railway and can be obtained at all Underground stations.

Buses and taxis

London's red buses and black cabs are as iconic as Big Ben or St Paul's Cathedral and make for a good alternative to the sometimes crowded tube. A single journey on London buses costs a flat fee of £1 with Oyster, or £2 cash. Trafalgar Square is the central hub for London's night buses, if you are travelling outside of the Tube's operating hours (see above). A more expensive, but nonetheless reliable, method of transport is the ubiquitous black cab. Prices vary but an average 2 mile trip in central London can cost between £6.60 and £9. It's important to only use licensed taxis – avoid unlicensed minicabs at all costs.

Other ways around

Walking around London is great for those wanting a less-frenetic or greener option to buses or taxis. London has a handful of designated routes and the most popular are The London Loop, The Thames Path (Hampton Court to the Thames Barrier) and the Jubilee Walkway. Routes can be downloaded from the Transport for London website (see below). If messing around on the river is your thing, sightseeing boats and clippers run to and from Embankment and the Woolwich Ferry Terminal in the south of the capital.

Useful websites

www.heathrowairport.com
www.gatwickairport.com
www.stanstedairport.com
www.stpancras.com
www.tfl.gov.uk
www.visitlondon.com

GFG recommends

Central London hotels with GFG recommendations include Rhode's W1 Brasserie, Galvin at Windows and Theo Randall at the InterContinental.

MAPS

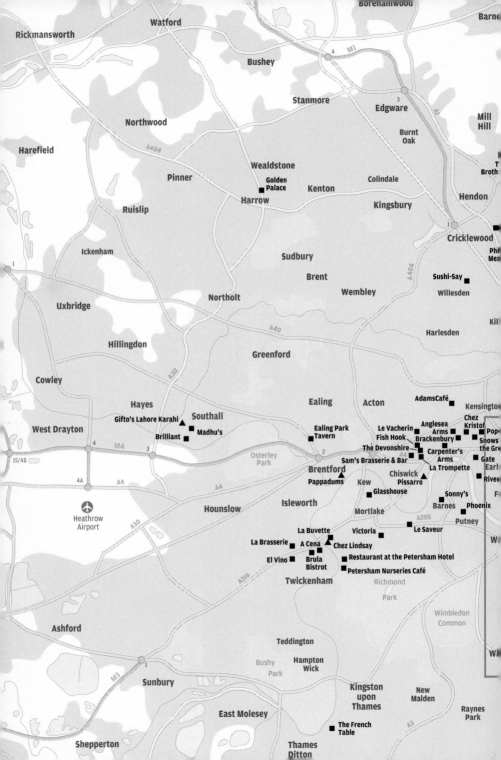

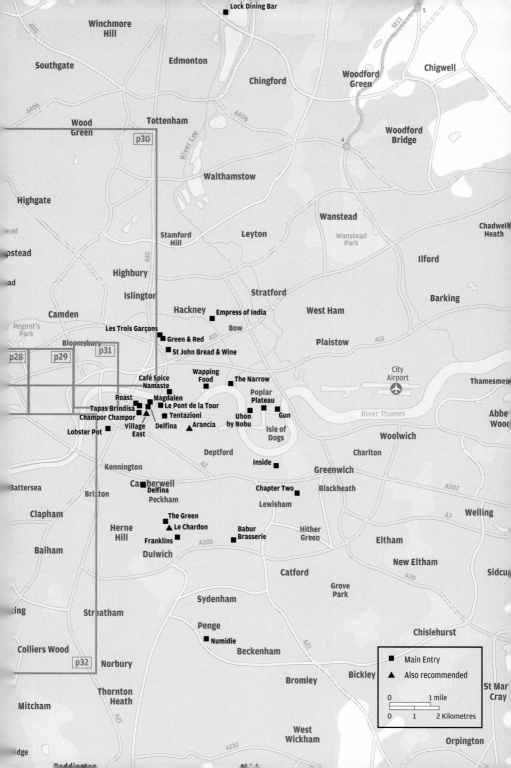

Lock Dining Bar

Winchmore Hill

Southgate

Edmonton

Chigwell

Chingford

Woodford Green

Wood Green

p30

Tottenham

Woodford Bridge

Walthamstow

Highgate

Stamford Hill

Leyton

Wanstead

Wanstead Park

Chadwell Heath

Ilford

Highbury

Islington

Stratford

West Ham

Barking

Camden

Bloomsbury

p28 p29 p31

Hackney

Bow

Empress of India

Plaistow

Regent's Park

Les Trois Garçons

Green & Red

St John Bread & Wine

City Airport

Thamesmead

Café Spice Namaste

Wapping Food

The Narrow

Poplar Plateau

Roast

Magdalen

Le Pont de la Tour

Gun

Ubon by Nobu

Tapas Brindisa

Champor Champor

Tentazioni

River Thames

Abbe Wood

Lobster Pot

Village East

Delfina

Arancia

Isle of Dogs

Woolwich

Deptford

Charlton

Kennington

Inside

Greenwich

Blackheath

Welling

Camberwell

Delfina

Peckham

Chapter Two

Lewisham

Hither Green

Eltham

New Eltham

Sidcu

Battersea

Brixton

Clapham

Balham

Herne Hill

The Green

Le Chardon

Franklins

Dulwich

Babur Brasserie

Catford

Grove Park

Streatham

Sydenham

Penge

Numidie

Beckenham

Chislehurst

Colliers Wood

p32

Norbury

Bromley

Bickley

St Mar Cray

Thornton Heath

Mitcham

West Wickham

Orpington

■ Main Entry

▲ Also recommended

0   1 mile

0   1   2 Kilometres

MAPS

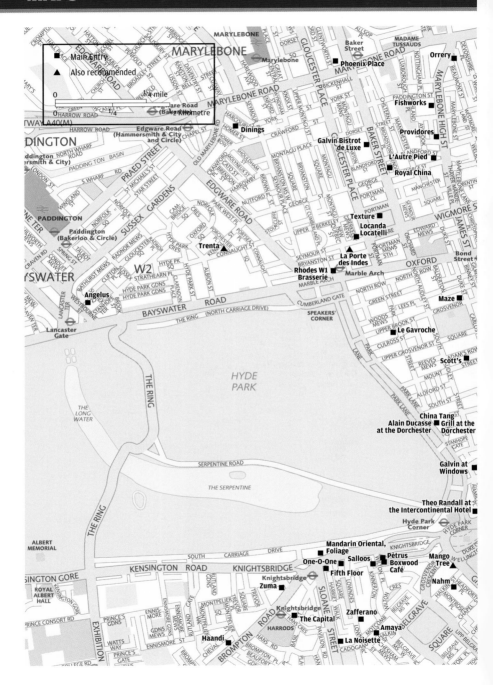

- ■ Main Entry
- ▲ Also recommended

0   1/4 mile
0   1/4   1/2 Kilometre

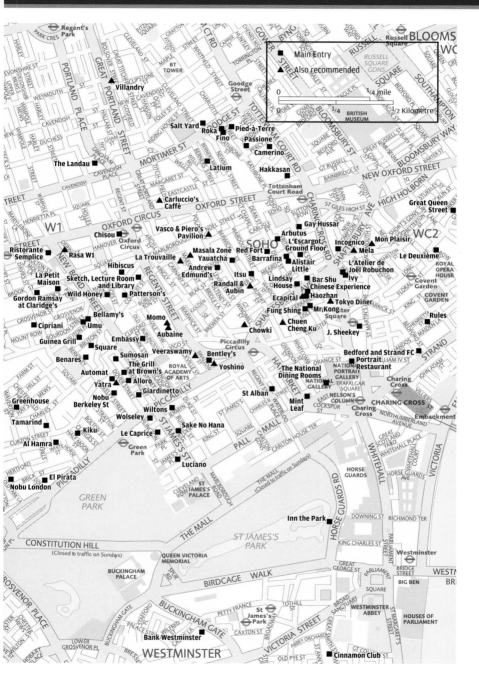

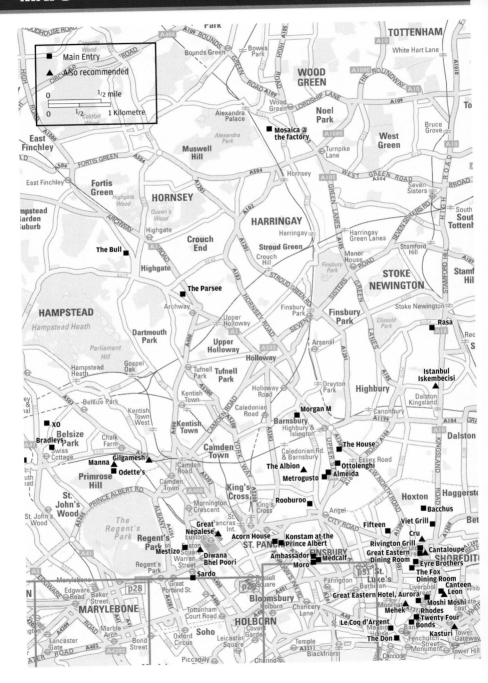

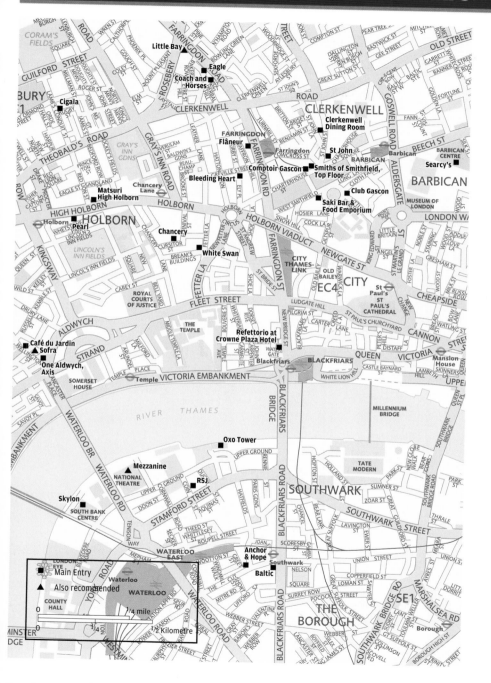

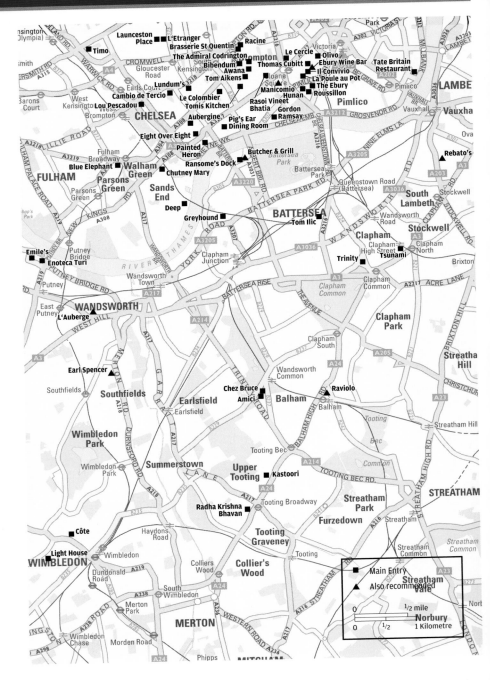

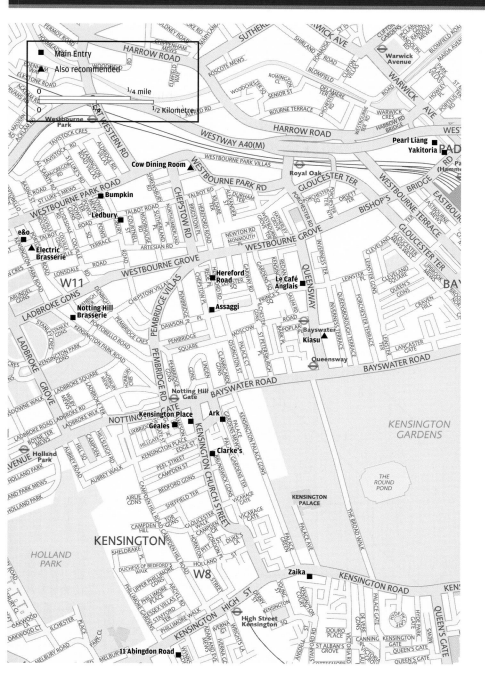

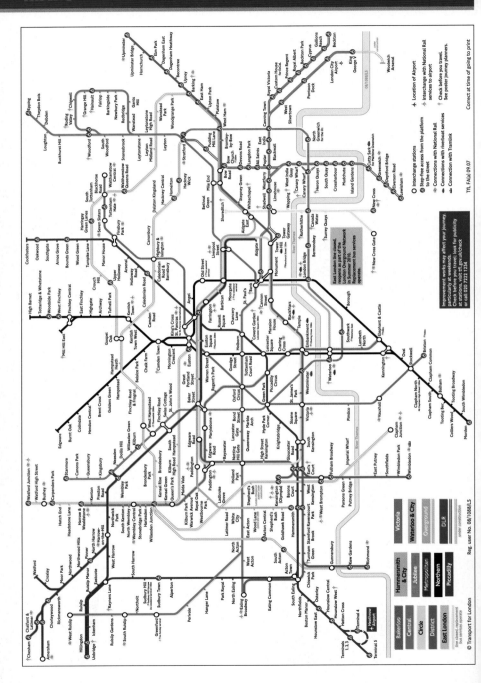

CENTRAL

Belgravia, Bloomsbury, Chelsea,
Chinatown, Clerkenwell, Covent Garden,
Euston, Fitzrovia, Green Park, Holborn,
Hyde Park, Knightsbridge, Lancaster Gate,
Leicester Square, Marble Arch,
Marylebone, Mayfair, Oxford Circus,
Piccadilly, Soho, St James's Park,
Tottenham Court Road, Trafalgar Square,
Victoria, Westminster

▌Belgravia
Le Cercle
Imaginative French-style tapas
1 Wilbraham Place, SW1X 9AE
Tel no: (020) 7901 9999
⊖ **Sloane Square**
French | £34
Cooking score: 5

🍷 **V**

The younger sibling of Club Gascon (see entry), Le Cercle is in much the same business – tapas-sized portions of high-class, innovative cooking, loosely based on the traditions of southwest France. It's a windowless basement room off Sloane Street, cleverly done in neutral tones to mitigate the subterranean feel. Thierry Beyris is a formidable talent, both in imagination and in execution, as is witnessed by dishes such as cod with an artichoke emulsion and artichoke chips, wood pigeon with hazelnut mash and a rocket and truffle vinaigrette, or steamed brill with barley risotto, chorizo and spring onions. The menu, as at Club Gascon, is divided into French-titled categories, and you might want to play the game of sampling something from each, leaving space for the gourmandises of course. These include chocolate sorbet macaroon and redcurrant coulis, and 'luscious pears' with caramelised popcorn and sesame ice-cream. Every item on the menu has a suggested wine or other drink appended to it, and much is available by the glass. This encourages exploration of the lesser-known byways of French wine, such as the Jura, as well as the *sud-ouest* itself. Prices open at £18, with glasses from £4.50.
Chef/s: Thierry Beyris. **Open:** Tue to Sat 12 to 3, 6 to 11. **Closed:** Christmas to New Year. **Meals:** Meals: alc (main courses £4.50 to £35). Set L £15, Set D 6 to 7 £19.50. Bar menu available. **Service:** 12.5% (optional). **Details:** Cards accepted. 70 seats. Air-con. Music. Children's portions.

Nahm
Top-drawer Thai food
Halkin Hotel, 5 Halkin Street, SW1X 7DJ
Tel no: (020) 7333 1234
www.nahm.como.bz
⊖ **Hyde Park Corner**
Thai | £47
Cooking score: 3

🍴 **V**

A swish dining room in the Halkin Hotel provides a sleek, minimalist backdrop for David Thompson's highly personal take on Thai cuisine. After a taster of salted chicken and longan wafers, expect inventive salads such as poached chicken with banana blossoms ahead of cleansing soups. Other courses focus on intense curries including a 'green' version with braised salted beef, wild ginger, apple and pea aubergines. At lunch, the menu focuses on one-plate street dishes, with rice and noodles as the mainstays: look for chicken 'pilaff' with sweet chilli sauce or kanom kin (noodles) with rich fish and wild ginger curry. Prices on the pedigree wine list can seem intimidating; there is precious little below £30.
Chef/s: Matthew Albert. **Open:** Mon to Fri L 12 to 2.30, all week D 7 to 10.30 (10. Sun). **Closed:** bank hols. **Meals:** Set D £49.50. **Service:** 12.5% (optional). **Details:** Cards accepted. 78 seats. Air-con. Separate bar. Wheelchair access. Music. Children's portions.

Noura Brasserie
Sleek venue serving authentic Lebanese food
16 Hobart Place, SW1W 0HH
Tel no: (020) 7235 9444
www.noura.co.uk
⊖ **Victoria**
Middle Eastern | £36
Cooking score: 3

V

Imported from Paris and now spreading its tentacles across central London, the Noura mini-chain aims to bring traditional Lebanese cooking to a wider audience by offering flexibility and all-day opening. The Hobart

Place original trades on sleek, minimalist elegance and offers an extensive menu of dishes with an authentic stamp. A vast assortment of hot and cold mezze is tailor-made to suit most dietary preferences: opt for a mixed platter or choose individually from a list that includes everything from hummus, kebbeh nayeh (lamb 'tartare' with cracked wheat) and moujaddara (lentils and rice topped with seared onions) to fatayer (pastry parcels of baked spinach) and samke harra (fish 'ratatouille'). Main courses are mostly high-protein chargrills and kebabs, ranging from marinated chicken to red mullet with tarator sauce, and there are some tantalising desserts to round things off. Heavyweight names from France and Lebanon hold centre stage on the concise wine list. Prices start at £23 for Château Ksara. See the website for details of other branches.

Chef/s: Badih el Asmar. **Open:** all week 11.30 to 11.30. **Meals:** alc (main courses £11.50 to £22). Set L £18 to £30, Set D £30 to £40. **Service:** not inc. **Details:** Cards accepted. 120 seats. 15 seats outside. Air-con. Wheelchair access. Music. Children's portions. Car parking.

Olivo
Lively Sardinian restaurant
21 Eccleston Street, SW1W 9LX
Tel no: (020) 7730 2505
www.olivolondon.com
⊖ Victoria
Italian | £30
Cooking score: 2

The buzzy, convivial ambience generates the perfect atmosphere for the Sardinian-orientated food. Wooden floors, tightly-packed tables and a lack of napery help crank up the volume and lend an informal air to proceedings. Chargrilled stuffed baby squid with plum tomatoes and basil is a good way to start, or there's pasta, which comes in starter of main-course portions – try a Sardinian spaghetti dish with grated grey mullet roe as a second course before sautéed lamb's sweetbreads with white beans and artichokes. Desserts include the usual pannacotta,

semifreddo or chocolate and almond tart. Staff 'have a passion for food'. Prices on the short but appealing patriotic all-Italian wine list open at £15.50.

Chef/s: Sandro Medda. **Open:** Mon to Fri L 12 to 3, all week D 7 to 11 (10 Sun). **Closed:** bank hols. **Meals:** Set L £19.50 (2 courses) to £22.50. **Service:** not inc. **Details:** Cards accepted. 45 seats. Air-con. No music. Children's portions.

La Poule au Pot
Rigorously authentic French restaurant
231 Ebury Street, SW1W 8UT
Tel no: (020) 7730 7763
⊖ Sloane Square
French | £38
Cooking score: 2

V

Here is a little corner of provincial France on a smart London street. The décor features the kind of bistro clutter that others have long since chucked out in favour of blank minimalism, while the service is all old-school French bonhomie. Test your linguistic skills with a menu that offers simple cuisine bourgeoise, not excluding foie gras poelé with a glass of sweet Monbazillac. Other starters might be smoked salmon paupiette stuffed with crab, or nine snails, and then there is a wide range of fish or meat to choose from for main. Grilled daurade fillets in white wine and fennel, or rabbit in mustard, are likely to be the order of the day. Choose from the likes of crème brûlée, tarte Tatin or chocolate mousse to finish. Wines are of course exclusively French, with house Sauvignon and Merlot at £14.50.

Chef/s: Kris Goleblowski. **Open:** all week 12.30 to 2.30, 6.30 to 11. **Closed:** 25, 26 Dec. **Meals:** alc (main courses £16 to £25) Set L £17.75 (2 courses) to £19.75. **Service:** 12.5% (optional). **Details:** Cards accepted. 65 seats. 35 seats outside. No music. Wheelchair access. Children's portions.

READERS RECOMMEND
Volt
Modern European
17 Hobart Place, SW1W 0HH
Tel no: (020) 7235 9696
www.voltlounge.com
'Italian food in super-hip surroundings.'

▌Bloomsbury
Cigala
Fiery, intriguing Iberian
54 Lamb's Conduit Street, WC1N 3LW
Tel no: (020) 7405 1717
www.cigala.co.uk
⊖ Holborn
Spanish | £39
Cooking score: 1

V

Immensely popular and buzzing, this no-frills Spanish restaurant with its picture windows, unadorned cream walls, rough-hewn wooden floorboards and chunky alfresco seating makes a great pit stop for tapas. Tuck into grilled chorizo, exemplary patatas bravas topped with a punchy sauce laced with red chilli and crushed coriander, chicken croquetas, or grilled quail with tomato and red onion salad. On the restaurant menu, daily changing dishes incorporate imaginative ingredients, say cebreiro (traditional cow's milk mountain cheese) and there are two varieties of paella. Other robust mains might be grilled black bream with braised chard and anchovies, or roast pork belly with lentils and romesco sauce. A short, patriotic drinks list encompasses Cava, sherries and regional wines, around fifteen of which are available by the glass, priced between £3.50 to £8.
Chef/s: Johnny Murray and Jake Hodges. **Open:** Mon to Fri 12 to 10.45 (12.30 Sat, 12.30-9.30 Sun). **Closed:** D 24 Dec, 25 and 26 Dec, 1 Jan, Easter Sun. **Meals:** alc (main courses £12 to £18). Set L Mon to Fri £15 (2 courses) to £18, Set L and D Sun £10.50 (1 course). Tapas menu available. **Service:** 12.5% (optional). **Details:** Cards accepted. 60 seats. 20 seats outside. Air-con. Separate bar. No music. Wheelchair access. Children's portions.

READERS RECOMMEND
Norfolk Arms
Gastropub
28 Leigh Street, WC1H 9EP
Tel no: 020 7388 3937
www.norfolkarms.co.uk
'Homely gastropub with a Spanish element'

Number 12
Modern British
12 Upper Woburn Place, WC1H 0HX
Tel no: (020) 7693 5425
'British cooking with a twist in Bloomsbury'

Patisserie Deux Amis
French
63 Judd Street, WC1H 9QT
Tel no: 020 7383 7029
'A real neighbourhood secret'

Tas
Middle Eastern
22 Bloomsbury St, WC1B 3QJ
Tel no: (020) 7637 4555
www.tasrestaurant.com
'Inventive. good-value menu in a modern setting'

▌Chelsea
The Ebury
Evolving menu
11 Pimlico Road, SW1W 8NA
Tel no: (020) 7730 6784
www.theebury.co.uk
⊖ Sloane Square
Modern European | £30
Cooking score: 5

The Ebury seems to have evolved into a fully fledged restaurant, albeit one with a lively bar attached. Natural light pours in through windows ribboning round this imposing corner building. Downstairs, the bar-cum-dining room buzzes informally as the Sloane set rub shoulders with office workers stopping off for a drink before heading home. Upstairs, in the chandeliered clubroom a jazz trio

Antonio Carluccio OBE

Why did you become a chef?
Passion and greediness.

Who was your main inspiration?
My mother and Pellegrino Artusi.

Where do you eat out?
Mainly in ethnic restaurants and sometimes Italian ones.

Where do you source your ingredients?
Italy for authentic items and Britain for meat and fish.

Who is your favourite producer?
Mother (or Father) Nature.

What's the best dish you've ever eaten?
Pasta with truffles made with 40 egg yolks and one kilo of flour that I ate in an Italian town called Bra, the HQ of Slow Food.

Do you have a favourite local recipe?
Bacon and eggs.

What's your guilty food pleasure?
Tinned sweet condensed milk (or in a tube).

If you could only eat one more thing, what would it be?
My wife's souffle.

Which are your produest achievements?
The Neal Street Restaurant, Carluccio's, my OBE and Commendatore (Italian Knighthood).

provides a smooth backdrop to classy dining. Peter Woods's seasonal menu is mainly British inspired, but with a nod to mainland Europe, so expect a 'flawless' starter of soft poached egg, sautéed oyster mushrooms and brioche 'soldiers' served in neat lidded bowl, lamb's tongue salad teamed with pickled beetroot, or foie gras parfait, chicken livers and cured duck. For mains, seared gilthead bream with fennel reveals moist, flakey fish beneath a crispy skin, otherwise there could be lamb with potatoes boulangère and caramelised onion purée, and ribeye beef with bone marrow and Lyonnaise onions. Date and vanilla tart with nutmeg Chantilly cream is an appealing way to finish, with the all-French cheeseboard a savoury alternative. Service is cheerful and fast. Wines by the glass start with a Carignan Vieilles Vignes at a reasonable £3.50.

Chef/s: Peter Woods. **Open:** all week 12 to 3.30 (4 Sat and Sun), 6 to 10.30 (10 Sun). Dining room: Mon to Sat D only 6 to 10.30. **Closed:** 25 and 26 Dec. **Meals:** alc (main courses £10.95 to £16.50). **Service:** 12.5% (optional). **Details:** Cards accepted. 65 seats. Air-con. Wheelchair access. Music.

Hunan

Well-executed Chinese regional cooking
51 Pimlico Road, SW1W 8NE
Tel no: (020) 7730 5712
⊖ **Sloane Square**
Chinese | £34
Cooking score: 3

The home-style Hunanese cooking on offer at this restaurant is in neat contrast to the plutocrats' paradise in which it sits. Pimlico Road's idea of 'home-style' is soft furnishings in four figures in the nearby shops. The 'leave-it-to-us' menu is one way of going about it, with Michael Peng gladly accepting free rein to bring you a whole series of novel and unexpected dishes. Otherwise, there are various fixed-price menu options that take in dishes such as steamed monkfish and salmon rolls, whole prawn and spinach dumplings, and – unusually in Chinese cooking – lamb stir-fried with garlic shoots. Unusual bits of pig (ear and tongue) might turn up in a salad, while cuttlefish is labour-intensively stuffed and grilled. Finish with sweet red bean pancake and almond jelly. A much more extensive wine list than is the norm with Chinese food begins with nine house wines from £14, and there's Corton-Charlemagne if you want it.

Chef/s: Michael Peng. **Open:** Mon to Sat 12.30 to 2.30, 6.30 to 11.30. **Closed:** 25 Dec, Easter, bank hols. **Meals:** Set L from £24.80. Set D from £33.80. **Service:** 12.5% (optional). **Details:** Cards accepted. 44 seats. Air-con. Music.

Il Convivio

Contemporary flavours in a convivial setting
143 Ebury Street, SW1W 9QN
Tel no: (020) 7730 4099
www.etruscarestaurants.com
⊖ Sloane Square
Italian | £34
Cooking score: 2

Dante reputedly coined the term 'il convivio', and the poet's words are embossed on the deep-red walls of this cool Belgravia Italian. A sought-after conservatory with cedarwood decking and an electric roof provides alfresco dining all year round, while a skylight lends pleasant natural illumination to the main body of the restaurant. Contemporary themes and trends colour most dishes on the stylish menu, which might open with seared scallops, cauliflower purée, beetroot and hazelnut infusion or a risotto with chicory and suckling pig confit. Centrepieces could range from balsamic-caramelised black cod with grilled asparagus and Muscat grapes to milk-fed baby lamb with 'pappa al pommodoro' and a sauce of preserved lemons. Finish with Gianduia semifreddo, polenta crumble and blood oranges or explore the organic Italian cheeses. Italy and France share most of the honours on the wine list, which includes a few bargains among the pricier stuff. House Colonnara is £13.50 (£3.95 a glass).

Chef/s: Lukas Pfaff. **Open:** Mon to Sat 12 to 2.45, 7 to 10.45. **Closed:** bank hols. **Meals:** alc L (main courses £8.50 to £21). Set D £27.50 (2 courses) to £39.50 (4 courses). **Service:** 12.5% (optional). **Details:** Cards accepted. 65 seats. Air-con. Music.

Painted Heron

Accomplished Indian with radical ideas
112 Cheyne Walk, SW10 0DJ
Tel no: (020) 7351 5232
www.thepaintedheron.com
⊖ Sloane Square
Indian | £28
Cooking score: 3

 V

Hailed as an Indian restaurant for the twenty-first century when it opened, the Painted Heron is still going strong opposite the houseboats near Battersea Bridge. The décor aims for contemporary minimalism and the daily menu eschews most Indian names and terminology in favour of plain English (black tiger prawns in pickled lime marinade served with pomegranate chutney, for example). Some ideas are founded on the traditions of the subcontinent, witness spiced chick peas with raita and fried bread or diced mutton in slow-cooked Pakistani 'haleem' curry with wheat 'kernels'. But the kitchen also breaks the rules when it comes to wild Alaskan black cod in samphire marinade with tamarind rice noodles and coconut curry or Kashmiri-style venison with kohlrabi. The creative urge extends to the roll-call of side dishes, which calls into play asparagus, sugar snap peas and broad beans as well as a curry of strawberries and mini 'kumquat' oranges; naan bread flavoured with mango, coconut and pistachios simply adds to the unpredictability of it all. A dozen wines by the glass (from £4) head the racy global list.

Chef/s: Yogesh Datta. **Open:** Sun to Fri L 12 to 2.30, all week D 6.30 to 10.30. **Closed:** 25 and 26 Dec, 1 Jan. **Meals:** alc (main courses £11 to £18). Set menu £27.50. **Service:** 12.5% (optional). **Details:** Cards accepted. 75 seats. 20 seats outside. Air-con. Music.

Pig's Ear Dining Room

A versatile gastropub
35 Old Church Street, SW3 5BS
Tel no: (020) 7352 2908
www.thepigsear.co.uk
⊖ **Sloane Square**
Modern British | £30
Cooking score: 2

A perfectly contemporary London eating-place, the Pig's Ear is a gastropub that features a lively ground-floor bar and upstairs dining-room. It's Chelsea, but not as we used to know it. Hang loose with menus that deal in the likes of roast bone marrow with ginger salt and salad leaves, or smoked haddock kedgeree, to start. Then gather pace with crackled Tamworth pork belly with cabbage, carrots and apple purée, or roast cod with brown shrimps, spinach and gremolata. Sweet treats include ice cream and cookies, as well as banana Tatin with crème fraîche. Wines are predominantly French, with just a handful of southern Europeans and New Worlders. Prices open at £15, or £3.50 for a standard glass.
Chef/s: Chris Sharpe. **Open:** Mon to Sat 12 to 11, Sun 12 to 10.30. **Closed:** Christmas and New Year's Eve. **Meals:** alc (main courses £11.50 to £16.50). **Service:** 12.5% (optional). **Details:** Cards accepted. 35 seats. Air-con. Separate bar. Wheelchair access. Music. Children allowed.

Roussillon

French gem goes from strength to strength
16 St Barnabas Street, SW1W 8PE
Tel no: (020) 7730 5550
www.roussillon.co.uk
⊖ **Sloane Square**
French | £46
Cooking score: 6

🍷 V

The well-worn description 'understated elegance' is for once fully merited at this French restaurant in a quiet corner of Pimlico. Alexis Gauthier starts as he means to go on, offering excellent breads baked in-house, and containing anything from cumin to black pudding. Nibbles come in waves, and then the main menu business begins. Like the décor, the style is deceptively simple, with much use of superb raw materials. A straightforward seafood salad stops being straightforward when its principal components – a pair each of scallops and langoustines – are so great, their sea-fresh savour enhanced by note-perfect timing. Potato gnocchi are texturally spot-on, served with an array of seasonal vegetables, with a finely judged sherry vinegar reduction and a Roquefort tuile. Fish may be as uncomplicated as roasted monkfish with chicory both raw and braised, or the sea bass that came with ('slightly over-chewy') girolles. At inspection, meat options included a properly timed piece of superlative beef fillet, garnished with purple artichokes and slivers of olive. Cheese service is highly knowledgeable, and the French cheeses themselves top-notch, while the show-stopping dessert is the Louis XV praline creation, a textural marvel that uses brilliant Weiss chocolate from St-Etienne. An alternative might be plum and almond tartlet with plum compote. The lunch deal at £35, including half a bottle of wine, water and coffee, remains one of the great London bargains. Eighteen wines by the glass head up an expansive list that is most assured in France, especially the lesser-known southern appellations (remember the restaurant's name). Elsewhere, it looks a little more haphazard. Bottles start at around £18.
Chef/s: Alexis Gauthier, Gerard Virolle. **Open:** Mon to Fri L 12 to 2.30, Mon to Sat D 6.30 to 10.30. **Meals:** Set L £35 (3 courses), Set D £5 (3 courses). **Service:** 12.5%. **Details:** Cards accepted. 50 seats. Air-con. No music. Children allowed.

READERS RECOMMEND

Cheyne Walk Brasserie

French
50 Cheyne Walk, SW3 5LR
Tel no: 0207 3768787
www.cheynewalkbrasserie.com
'Compact and classy, with a great river view'

Special occasions

London's restaurants offer almost limitless possibilities, whether you are looking for cosseted intimacy, star-spangled jollity or simply the perfect night out.

Le Gavroche

Synonymous with classical French cuisine for more than 40 years and still an incomparable choice for 'special event dining'.

Gordon Ramsay

Flagship of the Ramsay brand and an unmissable experience. Expect consummate cuisine, and supremely orchestrated service.

The Ivy

Star-watching adds to the buzz of eating at this iconic theatreland venue. You must book well ahead.

Ledbury

The Ledbury ticks all the boxes: exciting modern food, razor-sharp service and a heavyweight wine list.

Lindsay House

Calm civility is the hallmark of Richard Corrigan's discreet Soho townhouse. Expect understated class and impeccably crafted food.

Locanda Locatelli

Big-occasion regional Italian food out of the top drawer, cooked by a charismatic master of his craft. A swanky, good-natured place, and you can even bring the kids.

Pétrus

Unashamed luxury drips from this dining room. Splash out on something special from the wine list: Ch. Pétrus '28, anyone?

Le Poule au Pot

Universally prized as a schmaltz-free romantic rendezvous. Old-fashioned flavours, close-packed tables, magnums of house wine – pure seduction.

Rules

Celebrate days gone by in this centuries-old bastion of Bulldog British cooking. Priceless archaic décor sets the tone, seasonality rules on the menu: it is all comfortingly reassuring if you fancy a break from the modern world.

Sketch Lecture Room and Library

Check your bank balance before committing to a mega-blow-out, but it's worth going for broke to experience the über-extravagant, fabulously flamboyant Lecture Room. The food challenges, the service pampers.

Manicomio

Italian
85 Duke of York Square, SW3 4LY
Tel no: 020 7730 3366
www.manicomio.co.uk
'Fine Italian restaurant and deli'

█ Chinatown

Chinese Experience

Excellent dim sum
118 Shaftesbury Avenue, W1D 5EP
Tel no: (020) 7437 0377
www.chineseexperience.com
⊖ **Leicester Square**
Chinese | £23
Cooking score: 2
V

On the touristy fringes of Soho Chinatown, this sleek-looking restaurant puts on a contemporary show with muted primary colours and pots of paper orchids. Daytime dim sum are one of the high spots, and the long list extends well beyond the usual steamed dumplings into the esoteric realms of Szechuan duck tongue with 'green bean sheet', deep-fried cuttlefish with sweetcorn and lychee 'snow balls'. 'Lai min' noodles are also worth ordering. Elsewhere, the kitchen plays to the gallery with a full quota of Cantonese favourites (aromatic crispy duck, steamed sea bass with ginger and spring onion, pork chop with garlic), but it's worth homing in on chef's specials such as air-dried beef in spiced honey sauce, stir-fried lamb with leeks and baked pak choi with milky cream.
Chef/s: Gun Leung. **Open:** all week 12 to 11.
Meals: alc (main courses L £8 to £10, D £10 to £15).
Set L £19.90 to £23 (all min 2). **Service:** 10%.
Details: Cards accepted. 130 seats. Air-con. Music.

Fung Shing

Acclaimed Cantonese cuisine
15 Lisle Street, WC2H 7BE
Tel no: (020) 7437 1539
www.fungshing.co.uk
⊖ **Leicester Square**
Chinese | £31
Cooking score: 2
V

Held in high regard for over 30 years both inside and outside London's Chinese community, Fung Shing continues to be popular with everyone who appreciates authentic Cantonese cooking, appealing to a broad mix of Westerners and Chinese. The dining room is calm and restful with Chinese paintings, neat aqua-marine tablecloths and smart-suited waiters. Dishes on the long and wide-ranging menu may read fairly similarly to their Chinatown neighbours, but what arrives on the plate is far better – sizzling, spicy prawns, crispy aromatic duck, crab with ginger and spring onion and sweet and sour chicken are among a selection which includes familiar favourites. The chef's specials list should tempt the more adventurous, perhaps braised sea cucumber with meat balls, squid stuffed with seafood, or ostrich with yellow bean sauce. The wine list is a decent selection and opens at £15.
Chef/s: Frank Cheung. **Open:** all week 12 to 11.30.
Closed: 24 to 26 Dec. **Meals:** Set L and D £18 to £30. **Service:** 10%. **Details:** Cards accepted. 100 seats. Air-con. Music. Children allowed.

Haozhan

New-wave Chinese raising the bar
8 Gerrard Street, W1D 5PJ
Tel no: 020 7434 3838
www.haozhan.co.uk
⊖ **Leicester Square**
Chinese | £30
Cooking score: 3

The received opinion is that if you want interesting Chinese food in London, avoid Chinatown, especially Gerrard Street. So it's

good to see a new-wave Chinese bucking the trend. The interior is clean and contemporary and the surprisingly short menu decidedly fusion in intent with styles borrowed from Japan, Malaysia and Vietnam. This is an interesting little restaurant in any language. Jasmine ribs are meaty and tender, deep-fried (but greaseless) curry soft-shelled crab 'excellent' and unusual marmite prawns have an 'edgy and subtle flavour'. Not all dishes are 'as good as the kitchen intended', but standouts have included a glorious, crispy quail with chilli and salt, and a hotpot of braised aubergine and minced pork with silky, creamy homemade tofu. Skip dessert. Service has 'ranged from disinterested to enthusiastic depending on who you get', while wines are a mixed bunch, ranging from £11 to a short list of reserve wines at overstated prices.
Chef/s: Chee Loong Cheong. **Open:** all week, 12 to 11.30 (12 midnight Fri to Sat, 11 Sun). **Closed:** 24 and 25 Dec. **Meals:** alc (main courses from £8.50 to £19). **Service:** 10% (optional). **Details:** Cards accepted. 75 seats. Air-con. Wheelchair access. Music. Children allowed.

Mr Kong

An unorthodox Oriental adventure
21 Lisle Street, WC2H 7BA
Tel no: (020) 7437 7341
⊖ Leicester Square
Chinese | £33
Cooking score: 2
V

A fire in the kitchen in the summer of 2007 closed this restaurant temporarily – the owners taking the opportunity to upgrade the three-tiered restaurant 'substantially'. It will open in February 2008. The menu, we are assured, will remain the same, offering much that is out of the ordinary, while the well-prepared likes of sweet-and-sour pork and crispy aromatic duck will continue to keep this place busy with tourists. It is for the recherché list of 'chef's specials' and 'manager's recommendations' that regulars rate this place so highly: a couple of soft-shell crabs encased in light, crisp batter and scattered with chillis,

followed by deep-fried pig's intestine stuffed with minced prawn. Duck wrapped with yam is less adventurous but no less delicious, while a side plate of crunchy pak choi points, like all the dishes, to fresh ingredients. Hotpots, such as pork belly with preserved vegetables and chicken with salted fish, are another speciality well worth trying here. House wine is £8.90.
Chef/s: K Kong and Y W Lo. **Open:** all week 12 to 2.45am (1.45am Sun). **Meals:** alc (main courses £6 to £16). Set L and D £9.30 (2 courses) to £22 (all min 2 to 8). **Service:** 10%. **Details:** Cards accepted. 110 seats. Air-con. Music.

ALSO RECOMMENDED
▲ Ecapital

8 Gerrard Street, W1D 5PJ
Tel no: (020) 7434 3838
⊖ Leicester Square

Essentially London's first entirely Shanghaiese restaurant. Generally sweeter and richer than Cantonese cooking, the traditional Shanghai options are highlighted in pink on the menu. To start try the cold combination platter (£6.50), which includes marinated meats, smoked fish and a crisp serving of what is known as vegetarian goose – dried tofu. Steamed dumplings with pork and a tasty soup stock (xiao long bao) are a Shanghai speciality that come served with a knowing smile. Main courses range from scallop, prawn and tofu hotpot (£8.50) and roast belly pork (£9.75) to fish dishes such as sea bass 'West Lake style' (£16.95). House wines are £11. Open all week.

■ Clerkenwell
READERS RECOMMEND
Konditor and Cook

Café
47 Grays Inn Road, WC1X 8LR
Tel no: (020) 7404 6300
'Perfect for a quick coffee and a piece of cake'

Covent Garden
Café du Jardin
Long-standing theatreland favourite
28 Wellington Street, WC2E 7BD
Tel no: (020) 7836 8769 and 8760
www.lecafedujardin.com
⊖ Covent Garden
Modern European | £31
Cooking score: 2

 V

A bastion of Covent Garden's theatreland scene for almost two decades, this veteran brasserie is driven by chef/proprietor Tony Howorth's enthusiasm. The fun-loving venue is spread over two floors, with a street-level, conservatory-style area providing the best views of the action and a live pianist playing below stairs in the evening. Brasserie stalwarts like confit of duck or calf's liver with 'cream whipped' potatoes and caramelised onions tend to be eclipsed by more contemporary ideas with an eclectic slant: tartare of blue fin tuna with sesame seed tuile could figure ahead of tempura of shrimps with chorizo and lime-scented rice. The international wine list is stuffed with gilt-edged drinking, especially from France, Italy and Australia, while the separate list of 'fine wines' ought to attract aficionados. Prices start at £11.50 (£3.85 a glass) for house vins de pays. Le Deuxième is part of the same stable (see entry), as is the Forge at 14 Garrick Street, WC2.
Chef/s: Tony Howorth. **Open:** all week 12 to 3, 5.30 to 12 (12 to 11 Sun). **Closed:** 24 and 25 Dec. **Meals:** alc (main courses £10 to £17.50). Set L and D £11.95 (2 courses) to £15.50 (3 courses). **Service:** 15% (optional). **Details:** Cards accepted. 100 seats. 20 seats outside. Air-con. No music. Wheelchair access. Music. Children allowed.

Le Deuxième
Lively brasserie with eclectic overtones
65A Long Acre, WC2E 9JH
Tel no: (020) 7379 0033
www.ledeuxieme.com
⊖ Covent Garden
Modern European | £32
Cooking score: 2

V

Like its elder brother Café du Jardin (see entry), Le Deuxième is in the heart of Covent Garden's cultural maelstrom, within earshot of the Royal Opera House. It copes efficiently with the crowds, offering a range of attractive fixed-price deals at peak times. European brasserie food with a few Oriental flashes is the order of the day, and the kitchen moves easily between escargots bourguignon and freshwater shrimp tempura with sweet Thai dressing. Pasta has its say and main courses are a lively assortment ranging from fillet of veal with Mozzarella, rösti and red pepper chutney to rare, grilled tuna with choi sum, water chestnuts and sesame glaze. Desserts are in the classic mould of lemon tart or warm chocolate fondant. The auspicious wine list is packed with quality drinking, especially from the French regions, Italy and Australia. Further treasures are on the 'fine wine list'; house recommendations start at £12.50. (The Forge at 14 Garrick Street, WC2 is from the same stable).
Chef/s: Simon Conboy. **Open:** Mon to Fri L 12 to 3, D 5 to 12, Sat 12 to 12, Sun 12 to 11. **Closed:** 24 and 25 Dec. **Meals:** alc (main courses £14.50 to £16.50). Set L and D £11.95 (2 courses) to £15.50 (3 courses). **Service:** 15%. **Details:** Cards accepted. 55 seats. Air-con. No music. Wheelchair access.

Great Queen Street

Scrupulously seasonal British brasserie
32 Great Queen Street, WC2B 5AA
Tel no: 020 7242 0622
⊖ **Covent Garden**
British | £25
Cooking score: 4
 £30

More gastro than pub, this is the epitome of
moderately priced good eating with integrity:
a scrupulously seasonal Brit brasserie in a
former down-at-heel pub in Covent Garden.
In an area where sound cooking is curiously
scarce, it's a dream team, with The Eagle, The
Anchor and Hope, and St John in its lineage.
Notably, the head chef is Tom Norrington-
Davies, the serving staff are equally
committed, brimming with knowledge and
enthusiasm. The short, daily changing menu is
wholly appealing, and items such as the own-
made potted shrimps with a piquant lemony
edge set the tone. Invariably there's soup,
perhaps wild garlic, and a salad starter. The
roast beetroot, mint and delectable goat's
cheese curd with textural toasted crumbs is
scrape-the-plate moreish. Impeccable
sourcing defines the main dishes, as found in
the cod with roasted tomatoes on the vine and
garlic aïoli, duck confit of impeccable
crispness with braised lettuce and peas.
Desserts all come in at under £5, including
lemon pots and fabulous caramel custard with
muscat. The well-chosen, mostly lesser-
known French appellation wine list includes
375ml carafes and house wines from £10.
Chef/s: Tom Norrington-Davies. **Open:** Mon to Sat L
12 to 3, Tue to Sat D 6 to 10.30. **Closed:** Christmas.
Meals: alc (main courses £6 to £15). **Service:** not
inc. **Details:** 70 seats. Separate bar. No music.
Wheelchair access. Children allowed.

L'Atelier de Joël Robuchon

Beautifully crafted dishes
13-15 Well Street, WC2H 9NE
Tel no: (020) 7010 8600
www.joelrobuchon.co.uk
⊖ **Leicester Square**
French | £66
Cooking score: 6

It looks fittingly discreet from the outside,
inside it's a show-stopper – Joël Robuchon's
London outpost seduces most who cross its
threshold. It's arranged on three levels: the
unabashedly luxurious fine diner on the
ground floor (where counter seating
grandstands the kitchen), the monochrome
first-floor dining room 'La Cuisine' (similar
menu, less atmosphere), and a top-floor bar.
There's a broad range of dishes in the
repertoire, all carried off with the same sure
touch and stunning presentation. While prices
on the à la carte will make you gasp, it's the
equally expensive list of small tasting plates
that is the main draw and there was not a dud
note among the beautifully crafted dishes tried
at inspection. Fresh mackerel on a thin tart
with Parmesan shavings and olives came
bursting with flavour, while finely chopped
pig's trotter spread on parmesan toast was
refined and gutsy at the same time. A sense of
comfort pervades the menu, exemplified by
dishes such as a pair of exquisite miniature beef
and foie gras burgers served with lightly
caramelised bell peppers, and Robuchon's
signature truffle mashed potato, a small dollop
of which came with quail stuffed with foie
gras. Green chartreuse soufflé with pistachio
ice cream, or chocolate fondant with fresh ice
mint sorbet, are both worth the 15-minute
wait. Service can be a lottery; pedestrian at
times, effortlessly accomplished at others.
Wine selections open at £18.
Chef/s: Frederic Simonin. **Open:** Daily, ground floor
L 12 to 2.30 D 5.30 to 10.30, La Cuisine L 12 to 2.30
D 7 to 10.30. **Closed:** Summer closed Sat L and Sun
La Cuisine. **Meals:** alc (main courses £15 to £36) Set
menu L £35 (4 courses, small portions) D pre-
theatre £35 (as before). **Service:** 12.5%.
Details: Cards accepted. 101 seats. Air-con.
Separate bar. Wheelchair access. Music.

Send your reviews to: www.which.co.uk/gfgfeedback

One Aldwych, Axis

Urban hotel dining
Aldwych, WC2B 4RH
Tel no: (020) 7300 0300
www.onealdwych.com
⊖ Covent Garden
Modern European | £35
Cooking score: 3

⊨ V

Axis has been dealt the slickest of twenty-first century makeovers. A spiral staircase sweeps down to the high-ceilinged dining room where waves of sea green silk cascade down walls, there s a screen of slender metal tree trunks and, at well-spaced tables, leather armchairs qualify for the most comfortable in town. The modern British menu reads simply and enticingly and delivers the flavours it promises with creditable panache, say Cheddar Gorge cheese soufflé with Russet apple chutney and Denham Estate venison with parsnip purée, Brussel sprouts and juniper jus. If the pricey carte is beyond your budget, the set price menu (lunchtime and pre/post theatre) is very good value considering the theatreland location, smart setting, level of cooking and swift, professional service: celeriac velouté with sautéed snails, steak and kidney pudding with a fresh oyster and mash, then dark chocolate and pumpkin mousse, all for £17.50, have been recent successes. Although wine prices are highish, there s a good selection by the glass. Bottle prices start at £19.95.
Open: Mon to Fri L 12 to 2.30, Mon to Sat D 5.45 to 10.30 (11.30 Sat). **Closed:** Christmas, New Year, bank hols. **Meals:** alc (main courses £14.40 to £43) Set L and D (before 7.15pm and after 10pm) £17.50 (2 courses) to £20.50. **Service:** 12.5% (optional). **Details:** Cards accepted. 110 seats. Air-con. Wheelchair access. Music. Children's portions.

Rules

Welcoming and resolutely British
35 Maiden Lane, WC2E 7LB
Tel no: (020) 7836 5314
www.rules.co.uk
⊖ Covent Garden
British | £43
Cooking score: 3

This time-honoured restaurant is reputedly the oldest restaurant in London. It boasts a priceless décor, the erstwhile design fit for King George III, who ruled the country when the restaurant first opened. Reassuringly, you may find yourself being seated next to a bust of Lord Nelson, but this historic setting is far from stuffy, possibly due to the relaxed co-existence of visitors and business suits, and the welcoming service, straight from the school of politesse. The cooking is utterly, traditionally British (puds, pies, game), but it is not old-fashioned. Start with a delicious pancake filled with lobster and asparagus and served with field mushrooms. The restaurant supports 'Keep Britain Farming', and has its own estate in the High Pennines, so not surprisingly one main course featured an exemplary roast saddle of Wiltshire rabbit paired with foie gras and a summer truffle risotto. Warm Eccles cakes with butterscotch sauce is a sure way of putting you in a positive mood to tackle the modern world. Wines, mainly sourced from France, and notably strong in the Rhone Valley, start from £17.95, with a wide selection by the glass or in jugs of 50cl.
Chef/s: Richard Sawyer. **Open:** all week 12 to 11.45 (10.45 Sun). **Closed:** 24 to 27 Dec. **Meals:** alc (main courses £17 to £24.50). **Service:** 12.5% (optional). **Details:** Cards accepted. 93 seats. Air-con. No music. No mobile phones. Children's portions.

ALSO RECOMMENDED

▲ Bedford and Strand

1a Bedford Street, WC2E 9HH
Tel no: 020 7836 3033
www.bedford-strand.com
⊖ Covent Garden

First impressions might suggest that this relatively recent arrival to Covent Garden is owned by the corporate big-boys. However, this is a one-off that's owned by a team of young wine enthusiasts, a passion that's evident in a short, keenly priced (three house bottles for £12.50) list that offers a genuinely eye-opening selection – anyone for Brazilian Chardonnay? On the food front, starters kick off with bistro classics such as soupe de poisson (£5.95), while mains range from a fillet of sea bass with ratte potatoes, rocket salad, lemon and smoked paprika aïoli, to pork and leek sausages (£9.95) and shepherd's pie (£8.95). To finish, there's chocolate fondant (£5.50) for pud. Closed Sun.

▲ Mela

152-156 Shaftesbury Avenue, WC2H 8HL
Tel no: (020) 7836 8635
www.melarestaurant.co.uk
⊖ Leicester Square

For those tired of the Bengali cooking common to most high streets, Mela comes as a pleasant surprise. Situated on the outskirts of theaterland, one can be forgiven for thinking that the location (and the garishishly-hued exterior) masks a tasteless experience within. Not so. The Indian 'country-style' menu is as surprising as the choice of lighting (bright). Highlights are mussels hara masala, pot-roast quail marinated in ginger and garlic with mango, and Hyderabadi crab curry. Main courses range between £7.25 and £21.95. House wine starts at £10.50.

▲ Mon Plaisir

21 Monmouth Street, WC2H 9DD
Tel no: (020) 7836 7243

For 35 years, Mon Plaisir has stood like an outpost of France in Covent Garden, and remains a popular choice for pre-theatre meals before 8pm. Those with more time to enjoy their meal can choose from the full repertoire of French classics, ranging from onion soup (£6.75) to steak tartare (£17.45) and coq au vin (£14.50), as well as more inventive offerings such as crab and cauliflower pannacotta with curry (£8.50), or lamb rump with confit garlic and truffle bread-and-butter pudding (£16.95). Finish with raspberry crème brûlée or floating islands. House wines are £12.75 a bottle, or £8.75 for a 50cl carafe.

▲ Sofra

36 Tavistock Street, WC2E 7PB
Tel no: (020) 7240 3773
www.sofra.co.uk
⊖ Covent Garden

The complimentary olives and bread offered to punters perusing the menu at this popular Turkish restaurant exemplify the customer-friendly approach that has kept Sofra on the London scene for more than a quarter of a century. It is open daily from noon to midnight, so is an ideal spot for lunch or a pre- or post-theatre meal. The meze platter (£7.95) provides a good taster for first-timers, while regulars may prefer individual portions of hoummus, cacik or lentil kofte (£3.95). Typical mains are chargrilled chicken, lamb or beef or the lighter cod with coriander and spring onions (£9.95). Honey-glazed shoulder of lamb from the specials menu was good value at £10.95. Desserts (£3.45) include Middle Eastern favourites like creamy coconut rice pudding with rosewater, while tiramisu and crème brûlée cater for the less adventurous. Wines start at £11.65. Other branches are at 18 Shepherd Market, (020) 7493 3320 and 1 Christopher Place (020) 7224 4080, both in W1.

READERS RECOMMEND
Orso
Italian
27 Wellington Street, WC2E 7DA
Tel no: (020) 7240 5269
www.orsorestaurant.co.uk
'Old-fashioned country cuisine'

▌Euston

ALSO RECOMMENDED
▲ Great Nepalese
48 Eversholt Street, NW1 1DA
Tel no: (020) 7388 6737
⊖ Euston

Located on a street just a few minutes away from Euston, you could do worse than to wheel your case over to the Great Nepalese if you are experiencing delays. You will find plenty of warming usual curry-house staples, but more interesting is the wide range of Nepalese specialities. To start try chicken pakora, topped with home-made tomato pickle (£4.35), or haku choyola – barbecued diced mutton with hot spices, garlic and ginger (£4.25). To follow order fish bhuna (£6.75), or nargis kofta, which is boiled eggs covered with minced lamb, barbecued in a charcoal oven with almonds, cream and spices (£6.50). Or try the Nepalese hariyo hash – duck cooked with mint, coconut and cream (£11.95). Set meals are available and wines start at £9.50. Open all week.

▌Fitzrovia
Camerino
Good-value Italian plays to its strengths
16 Percy Street, W1T 1DT
Tel no: (020) 7637 9900
www.camerinorestaurant.com
⊖ Goodge Street
Italian | £33
Cooking score: 3

Just off the bottom of Charlotte Street, Camerino attracts a less touristy crowd than the row's other eateries, with local media execs appreciating the well-spaced tables for quiet business lunches. Red drapes, spherical glass lights and swirly patterns on the walls might suggest modern Italian on the menu, but the cooking is straightforward. You're as likely to find a classic lasagne as roast salmon with spinach and balsamic sauce on the fixed-price menu (excellent value for this part of town). Strong, earthy flavours are in abundance – witness a starter of smoked duck breast with marinated mushrooms – while home-made pasta is the highlight of a meal here, whether a light fettuccine with tomato sauce and basil or a more substantial penne with mussels, garlic and tomato sauce. Desserts continue the theme of well-prepared simplicity with pears poached in red wine, tiramisu or Italian cheeses. House Chardonnay is £17.50 on a reasonably priced, all-Italian wine list.
Chef/s: Valerio Daros. Open: Mon to Fri L 12 to 3, Mon to Sat D 6 to 11. Meals: alc (main courses £18.50 to £20.50). Set L and D 6 to 7 £19.50 (2 courses) to £23.50. Service: 12.5% (optional). Details: Cards accepted. 70 seats. 8 seats outside. Air-con. Wheelchair access. Music. Children's portions.

Fino
Modern tapas served in style
33 Charlotte Street (entrance in Rathbone Street), W1T 1RR
Tel no: (020) 7813 8010
www.finorestaurant.com
⊖ Goodge Street
Spanish | £30
Cooking score: 2

The Hart Brothers' Charlotte Street restaurant is a tapas joint in the loosest sense of the word, bearing little relation to either the British 'sun, sea and sangria' or Spanish spit-and-sawdust model. There is a counter by the semi-open kitchen where one can order a caña and tortilla from an extensive menu of tapas standards, but nearly all opt for a sit-down tapas feast in the somewhat corporate looking basement dining room. Tapas are largely successful, with a range of basics, e.g. pa amb tomaquet, £3.50, or tortilla £5, supplemented by seasonal treats.

Be warned, it soon adds up once you hit the good stuff like jamon Jabugo, £16.50, or tiger prawns, £4.50 each. The wine list is exclusively Iberian with lesser-known regions like Utiel Requena and Toro represented, as well as a super sherry list, much of which is available by the glass. House wines kick off at £16.00

Chef/s: Jean Philippe Patruno. **Open:** Mon to Sat L 12 to 2.30, D 6 to 10.30. **Closed:** Christmas, bank hols. **Meals:** alc (main courses £7 to £16.50). Set L £17.95 to £30 (inc wine; all min 2 or more), Set D £17.95 to £28 (min 2). **Service:** 12.5% (optional). **Details:** Cards accepted. 90 seats. Air-con. No music. Wheelchair access. Children allowed.

Latium

Regional food in sleek surroundings
21 Berners Street, W1T 3LP
Tel no: (020) 7323 9123
www.latiumrestaurant.com
⊖ Goodge Street
Italian | £30
Cooking score: 2

Maurizio Morelli's sleekly attired, minimalist restaurant takes it name from the Italian region of Lazio (Latium), and his food has a strong regional bias. The kitchen flaunts its 'passion for ravioli' with a full menu devoted to these stuffed morsels: among the possibilities might be a version filled with Taleggio, Swiss chard and walnuts or veal with courgette and Pecorino. The regular seasonal carte could open with foie gras terrine and Morello cherry bread or pea soup with chervil and Ricotta, while main courses might range from grilled tuna with braised baby lettuce, red wine vinegar, capers and shallot dressing to poached beef fillet with spinach, pickled baby carrots, toasted hazelnut and tomato broth. Regional cheeses are alternatives to desserts such as chocolate and almond tart with Amaretto sauce. The all-Italian wine list has plenty of good stuff from Piedmont and elsewhere. Prices start at £14.50 and around a dozen are available by the glass.

Chef/s: Maurizio Morelli. **Open:** Mon to Fri L 12 to 2.45, Mon to Sat D 6 to 10.30 (11 Sat). **Closed:** bank hols. **Meals:** Set L and D £24.50 (2 courses) to £32.50. **Service:** 12.5% (optional). **Details:** Cards accepted. Air-con. Wheelchair access. Music.

Passione

Sassy southern-Italian food
10 Charlotte Street, W1T 2LT
Tel no: (020) 7636 2833
www.passione.co.uk
⊖ Goodge Street
Italian | £41
Cooking score: 4

Trendy Charlotte Street throngs with bustling restaurants and informal eateries and Gennaro Contaldo's intimate restaurant, hidden behind a narrow, unassuming shop-front flanked by potted bay trees, draws a loyal crowd for simple, modern Italian food. Lightwood chairs and a dark wood floor create a clean, convivial ambience, and the contemporary regional Italian cooking echoes this feeling. The menu is a sensible length, with a balance between meat, fish and vegetables, the carefully sourced ingredients include wild produce where possible, and dishes look good. They range from the robust and hearty, such as a main course of rabbit with pistachios, sun-dried tomatoes, black olives and sautéed potatoes, a simple risotto (wild sorrel, butter and parmesan) and pasta dishes (ribbon pasta with truffle sauce), to the sophisticated, perhaps pan-fried turbot with parmesan, asparagus and pea shoots. Flavours are paramount throughout. Desserts include liquorice pannacotta with berry sauce, a classic tiramisu, or round off with the aged-pecorino cheese served with chestnuts, honey and crispy Sardinian bread. The all-Italian wine list starts at £14.50, with little choice by the glass.

Chef/s: Mario Magli. **Open:** Mon to Fri L 12.30 to 2.15, Mon to Sat D 7 to 10.15. **Meals:** alc (main courses £21 to £26). **Service:** 12.5% (optional). **Details:** Cards accepted. 42 seats. 6 seats outside. No music.

Pied-à-Terre

Meticulously rendered French food
34 Charlotte Street, W1T 2NH
Tel no: (020) 7636 1178
www.pied-a-terre.co.uk
⊖ **Goodge Street**
French | £58
Cooking score: 8

🍷 V

Design makeovers continue to proceed at a stately pace at Pied-à-Terre, in what has always felt a rather womb-like interior. The narrow space could easily feel cramped, and yet doesn't because of some clever mirroring, artfully directed lighting and a large skylight. Staff are supremely capable and courteous, the sommelier knowing what you have ordered and making apposite, sensible suggestions. This contributes to the sense of a quality restaurant firing on all cylinders. Nibble an olive or two, glance at the menus, recline into the wine list, and all seems right with the world, an impression reinforced when the excellent breads and row of canapés arrive. Shane Osborn's cooking has pursued an interesting trajectory in recent years. He is one of those chefs who has journeyed out to the wilder shores, picked up some ideas and then headed back to safe harbour again, combining modern juxtapositions with classical technique. This results in dishes like slices of bluefin tuna wrapped in Parma ham, topped with soft-boiled quail eggs, and encircled with new season's broad beans and a parsley purée. Impressive, both for the standard and the timing of the tuna. A main course of blackleg chicken from Landes reminds us that chicken doesn't have to be the less exciting option. It came as a beautifully tender breast served with English spring vegetables, a smooth-textured garlic purée, well-made gnocchi and a top-notch reduction of the cooking juices. Kid goat has often cropped up on the menu here, perhaps with caramelised endive and roasted shallots, or there may be Devon venison loin, roasted and poached, served with Savoy cabbage, bacon, quince purée and walnuts. Excellent French cheeses

are the alternative to the fiendishly inventive desserts, which might take in mandarin parfait with toasted marshmallow, citrus filo, fromage frais sorbet and blood orange foam. There is an incredibly good wine list, or rather lists, a volume each for reds and whites. Growers are carefully selected, and the range is as inspiring in the New World as in the Old. California and Australia are both sensational, there are pedigree Italians and Germans, and lovers of classical French stuff will be in clover. Prices start at £22 for a Rueda white, with glasses from £5.

Chef/s: Shane Osborn. **Open:** Mon to Fri L 12.15 to 2.35, Mon to Sat D 6.15 to 10.45. **Closed:** Last week Dec. **Meals:** Set L £24.50 (2 courses) to £30, Set D £49.50 (2 courses) to £62.50. **Service:** 12.5% (optional). **Details:** Cards accepted. 46 seats. Air-con. Wheelchair access. Music.

Roka

Terrific Japanese food
37 Charlotte Street, W1T 1RR
Tel no: (020) 7580 6464
www.rokarestaurant.com
⊖ **Goodge Street**
Japanese | £35
Cooking score: 4

An open aspect on this stylish corner site ensures a generous amount of foot traffic and helps to maintain the bustling atmosphere, but sound effects 'can reach soprano levels'. The izakaya concept is taken a step further here, with a small army of chefs working on the robata grill. The DNA connection with Roka's older sibling, Zuma, is also evident when it comes to the menu, which is divided into snacks, sashimi and Roka dishes. Although underpinned by Japanese influences, the cooking has a distinct cross-cultural slant. A delicate maki roll of king crab leg tempura is a sensible way to kick things off, then flame-grilled tofu, artfully arranged, made special by a piquant dip of crushed yuzu and barley miso. Tasty baby pork ribs, which had been slowly pre-cooked with citrus fruit and spices before being placed on the grill, hit all the right notes, too. Finish with honey chawan mushi (egg custard) served with a medley of fruits. The erudite service is pleasant, helpfully guiding you through the menu. Wines and sake, in tune with the style of food, start high at £21.

Chef/s: Nicholas Watt and Rainer Becker. **Open:** Mon to Sat L 12 to 2.30, all week D 5.30 to 11.15 (10 Sun); summer all week 12 to 11.15. **Meals:** alc (main courses £7 to £55). Set L £15 to £25, Set D £50 to £75. **Service:** 13.5% (optional). **Details:** Cards accepted. 88 seats. 20 seats outside. Air-con. Wheelchair access. Music.

Salt Yard

A vibrant sweep of the Med
54 Goodge Street, W1T 4NA
Tel no: (020) 7637 0657
www.saltyard.co.uk
⊖ **Goodge Street**
Mediterranean | £25
Cooking score: 2

V

Billed as a 'charcuterie bar and restaurant', Salt Yard, which takes inspiration from Italy as well as Spain, is not your average tapas joint. Kick off with 18-month cured Serrano ham and a selection of three Pecorinos with truffle honey, say. Hot dishes range from respectful treatments of crowd-pleasers such as crisply battered, squeaky fresh squid with a gentle aïoli to creative spins on classic tapas such as morcilla croquetas and dishes that are effectively mini main courses: try the meltingly tender, braised beef cheek with farro, peas and broad beans. Special mention must go to the signature dish of courgette flowers stuffed with Monte Enebro cheese and drizzled with honey, one of several notable vegetarian options. Good-value prices draw a lively young crowd, though popularity means that table turning can operate, something that is handled with tact by the brisk staff. Sit for preference on the ground floor, higher on atmosphere if lower on space than the somewhat stark basement where an open kitchen forms the focal point. A snappy Spanish and Italian wine list offers eight sherries by the glass. House wine is £14.50.

Chef/s: Benjamin Tish. **Open:** Mon to Fri L 12 to 3, Mon to Sat D 6 to 11. **Closed:** bank holidays. **Meals:** alc (tapas £3 to £8.50, charcuterie £7.50 to £13). **Service:** 12.5% (optional). **Details:** Cards accepted. 70 seats. 12 seats outside. Air-con. Wheelchair access. Music. Children allowed.

Sardo

Upmarket Sardinian offerings
45 Grafton Way, W1T 5DQ
Tel no: (020) 7387 2521
www.sardo-restaurant.com
⊖ **Warren Street**
Italian | £30
Cooking score: 4

Don't be deceived by this Sardinian specialist's off-the-beaten-track location and pleasantly rustic interior: the family-run restaurant is one of the unsung heroes of the London restaurant scene and a first meal here can feel like stumbling across a well-kept secret, though with booking advised even early in the week, Sardo obviously has a considerable number of fans. A terrific bread basket (including the moreish olive focaccia) and a smashing bowl of juicy olives set the tone for simple cooking with an emphasis on unfussy flavour and top-quality ingredients. At inspection, sun-dried fillet of tuna made a memorable starter, the pungency of the fish nicely offset by French beans and sun-dried tomatoes. To follow, pasta parcels filled with pecorino cheese and potatoes with a sauce of fresh tomatoes and mint was fresh tasting and light; for something heartier, there are deftly handled meat and fish grills. Desserts take in the classics – lemon tart, pannacotta, tiramisu. Charming, knowledgeable service. The bulk of the Sardinian bottles on the wine list are under £30, with more elevated – but still reasonable – prices for big hitters from the rest of Italy. House wine is £14.

Chef/s: Roberto Sardu. **Open:** Mon to Fri L 12 to 3, Mon to Sat D 6 to 11. **Closed:** 25 Dec, bank hols. **Meals:** alc (main courses £12 to £16.50). **Service:** 12.5% (optional). **Details:** Cards accepted. Air-con. Wheelchair access. Music.

ALSO RECOMMENDED

▲ Villandry

170 Great Portland Street, W1W 5QB
Tel no: (020) 7631 3131
www.villandry.com
⊖ Great Portland Street

The steady encroachment of dining tables as the retail grocery side is scaled down finds the denizens of Fitzrovia mourning the loss of their much-loved food emporium – vociferously, if our reader feedback is anything to go by. For everyone else, casual all-day dining ranges from coffee and croissants to plates of charcuterie and salads, with a large bar serving food at lunch and dinner. In the more formal, light, spacious dining room, fried organic egg with Toulouse sausage and sautéed wild mushrooms (£9.50), fillet of sea bass with artichoke and salsify lyonnaise and truffle dressing (£22.50) and tarte Tatin with vanilla ice cream (£5.75) typify the pricey, French-led menu. House wine is £13.50. Closed Sun D.

READERS RECOMMEND

Pescatori

Seafood
57 Charlotte Street, W1T 4PD
Tel no: (020) 7580 3289
'Rustic cooking focusing on fresh fish'

▌Green Park

Al Hamra

Mezze in the market
3133 Shepherd Market, W1J 7PT
Tel no: (020) 7493 1954
www.alhamrarestaurant.co.uk
⊖ Green Park
Middle Eastern | £28
Cooking score: 2

♀ V £30

There's a relaxed, continental feel to this popular Lebanese restaurant. Meat and vegetarian mezze dishes, include hummus, tabbouleh and arayes al Hamra, a speciality

dish of minced lamb made with onion, sesame seeds and pine nuts on a pizza-style dough base. Mains incline more towards meat eaters: skewered lamb chunks and whole boneless baby chicken, say. Desserts are less numerous with a Lebanese milk pudding topped with crushed pistachios the only one on offer at inspection. The restaurant serves French wine from £15 a bottle and Lebanese wine at £21.50. But note the minimum charge of £20 per person, so it's not the place to go if you are after a light bite. Alfresco seats fill up quickly in the summer, so book ahead.
Chef/s: Mahir Abboud. **Open:** all week, 12 to 11.30. **Closed:** 22 Dec to 2 Jan. **Meals:** alc (main courses £13 to £22.50). Set L £20 to £25, Set D £25 to £30. Cover £2.50. **Service:** not inc. **Details:** Cards accepted. 65 seats. 24 seats outside. Air-con. Wheelchair access. Music. Children's portions. Children allowed.

Greenhouse

Finely tuned French gastronomie
27a Hays Mews, W1J 5NY
Tel no: (020) 7499 3331
www.greenhouserestaurant.co.uk
⊖ Green Park
Modern European | £67
Cooking score: 6

The name is misleading, though the restaurant is reached via a fairy-lit decked walkway lined with elegantly clipped trees, The Greenhouse has recently been refurbished and is the height of sophisticated urbanity. Lyon-born Antonin Bonnet used to be the private chef for Marlon Abela, who also owns Umu (see entry), and one can only say that Mr Abela has shown the utmost generosity in sharing the Frenchman's talent with a wider public. Bonnet's repertoire includes a seven-course tasting menu and a seasonal menu based around a theme ('Crustacean & Shellfish', at inspection), alongside an à la carte that might start with a dish that has the smooth-textured sweetness of pan-fried scallop set off by the crunch of salted, toasted almonds and the juiciness of golden raisins scattered in a celeriac couscous. To follow, Bresse pigeon breasts served just the right side of rare served on top of a pungent cream made from the giblets and almonds, the legs served confit on the side, a ravioli filled with pigeon liver and cool cucumber relish acting as a palate cleanser amid the richness. Desserts, many based vogueishly around ice cream, might include pineapple carpaccio with crunchy cereals and coconut ice cream, but at inspection the intermittent wafts from a passing cheese trolley proved irresistible, the predominantly French board kept in tip-top condition. A 100-page wine list showcases one of the world's finest cellars, with a by-the-glass selection that would be the entire wine list of a lesser establishment. House wine is £21.00 and swiftly accelerates in price. **Chef/s:** Antonin Bonnet. **Open:** Mon to Sat L 12 to 2.30, D 6.45 to 11. **Closed:** Christmas, bank hols. **Meals:** Set L £29 to £60, Set D £60 to £75. **Service:** 12.5% (optional). **Details:** Cards accepted. 70 seats. Air-con. Separate bar. No music. Wheelchair access. Children's portions.

▌Holborn

Chancery

European cuisine for London's legal eagles
9 Cursitor Street, EC4A 1LL
Tel no: (020) 7831 4000
www.thechancery.co.uk
⊖ Chancery Lane
Modern European | £30
Cooking score: 4

The restaurant's name is a clue to its location, just off Chancery Lane in the moneyed backwaters of central London's 'lawyerland'. Inside, the fabric of the high-ceilinged building has been brought up-to-date with mahogany parquet floors, brown leather chairs and abstract oils on dark brown walls. It is a place of fluctuating moods, veering from the frenzied hubbub of power lunches to more genteel, informal intimacy at night. Terse dish descriptions suggest that the kitchen is familiar with the prevailing culinary *lingua franca*, and influences from the Mediterranean loom large. Crisp red mullet with beetroot

Aiden Byrne **Grill at the Dorchester**

Why did you become a chef?
It was the first thing I fell in love with.

Which of today's chefs do you admire?
Tom Aikens.

Where do you eat out?
The Square, Tom Aikens, Sketch, the Fat Duck.

Where do you source your ingredients?
Mainly from the British Isles, and my favourite producer is Richard Vine from R.V. Salads.

What's your favourite cookery book?
I would have to say *L'Encyclopedia Culinaire du XXIe Siecle* by Marc Veyrat.

What's the best dish you've ever eaten?
Probably Heston Blumenthal's salmon with liquorice.

Do you have a favourite local recipe?
Being based in London you don't really get local recipes, but I do love the asparagus season.

What's the hardest thing about running a restaurant?
Keeping the staff motivated 18 hours a day.

What's coming up next for you?
A cookery book and hopefully more accolades.

carpaccio or rabbit beignet with quinoa, blood orange and cardamom dressing lay down colourful markers, ahead of Manuka smoked monkfish and tiger prawns with Puy lentils and confit tomato ravioli or fillet of pork wrapped in Parma ham with pearl barley and salsify. The kitchen's light touch and eye for clear presentation extends to desserts such as retro banana split with chocolate ice cream and a boozy 'B52' parfait blitzed with Kahlua, Baileys and Grand Manier. The concise wine list offers a sharp selection of international names with a sound pedigree. House recommendations start at £15 (£5.50 a glass). Andrew Thompson and Zak Jones also run the Clerkenwell Dining Room (see entry).

Chef/s: Andrew Thompson. **Open:** Mon to Fri L 12 to 2.30, D 6 to 10.30. **Closed:** 22 Dec to 2 Jan, bank hols. **Meals:** Set L and D £15.50 (2 courses) to £20.50, Set D £32. **Service:** Service: 12.5% (optional). **Details:** Cards accepted. 50 seats. Air-con. Wheelchair access. Music.

Matsuri High Holborn
Modern design and traditonal Japanese cooking
71 High Holborn, WC1V 6EA
Tel no: (020) 7430 1970
www.matsuri-restaurant.com
⊖ Holborn
Japanese | £45
Cooking score: 3

Matsuri stands out from the crowd in busy mid-town, thanks to its well-appointed interior design. Natural light from the lofty floor-to-ceiling windows helps to illuminate the main dining room, and the space is both attractive and functional. In contrast to its modern design, Matsuri continues to serve traditional Japanese dishes, and the menu here covers many of the classics, including teppanyaki, which can be enjoyed in the rather austere basement room. A typical meal could start with dobinmushi, a clear vegetable soup served in an earthenware teapot, followed by a platter of sushi or sashimi, brimming with scallops, 'so fresh it tasted velvety', and firm, tasty pieces of o-toro, salmon and turbot. For main course, beef teriyaki made with excellent

quality ribeye, and to finish a rather workmanlike raspberry sorbet. Moderate prices, especially at lunchtimes, ensure a loyal following from nearby offices, and service has been singled out as being 'particularly courteous'. There is a fair selection of wines as well as hot and cold sakes with prices starting from £16. The original branch in St James is on 15 Bury Street, London SW1Y 6AL, tel (020) 7839 1101.

Chef/s: Hiroshi Sudo. **Open:** Mon to Sat L 12 to 2.30, D 6 to 10. **Closed:** Christmas, bank hols. **Meals:** alc (main courses £16 to £35). Set L £8.50 (2 courses) to £22, Set D £35 (4 courses) to £70. **Service:** 12.5% (optional). **Details:** Cards accepted. 100 seats. Air-con. Wheelchair access. Music.

Pearl
Insightful cooking and a sumptuous interior
252 High Holborn, WC1V 7EN
Tel no: (020) 7829 7000
www.pearl-restaurant.com
⊖ Holborn
Modern European | £50
Cooking score: 5

🌡 🛏 V

Connected to an elegant hotel in a striking landmark building built originally for the Pearl Assurance Company, Pearl's opulent dining room, with its stylish bar, is a thoughtful blend of modern furnishings and Edwardian architecture. The cooking here is far from precious, and good technique is used to mobilise a trio of excellent amuse-bouche – rabbit rillette, imam bayaldi, hummus – served with olive ciabatta, and a vivacious starter of warm, fleshy mackerel fondant with à la grecque vegetables. Jun Tanaka's adventurous ideas are enhanced on the plate by skilful cooking, fine presentation and interesting variations of flavour and texture, but appear to work best when not preoccupied with multiplicity of flavours: an osso buco raviolo with Jerusalem artichokes plus a foam, jus and oil, was packed with so much meat that it was trying to burst out. To finish, a delectable prune custard tart with walnut ice cream put the meal firmly back on course. The enthusiastic service team is young and relaxed, but a little green. The stellar wine list includes a fine collection from the USA and starts at £18, but is marred by the high pricing policy – for example, 30 wines come by the glass and start at £5, but more than half are over £10. **Chef/s:** Jun Tanaka. **Open:** Mon to Fri L 12 to 2.30, Mon to Sat D 6 to 10. **Closed:** Christmas to New Year, Easter, last 2 weeks Aug. **Meals:** Set L £25 (2 courses) to £28, Set D £29.50 (2 courses) to £55. **Service:** 12.5% (included). **Details:** Cards accepted. 70 seats. Air-con. No mobile phones. Wheelchair access. Music.

White Swan

Multi-faceted dining experience
108 Fetter Lane, EC4A 1ES
Tel no: (020) 7242 9696
www.thewhiteswanlondon.com
⊖ **Chancery Lane**
Gastropub | £34
Cooking score: 3

Tom and Ed Martin's flagship city dining pub continues to thrive, drawing in drinkers to the buzzing groundfloor bar, and diners up the big, mirror-lined staircase to the more formal dining room above. The latter is a stylish space: polished wooden floors are reflected back from a mirrored ceiling along with the white-clad tables. Appealing, crowd-pleasing menus come bolstered by daily specials, the kitchen looking to Britain and Europe for inspiration. Start with Denham Estate venison carpaccio with caramelised apples, watercress and parsnip cream, or scallops with bacon blini, pea purée and truffle oil. The main course repertoire extends to line-caught sea bass with Jerusalem artichoke purée, sun-dried tomato and fennel foam, and roast duck breast with Bordelaise jus. Desserts embrace banana and toffee cheesecake as well as milk and white chocolate mousse with raspberry jelly. The international wine list is pretty extensive, with a dozen good-quality bottles served by the glass. Prices by the bottle open at £14.50.

Chef/s: Grant Murray. **Open:** Mon to Fri L 12 to 3, D 6 to 10. **Closed:** Christmas, New Year, bank hols. **Meals:** alc D (main courses £13 to £19.50). Set L £20 (2 courses) to £25. Bar menu available.. **Service:** 12.5% (optional). **Details:** Cards accepted. 40 seats. Air-con. Music. Children's portions.

READERS RECOMMEND

The Terrace
Caribbean
Lincolns Inn Fields, WC2A 3LJ
Tel no: 020 7430 1234
www.theterrace.info
'Hidden café in a city oasis'

The Bountiful Cow
British
51 Eagle Street, WC1R 4AP
Tel no: (020) 7404 0200
'A peculiar combo of jazz bar and steak house'

Vivat Bacchus
Global
47 Farringdon Street, EC4A 4LL
Tel no: (020) 7353 2648
www.vivatbacchus.co.uk
'Eclectic menu with an epic wine list'

▮ Hyde Park

Alain Ducasse at The Dorchester
Ultra-refined French cooking
The Dorchester Hotel, 53 Park Lane, W1K 1QA
Tel no: 020 7629 8866
www.alainducasse-dorchester.com
⊖ **Hyde Park Corner**
French | £75
Cooking score: 4

Alain Ducasse is a man with an empire; he runs restaurants all over the world. London, however, has proved a tough nut to crack – the Philippe Starck designed Spoon at the Sanderson hotel didn't take – so much is riding on Alain Ducasse at the Dorchester with its accent on an ultra refined style of

French haute cuisine and big money. Neither the dining room nor the menu are intended to challenge. The food plays safe, combining generally top class materials with treatments that are straight Escoffier, lightly dusted with contemporary ingredients like squid bonbons, coco chutney, or ponzu dressing. While precise cooking yielded soft-boiled organic egg, crayfish and wild mushrooms served with a luscious sauce Nantua, and 'a rich, light and boozy' rum baba has been a hit at dessert stage, other areas could use a rethink (a winter pre-starter of crudité, for example). On the whole techniques are well drilled, but central ingredients tend to outshine their accompaniments, as in an impeccably rendered, tender, pink venison fillet served with a dull tangle of fruit and vegetables and an ungenerous serving of Grand Veneur sauce – a worry, for at these prices every dish needs to deliver consistent impact on the plate. Wines contribute energetically to the cost. The list offers encyclopaedic coverage of France with forays further afield, but budget options are hardly to be expected – the baseline is £25.
Chef/s: Jocelyn Herland. **Open:** Tue to Sat L 12 to 2, D 6.30 to 10. **Closed:** 10 to 31 Aug, 26 to 30 Dec. **Meals:** alc (£55 for 2 courses) to £75. Set L £35 (3 courses). **Service:** 12.5% (optional). **Details:** Cards accepted. 82 seats. Air-con. Wheelchair access. Music.

China Tang at The Dorchester

The Dorchester Hotel, 53 Park Lane, W1K 1QA
Tel no: (020) 7629 8888
www.thedorchester.com
⊖ Hyde Park Corner
Chinese | £40
Cooking score: 2

🍽 V

If looks alone could make a restaurant, China Tang would have nothing to worry about. A brainchild of David Tang, owner of the fashion house, Shanghai Tang, it has quickly established itself on the itinerary of the jet set. Easy to see why given the salubrious location – a subterranean space of the Dorchester

Hotel, with a glittery dining room, designed to resemble a cruise liner in the 1920's, flushed with silk embroidery covers, elegant lattice screens and glorious antiques. Service, on the other hand is somewhat lacking in charm and somnolent. The menu does not stray beyond Cantonese, although Peking duck (£48) has received much praise. The flavours pander more to westernised palates; pleasures are flickering, fried bean curd with spicy salt and pepper was exemplary but the spell was broken by an ordinary crispy rice noodles with pork, before roast duck in glass noodles restored proceedings. Desserts steer well away from the Orient, despite mangosteen making a brief appearance in a meringue. The glamour may be infectious but any slight frivolity can be hideously expensive; a bowl of boiled rice is £3, a plate of bean sprouts will set you back £8, but highly respectable dim sum is economical option at lunchtime. The wine list, focusing on prestige labels can easily burn a hole in your pocket, with no bottles under £29. Cognac, the tipple of choice for the Chinese old rich is well represented and features an 1853 Hennessey for £19,000.
Chef/s: Ringo Chow. **Open:** all week, L 11 to 3.30 D 5.30 to 12. **Meals:** alc (main courses from £10 to £150). Set L £15 (2 courses). **Service:** 12.5%. **Details:** Cards accepted. 150 seats.

Grill at The Dorchester
Talented chef attracting industry attention
The Dorchester Hotel, 53 Park Lane, W1A 2HJ
Tel no: 020 7629 8888
www.thedorchester.com
⊖ Hyde Park Corner
Modern British | £60
Cooking score: 5

🍽 V

It appears we are witnessing a mini-stampede of leading chefs to this exclusive corner of Park Lane. Aiden Byrne has breathed new life into the Grill's previously outmoded menu (though the same can't be said for the new décor – a riot of tartan and murals of burly Highlanders). Highlights at inspection included a serving of Dublin Bay prawns, some pan-fried, another in tempura, brilliantly paired with a purée of broccoli and gnocchi filled with a little ricotta cheese. Every dish seems to be accompanied by a second instalment, in this case a glass filled with alternating layers of broccoli purée and ricotta topped with langoustine caviar. While the menu descriptions intrigue for their intricacy and imagination, the 'ambitious and restless' cooking doesn't always deliver. Experimentation can go astray, as in the case of a John Dory, its skin rubbed with almonds and red pepper, served with a courgette fritto, along with a chorizo risotto, red pepper tuile and parmesan. With so many competing flavours, this one failed to make its point. Nevertheless, this is a chef to watch. When the ideas do work, the results can be thrilling, and a banana and peanut crumble, accompanied by a 'divine' palm sugar ice cream and pineapple roasted with Malibu, was a case in point. The wine list, as substantial as the dining room, matches the Park Lane location in price. France takes centre stage, but other countries are equally well represented, including an impressive flight of Harlan. The section entitled '30 under 30' does provide refuge for more modest pockets.

Chef/s: Aiden Byrne. **Open:** all week L 12 to 2.30 (12.30 to 3 Sun), D 6.30 to 11 (6 to 11 Sat, 7 to 10 Sun). **Meals:** alc (main courses £26 to £32) Set L £25 (2 courses) to £27.50. **Service:** 12.5% (included). **Details:** Cards accepted. 75 seats. Air-con. Separate bar. No mobile phones. Wheelchair access. Music. Children's portions. Children allowed.

READERS RECOMMEND

Cookbook Cafe
Modern British
1 Hamilton Place, W1J 7QY
Tel no: (0207) 318 8563
www.cookbookcafe.co.uk
'Food, events and recipes – a real winner!'

The Conservatory at the Lanesborough
Modern European
Hyde Park Corner, SW1X 7TA
Tel no: (020) 7259 5599
www.lanesborough.com
'Glass-roofed room with a Chinoiserie theme'

Knightsbridge

Amaya
Stylish restaurant pulls out the stops
15 Halkin Arcade, Motcomb Street, SW1X 8JT
Tel no: (020) 7823 1166
www.amaya.biz
⊖ Knightsbridge
Indian | £44
Cooking score: 3

Few restaurants can boast such a captivating interior, 'a hedonistic mix of informality and style' and in the evening, the atmosphere simply rocks with a decidedly fashionable crowd. But it's worth concentrating on the grazing menu, which offers Indian street food elevated to Belgravia. Delivered from an open-plan kitchen and based on three different cooking methods (tandoor, charcoal grill, iron skillet), much of the cooking is enticing. Subtle spicing helped to elevate a pair of grilled lamb chops delicately imbued with ginger, lime and coriander, fresh spotted grouper came with a mustard, chilli, peanut mix and was served with pandan leaves, and staples – naan, basmati rice – are praiseworthy. If there is a niggle, it's the small portions 'which may be helpful for achieving size zero' but can result in having to order more 'leading to a surprising uplift to the final bill'. Service is well-mannered and fleet-footed. Wines, thoughtfully assembled, start from £18.50 but rise steeply, although there are 35 by the glass from £6.10.

Chef/s: Karunesh Khanna. **Open:** all week L 12.30 to 2.30 (to 3 Sun), D 6.30 to 11 (10.30 Sun). **Closed:** 25 Dec. **Meals:** Set L £16, Set D £38. **Service:** 12.5%. **Details:** Cards accepted. 99 seats. Air-con. Separate bar. Wheelchair access. Music. Children allowed.

Boxwood Café

Swish brasserie with prices to match
Berkeley Hotel, Wilton Place, SW1X 7RL
Tel no: (020) 7235 1010
www.gordonramsay.com
⊖ **Knightsbridge**
Modern British | £45
Cooking score: 3

With its own entrance at the Berkeley Hotel, the Boxwood sits on a spacious corner plot just below street level. The split-level dining room exudes an urbane air and is modern in design, with art deco lighting, shimmering gold effect walls and muted brown colours. The bustling atmosphere from a cosmopolitan crowd effortlessly captures that Knightsbridge buzz, and, while it may be one of the least prominent restaurants of the Gordon Ramsay group, it can still pack a punch. Highlights of its brasserie-style menu have included a starter of plump-baked queen scallops paired with a silky sea urchin butter, decorously presented over a cast-iron skillet filled with rock salt. Mains might feature moist chicken, grilled and then poached, and enhanced by a fragrant broth infused with thyme. To finish, perhaps a bulls-eye carpaccio of pineapple and roasted mango befittingly accompanied by a fine Campari and blood orange granita. The well-constructed wine list starts from £20, though there are some 30 on offer by glass from £5 for the more budget conscious.
Chef/s: Stuart Gillies. **Open:** all week 12 to 3 (4 Sat and Sun), 6 to 11. **Meals:** alc (main courses £10.50 to £28). Set L £25, Set D £55. **Service:** 12.5%. **Details:** Cards accepted. 140 seats. Air-con. No mobile phones. Wheelchair access. Music. Children's portions.

Brasserie St Quentin

A dynamic Knightsbridge eatery
243 Brompton Road, SW3 2EP
Tel no: (020) 7589 8005
www.brasseriestquentin.co.uk
⊖ **South Kensington**
French | £49
Cooking score: 3

Evoking traditional French brasserie style, this long-running west London restaurant none the less moves with the times, inspired by a youthful kitchen team with fresh ideas. Among starters on the regularly changing menu, classic fish soup with aïoli and croûtons might rub shoulders with linguini with foie gras and peas, or a pigeon terrine with pear chutney. Main courses show similarly broad scope, ranging from good old-fashioned ribeye of Buccleuch beef with béarnaise and chips, or calf's liver with port-glazed shallots and mash, to dishes with a more contemporary feel, such as crab-crusted halibut with baby leeks, lemongrass and ginger broth. End perhaps with hot chocolate fondant with burnt orange ice cream, or caramelised banana terrine. A predominantly French wine list opens with house selections at £14.50.
Chef/s: Gary Durrant. **Open:** all week 12 to 3, 6 to 10.30 (10 Sun). **Closed:** 23 to 30 Dec. **Meals:** alc (main courses £10.50 to £25). Set L and D 6 to 7.30 to £18 (3 courses). **Service:** 12.5% (optional). **Details:** Cards accepted. 55 seats. Air-con. No music.

The Capital

Refined haute cuisine
22-26 Basil Street, SW3 1AT
Tel no: (020) 7591 1202
www.capitalhotel.co.uk
⊖ **Knightsbridge**
French | £55
Cooking score: 7

🍷 🍽 V

Hidden away down a side street behind Harrods, The Capital makes a virtue of discretion, going about its business with cool

Best for business

London has no shortage of places to take clients who need to be impressed.

Hibiscus

Claude Bosi transplants the idiosyncratic cooking of Hibiscus from Ludlow to city premises just off Regent Street. The décor is easy on the eye, and the location perfect for Mayfair types.

Le Gavroche

The Roux institution may have been in and out of fashion over the decades, but the stylish French cooking, impeccable service and womb-like basement room are the last word in class.

The Capital

Grand hotel dining-rooms can be anonymous places, but the Capital has always offered luxe style on a human scale. Eric Chavot's high-gloss cooking is full of personality.

The White Swan

The Martin brothers' reconstructed gastropubs in the City are worth a look. The White Swan on Fetter Lane is the flagship, comprising a bustling bar with a formal dining-room.

Lindsay House

Richard Corrigan offers a mix of new-wave Irish and European cookery at Lindsay House in Soho. You may be within a stone's-throw of central London at its lewdest, but the feel is more country-house hotel.

L'Atelier du Joël Robuchon

Once part of a movement in which France's culinary glitterati began establishing outposts

all over the world, Parisian star Robuchon brings up-to-the-minute, modern cuisine to a sexily lit venue near Leicester Square.

Galvin Bistrot de Luxe

Galvin Bistrot de Luxe on Baker Street brings high-end French comfort food at less-than-drop-dead prices to an area in need of culinary regeneration.

Zuma

Restful Zen garden landscaping comes to a Knightsbridge office block, and so do fabulously fresh sushi and sashimi.

Aubergine

Top-drawer dining in Chelsea. The room is genteel and civilised, and the cooking is contemporary as well as being polished.

Send your reviews to: www.which.co.uk/gfgfeedback

aplomb. Two grand chandeliers hang from the lofty ceiling of the wood-panelled dining room, although it feels remarkably cosy, with just nine well-spaced tables. Over the years, Eric Chavot has become a grand master of refined French haute cuisine, bringing the best out of top-drawer ingredients and allowing flavours and textures to do their work cohesively. A single plump seared scallop sits on a pool of foaming tomato and lemon 'sauce vierge', garnished with a slice of Melba toast and intense tapenade, while unctuous foie gras terrine arrives in a little jar topped with apple foam, all accompanied by a pool of apple compote on the side, some celeriac rémoulade and a slice of gingerbread. By contrast, an inspector who has always viewed The Capital as 'a bastion of reliability' found little to applaud when it came to a main course involving 'seriously overcooked' sea bream. That said, the kitchen has more than proved its worth on other occasions with exemplary roasted lobster with tagliolini pasta and sauce vierge. The cheeseboard is an absolute stunner, comprising 17 species from arguably 'the best affineur in France', Bernard Antony: choice, quality and ripeness are beyond reproach, from two-year-old aged Comte to rarities like Tomme de Carayac. Desserts have displayed plenty of top-end technique and execution, as in homemade yoghurt with an intense red fruit and prune compote and a silky Jivara chocolate ice cream embellished with a thin stick of chocolate or a neatly balanced assemblage of Calvados jelly, apple jelly and hot caramelised apple contrasting with a textbook crème brûlée. Coffee is excellent, although petits fours seem to have moved into fashionable Spanish territory, with variable results. The wine list is a very grand affair covering the classic French regions in exhaustive detail and providing some seriously fine alternatives from Italy, Australia and Germany. Expect to pay at least £30 for even the humblest offerings, although there are also plenty of half-bottles and a few options from £6 a glass.

Chef/s: Eric Chavot. **Open:** all week L 12 to 2.30, D 6.45 to 10.30. **Meals:** Set L £29.50 to £68, Set D £55 to £68. **Service:** 12.5% (optional). **Details:** Cards accepted. 34 seats. Air-con. No mobile phones. Music.

Fifth Floor
Harvey Nic's flagship brasserie
Harvey Nichols, 109-125 Knightsbridge, SW1X 7RJ
Tel no: (020) 7235 5250
www.harveynichols.com
⊖ **Knightsbridge**
Modern British | £42
Cooking score: 3

🍷 **V**

The fifth-floor food court at Harvey Nichols offers a sushi bar, wine boutique, food hall, café and bar, but the culinary centre of gravity remains with the restaurant. The kitchen continues to deliver, sending out decent renditions of uptown brasserie cooking for which the place has always been renowned. This is the sort of place where you could eat smoked mackerel, celeriac and apple remoulade with lemon and fennel syrup, or a simple Colston Bassett Stilton with wild rocket and olive oil. Main courses may include fish cakes with buttered spinach, mixed leaves and pickled ginger buerre blanc, or honey roast loin of Middle White pork with pommes mousseline, chestnuts and sage jus. Expect fresh orange segments with crème fraîche and orange sorbet and French meringue, or chocolate fondue for two for dessert. Harvey Nichols' own-label house wine starts at £14.
Chef/s: Jonas Carlson. **Open:** all week L 12 to 3 (3.30 Fri, 4 Sat and Sun), Mon to Sat D 6 to 11. **Meals:** alc (main courses £14.50 to £19.50). Set L £19.50 (2 courses) to £24.50. Set D £19.50 (2 courses) to £39.50. Bar menu available. **Service:** 12.5% (optional). **Details:** Cards accepted. 45 seats. Air-con. Wheelchair access. Music. Children's portions.

Foliage at the Mandarin Oriental

Modern food in serene surroundings
66 Knightsbridge, SW1X 7LA
Tel no: (020) 7235 2000
www.mandarinoriental.com
⊖ Knightsbridge
Modern European | £65
Cooking score: 5

Glide past the marble foyer of this opulent Knightsbridge hotel to reach the verdantly-themed Foliage restaurant, which soothes visitors with its mood of calming serenity. Subtle peppermint hues complement the cream leather chairs and varnished walnut, floor-to-ceiling windows provide stunning views of Hyde Park and the 'foliage' motif is completed by leafy patterns encased in glass. Meals begin on a positively appetising note with, say, a 'wispy' horseradish and potato velouté with beef carpaccio. Dish descriptions are concise and accurate: a starter of crab, langoustine and fennel is exactly that – a pile of crabmeat placed in the middle of a confit of fennel with a langoustine bisque. This is intricate and inventive food, with more than enough to stimulate the senses. Occasional touches of 'over extemporation' may dull the impact, but when everything gels, the results are 'stupendous': a picture-perfect dish of sea bass ingeniously paired with a blood orange purée, red pepper confit and a sensational cucumber foam has been 'as refreshing as a puff of fresh oxygen'. Elsewhere, chicken cooked 'sous vide' and partnered by broccoli purée, gem lettuce and Gewürztraminer creates a suitably 'evanescent' impression. By and large, the carbohydrate count is kept low, which should enable the ladies-who-lunch to squeeze into their little black numbers from nearby Harvey Nicks. Desserts, such as a fragile coffee pannacotta with hazelnut and frangelico, are exquisitely crafted, the nimble pastry work shining right through to the petit fours. Service is 'fantastic', unfailingly cordial and guaranteed to lift the most elegiac mood. France is the focus of the patrician, 40-page wine list, but other countries are not ignored and the 'Super Tuscans' get special coverage. Prices start at £17, choice by the glass (from £5.50) is commendable and lovers of sweet wines will find plenty to smile about.
Chef/s: Chris Staines. **Open:** all week 12 to 2.30, 7 to 10. **Closed:** 26 Dec, 1 Jan. **Meals:** Set L £29 (4 courses), Set D £65 (4 courses). **Service:** 12.5%. **Details:** Cards accepted. 45 seats. Air-con. Separate bar. Wheelchair access. Music. Children's portions.

Haandi

Classy North Indian food near Harrods
136 Brompton Road, SW3 1HY
Tel no: (020) 7823 7373
www.haandi-restaurants.com
⊖ Knightsbridge
Indian | £33
Cooking score: 4
V

Situated directly opposite Harrods, this stylish Indian restaurant is one of an international quartet and it puts on a high-class show. Shades of brown, beige and yellow define the long dining room, where a glass-fronted kitchen is the main focus of attention. Behind the façade, a team of chefs gets to work on native specialities from the Punjab and North West Frontier. The tandoor gets plenty of use and its output ranges from chicken burra tikka to barbecued lobsters laced with garlic and tomato chutney. Other dishes are cooked – and served – in eponymous 'haandis' (wide-bellied, narrow-necked pots) and the choice extends from classic rogan josh and ubiquitous chicken tikka masala to chicken chennai (a South Indian speciality with coconut, curry leaves and mustard seeds). Goa contributes a fish curry and a pair of vindaloos, while the vegetarian contingent includes Punjabi aloo choley – a chick pea dish best eaten with fried batura bread. The lengthy international wine list offers plenty of suggestions for matching with particular dishes. House selections start at £12.95. A second London branch is at 301–303 Hale Lane, Edgware; tel: (020) 8905 4433.

Chef/s: Ratan Singh and Arjun Singh. **Open:** all week 12 to 3, 5.30 to 11 (11.30 Fri and Sat). **Closed:** 25 Dec. **Meals:** alc (main courses £6.50 to £16.50). Set L £4.99 to £11.95 (all 1 course).. **Service:** 12.5% (optional). **Details:** Cards accepted. 95 seats. 8 seats outside. Air-con. Music. Children allowed.

La Noisette

New addition to the Ramsay empire
164 Sloane Street, London, SW1X 9QB
Tel no: (020) 7750 5000
www.gordonramsay.com/lanoisette
⊖ **Knightsbridge**
French | £62
Cooking score: 4

By backing former Greenhouse chef Bjorn van der Horst, Gordon Ramsay is hoping to reverse the run of bad luck that has dogged restaurants on this site. While it's hard to understand why a restaurant on this street has never succeeded, when you enter the brown, dimly lit dining room on the first floor you begin to see why. The kitchen cooks in the modern medium – think froth, espuma – and is undeniably talented, with pea velouté topped with a sabayon of ham, accompanied by a refreshing lollipop of mint sorbet. Techniques are varied: a starter of pan-seared foie gras comes with espresso syrup and Amaretto foam, while main-course milk-fed Somerset veal has pancetta, gnocchi and parmesan for company. A pre-dessert of mango sorbet placed over vanilla foam and a blackcurrant espuma visually resembled a dish of egg and bacon, and desserts take a cross-cultural road, with a honey and lychee ravioli, green tea and Japanese pepper cake. The highlight at inspection was an unusual red wine soufflé with a fromage blanc sorbet, shallot crystalline, and chives. The lengthy wine list is arranged by grape varietals, including the lesser-known Grüner Veltliner. Prices, starting at £20 or £7 for a glass, reflect the Knightsbridge location.

Chef/s: Bjorn van der Horst. **Open:** Mon to Fri L 12 to 2.30, Mon to Sat D 6 to 10.30. **Closed:** One week at Christmas. **Meals:** Set L £21 (up to 7pm) Set Dinner £55 to £65. **Service:** 12.5% (included).

Details: Cards accepted. 55 seats. Air-con. Separate bar. No music. No mobile phones. Wheelchair access. Children allowed.

★ BEST FISH RESTAURANT ★

One-0-One

Creative, confident fish cookery
Sheraton Park Tower, 101 Knightsbridge, SW1X 7RN
Tel no: (020) 7290 7101
www.oneoonerestaurant.com
⊖ **Knightsbridge**
Seafood | £55
Cooking score: 5

All is sleek designer chic at the restaurant at the base of the Sheraton Park Tower, a recent makeover finally pulling the restaurant together, allowing it to stand alone from the hotel. Closure allowed Pascal Proyart time to rework ideas to stunning effect. His new menu is divided into four sections, two devoted to fish, two mixing meat and fish. The culinary idiom is essentially modern French with Asian undertones, but the USP here is the serving of small tasting dishes. The cooking is creative and confident, full of twists and turns and surprising technique, but with a strong sense of direction and purpose. Norwegian red king crab with sweet chilli, ginger and spiced cuttlefish tagliatelle certainly packed a punch, full of flavour it slightly outshone a chilled version served with aïoli sauce. Similarly, a slow-poached Norwegian cod loin with chorizo carpaccio, squid à la plancha with olive oil, garlic and anchovies delivered layers of savoury complexity while scallop with pork belly was succulent and subtle. Lunch is quite a bargain: pheasant with vine leaf and autumn truffle, endive and foie gras charlotte, chestnut mousse and wild cranberry sauce poivrade, and chocolate soufflé with a delicate, fresh mint ice cream being the highlights of a £24 four-plate lunch. Service is friendly and easy-going, yet polite and correct. Predominantly French wines aim for the upper end of the market; house wine is £22.

Chef/s: Pascal Proyart. **Open:** all week, L 12 to 2.30 (12.30 Sat and Sun), D 6 to 10. **Meals:** alc (main courses £8 to £17). Set L £15 (2 courses) to £35. **Service:** not inc. **Details:** Cards accepted. 50 seats. Air-con. Separate bar. Wheelchair access. Music. Children's portions. Children allowed.

Pétrus

Sublime, masterly food
The Berkeley, Wilton Place, SW1X 7RL
Tel no: (020) 7235 1200
www.marcuswareing.com
⊖ Knightsbridge
French | £75
Cooking score: 8

🍷 V

The Château Pétrus label is etched onto the front door handle, a sure sign that Marcus Wareing's ultra-exclusive restaurant means business. Nestling within the high-flown Berkeley Hotel and discreetly divided into three parts, the dining room exudes sexy warmth, style and class. Its walls are clothed in soft velvet and enunciated by a sensual claret colour scheme; elegant lampshades and petite chandeliers hang from the ceiling, and a smartly designed abacus replete with blown-glass beads guards the impressive wine store. Sink into one of the generously proportioned leather chairs to enjoy an appetiser of hummus while perusing the menu. To start, there is always something tantalising, perhaps warm mushroom velouté with cold cep foam, a dish that manages to deliver a 'clever interplay of hot and cold sensations'. The kitchen is never afraid to innovate, turning out an exquisite ballotine of tuna with spiced pineapple carpaccio alongside marinated mooli, mint and a cardamom foam, which resulted in a rare 'Umami' moment for one recipient. The sheer consistency and refinement of the food never fails to turn heads: one reporter's 'simply faultless' main course of entrecôte of veal with white asparagus, Jersey Royal new potatoes and morel mushrooms came topped with a dazzling piece of cromesquis made with the veal meat. Endorsements suggest that Wareing

Pascal Sanchez   **Sketch**

Why did you become a chef?
I was inspired by my mother's passion for cooking.

Which of today's chefs do you admire?
Pierre Gagnaire.

Where do you source your ingredients?
I source my shellfish locally from Premier Shellfish in London, along with fresh ingredients from France, Spain and Italy.

Who is your favourite producer?
Bastellica — they are based in South-West France and I consider their organic herbs to be the best.

What's the best dish you've ever eaten?
A Gruyere soup in Switzerland. It was from a small family-run establishment located in the Swiss Alps.

Do you have a favourite local recipe?
Fish soup from Marseille.

What's your guilty food pleasure?
Sweet pastries, especially the ones filled with chocolate cream.

If you could only eat one more thing, what would it be?
Kobe beef.

What's coming up next for you?
Fine-tuning our menus and our style at Sketch.

is at the top of his game: those who are analytically inclined note that flavours are pronounced, never too assertive; pristine ingredients and excellent technique are mobilised to conjure up dishes that lack nothing. Meals proceed at a measured pace, and napkins are changed before the final act: that signals the imminent arrival of an exquisite pre-dessert, perhaps a ravishing Sauternes jelly with vanilla yogurt and apple granita. Desserts here are amongst the best in class and they are Wareing's way of celebrating his Lancastrian roots. Few can resist the prospect of a supremely simple custard tart with vanilla and poached English rhubarb or a friable Eccles cake with Earl Grey tea cream, spiced prune and milk foam, before the irresistible bon-bon trolley appears. Service is impeccable, with much pampering and TLC dispensed with palpable largesse. Well-groomed courtesy extends to the sommelier, who proffers helpful advice without any hint of snobbery. The wine list itself is a shining model of care and grandiloquence, spread over 40 pages and brimming with superstars from every region. France takes centre stage but other countries are not ignored, and it's good to see Slovakia, Slovenia and Israel making an appearance among the wine world's veterans. Prices start from £20, with selections by the glass from £5, but since this restaurant is named after the world's most expensive wine, it is bound to be a magnet for financial big-hitters. Some 40 examples from the Château Pétrus dynasty are on show, going back to 1924 and including the legendary 1928 vintage for a mere £11,600.
Chef/s: Marcus Wareing. **Open:** Mon to Fri L 12 to 2.30, Mon to Sat D 6 to 11. **Closed:** 1 week Christmas. **Meals:** Set L £30 to £80, Set D £60 to £80. **Service:** not inc. **Details:** Cards accepted. 70 seats. Air-con. No music. No mobile phones. Wheelchair access. Children's portions.

Racine

Authentic French bistro
239 Brompton Road, SW3 2EP
Tel no: (020) 7584 4477
⊖ South Kensington
French | £33
New Chef

A chirpy 'Bon Soir' greets you as you enter Racine thus setting the tone for an unremittingly gallic experience. Chef and founder Henry Harris may have moved on, but this unpretentious Knightsbridge 'bistro deluxe' remains – five years later – ahead of the competition with classic dishes like soupe a l'oignon, or steak tartare often bettering what you mght find in Paris. With its wooden floor, dark brown leather banquettes, and light walls, it's a serious, smart looking spot, nicely in keeping with the straightforward cuisine. The generously priced prix fixe menu is on at lunch and dinner until 7.30pm, with house wines on the all-French list starting at £15.50. There are daily specials too, usually simple seasonal dishes like new season's asparagus with hollandaise, or ris de veau aux champignons sauvages. The carte offers all the bistro favourites – choucroute alsacienne, tête de veau, sauce ravigote – rendered with true flavours and the minimum of dressing-up. Service from black and white clad waiters is professional yet jolly, and refreshingly unparsimonious. When refills of tap water, baguette and pats of foil-wrapped Echiré butter arrive unbidden, you sense they know that such small things make all the difference.
Chef/s: Henrik Ritzen. **Open:** all week 12 to 3 (3.30 Sat and Sun), 6 to 10.30 (10 Sun). **Closed:** 25 Dec. **Meals:** alc (main courses £13.25 to £20.75). Set L £17.50 (2 courses), Set D £19.50 (3 courses). **Service:** 14.5% (optional). **Details:** Cards accepted. 67 seats. Air-con. No music. Wheelchair access. Children's portions.

Salloos

Subtlety and spice from the subcontinent
62-64 Kinnerton Street, SW1X 8ER
Tel no: (020) 7235 4444
⊖ Knightsbridge
Indian | £34
Cooking score: 3

Tucked away in a quiet corner of Knightsbridge (yes, they do exist), Salloos is a long-standing south-Asian restaurant that offers comfort, carefully cooked dishes and consistency. That last asset is borne out by the fact that Abdul Aziz has now entered on his fourth decade at the stoves here. At the stoves, and at the tandoor, for there is fine clay-oven cooking here too. The tandoori prawns are usually great. Lamb cooked with spinach, fenugreek and ginger, or chicken karahi, are reliable main courses, and might be preceded by a bowl of chicken and almond soup. Spicing tends to be fiery, so have plenty of water on hand. Haleem akbari is a recommended speciality – shredded lamb in wheatgerm, lentils and spices. Round things off with cool pistachio kulfi. House wines from Corney and Barrow are £15.50, or £4.50 a glass.

Chef/s: Abdul Aziz. **Open:** Mon to Sat 12 to 2.30, 7 to 11. **Closed:** 25 and 26 Dec. **Service:** 12.5% (optional). **Details:** Cards accepted. 65 seats. Air-con. No music. Children allowed.

Zafferano

Top-notch seasonal food
15 Lowndes Street, SW1X 9EY
Tel no: (020) 7235 5800
www.zafferanorestaurant.com
⊖ Knightsbridge
Italian | £39
Cooking score: 6

V

From the outside, Zafferano still looks discreetly serious, but the interior has been lightened up of late with stone flooring, orange and brown banquettes and a 'capricious' bar. It feels reassuring and hospitable, with no designer-led frivolities to distract from the main business of the day. This is a 'very fine restaurant' and its enduring success hinges on Andy Needham's approach to thoroughbred Italian cooking. Much depends on sourcing, and Zafferano has an enviable, unchallenged reputation for garnering faultless raw materials that are at their seasonal peak. First courses lay down a marker for what is to follow: having sampled a refreshing assemblage of spring vegetables with superb leaves and a light vinaigrette, one well-travelled correspondent noted that 'hardly a restaurant in the UK seems capable of producing a salad of this quality'. Homemade pasta is another star turn, impeccably fresh, perfectly timed and silky, with fascinating fillings and accompaniments (veal shank ravioli with saffron or linguine with bottarga, thyme and fresh tuna, for example); gnocchi are also 'a revelation'. Following the traditional four-course format and framework, centrepiece dishes prove their worth with up-front flavours and forceful simplicity, witness roast partridge with lentils and pumpkin cream, or red snapper with fennel and Taggiasche olives. There is a complete truffle menu in season, while desserts set out to tantalise with the likes of chestnut semifreddo, orange and pine nut tart with Cointreau cream or a near-legendary tiramisu. The wine list is an Italian gem aimed at those with plenty of disposable income. Premier-league names abound, with gilt-edged stuff from Piedmont and Tuscany in particular. Dessert wines venture into rarefied territory while, back on terra firma, house selections start at £17.50.

Chef/s: Andy Needham. **Open:** all week 12 to 2.30, 7 to 11. **Closed:** 24 Dec to 2 Jan, bank hol L. **Meals:** Set L £25.50 (2 courses) to £34.50, Set D £29.50 (2 courses) to £45. **Service:** 13.5% (optional). **Details:** Cards accepted. 75 seats. Air-con. No mobile phones. Wheelchair access. Music.

Which? Campaigns

To find out more about Which? food and drink campaigns, please visit:
www.which.co.uk

Zuma

High fashion and seductive flavours
5 Raphael Street, SW7 1DL
Tel no: (020) 7584 1010
www.zumarestaurant.com
⊖ **Knightsbridge**
Japanese | £67
New Chef

♨ V

Designed to resemble a Japanese Zen garden in a Knightsbridge office block, Zuma exudes ultra-cool cosmopolitan style. The interior is homage to industrial chic: everywhere there are monumental unyielding surfaces, pink marble pillars, rough-hewn wood, steel, glass and concrete. It might seem hard-edged and architecturally primeval, but the place generates its own warmth and animated atmosphere. By day, Zuma is genteel and calming; at night it buzzes as the beautiful people come out to play. The overtly intricate menu divides up into appetisers and salads, tempura, fabulously fresh sushi and sashimi, plus offerings from the flaming robata grill. Exquisite miniature dishes arrive in waves and the idea is to share. Among the palate-arousing openers are fried soft shell crab with wasabi mayonnaise and mizuna or slices of yellowtail pointed up with green chilli relish, ponzu and pickled garlic. These are the prelude to skewers of yakitori and other grills ranging from ribeye steak with wafu sauce and garlic crisps to scallops paired with grated apple and sweet soy. There are also specialities and 'new dishes' including seared miso-marinated foie gras with a compote of umeboshi (fiercesome salted plums) or marinated langoustines with chilli, ginger and lime. Desserts turn westwards for European-inspired offerings like green tea and banana cake, hot chocolate fondant and intriguing sorbets. To drink, the vintage selection of aged sakes aims to seduce initiates and novices alike. Those who prefer the juice of the grape should explore the exquisite compendium of fine wines – especially if price is no deterrent.

Stellar selections shine out from every page, prices start at around £20, and there are a dozen good choices from £5.90 a glass. **Chef/s:** Ross Shonan. **Open:** all week L 12 to 2.30 (from 12.30 Sat, Sun) D 7 to 11. **Closed:** 24, 25 Dec, 1 Jan. **Meals:** Set D £96 (min 2).. **Details:** Cards accepted. 127 seats. Air-con. Separate bar. Wheelchair access. Music. Children allowed.

■ Lancaster Gate

Angelus

4 Bathurst Street, W2 2SA
Tel no: 020 7402 0083
www.angelusrestaurant.co.uk
⊖ **Lancaster Gate**
French | £36
Cooking score: 4

♀

Thierry Tomasin, the free thinking yet focused ex-head sommelier from Le Gavroche and former general manager of Aubergine, itching to break the bonds of fine dining gives this former pub a rare edge. It's in an area of London that 'desperately needs a good quality restaurant'. The space is rather cramped but dark wood, mirrors, chandeliers, buttoned back leather banquettes, and 'oddly positioned' white-clad tables hit all the right Parisian brasserie notes. The carte has great appeal, taking in starters of 'very tasty' foie gras crème brûlée, and a generous warm scallop salad with Charlotte potatoes and truffled vinaigrette, while lighter main courses could include john dory with viennoise crust, pak choi and vin juane sauce with clams. Output is variable but, at its best, sound judgement is evident: in, for example, 'delicious and perfectly prepared' pigeon 'façon Bécasse' with buttered Savoy cabbage and marjoram. The wine list accords pride of place to the French regions, but there are a few from other wine growing regions, including the southern hemisphere. House wine is £13. **Chef/s:** Olivier Duret. **Open:** Tue to Sun 12 to 11. **Closed:** 23 Dec to 3 Jan. **Meals:** alc (main courses £16 to £20). **Service:** 12.5%. **Details:** Cards

Best set menus

Highly regarded restaurants often offer a great set lunch deal as an introduction to their pricier carte. Prices below are for three courses, unless otherwise stated.

Wild Honey

Reporters are full of praise for the comforting wood-panelled space, the quality of the food and the wonderful wine policy. The excellent set lunch, in particular, has been singled out. £15.50.

One-O-One

Pascal Proyart is back at the stoves with renewed vigour, delivering a fish-based haute Brittany cooking. Lunch offers two to six small tasting dishes for £15–£35.

Le Gavroche

The absolute classic. For £46, the set lunch delivers haute level cooking and includes half a bottle per person of proper wine.

Galvin Bistro de Luxe

Readers continue to be impressed by the Galvin brothers comfortable restaurant, with a dream line-up of bistro dishes for £15.50.

Tom Aikens

Tom Aikens stellar cooking offers endless culinary surprises, so you might like to checkout the £29 set lunch.

L'Autre Pied

New opening from the highly acclaimed Pied à Terre stable, so expect high-gloss proficiency. The set lunch is excellent value at £19.95.

Le Cercle

The younger sibling of Club Gascon offers tapas-sized portions based on the traditions of south-west France. £15.

Rasoi Vineet Bhatia

Vineet Bhatia brings a new-wave sensibility to Indian cooking. His meticulous technique comes at a price not normally charged for Indian food, so the set lunch is good value at £26.

Axis, One Aldwych

A makeover of this coolly spacious room, great British ingredients and a lunchtime, pre- and post-theatre menu for £17.50 make an unbeatable combination for this otherwise poorly served theatre-land location.

Ristorante Semplice

Exceptional ingredients simply prepared at this small-but-sassy modern Italian. The set lunch (£18) is a perfect intro to the pricier evening carte.

Send your reviews to: www.which.co.uk/gfgfeedback

accepted. 35 seats. 12 seats outside. Air-con. Separate bar. No mobile phones. Wheelchair access. Music. Children allowed.

Leicester Square

Incognico

Assured modern food for theatre-goers
117 Shaftesbury Avenue, WC2H 8AD
Tel no: (020) 7836 8866
www.incognico.com
⊖ Leicester Square
Modern European | £51
Cooking score: 4

V

A prime West End theatreland location is one of the enduring attributes of this pleasing, understated venue close to Cambridge Circus. The conservative, brasserie décor reminded one reporter of restaurants in Florence, with its polished wooden floors, high ceilings inlaid with shiny tiles and massive lamps dangling from heavy chains. Large mirrors adorn the walls and gentle light streams in from tall windows: it makes a sedate and comfortable setting for precise, uncomplicated modern food based on top-drawer ingredients. Well-judged mainstream starters encompass everything from grilled fillet of mackerel with beetroot and potato to a salad of endive, apple, hazelnuts and Gorgonzola. Mains continue the momentum with non-controversial dishes like roast cod wrapped in Parma ham with pea purée, honey-roast duck breast or rump of lamb with potato mille-feuille, diced tomato and tarragon jus. Desserts end proceedings on a familiar note with, say, vanilla pannacotta and poached rhubarb or apple and cinnamon crumble. Europe takes up the lion's share of the varietally arranged wine list, which offers a good spread of reputable names and vintages. Prices start at £18.50 (£4.75) for vins de pays. **Chef/s:** Dafydd Watkin. **Open:** Mon to Sat 12 to 3, 5.30 to 11. **Meals:** alc (main courses £12.50 to £18.50). **Service:** 12.5% (optional). **Details:** Cards accepted. 85 seats. Air-con. Music.

The Ivy

The galactico of the London scene
1-5 West Street, WC2H 9NQ
Tel no: (020) 7836 4751
⊖ Leicester Square
Modern British | £40
Cooking score: 4

The fame of this quintessential celebrity restaurant remains undimmed and, should you not find yourself sitting next to an Oscar winner or A-lister, the consistent quality of cooking, deferential service and infectiously upbeat atmosphere guard against any disappointment. The menu never changes but its length and variety ensure there's always something you'll want to eat whatever your mood: bang-bang chicken or Thai-baked sea bass with fragrant rice and a soy dip, say, or smoked haddock and salmon kedgeree, even a shared dish of roast poulet des Landes with Madeira jus and dauphinoise potatoes. At inspection, perfectly poached eggs Benedict atop soft folds of ham, a crisp muffin and a well-balanced hollandaise sauce was followed by a fine piece of battered haddock with proper chips and minted pea purée (aka mushy peas) with a tangy Welsh rarebit to finish. You won't, however, get to eat any of it unless you are prepared to book months ahead or eat off-peak: at pre-theatre, say, or a late weekend lunch (when a set menu is offered). House Chilean Sauvignon is £15.25 but the rest of the global wine list offers slim pickings until you've passed the £30 mark. **Chef/s:** Alan Bird. **Open:** all week 12 to 3.30 (4 Sun), 5 to 12. **Closed:** 25 and 26 Dec, 1 Jan, Aug bank hol. **Meals:** alc (main courses £12 to £35). Set L Sat and Sun £21.50. Cover £2. **Service:** not inc. **Details:** Cards accepted. 100 seats. Air-con. No music. No mobile phones. Wheelchair access. Children's portions.

J. Sheekey

A venerable seafood establishment
28-32 St Martin's Court, WC2N 4AL
Tel no: (020) 7240 2565
www.j-sheekey.co.uk
⊖ **Leicester Square**
Seafood | £34
Cooking score: 4

It might have a lower profile than its nearby sibling The Ivy but this theatreland fish specialist pulls off the same trick of making ordinary mortals feel like A-list stars, from the welcome of the unfailingly polite liveried doormen and the graciousness of the staff within to the mirrored windows guarding the wood-panelled dining room from prying eyes. Menus offer an undemanding mix of simply prepared fish and shellfish, British comfort food and classic matches from around the world. Starters could be one of several things on toast (potted shrimps, herring roe or crab pâté), a plateau de fruits de mer, or an Arbroath smokie with endive salad and soft-boiled quails' eggs. Follow, perhaps, with fish pie or fillet of cod with a crab risotto and tarragon dressing. Fishcakes with sautéed spinach and sorrel sauce, in which the salmon:potato ratio was firmly in favour of the fish, impressed at inspection. Puds include the sweet and tart Ivy classic, Scandinavian iced-berries with a hot white chocolate sauce. The wine list has a strong bias towards France, with cheaper bottles of white from the south and south-west for under £30 giving way to a strong showing from Burgundy. House wine is £15.25 and there are 20 available by the glass, mostly around the £7.50 mark.
Chef/s: Martin Dickinson. **Open:** all week 12 to 3 (3.30 Sun), 5.30 (6 Sun) to 12. **Closed:** 25 and 26 Dec, 1 Jan, Aug bank hol. **Meals:** alc (main courses £11 to £35). Set L Sat and Sun £21.50. **Service:** not inc. **Details:** Cards accepted. 106 seats. Air-con. No music. No mobile phones. Wheelchair access. Children's portions.

Heston Blumenthal **London tbc**

Why did you become a chef?
Aged 16, my father took us to the restaurant l'Oustau de Baumaniere in Provence. I was captivated by the sights, the smells, the sounds, the whole dining experience.

Who was your main inspiration?
Harold McGee.

What's your favourite cookery book?
At the moment I am reading **The Encyclopaedia of Practical Cookery**, published in 1895 and edited by Theodore Francis Garrett.

What's the best dish you've ever eaten?
Shopping for, preparing and cooking barbecues with the kids.

Do you have a favourite local recipe?
Eton Mess, a dessert we serve at the Hinds Head, from our local Eton College tuck shop.

What's your guilty food pleasure?
Tomato ketchup.

If you could only eat one more thing, what would it be?
A menu I discovered recently from the court of King James, comprising of 174 courses; one included 48 desserts and another 12 puffins. And that was just for two people.

What's coming up next for you?
The development of the Fat Duck historic British menu.

National Portrait Gallery, Portrait Restaurant

Picture-perfect British cooking
Orange Street, WC2H OHE
Tel no: (020) 7312 2490
www.searcys.co.uk
⊖ Leicester Square
Modern British | £29
Cooking score: 2

V

Ask for a window seat when booking a table at the National Portrait Gallery's rooftop restaurant: the reward is fine views over Trafalgar Square and over London landmarks. The venue attracts a mixed clientele, from business lunchers to tourists, who are drawn not only by the view but by an eclectic menu of sparky modern British cooking. Pressed game confit typically opens proceedings, partnered with a rhubarb and sultana chutney with fig, red wine and nut bread, or you might opt for smoked black pudding with a poached egg on a spinach and bacon salad. To follow, monkfish is wrapped in bacon and served with buttered marsh samphire, while daily specials could include braised lamb shank with honey-roasted root vegetables, garlic and parsley mash and a rosemary and port jus. Caramelised citrus tart with kumquat syrup and Valrhona chocolate sorbet rounds things off nicely, and house wines are £15. **Chef/s:** Katarina Todosijevic. **Open:** all week L 11.45 to 2.45 (11.30 to 3 Sat and Sun), Thur and Fri D 5.30 to 10. **Closed:** 25 Dec. **Meals:** alc (main courses £15 to £32). Brunch, lounge and pre-theatre (Thur and Fri 5.30 to 6.30) menus available. **Service:** 12.5% (optional). **Details:** Cards accepted. 120 seats. Air-con. No music. Wheelchair access. Children's portions.

ALSO RECOMMENDED

▲ Tokyo Diner

2 Newport Place, WC2H 7JJ
Tel no: (020) 7287 8777
www.tokyodiner.com
⊖ Leicester Square

The word 'diner' gives you a clue as to what to expect. This Japanese eatery is low on frills but scores when it comes to serving fresh food at very favourable prices. Bento boxes are particularly good value. These compartmented containers provide a satisfying meal, with salmon sashimi, rice, a main-course dish such as chicken teryaki, sunomono (a vinegared salad) and pickles. The Agadashi set lunch, based on miso soup, is ideal for those who want a light midday meal. Open from noon until midnight, the Tokyo Diner has a special late-night menu from 11.30pm.

▮ Marble Arch

Locanda Locatelli

A peerless reputation for seasonal food
8 Seymour Street, W1H 7JZ
Tel no: (020) 7935 9088
www.locandalocatelli.com
⊖ Marble Arch
Italian | £56
Cooking score: 6

🍾 **V**

Part of the Churchill Hotel, but clearly a separate operation, Locanda Locatelli is smartly swanky, with plenty of wood, leather and spotlights. It can be difficult to book a table here, and with good reason, as the Guide receives a steady stream of praise for Giorgio Locatelli's 'true Italian cuisine' and the restaurant's 'excellent service'. Although Locatelli could be described as a 'celebrity chef' (the book, the TV series . . .), his reputation was built and continues to be maintained in the kitchen (using the finest ingredients) and he delivers a menu that is laid out along traditional Italian lines. After antipasti, start with perfectly cooked fresh

linguine with delicate langoustines, garlic and sweet chilli in a tomato sauce, say, or with pappardelle, broad beans and fresh peppery rocket. At inspection, a main course of chargrilled rolled pork was 'bursting with fresh herbs', and came with meat jus and deep-fried courgettes in batter, while a dish of grilled tuna with rocket salad and tomatoes, simply served with a wedge of lemon, showed off the freshness and quality of the raw materials. Side orders could include roast potatoes pungent with the scent of rosemary, while the foccacia and breadsticks are repeatedly pronounced 'excellent'. A chocolate tasting dessert, including everything from parfait to ice cream, gave Amadei chocolate the attention it deserves, while a perfect vanilla pannacotta with berries, red fruit sauce and stracciatella (chocolate chip) ice cream on a biscuit base also hit the spot. Coffee is 'as good as you would expect', and comes with a chocolate truffle and an 'outstandingly good' Amaretto biscuit. The wine list is all-Italian, apart from champagne. Whites and reds are arranged by region, and feature well-known growers such as Gaia and Antinori. There is a good range of wines by the glass, priced from £3.50 to £18.
Chef/s: Giorgio Locatelli. **Open:** all week 12 to 3 (3.30 Sun), 7.00 to 11 (11.30 Fri and Sat, 10.00 Sun). **Closed:** bank hols. **Meals:** alc (main courses £12 to £29.50). **Service:** not inc. **Details:** Cards accepted. 70 seats. Air-con. No mobile phones. Wheelchair access. Music. Children's portions.

Rhodes W1 Brasserie

Best-of-British brasserie
Cumberland Hotel, W1A 4RS
Tel no: (020) 7479 3838
www.garyrhodes.com
⊖ **Marble Arch**
Modern British | £23
Cooking score: 3

The Gary Rhodes-accented dishes are exactly what you would expect from this longstanding TV chef. The vibrant, unfussy modern British cooking with a European

twist here and there delivering the likes of 'beautifully presented' mackerel rillette on soft potato with dill, spring onion and a radish salad. There's a tempting grill section for mains, offering a variety of fish or steaks, such as the thick slab of hake smothered in Montpellier butter tried at inspection, otherwise there could be calf's liver in a rich gravy with a side of 'smooth and very moreish' mash. A tangy lemon curd tart was 'flawless', brilliantly matched by a scoop of cocoa sorbet. Friendly, efficient and well-trained staff lift the experience, although the dimly lit surrounds (plush red velvet banquettes and dark wood tables) give the place a nightclub feel and the music from the adjacent bar can get loud and might not be to everyone's taste. A surprisingly reasonable and concise wine list starts at £3.50 a glass and £16.00 a bottle.
Chef/s: Gary Rhodes. **Open:** Daily, L 12 to 2.30, D 6 to 10.30. **Meals:** alc main courses £13 to £22. **Details:** Cards accepted. 142 seats. Separate bar. Wheelchair access. Music. Children allowed.

Texture

Striking culinary imagination
34 Portman Street, W1H 78Y
Tel no: 020 7224 0028
www.texture-restaurant.co.uk
⊖ **Marble Arch**
Modern European | £45
Cooking score: 4

The cool, stylish, ornately plastered white room is divided by glass displays and contemporary art, while bare wood tables, cream leather chairs and modern lighting create a buzzy, high volume look. The cooking essays a degree of experimentation, new Nordic cuisine with more than a hint of contemporary French fashion to it (Agnar Sverrisson was formerly head chef at Le Manoir aux Quat'Saisons) and technique is versatile enough to attempt, for example, chargrilled pigeon with sweetcorn, bacon popcorn and red wine essence. Best value is at lunch when a range of ten starter sized dishes,

all priced at £8.50, is offered, otherwise there's a pair of tasting menus from £55 or a more conventional three-course à la carte. At inspection, a great piece of roast Icelandic lamb gained punch from a side bowl of deeply flavoured lamb broth, but on the downside flavours don't always pack a punch: Mediterranean tuna, smoked, Asian flavours, arrived under a porcelain dome that, when lifted, released an aromatic puff of wood smoke, but failed to follow through with any definite flavour. Service is well drilled and co-founder Xavier Rousset's classy wine list is particularly strong in France. Entry level is £18 with reasonable action under £30.
Chef/s: Agnor Sverrison. **Open:** Tue to Sat L 12 to 2.30, D 6.30 to 11. **Closed:** Christmas, New Year. **Meals:** Tasting Menu £55 to £59. **Service:** 12.5%. **Details:** Cards accepted. 60 seats. Air-con. Separate bar. Wheelchair access. Music.

ALSO RECOMMENDED
▲ La Porte des Indes
32 Bryanston Street, W1H 7EG
Tel no: (020) 7224 0055
www.pilondon.net
⊖ Marble Arch

Exotic and evocative, with dark red wooden floors, colourful draped fabrics, huge murals of jungle scenes, spectacular flower arrangements and a cascading waterfall, it is perhaps the grandest setting of all London's Indian restaurants. Conventional dishes such as a classic chicken tandoori (£11.90) and pork vindaloo (£12.90) share the billing with colonial French (Creole) inspired dishes, including a starter of parsee fish (sole fillets encased in a mint and coriander chutney and lightly steamed in banana leaves; £9.50) or, for main course, chumude karaikal (seared beef tenderloin with roasted cinnamon, aniseed, cloves and black pepper sauce). Good house menus plus global wines from £18. Closed Sat L.

▲ Trenta
30 Connaught Street, W2 2AF
Tel no: 020 7262 9623

This pint-sized Italian restaurant, formerly Al San Vincenzo, occupies the ground floor and basement of a narrow terraced house not far from Marble Arch. Dark wooden floors and modern artwork on red-painted walls set an intimate scene for some accomplished cooking, the set-price two-course lunch (£13.50) and dinner (£19.50) menus are traditionally laid out and offer a good choice. From antipasti such as mixed seafood platter and interesting pasta options, say, spaghetti with clams, chilli and garlic, the menu extends to lamb steak with garlic and rosemary, and grilled prawns with balsamic mayonnaise. Desserts include chocolate pannacotta. Wines from £14.50.

Marylebone
Dinings
Tiny restaurant in an unlikely backstreet
22 Harcourt Street, W1H 4HH
Tel no: 020 7723 0666
⊖ Marylebone
Japanese | £36
Cooking score: 3

V

This 'really titchy' newcomer, located in an anonymous backstreet, provides little in the way of creature comforts. The sushi bar on the ground floor is snug at best, but the achingly hard wooden chairs and harsh concrete floor in the basement dining room will not please everyone. However the cooking from ex-Nobu chef, Tomanari Chiba, is vibrant and delicate. The menu is neatly divided into cold or hot tapas and the cooking punches well above its weight, with high quality sushi and tempura – tuna belly and freshwater eel sushi, in particular, were considered 'exemplary' at inspection. Contemporary dishes are equally successful: the interplay of flavours of a saver fish sashimi served with a spring onion and horseradish ponzu sauce was well managed, and from the hot section, a slow roasted

Iberian pork shoulder was cunningly paired with a piquant dressing of coriander, tomato and lemon yuzu. Even dessert, never the strongest aspect of an Oriental menu, did not disappoint with a textbook crème brulée made with macha green tea. Sweet natured service hits the spot, and the brief wine list provides a selection of shochu and sake. House wine from Porter Mill is £14.50 a bottle, £4.20 a glass or alternatively try a glass of Umeshu plum wine at £3.80.

Chef/s: Tomanari Chiba. **Open:** Mon to Fri L 12 to 3. Mon to Sat D 6 to 10.30. **Closed:** 25 and 26 Dec. **Meals:** alc (main courses (£4 to £16). **Service:** 10%. **Details:** Cards accepted. 28 seats. Music. Children allowed.

Duke of Wellington

Neighbourhood pub with lots of promise
94a Crawford Street, W1H 2HQ
Tel no: (020) 7723 2790
⊖ Baker Street
Gastropub | £25
Cooking score: 1

Occupying a corner site, this updated neighbourhood boozer has adopted the gastro-pub formula of dark timber flooring, funky lighting, leather banquettes, abstract artwork and bare tables. Although still (just) a pub standing at the bar watching the plates of food going by it is hard to resist. The cooking style focuses on using well-sourced, good quality ingredients. Flavours are robust and clear, and portions generous; witness a main course confit of duck leg with sarlardaise potatoes, pickled red cabbage and Griottine cherry jus. Start with ham hock and parsley terrine with piccalilli, and finish with rum baba with Chantilly cream. There s a small, smarter restaurant upstairs, but the menu remains pretty much the same. Like the food the wine list aims at good value, with house opening at £14.50.

Chef/s: Fred Smith. **Open:** Mon to Fri L 12 to 3 Sat to Sun 12.30 to 4.30 all week D 6.30 to 10. **Closed:** 25 to 26 Dec, 31 Dec. **Meals:** alc (main courses £11 to £16). **Service:** not inc. **Details:** Cards accepted. Air-con. Music. Children's portions.

FishWorks

Marylebone branch of strong seafood chain
89 Marylebone High Street, W1U 4QW
Tel no: (020) 8994 0086
www.fishworks.co.uk
⊖ Marylebone
Seafood | £30
Cooking score: 2

There's now a whole shoal of FishWorks restaurants across London, with branches in Fulham, Chiswick, Islington, Notting Hill, Parsons Green, Primrose Hill and Richmond as well as Marylebone, all swimming smoothly along to Mitch Tonks' tried-and-tested formula of wet fish counter out front and stylish brasserie out back. It's all very lively, simple and unfussy, letting the fresh fish and its straightforward treatment speak for themselves. Selection depends on the day's intake of fish – it's a broad menu but dishes do run out and you may have to forsake your first choice. A fresh-tasting taramasalata served with bread, pesto and tapenade or whitebait with aïoli gets things off to a swinging start. Mains range from fresh Isle of Lewis langoustines to more substantial grilled swordfish with Moroccan spices and tomato salad, and a fulsome zuppa del pescatore with saffron and thyme. Service can occasionally be shaky, with staff sometimes slow to take orders and clear between courses. Choose from around a dozen house wines starting at £3.75 a glass; otherwise European whites dominate the list, with a clutch of fish-friendly reds also suggested.

Chef/s: Jack Scarterfield. **Open:** Tue to Sun L 12 to 2.30, Tue to Sat D 6 to 10.30. **Closed:** 24 Dec to early Jan, day after bank hols. **Meals:** alc (main courses £12 to £25). **Service:** not inc. **Details:** Cards accepted. 48 seats. Air-con. Music. Children's portions.

Galvin Bistrot de Luxe

Elementary French food on Baker Street
66 Baker Street, W1V 7DH
Tel no: (020) 7935 4007
www.galvinuk.com
⊖ Baker Street
French | £28
Cooking score: 5

With its reasonable prices, simple food and informal atmosphere, brothers Chris and Jeff Galvin have made such a success of this formerly ill-fated site on Baker Street that their family name is in danger of upstaging that of Sherlock Holmes. Everything about this place feels so right: the bentwood chairs, starched white tablecloths and wood-panelled walls are absolutely *comme il faut*. There's 'excellent', well-timed service and a menu so stuffed full of good things that you're planning a return visit before you've even ordered. From a dream line-up of bistro dishes cooked with skill come six escargots bourguignonne, which slip from the shell, dripping garlicky juices, a chunkily chopped steak tartare topped with a quivering egg yolk, six fines de claire oysters accompanied by stubby sausages of cigar-shaped chorizo. There's an element of comfort food to the cooking but the brothers' respect for provincial French recipes prevents things from getting too cosy: veal brains may be roasted and served in beurre noisette or, à la forestière, as part of a flavourful assiette of veal that also includes roast rump and melt-in-the-mouth braised cheek. Desserts set out to delight, especially an oeufs a la neige, which skims the surface of the lightest of crème anglaises. A commitment to good value means that South and Southwest France are the strengths of the wine list, while offering four beers specifically chosen to match the food is typical of the democratic feel of the place. House wine is £13.95 a bottle, with a dozen available by the glass.

Chef/s: Jeff and Chris Galvin, Sian Rees. **Open:** all week 12 to 2.30, 6 to 11 (12 to 9.30 Sun). **Closed:** 25, 26 Dec, 1 Jan. **Meals:** Set L £15.50, Set D 6 to 7

£17.50. **Service:** 12.5% (optional). **Details:** Cards accepted. 90 seats. Air-con. Separate bar. Wheelchair access. Music. Children's portions.

L'Autre Pied

Relaxed, good-value sibling of Pied à Terre
57 Blandford Street, W1U 3DB
Tel no: (020) 7486 9696
www.lautrepied.co.uk
⊖ Bond Street
Modern European | £35
Cooking score: 5

Found on a quiet side road off bustling Marylebone High Street, L Autre Pied is the second opening from the pair behind the highly acclaimed Pied à Terre – David Moore and Shane Osborn (see entry). But this is no pared down version of the Charlotte Street original. The slightly cramped room and low-key decor give a hint that the drill is simpler the food is less intricate and prices commensurately lower. However, chef Marcus Eaves previously worked at Pied à Terre and with a pedigree like that one would expect a certain level of high-gloss proficiency it is not lacking. Slow-cooked ox cheeks with oxtail beignets and cauliflower cream set the pace, proving a hit at inspection, and a similarly engaging butternut squash velouté from the set lunch menu combined crushed white beans and a sage beignet with an intense flavour. Main courses demonstrate skilful timing of meat and fish and an understanding of complementary flavours, so that haunch of venison is intelligently partnered with butternut squash, orange purée and a port sauce, while plaice appears successfully teamed with braised oxtail and Puy lentils. At times, the cooking has an appealing straightforwardness, expressed, for example, in braised blade of beef with horseradish pomme purée and beetroot consommé, again from the set lunch menu excellent value at £16.50 for 2 courses. Finish with warm financier with almond milk and coffee sorbet. The well-chosen wine list starts at £11.50.

Chef/s: Marcus Eaves. Open: all week L 12 to 2.45 D 6 to 10.45. Closed: Christmas. Meals: alc (main courses £16.95 to £21.50). Set L and pre-theatre £16.50 (2 courses). Service: 12.5% (optional). Details: Cards accepted. 53 seats. Air-con. No music.

Orrery
Light touch from a new kid on the block
55 Marylebone High Street, W1M 3AE
Tel no: (020) 7616 8000
www.orrery.co.uk
⊖ Baker Street
French | £50
Cooking score: 5

🍷 V

At this vibrant first-floor Marylebone dining room, mirrored walls help even those not facing the windows to enjoy the verdant view over a churchyard. The civilised, light coloured long room with tables smartly set with white napery gives out an air of quiet restraint, service is excellent and there's no doubting the quality of Tristan Mason's cooking, which has truly come of age: he trusts his judgement, lets ingredients speak for themselves and allows modern ideas to impinge freely on classic French ideas. Saucing, texture and balance are spot on. Witness a sureness of touch with richer dishes that coaxes astonishing depth of flavour out of foie gras ballottine with pain d'epice, haricots verts and hazelnuts, or the extravagant success of a slow roast rib of beef served with beetroot risotto and baby turnips. Fish and meat pairings are popular: scallops with confit chicken and celeriac purée, viennoise-crusted roast turbot with oxtail and salsify, daube of veal cheek with crayfish, orange and turnip purée – the latter delivering 'exquisite layers of flavour'. Pre-desserts may well be as 'artfully composed as the dessert itself', the latter perhaps offering almond cake, toffee and candied apple. The impressively comprehensive wine list is now organised stylistically, but continues to offer some 16 or so sommeliers choice by the bottle (from £26) or by the glass (from £7).
Chef/s: Tristan Mason. Open: all week L 12 to 2.30, D 6.30 to 10.30. Closed: Christmas, 1 Jan. Meals: alc (main courses £25 to £38). Set L £25, tasting menus £46 to £59. Service: 12.5% (optional). Details: Cards accepted. 80 seats. Air-con. No music. Wheelchair access.

Phoenix Palace
Opulent surroundings
3-5 Glentworth Street, NW1 5PG
Tel no: (020) 7486 3515
⊖ Baker Street
Chinese | £25
Cooking score: 2

V

Just around the corner from Baker Street tube station, this busy, bustling restaurant is one of central London's best venues for reliably good Chinese cooking. The large dining room, patrolled by brisk staff wearing snazzy gold uniforms, is smarter and more elaborately decorated than most of those in Chinatown. A comprehensive (and bewilderingly long) Cantonese menu ranges from crowd-pleasers such as sesame prawn toast, crispy chilli beef and sweet and sour pork to more unusual (to western eyes) dishes such as kung po spicy hare, one of several game options. The quality of cooking is accomplished throughout and lotus root with minced pork, prawns and salted fish, and roast chicken stuffed with mashed prawns both impressed at inspection. The daytime dim sum is held in justifiably high regard and is particularly popular at the weekend with families, making Phoenix Palace even noisier than it is normally. House wine is £10.
Chef/s: Mr Tan. Open: all week 12 to 11.30 (10.30 Sun). Meals: alc (main courses £6 to £28). Set D £15.80 (2 courses) to £26.80. Service: 12.5%. Details: Cards accepted. 250 seats. Air-con. Music.

Providores

Marylebone's foremost Oceanic eaterie
109 Marylebone High Street, W1U 4RX
Tel no: (020) 7935 6175
www.theprovidores.co.uk
⊖ **Baker Street**
Asian fusion | £50
Cooking score: 4

The ground floor operates variously as a tapas bar, café and meeting place while Providores, the main dining room, is on the first floor. Peter Gordon's grasp of the complexities of the world larder and his juggling of contrasting flavours – none of his dishes has fewer than six ingredients – make for food that is 'entertaining on the plate'. Straightforward cooking techniques – grilling, roasting and frying – are at the heart of the cooking, and the kitchen's sound culinary sense keeps everything on track: for example, crisp, spiced nori soft-shell crab with avocado sesame purée, pickled tomato, hijiki and peanut sprout salad with wasabi-tobikko ginger dressing, proved to be 'very fine' at inspection. Brown shrimp and coconut-crusted sea bass, which came with fennel, orange, green olive, smoked eel and dill salad, ponzu dressing and soy tapioca, had a fresh and vibrant appeal, while accompanying steamed sugar snaps, sweet potato and miso mash were full of flavour. To finish, a banana and pecan charlotte filled with lime custard and topped with slices of cooked pears seemed positively homely. The wine list is almost exclusively from New Zealand with prices starting at £14.50 a bottle.
Chef/s: Peter Gordon, Michael McGrath, Jeremy Leeming. **Open:** all week 12 to 2.45, 6 to 10.30 (10 Sun), tapas room all week 9 to 10.30 (10 to 10 Sun). **Closed:** Easter Sun and Mon. **Meals:** alc (main courses £18 to £24.50). **Service:** 12.5% (optional). **Details:** Cards accepted. 86 seats. 6 seats outside. Air-con. No music. Wheelchair access.

Royal China

An expanding family of Cantonese masters
2426 Baker Street, W1M 7AB
Tel no: (020) 7487 4688
www.dorchestergroup.com
⊖ **Hyde Park Corner**
Chinese | £29
Cooking score: 3

V

The opening of a Fulham outpost in early 2007 brought the number of London branches of this well-respected mini chain to five. Though each restaurant has its own character – Bayswater and Baker Street are large and bustling, Riverside has a notable Thamesside terrace while St John's Wood and Fulham have a neighbourhood vibe – each follows the same glitzy design template of golden geese taking flight on black lacquered walls and offers the same menu of classic Cantonese cooking. Dim sum, is famously good for textbook versions of the likes of steamed prawn dumplings, roast pork puffs, fried turnip paste with dried meat and braised noodles with ginger and spring onion. It takes some time to fully peruse the evening à la carte – soups alone take up two pages – from which a meal might begin with spicy smoked shredded chicken ahead of chicken with yellow bean sauce, honey-roasted pork or the chain's speciality of seafood: steamed eel with black bean sauce. Faster (and more unusual) ordering can be facilitated by turning to the page of 'chef's favourites', such as stewed pork belly with preserved cabbage, or one of several set menus, including a vegetarian option. House French is £15. Other branches in St John's Wood, Bayswater and Canary Wharf.
Chef/s: Ringo Chow. **Open:** all week 11 to 3.30 (4 Sun), 5.30 to 11.30. **Closed:** 25 Dec. **Meals:** alc (main courses L £8 to £15, D £10 to £25). **Service:** 12.5% (optional). **Details:** Cards accepted. 100 seats. Air-con. Separate bar. Wheelchair access. Music. Children allowed.

108 Marylebone Lane

Modern European
108 Marylebone Lane, W1U 2QE
Tel no: (020) 7969 3900
www.108marylebonelane.com
'Solid restaurant with an eclectic menu'

Eat and Two Veg

Vegetarian
50 Marylebone High Street, W1U 5HN
Tel no: (020) 72588595
www.eatandtwoveg.com
'Fantastic variety on the menu; great for breakfast'

Kandoo

Persian
458 Edgware Road, W2 1EJ
Tel no: (020) 7724 2428
'Superior Persian food in a canteen setting'

Levant

Middle Eastern
Jason Court, Wigmore Street, W1U 2SH
Tel no: (020) 72241111
'Wilfully exotic environs for mezze'

Original Tagines

Moroccan
7A Dorset Road, W1U 6QN
Tel no: (020) 7935 1545
'No-nonsense, good value North African food'

Star Polska

Polish
69 Marylebone Lane, W1U 2PH
Tel no: (020) 7486 1333
'Cosy location for hearty, traditional food'

deVille

Modern European
Mandeville Place, W1U 2BE
Tel no: (020) 7935 5599
www.mandeville.co.uk
'High style and accomplished cooking'

█ Mayfair

Alloro

Top spot for business lunches
19-20 Dover Street, W1S 4LU
Tel no: (020) 7495 4768
www.alloro-restaurant.co.uk
⊖ Green Park
Italian | £50
Cooking score: 2

🍷 V

Alloro caters for a well-heeled rather than hip crowd, and, as such, the décor is stylish, the service attentive and the cooking confident, though not attention-grabbing. A daily special might be roast lamb, while on the menu, prawns cooked with saffron and artichokes looks an adventurous choice. For starters, borage soup with sautéed red mullet fillets and Sicilian olive oil sounds more interesting than it was, while the pan-fried sea bream on a spinach salad tasted sprightly and fresh. The cheese board offers a diverse selection, and the sweet-toothed will enjoy an untraditional banana mousse. Less pleasing are the supplements sprinkling the set menus, which start at £26 for two courses. A reader praised the sommelier's guidance on the excellent wine list, which favours northern Italian producers. The mark-ups are on the high side, but there are eight decent house wines, from £18, which are also available by the glass.

Chef/s: Daniele Camera. **Open:** Mon to Fri L 12 to 2.30, Mon to Sat D 7 to 10.30. **Closed:** Bank hols, Christmas. **Meals:** Set L £26 (2 courses) to £29, Set D £28.50 (2 courses) to £36. **Service:** 12.5% (fixed). **Details:** Cards accepted. 66 seats. 4 seats outside. Air-con. No music. Children allowed.

Automat

Quality American diner
33 Dover Street, W1S 4NF
Tel no: (020) 7499 3033
www.automat-london.com
⊖ **Green Park**
American | £40
Cooking score: 1

Two years after opening, this all-day diner continues to pack customers in at an impressive rate. The three separate dining areas include a high turnover overspill zone by the front door, a stunning railway carriage mock-up section and the restaurant proper, which is an airy split-level eatery, with tiled walls and open kitchen. Superb steaks go against the current trend towards local produce, as all are imported from the US, with other main courses taking in roasted black cod, or baked lobster with cauliflower cheese, but prices are more Mayfair restaurant than American diner. If you want to keep the bill in check, visit for lunch and stick to soft-shell 'po boys', a burger (with good chips), or perhaps 'a positively sinful' macaroni cheese. Desserts, such as New York cheesecake, are equally well made. The succinct wine list is well thought-out though pricey; house French is £14.

Chef/s: Shaun Gilmore. **Open:** brasserie Mon to Fri 12 to 1am, breakfast 7 to 11, Mon to Fri L 12 to 3, Mon to Sat D 6 to 11, weekend brunch 11 to 4. **Service:** 12.5% (inc). **Details:** 90 seats. Air-con. Wheelchair access. Children allowed.

Bellamy's

Classy French brasserie in a discreet mews
18-18a Bruton Place, W1J 6LY
Tel no: (020) 7491 2727
www.bellamysrestaurant.co.uk
⊖ **Green Park**
French | £45
Cooking score: 5

Its dark green canopies and outside planters pick this French brasserie-cum-deli out from the crowd in its quiet Mayfair mews just off Berkeley Square. Walking through the well-stocked shop (where there is a new eight-seater oyster bar) really whets the appetite and heightens anticipation, while the dining-room itself comes classily decked out with dark leather banquettes and matching chairs. The atmosphere is buzzy and relaxed, and service generally friendly and enthusiastic, while the cooking is fittingly classic French brasserie, driven by well-sourced produce, intelligent simplicity and assured execution. The menu divides up comfortably into entrées, caviar, salads, fish and meat options, so maybe opt for lobster bisque or a terrine of foie gras to start (there is also Beluga caviar for the Mayfair-smart), while to finish, a tarte au citron or crêpes aux griottines could catch the eye. In between, perhaps try the John Dory à la planche with tomato and tarragon, or sliced entrecôte of beef with pommes frites. The short patriotic French wine list starts out life at £22, with a good selection by glass, before accelerating up to £650 for those wanting to push the boat out. (The Oyster Bar option delivers open sandwiches like lobster or salmon roe, or cold dishes such as potted shrimps alongside its namesake mollusc and a variety of shellfish.)

Chef/s: Stéphane Pacoud. **Open:** Mon to Fri L 12 to 2.15, Mon to Sat D 7 to 11.30. **Closed:** Bank hols. **Meals:** Set L and D £24 (2 courses) to £28.50. Oyster bar menu available. **Service:** 12.5%. **Details:** Cards accepted. 80 seats. Air-con. Separate bar. Wheelchair access. Children's portions.

Benares

East meets West in glamorous surroundings
12A Berkeley Square House, Berkeley Square, W1J 6BS
Tel no: (020) 7629 8886
www.benaresrestaurant.com
⊖ **Green Park**
Indian | £45
Cooking score: 3

This supremely swish restaurant and cocktail bar would not disgrace one of India's Oberoi hotels, the luxury chain where Benares's talented chef-proprietor Atul Kochhar did his training. Many of the subtly spiced dishes display a prominent European influence, but flavours are always balanced and ingredients intelligently paired. Chicken tikka with foie gras and smoked duck breast, for instance, might be followed by a bouillabaisse–style Indian fish stew with saffron and potatoes made with whatever's freshest at market. More traditional tastes are accommodated by a rogan josh. High prices are commensurate not only with the skill of the kitchen but the Mayfair location and glamorous sheen of the décor. Lunch and weekend menus provide a cheaper way in and, although choice is restricted to three options per course, the £29.95 price commendably includes a glass of wine, coffee and petits fours. The lengthy wine list requires proper consideration, not only for its selection of aromatic grapes from Europe's cool-climate regions (German Riesling especially), but for a handful of quirky inclusions such as Domaine Roxane Matsa 2004 from Greece at £28.00. At the other end of the scale, big money can be blown on 10 or so Super Tuscans.

Chef/s: Atul Kochar. **Open:** Mon to Sat L 12 to 2.30, D 5.30 to 11, Sun L 12.30 to 3, D 6 to 10.30. **Closed:** 25 Dec, 1 Jan. **Meals:** Set L and D £24.95 (2 courses) to £29.95 (3 courses). **Service:** 12.5%. **Details:** Cards accepted. 133 seats. Air-con. Separate bar. Wheelchair access. Music. Children's portions. Children allowed.

Le Caprice

Classy brasserie continues to shine
Arlington House, Arlington Street, SW1A 1RJ
Tel no: (020) 7629 2239
www.le-caprice.co.uk
⊖ Green Park
Modern European | £45
Cooking score: 4

For twenty-seven years Le Caprice has been a perennial favourite of London's café society and its popularity remains undiminished despite an ever-expanding restaurant scene. The L-shaped room is predominately monochrome with lots of glass and mirrors placed strategically so that you can see most of the people in the room. The atmosphere shimmers and when it comes to service there are few slicker operations in town. An inspection meal found the kitchen on top form, happy to see that among the calf's liver and fish and chips, current trends are not ignored. An innovative starter of sea trout and foie gras tempura, shaped as a maki roll, placed over a banana leaf, proved a complex of contrasting textures and flavours. The main course saw a return to the classics with a superb roast Goosnargh duck, cep pithiviers ('excellent pastry work') and a fine Madeira sauce. This was classy stuff. For dessert, a rhubarb crumble was singled out for particular praise, and so, too, the sourdough bread. The wine list is well thought out, though prices reflect the swanky St. James location, starting at £18.50 for the house variety.

Chef/s: Paul Brown. **Open:** all week, L 12 to 3 (5 Sun); D 5.30 to 12. **Closed:** 25 and 26 Dec, 1 Jan, Aug bank hol. **Meals:** alc (main courses £13.25 to £26.50). Cover £2. **Service:** 12.5% (included). **Details:** Cards accepted. 90 seats. Air-con. No mobile phones. Wheelchair access. Music. Children's portions.

Chisou

Accomplished Japanese food
4 Princes Street, W1B 2LE
Tel no: (020) 7629 3931
⊖ Oxford Circus
Japanese | £33
Cooking score: 4

Not all Japanese eating in the capital comes at arm-and-a-leg prices in designer surroundings. Chisou has the ambience of a simple Tokyo eatery, the kind of place you might stop off at on the way home from work. The menu is easily navigated, the appetisers including good sunomono (vinegar-dressed) seafood, or more recherché items such as monkfish liver in ponzu, spring onions and grated daikon. Sashimi and sushi include a full roll-call of tuna preparations, and there are the usual teriyaki dishes, which take in mackerel as well as chicken and beef. Set-price lunches look good value, and there is a handful of standard rice-bowls with toppings such as barbecued eel, or prawn and vegetable tempura. A full list of sakes complements the brief listing of grape wines, which start with Chilean house wines at £13.70 (£3.70 a glass). **Chef/s:** Kodi Aung. **Open:** Mon to Fri 12 to 2.30, Sat 12.30 to 3, Mon to Sat 6 to 10.15. **Closed:** Christmas and bank hols. **Meals:** alc (main courses £7 to £23.50). Set L £11.50 to £18. **Service:** not inc L, 12.5% D. **Details:** Cards accepted. 54 seats. Music.

Cipriani

An elegant slice of Venice
23-25 Davies Street, W1K 3DE
Tel no: (020) 7399 0500
www.cipriani.com
⊖ **Bond Street**
Italian | £50
Cooking score: 4

This Mayfair spin-off from the Ciprianis – the people behind Harry's Bar in Venice – has proved a big hit with the glitterati ever since it opened in 2004 in a swanky location just off Berkeley Square. The modern glass-front conceals an opulently appointed dining room modelled on its Venice original – spacious and stylish, it oozes class and Art Deco style. Think Venetian chandeliers, chequered white marble floors, teak panelling and dark brown leather seating. An equally smart bar adds further buzz to the upbeat proceedings, while an army of white-jacketed waiting staff offer slick, knowledgeable Latin service. It is contemporary yet clubby, with 'bags of experience factor' and a high-price tag to match. The lengthy repertoire of straightforward, accomplished, classic Italian cooking comes driven by tip-top ingredients and peppered with Cipriani flashes. Take main-course beef medallions alla Rossini, or perhaps wild sea bass served with cherry tomatoes and black olives. The dessert trolley offers a selection of Cipriani cakes, or perhaps crêpes a la crème, while the heady prices continue with the predominantly all-Italian wine list that steps out at £26, though 'a Bellini for aperitifs should not be missed'.

Chef/s: Giuseppe Marangi. **Open:** all week 12 to 3, 6 to 11.45 (11 Sun). **Meals:** alc (main courses £15 to £38). Set L £29.40 (3 courses) to £36.80, Set D £36.80 (3 courses) to £42. **Service:** 12.5% (optional). **Details:** Cards accepted. 120 seats. Air-con. No music. Wheelchair access. Children's portions.

El Pirata

Authentic tapas hidden away in Mayfair
56 Down Street, W1J 7AO
Tel no: (0207) 491 3810
www.elpirata.co.uk
⊖ **Green Park**
Spanish | £27
Cooking score: 1

Located in a quiet Mayfair back street, this welcoming bar and restaurant offers authentic Spanish cooking at good-value prices. The cheerful ground floor dining room with its crowded tables and walls bright with Picasso and Miro reproductions, is preferable to the basement. The tapas menu has a good balance of meat and seafood, with staples from the Spanish repertoire such as a 'silky and rich' arroz negro, piquillo peppers stuffed with seafood, meat balls, chicken croquettes, and bean stew with chorizo sausage and pancetta. Look to the specials list for main courses of roasted suckling pig with patatas a la pobre, or a zarzuela (casserole of seafood). The wine list is a well-chosen, all-Spanish affair and opens with good everyday drinking at £15.

Chef/s: Ramon Castro. **Open:** Mon to Fri 12 to 11.30, Sat 6.30 to 11.30. **Closed:** Christmas, bank hols. **Meals:** Set L Mon to Fri £9. **Service:** 10% (optional). **Details:** Cards accepted. 90 seats. 16 seats outside. Air-con. No mobile phones. Wheelchair access. Children's portions. Children allowed.

Budget eating

The capital might be associated with fine dining, but when it comes to eating out, London prices can be good news.

Ottolenghi

Ottolenghi's internationally-inspired cooking and baking comes in snack-sized portions; order three for a full meal.

Rooburoo

An unlikely find amidst the greasy spoons of Chapel Market, this inventive Indian restaurant is open all day for inspired snacking or main courses at £10 or less.

Salt Yard

The nicely-priced tapas at this 'charcuterie bar and restaurant' might include pheasant ravioli or char-grilled baby squid with caramelised onions and capers.

Leon

The darlings of healthy fast food, the Leon chain offers a feisty skit through favourite international dishes, from Moroccan meatballs to grilled halloumi.

Canteen

This sleek British restaurant does the culinary flag-waving so well you may have to queue at weekends. Expect traditional recipes, presented with a modern edge as sharp as the diner-style décor.

Kastoori

A unique mix of Gujurati and Ugandan influences has made Kastoori a long-standing vegetarian favourite. Try samosas and dosas, or continent-crossing curries.

El Pirata

Amazing: a bargain eatery in Mayfair. The food is authentically Spanish, from piquillo peppers stuffed with seafood to bean stew with chorizo and pancetta.

Ma Cuisine

Plastic tablecloths actually enhance the atmosphere of this French bistro, where Gallic classics are served with a smile. Further branches have opened in Twickenham and Barnes.

Brilliant

Over 30 years old and sporting a modern new look, this Indian restaurant continues to be as good as its name. Despite the length of the menu, the cooking shows no signs of short cuts.

Embassy

An ambassador for British seafood
29 Old Burlington Street, W1S 3AN
Tel no: (020) 7851 0956
www.embassylondon.com
⊖ **Green Park**
Modern British | £40
Cooking score: 4

Readers of the tabloids might know Embassy as a late-night club where C-list celebs are snapped by the paps falling onto the pavement in the small hours of the morning. But there's more to the place than drinking and dancing: there's also a chandelier-lit dining room that's especially pleasant when the sun shines, whether on the alfresco pavement terrace or through the full-length windows. Fish and seafood are particular strengths of the modern menu, from starters such as a salad of roast scallops with walnuts and piccalilli to main courses like Cornish hake with caramelised chicory, garlic and Merlot jus. The Mayfair location dictates a fair number of top-end ingredients for top-end prices and the kitchen is adept at pairing them intelligently, so that roast foie gras with rhubarb and raisins might be followed by Iberico pork with spinach and goats' cheese gnocchi, piquillo peppers, sage and brown butter. Finish with something sweet such as spiced pecan pie with maple syrup ice cream before heading on down to the dance floor. House French is £16.50 on a surprisingly short global wine list, about half of which is surprisingly priced under £30.
Chef/s: Garry Hollihead. **Open:** Tue to Sat D 6 to 11.30. **Meals:** alc (main courses £14 to £28). Set D £17 (2 courses) to £20. **Service:** 12.5% (optional). **Details:** Cards accepted. 120 seats. Air-con. Wheelchair access. Music.

Readers recommend

A 'readers recommend' review is a genuine quote from a report sent in by one of our readers. We intend to follow up these suggestions throughout the year to come.

Galvin at Windows

French cuisine hits great heights
Hilton Hotel, 22 Park Lane, W1Y 4BE
Tel no: (020) 7208 4021
www.hilton.co.uk/londonparklane
⊖ **Hyde Park Corner**
French | £58
Cooking score: 6

🍴 **V**

Galvin at Windows is the special occasion restaurant to beat all others. From its 28th floor perch atop the Hilton Park Lane, it offers glorious wraparound views over London and even Her Majesty's back yard. Since May 2006, it's had the additional draw of two of London's best-regarded chefs, Chris Galvin and André Garrett, in the kitchen. Their modern French menu displays both a light touch and a classical bent, an approach that gives prime seasonal ingredients a real chance to show off. A glossy slab of pork knuckle, foie gras, cured ham and black pudding terrine arrived prettily presented and at a perfect temperature but no amount of cute salad leaves or artful dots of apple purée could conceal its wonderful bold rusticity. Main courses – maybe a tranche of pearly white halibut with crushed Jersey Royals and crab or Anjou pigeon with petit pois a la française and pommes cocotte – are somewhat more refined, yet still generous and bursting with vibrant flavours. Perhaps inevitably, perhaps unfairly, this skyscraping destination takes a knocking for its conservative interior, its extensive but expensive wine list (take your pick from £22 a bottle), and the tourist-friendly appeal of its views. But if it's only for mugs and the expense account set, how else do you explain the terrific set-lunch deal, at just £45 for three courses, two glasses of wine, coffee, and petits fours?
Chef/s: Chris Galvin and André Garrett. **Open:** Sun to Fri L 12 to 2.30, Mon to Sat D 6 to 10.30.
Meals: alc (main courses £15 to £29.50). Set L £28, Set D £65. **Service:** 12.5% (optional). **Details:** Cards accepted. 108 seats. Air-con. No music. Wheelchair access.

Le Gavroche

Peerless cuisine from a Mayfair legend
43 Upper Brook Street, W1K 7QR
Tel no: (020) 7408 0881
www.le-gavroche.co.uk
⊖ **Marble Arch**
French | £95
Cooking score: 8

🍾 **V**

The opulent basement dining room hasn't changed over the years: it remains a 'masculine refuge', with luxurious drapery, plush velvet chairs and dark green walls busily covered with paintings. The whole operation runs on ultra-smooth casters, thanks to legions of meticulous staff who tour the tables discreetly, attending to every need. Old-school, special-event dining doesn't come more assured than this, and the whole experience is gilded with trappings and protocol from a bygone era – the silver domes, the tactfully unpriced menus for ladies, the regimented dress code for gentlemen. Michel Roux Jnr wears the mantle with confidence and – judging by recent feedback – the food has moved up a gear of late. Technical finesse has never been in doubt here, but the kitchen is now able to match the standard of its high-art desserts right across the board. There are also signs of a lighter touch and clarity, which helps to temper the prevailing mood of luxury-laden richness: a two-part crab starter involves a refreshing salad with premier-cru tomatoes and a perfectly balanced lime and coriander dressing, plus fried soft-shell crab totally devoid of greasiness. By contrast, lightly seared scallops are served around a few leaves with an outer ring of carrot 'spaghetti', all resting in a mustard tarragon sauce that keeps its primary flavours persuasively in check. Main courses really highlight what the kitchen is capable of in terms of sheer technique, timing and professional élan. Turbot is cooked on the bone, its 'tremendous' flavour enhanced by a textbook butter and chive sauce, plus a courgette roll filled with ratatouille and some chickpea chips. Likewise, fillet of beef (again of faultless quality) is served with a dazzling port sauce reduced to glorious thickness and intensity; its hand-picked companions are a slab of über-rich foie gras and some macaroni. Then came a staggeringly accomplished assiette of raspberry desserts: a peerless soufflé, a sorbet bursting with fruity intensity, a gossamer mille-feuille and – best of all – an extraordinary beignet, with a pot of raspberry coulis and a white chocolate tuile for dipping. The wine list is a French aristocrat, running to 42 pages of top-notch wines from the finest growers in all the major regions. Rarefied vintages are covered 'in loving depth', including Romanée Conti going back to 1971; also note the glorious Gewürztraminers, the fabulous selection from Languedoc Roussillon and the choice of dessert wines. Prices are unrelenting, although there is – apparently – 'one obscure bottle of white at just £20'. Wines by the glass are not advertised, but some can be provided on request. In a novel move, the restaurant has also introduced its own beer menu.

Chef/s: Michel Roux. **Open:** Mon to Fri L 12 to 2, Mon to Sat D 6.30 to 11. **Closed:** Christmas and New Year, bank hols. **Meals:** alc (main courses £26.50 to £64.80). Set L £48. **Service:** 12.5% (optional). **Details:** Cards accepted. 70 seats. Air-con. Separate bar. Children allowed.

Giardinetto

Upmarket Italian food
39-40 Albemarle Street, W1S 4TE
Tel no: (020) 7493 7091
www.giardinetto.co.uk
⊖ **Green Park**
Italian | £49
Cooking score: 3

Money has been lavished on this upmarket Italian restaurant and Maurizio Vilona's classic Genovese and Ligurian cooking certainly lives up to the swish Mayfair address. With buzzers to be pushed to gain access, you expect to find a stylish interior and the minimalist, split-level dining area, with its light plank flooring, copper and terracotta walls and linen-clothed tables provide the backdrop for some honest and passionate Italian cooking. The intention is to create a liaison of traditionalism and modernity, as is apparent in a main course of duck breast with caramelised oranges and ribiola cheese. Precede with an antipasto of steak tartare Piedmont style or traditional Ligurian ravioli filled with ham, spinach, eggs, herbs and beef fillet ragu. Finish with a classic apricot tart. The lighter lunch menu is excellent value. The all-Italian wine list is extensive and expensive, but a Puglian white starts proceedings at £17 and there's over 20 wines by the glass.

Chef/s: Maurizio Vilona. **Open:** Mon to Fri L 12 to 3, Mon to Sat D 7 to 11. **Meals:** alc (main courses £18 to £27.50). Set L £22. **Service:** 12.5% (optional). **Details:** Cards accepted. 54 seats. Air-con. Wheelchair access. Music.

Gordon Ramsay at Claridge's
Consistent standard at this Art Deco jewel
Brook Street, W1A 2JQ
Tel no: (020) 7499 0099
www.gordonramsay.com
⊖ **Bond Street**
French | £72
Cooking score: 5
⌖ V

Claridges just the mention of the name conjures up a sense of bygone days, when aristocratic hotels ruled the social fabric of London. Walking into the lobby, you may think that things have not changed all that much, but the dining room divides opinion with its pink and peach walls, purple chair covers and oversized layered lamp fittings. Mark Sargeant cooks in a diligent and decisive manner, his modern cooking has a strong classical foundation, so doesn't take too many risks. An amuse of celeriac velouté with Granny Smith apple and horseradish, for example, may precede a starter of perfectly seared scallops with sweetcorn purée, spring truffles and beurre noisette. Dishes are labour-intensive and since combinations are generally tried and tested, rely for effect on finesse: for example, a salt marsh lamb, rubbed with crystallised walnuts and cumin, turned round

a lining of parsnip purée, which in turn was paired with sweetbreads, roasted with thyme, and a superb filo pastry enveloping a confit of the lamb. When this energetic approach is applied to desserts it yields a 'faultless' lime-roasted pineapple, partnered with mascarpone cheese, served with pain perdu and a shot glass filled with alternating layers of pineapple jelly, cream and granite. Fresh-faced service, 'high in count', is polite but at inspection lacked attention to detail. The outstanding wine list, with limited choices under £30, can 'bling it with the best of them', starts at £20, and swiftly moves swiftly to £10,000 for a 1900 Ch. Lafite Rothschild. All the major wine regions are fully represented, with superb vintages from Italy and Spain as well as France, and there are three pages devoted to sweet wines.

Chef/s: Mark Sargeant. **Open:** all week 12 to 2.45 (3 Sun), 5.45 to 11 (6 to 10.30 Sun). **Meals:** Set L £30 to £75, Set D £65 to £75. **Service:** 12.5% (optional). **Details:** Cards accepted. 100 seats. Air-con. No music. No mobile phones. Wheelchair access. Children's portions.

The Grill at Brown's
A very British menu
30 Albemarle Street, W1S 4BP
Tel no: (020) 7518 4060
www.roccofortehotels.com
⊖ **Green Park**
British | £40
Cooking score: 4

It's appropriate that London's oldest five-star hotel is home to some of the capital's most traditional British dishes. That's not to say that there's anything fuddy-duddy about The Grill at Brown's: the nineteenth-century effect of the sombre wood-panelling, huge fireplace and carving trolleys is tempered by modern fabrics and crisp blinds. Simple dishes made from sound ingredients is what the kitchen does best: potted Morecambe Bay shrimps ahead of calf's liver and bacon from the grill, say. More elaborate dishes, such as Atlantic sea bass with grilled baby fennel, tarragon and vermouth cream are available too, and it's worth some forward-planning to co-ordinate your visit with a dish of the day: boiled brisket of Scottish beef with dumplings and horseradish for Monday lunch, say. The brevity of the dessert list – Eton mess is among the five on offer – suggests that huge portions defeat all but the most determined diner. Burgundy and Bordeaux lead the wine list with some vertiginously priced vintages, but the rest of the predominantly French selection is not nearly so stiff. House Chardonnay and Cab Sav from the Languedoc is £25, while a dozen by the glass and half bottle underscore The Grill's business lunch credentials.

Chef/s: Laurence Glayzer. **Open:** all week 12 to 2.30, 7 to 10. **Meals:** alc (main courses £13 to £28). Set L Mon to Sat £25 (2 courses) to £30, Set L Sun £27 (2 courses) to £35, Set D £45. **Service:** not inc. **Details:** Cards accepted. 80 seats. Air-con. No music. Wheelchair access. Children's portions.

Guinea Grill

No-nonsense steak house in W1
30 Bruton Place, W1J 6NL
Tel no: (020) 7409 1728
www.theguinea.co.uk
British | £65
Cooking score: 2

V

Tucked away at the back of an old-fashioned pub in a Mayfair mews, business diners and savvy grill fans beat a path here for signature steak and kidney pies and prime steaks. The Grill has a separate entrance, and, while the setting may not be the grandest considering its moneyed location – the low-ceilinged room paying little lip service to modern fashion – it does come linen clad, relaxed and unbuttoned. With its selection of Scottish, dry-aged, 28-day hung steaks and signature pies taking centre stage, there is a clubby, masculine affinity to the menu. However, there are concessions to lighter dishes, such as roast fillet of sea bass served with creamed leeks and tomato rice. Like the menu price tags, the wine

hits W1 tariffs too, though the list – with France in ascendancy – does kick off at £16.50 and there is a good selection by glass.

Chef/s: Mark Newbury. **Open:** Mon to Fri L 12.30 to 2.30, Mon to Sat D 6 to 10.30. **Closed:** 24 to 26 and 31 Dec, 1 Jan. **Meals:** alc (main courses £12.50 to £34). Bar menu available. **Service:** 12.5%. **Details:** Cards accepted. 28 seats. Air-con. No music. Children allowed.

Hibiscus

Ludlow star rises in the West End
29 Maddox Street, W1S 2PA
Tel no: 020 7629 2999
www.hibiscusrestaurant.co.uk
◒ Oxford Circus
French | £55
Cooking score: 5

Claude and Claire Bosi have forsaken the small but glittering Ludlow constellation for the anonymity of an unprepossessing slice of West End real estate and the tooth-and-claw competitiveness of the London scene. The room looks like what it is, the entrance to a corporate building that has been pressed into service as a restaurant, and the decor makes discordant noises in a muted tone . Claude Bosi has made a name as an ambitious, idiosyncratic chef, and for one inspector a starter of paper-thin carpaccio of pollack interleaved with black radish, garnished with some truffles and finished off with almond oil and autumn truffle vinaigrette was simply sensational . Similarly, a highlight from the set lunch menu proved to be an appealingly crisp-skinned Cornish silver mullet well matched by a smoky, meaty ragout of Puy lentils deemed the best thing on the plate . But these same reporters have questioned whether dishes are being properly road tested . Witness an amuse bouche of chilled hibiscus flower soda with smoked olive oil (the preliminary taste was reminiscent of medicine), or a micro-serving of gritty couscous stained with the cooking juices of purple cauliflower, topped with a rapidly melting splodge of coconut ice-cream and surrounded by a moat of truffled cauliflower cream. And while one meal

Hari Nagaraj The Cinnamon Club

Why did you become a chef?
I had a genuine passion for food from an early age.

Which of today's chefs do you admire?
Heston Blumenthal.

Where do you source your ingredients?
Primarily small, specialist farms in the UK and some in Europe.

Who is your favourite producer?
We've recently starting using water buffalo from Laverstoke Park in Hampshire, which has proved to be very popular with guests.

What's your favourite cookery book?
Cooking Delights of the Maharajas by Dharamjit Singh.

What's the best dish you've ever eaten?
I'm still working on finding that.

Do you have a favourite local recipe?
I do love a good bread and butter pudding.

What's your guilty food pleasure?
Apart from the bread and butter pudding? It has to be home-made chips.

What's the hardest thing about running a restaurant?
Finding the right balance between consistency and creativity.

concluded with a brilliantly made, wispy-thin apple tart, with salted butter caramel and an unusual lentil and ginger ice cream , another meal saw the pastry base as an overly dense, almost oaty construction that refused the pressure of the spoon . Service is unobtrusive but marginally detached . The wine list is a touch meandering, mainly focused on France, and prices are on the elevated side, with bottles starting at £19.50 and climaxing with Chateau Latour 1982 at £3,750.

Chef/s: Claude Bosi. **Open:** Mon to Fri L 12 to 2.30, D 6.30 to 10. **Closed:** Last 2 weeks Aug, Christmas and New Year. **Meals:** Set L £21 (2 courses) to £25, Set D £55. **Service:** not inc. **Details:** Cards accepted. 45 seats. Air-con. No music. Wheelchair access. Children's portions. Children allowed.

Kiku

A long-standing Japanese stalwart
17 Half Moon Street, W1J 7BE
Tel no: (020) 7499 4208/4209
www.kikurestaurant.co.uk
⊖ **Green Park**
Japanese | £31
Cooking score: 4

🍷 **V**

This venerable Mayfair institution marks its 30th anniversary in 2008, and though the culinary landscape has changed greatly since it first opened, Kiku has not been left behind. Its décor keeps pace with the contemporary fashion for clean lines and natural materials, and it remains one of the prime spots for first-rate Japanese cuisine in London. The long menu is a comprehensive run through the repertoire, opening with a page of nigiri and hand-rolled sushi from salmon through to razor clam, whelks and sea urchin. Seafood figures strongly throughout the menu, whether it's a salad of marinated mackerel, yellow tail sashimi, deep-fried lemon sole, or grilled eel on rice with miso soup. Meat and vegetable dishes are also well represented, including teriyaki beef, and chicken and aubergine casserole. Various set dinner menus provide a good way to sample a range of dishes, while lunchtime brings a choice of noodles, zosui (Japanese porridge) and donburi. Wines from Corney & Barrow open with house French red and white at £14.50, with green tea, hot or cold saké and Japanese beer providing alternative options.

Chef/s: H. Shiraishi and Y. Hattori. **Open:** Mon to Sat L 12 to 2.30, all week D 6 to 10.15 (5.30 to 9.45 Sun). **Closed:** 25, 26 Dec and New Year. **Meals:** alc (main courses £6 to £35). Set L £13.50, Set D £46. **Service:** 12.5%. **Details:** Cards accepted. 95 seats. Air-con. Wheelchair access. Music. Children allowed.

Luciano

Italian food served with trademark gusto
72-73 St James's Street, SW1A 1PH
Tel no: (020) 7408 1440
www.lucianorestaurant.co.uk
⊖ **Green Park**
Italian | £38
Cooking score: 4

Marco Pierre White's chic, clubby St James's restaurant has been decorated with some new artwork since last year, seeing things take a decidedly adult turn. Glossy prints by Bob Carlos Clarke – the photographer who captured White's *enfant terrible* era so memorably in 'White Heat' – are on all the walls, with the more outré ones tucked away in the private dining room. The food at Luciano isn't exactly shy and retiring either. Undainty antipasti – a tennis ball sized burrata pugliese, and a Cornish crab salad with pane carasau, speak of full-on flavours and fuss-free presentation. Primi of oxtail fettuccine and a risotto alla milanese with osso buco ragu, were similarly straightforward. There are also more upscale (and pricey) dishes like fillet of beef with foie gras and truffle, presumably there to please the moneyed local crowd that demands such things. The presence of lots of champagne on what is otherwise a largely Italian wine list (starting at £14.95) says a lot. Prices overall aren't low, but given the glamorous surroundings and the postcode, aren't so unreasonable.

Chef/s: Marco Corsica. **Open:** Mon to Sat L 12 to 2.45, D 5.30 to 11.15. **Closed:** 25 and 26 Dec. **Meals:** alc (main courses £12.50 to £26). Set L and

D £42 to £45. **Service:** 12.5%. **Details:** Cards accepted. 50 seats. Air-con. Music. Children's portions.

Maze

Cutting-edge metropolitan cooking
10-13 Grosvenor Square, W1K 6JP
Tel no: (020) 7107 0000
www.gordonramsay.com
⊖ **Bond Street**
French | £45
Cooking score: 6
🍷 **V**

Since it opened in 2005, Gordon Ramsay's pace-setting restaurant has never lacked for enthusiastic, solid support. That is partly what lends it its air of confidence and assurance – that, and having been at the cutting edge of metropolitan food fashion from its inception. The space is slick and classically unadorned, with creams and browns being the predominant colours. The focus of Jason Atherton's menu is tapas-sized portions; the recommendation being for around five to eight per head. Just about everything on the menu sounds fascinating, the combinations unusual but sensible and the kitchen can deliver some real treats. For example, roasted sea scallops teamed with a slick of pea purée, a fried quail's egg and potato with Yorkshire ham and maple syrup giving an extra flavour dimension. None of this would work if the raw materials weren't so classy. Witness just-seared Landes foie gras anointing honey and soy roasted quail, the accompanying spiced pear chutney further deepening the savour of the dish. Or roasted rack of lamb served with a melting nugget of braised shoulder and four ways with onions, including mini-battered rings. That same level of complexity is maintained for desserts that might include an outstanding Madagascan vanilla rice pudding served with raspberry and lemon thyme jam, a dollop of mascarpone and pecan ice cream added at table, or peanut butter and cherry jam sandwich with salted nuts and cherry sorbet. Wines are a star turn. The list shimmers with class and convinces in all regions. In France,

Bordeaux and Burgundy are complemented by a great range from the Loire, some Rhône heavyweights and the estate du jour of regional France. Elsewhere Italy and the Antipodes shine brightest and there's a good global selection by the glass. House wines start at £20.
Chef/s: Jason Atherton. **Open:** all week L 12 to 2.45, D 6 to 11. **Meals:** alc (main courses £16.50 to £18.50). Set L and D £37 to £60. **Service:** 12.5% (optional). **Details:** Cards accepted. 90 seats. Air-con. No mobile phones. Wheelchair access. Music. Children's portions.

Nobu Berkeley St

High-end Japanese chain
15 Berkeley Street, W1J 8DY
Tel no: (020) 7290 9222
www.noburestaurants.com
⊖ **Green Park**
Japanese | £70
Cooking score: 5

V

Chain restaurants don't come much cooler than the Berkeley Street branch of Nobu, which has supplanted its Park Lane sibling as the venue of choice for paparazzi-eager celebrities. It's consequently popular with a moneyed international crowd, for whom Nobu is as globally recognisable a luxury brand as Louis Vuitton. Fortunately, there's substance behind the style. Sushi rolls – each grain of rice glistening separately – might be filled with the sweet crunch of tempura prawn or melt-in-the-mouth tuna with a spicy sauce. It's prettily presented, too: asparagus spears shoot out of the prawn tempura sushi, while the signature dish of black cod marinated in miso, the fish firm-fleshed and pearly, is served on a banana leaf. Elsewhere, the long menu might yield duck breast with wasabi salsa cooked in the wood oven, pan-fried Chilean sea bass with jalapeño dressing, tuna sashimi salad, salmon teriyaki donburi, and spicy seafood udon noodles. Glum staff, sadly, are a big let-down: at inspection 'we weren't offered the daily specials suggested to a neighbouring table, spilt soy sauce was not wiped away and

we were served starters and main courses and out of the door in under an hour', not the sort of meal pacing commensurate with the high-scoring bill (including 15% service) and it's this kind of attitude that has led another reporter to label Nobu Berkeley 'overpriced and a pale imitation of the original'. House Muscadet is £20 while an über-glam downstairs bar is notable for its sake-based Martini cocktails.
Chef/s: Mark Edwards. **Open:** Mon to Sat L 12 to 2.15, all week D 6 to 11 (12 Thur, Fri Sat, 9.15 Sun). **Closed:** 24, 25, 26 Dec. **Meals:** alc (main courses £9.50 to £29.50). Set D £60. Bar menu available. **Service:** 15%. **Details:** Cards accepted. 200 seats. Air-con. Separate bar. Wheelchair access. Music.

Nobu London

Godfather of new-wave Japanese cooking
19 Old Park Lane, W1K 1LB
Tel no: (020) 7447 4747
www.noburestaurants.com
⊖ **Hyde Park Corner**
Japanese | £60
Cooking score: 5

V

Nobu London opened in 1997, and since that time we have seen an explosion of new wave Japanese restaurants. It is a testament to Nobuyuki Matsuhisa that his ground-breaking cuisine still sets the culinary benchmark today, and the restaurant continues to be the dining choice of the A-list. All this glamour comes at a hefty price tag, but the first-floor dining room is surprisingly modest, with pale wood tables and green leather banquettes. The 'In & Out' bento box lunch can provide a worthy glimpse into some of the signature dishes, such as the black miso cod or rock shrimp tempura with ponzu, and at a fraction of the price. At inspection, a yellowtail sashimi 'any fresher you will have to catch it yourself', was cunningly enhanced by jalapeño peppers to provide a hot and sexy undertone, and sushi in the form of sea bream, salmon and prawn nigri, as well as tuna maki, were top notch. A spicy Anti-Cucho tea-smoked lamb partnered by a sublime aubergine and miso purée, revealed finely-balanced flavours, as did a dessert of Satandagi doughnut filled with warm dark chocolate and served with caramelised pistachios and an almond ice cream. Amenable service comes without any hint of snobbery 'and so it should, given the 15% service charge'. The appealing wine list starts from a towering base of £23 and includes an extensive selection of hot or cold sakes from £7.50.

Chef/s: Mark Edwards. **Open:** Mon to Fri 12 to 2.15, 6 to 10.15 (11 Fri), Sat 12.30 to 2.30, 6 to 11, Sun 12.30 to 2.30, 6 to 9.30. **Meals:** alc (main courses £11.50 to £29.50). Set L £25 to £60, Set D £70 to £90. **Service:** 15% (included). **Details:** Cards accepted. 150 seats. Air-con. No music. Wheelchair access.

Patterson's

Enterprising family-run restaurant
4 Mill Street, W1S 2AX
Tel no: (020) 7499 1308
www.pattersonsrestaurant.com
⊖ Oxford Circus
French | £57
Cooking score: 4

V

The Pattersons run their intimate Mayfair restaurant as a family affair, which is a rare thing in this affluent part of the capital. Maria takes care of business out front, while Raymond and his son Tom work the stoves. Their menus are full of neat, distinctive touches and clever flourishes: carpaccio and tartare of beef are paired with avocado, salt-cured duck breast is served with mango risotto and creamed pak choi, while seared fillet of sea bass might be presented on a roulade of artichoke, potato and spinach with Mediterranean vegetable salsa. Raymond hasn't lost touch with his Scottish roots and looks to his home town of Eyemouth for lobsters, crabs and langoustines (which might even have their own menus from time to time). To conclude, expect intricate modern desserts like strawberry and passion fruit consommé with coconut sorbet or an elaborate combo involving chocolate

marquise, chocolate and chilli mousse and lemongrass chocolate ice cream. Cheeses are sourced from La Fromagerie and France is also the main contender on the wine list, with the rest of the world playing second fiddle. Ten house selections start at £19 a bottle (£4.50 a glass).

Chef/s: Raymond and Tom Patterson. **Open:** Mon to Fri L 12 to 3, Mon to Sat D 6 (5 Sat) to 11. **Closed:** bank hols. **Meals:** alc (main courses £17). Set L £20 (3 courses), Set D £40 (3 courses). **Service:** 12.5% (optional). **Details:** Cards accepted. 75 seats. Air-con. Music. Children's portions.

La Petite Maison

A taste of Nice
54 Brook Mews, W1K 4EG
Tel no: (020) 7495 4774
www.lpmlondon.co.uk
⊖ Bond Street
French | £42
Cooking score: 3

La Petite Maison is, nutshell-wise, the London version of a long-standing restaurant in Nice, brought to us by the team behind those modern Japanese restaurants Roka and Zuma. The premise is simple, Niçoise dishes served in an attractive, light but noisy triangular-shaped room. Main courses are advertised for sharing with a couple designed for solo diners an impeccable roast baby chicken marinated in lemon, for example but ignore any attempt to persuade you that starters are sharing material . Shared or not, a packed with flavour plate of marinated sardines served with grapes, tomatoes and capers, or deep-fried courgette flowers with sage, anchovies and onions, typify the style. An underwhelming whole sea bream baked en papillote left one table gazing wistfully at those tucking into a whole roast black leg chicken with foie gras, undoubtedly the (pricey) star dish here which must be ordered in advance. To keep the bill in check, one dessert, say a dark chocolate tart with orange cream and several spoons, will suffice. Expect to pay at least £23 for even the humblest offerings on the Francophile wine list.

Chef/s: Raphael Duntoye. **Open:** Mon to Fri L 12 to 2.30pm, Mon to Sat D 6 to 11pm. **Meals:** alc (main courses £9 to £70). **Service:** 12.5%. **Details:** Cards accepted. 85 seats. Air-con. Wheelchair access. Music. Children allowed.

Ristorante Semplice
Simple, small-but-sassy establishment
10 Blenheim Street, W1S 1LJ
Tel no: (020) 7495 1509
www.ristorantesemplice.com
⊖ **Green Park**
Italian
Cooking score: 5
🍾

Semplice is an intimate *ristorante* off Bond Street, the new venture of business partners chef Marco Torri and manager Giovanni Baldino, ex Locanda Locatelli. It certainly lives up to its name. Relying on exceptional ingredients often imported directly from Italy, the kitchen has the self-confidence and skill to prepare them very simply, bringing out their full, remarkable flavours. The prosciutto of duck breast is home-cured; the carpaccio of beef comes from *Fassone* all-female Alba cattle for extra tenderness. Original pasta dishes are a delight: try the Campanian *paccheri* penne with lamb ragù and a touch of red chilli, or spaghetti *alla chitarra* with Italian rabbit and black olives. Fish courses sensibly may rely on Cornish cod served with a beetroot sauce or wild sea bass with chick peas. From the prix fixe menu, the Piedmontese roast baby chicken with spinach or Herwick shoulder of lamb with fennel, followed by a plate of prime Italian cheeses makes a great £15 lunch. Fresh, simple desserts like panna cotta with chocolate sauce and fresh raspberries. Giovanni, who comes from Franciacorta really knows his wines. The house *bianco* and *rosso* from top Sicilian estate Borgo Selene are first-rate value at £13.50. For something special, the Barbera d'Alba Conca Tre Pile, Aldo Conterno 2003 is a great bottle at under £50. Service is professional yet natural and warm-hearted. Outstanding espresso (Haiti Comet, Extra Superieur).

Chef/s: Marco Torri. **Open:** L Mon to Fri 12 to 2.30; D Mon to Sat 7 to 10.30. **Closed:** Sunday. **Details:** Cards accepted. 70 seats. Air-con. No music. Wheelchair access.

★ BEST NEW RESTAURANT ★

Sake No Hana
Alan Yau's homage to Japanese food
23 St James's Street, SW1A 1HA
Tel no: 020 7925 8988
⊖ **Green Park**
Japanese | £60
Cooking score: 5

Alan Yau s latest temple of cool has produced a reader response unlike any other new London opening. While some hail it as pure and unadulterated joy for people who understand and love Japanese food , others have taken issue with the tatami mat seating where you have to take your shoes off, and then lever yourself into a table sunken into a pit in the floor' (ordinary tables are available), or been thrown by a drinks list that offers no wine, but promises quality speciality sakes and champagnes at a price. The menu structure is quite complex, too, with multi-course tasting options – there are no starters or main courses, just an array of dishes some tiny, some large . The trick is to order the right combination of individual small dishes and those large enough to share and as for what to drink, the sake sommelier has been described as a star – take his advice. Among highlights have been a tiny appetizer of mountain yam, sliced finely 'rather like noodles', with salmon roe, a small piece of wasabi root and a dipping sauce of dashi, very good sashimi, Chilean sea bass with sweet miso, ginkgo nuts and shimeji mushrooms, takiawase of extremely tender pork rib, or poulet noir ni a pot of 'deeply flavoured' black leg chicken with soya bean, carrot, sugar snap and yuzu pepper and excellent eel rice. With so many menu options, however, execution is almost bound to be patchy, but when on song, dishes will amaze. As will the final bill.

Chef/s: Masakazu Kikuchihara, Noboru Ishii. **Open:** Mon to Sat L 12 to 3, D 6 to 11 (11.30 Fri and Sat). **Closed:** 24 and 25 Dec. **Meals:** alc (main courses from £8 to £70). **Service:** not inc. **Details:** Cards accepted. 77 seats. Air-con. Separate bar. No music. Wheelchair access.

Scott's

Cosmopolitan glitter
20 Mount Street, W1K 2HE
Tel no: (020) 7495 7309
www.scotts-restaurant.com
⊖ Green Park
Seafood | £50
Cooking score: 3

V

Occupying a smart address, Scott's relaunch has brought a well-stocked shiny seafood bar, acres of dark wood, big contemporary artwork, and slightly cramped white-clad tables. The burst of enthusiasm that characterised its early output seems to have settled down to a gentle simmer, but it still delivers modern dishes with varying degrees of input from the British repertoire: dressed crab at one end, roast saddle of rabbit with langoustines and barba di frate at the other and wood pigeon on toast with hedgehog mushrooms somewhere in between. Seafood is plentiful, with a range from caviar to oysters, to clams, to sea bass with scallops and wild chervil. The kitchen's output, and hence reports, are mixed, however, but highly rated dishes include potted shrimps, gutsy cods' tongues and ceps bordelaise (perfectly complemented by three unadvertised little bone marrow), and an excellent, creamy rhubarb ripple ice cream 'with lovely rhubarb compote'. The wine list covers the whole spectrum of style but some of the prices may raise an eyebrow. Wines under £20 can be found, however, and 23 types are available by the glass.
Chef/s: Kevin Gratton. **Open:** Mon to Sat 12 to 10.30, Sun 12 to 10. **Closed:** 25, 26 Dec, August Bank Hol. **Meals:** alc (main courses £13 to £39.50).

Service: 12.5%. **Details:** Cards accepted. 120 seats. 25 seats outside. Air-con. Separate bar. No music. Wheelchair access. Children allowed.

Sketch, Lecture Room and Library

Controversial, imaginative and expensive
9 Conduit Street, W1S 2XG
Tel no: (0870) 777 4488
www.sketch.uk.com
⊖ Oxford Circus
French | £90
Cooking score: 6

V

Sketch offers a myriad of dining options: Parlour, Gallery, Glade and the fine dining restaurant, Lecture Room and Library. The concept is a cavalcade of colours and designs, ranging from marble staircases to science fiction sets. The Lecture Room sits on the first floor, its dining room a celebration of comfort and flamboyance, matched by a menu predisposed to exuberance; stray away from the affordable lunch menu and 'you may need a defibrillator – the first two courses from the carte can easily take you past the £100 mark'. Following the outstanding breads, the opening act arrives in different vessels: cream of tuna, a jelly made with a few drops of Jack Daniel's and dusted with dark chocolate, 'sensational' tartlet of cuttlefish and a spoon of sea bream carpaccio. To follow, another flurry of small dishes, including a superb warm mousseline of chicken with green beans, a confit of salmon with caviar. The cooking can be cerebral, and there is no denying that Pierre Gagnaire is a culinary genius. However, without his presence, the intricate cuisine can get lost in translation, but when the techniques come together, the results can be breathtaking. Simmenthal beef, for example, first poached in port bouillon and served with braised lettuce, and paired with beef marrow and pochas beans, accompanied by a 'sublime' carmine sauce made from tomatoes, mustard and white wine, and rounded off by the second installment of consommé of vinegar and wild mushrooms. To finish, a plate of

textured desserts, 'resembling a small child's perfect birthday treat': a huge bowl filled with marshmallow, loukhoum, sable biscuit, crystallised and caramelised fruits as well as iced parfait of raspberries and pineapple pulp. The service is hard to fault, making you feel pampered and welcomed. France is the centerpiece of the lengthy wine list, particularly strong in Bordeaux, Burgundy and Rhone. Prices start from £19 but the list doesn't really get going until you reach £40.
Chef/s: Pierre Gagnaire and Pascal Sanchez. **Open:** Lecture Room/Library Tue to Fri L 12 to 4, Tue to Sat D 6.30 to 12. **Closed:** Bank hols, 21 Aug to 4 Sept, 25 to 30 Dec. **Meals:** (main courses £39 to £52). Set L £30 to £35, Set D £90. **Service:** 12.5% (optional). **Details:** Cards accepted. 50 seats. Air-con. No mobile phones. Wheelchair access. Music.

★ BEST WINE LIST ★

Square

Exemplary French cuisine
6-10 Bruton Street, W1J 6PU
Tel no: (020) 7495 7100
www.squarerestaurant.com
⊖ Green Park
French | £70
Cooking score: 8

The Square is a sure-fire gastronomic experience, rock-like in the consistent excellence of the ingredients and the reliably assured technique in the kitchen. The dining room has everything a serious restaurant should: high ceilings, full drop windows (looking out onto Bruton Street) and generously spaced tables. A few large, goodish pieces of abstract art adorn the walls. Lighting is excellent, with plenty of carefully directed ceiling spots and a few side lamps. Waiters and waitresses in smart black suits are extremely good, attentive and friendly; wine and water topped up effortlessly. The menu – nine starters, eight main courses and a couple of specials – is classical French, nicely balanced without too much elaboration. To start with, comes a little tray of delicious nibbles like anchovy bread stick, a warm broad bean

savoury beignet, and a slice of lovely smoked salmon and asparagus terrine flavoured with dill and a little pickled cucumber. For one inspector, dinner began with three roast langoustine tails of excellent flavour, each resting on a Parmesan gnocchi; the gnocchi had 'lovely soft texture and strong Parmesan flavour'. The renowned lasagne of Devon crab was then served in a soup bowl with a fluffy cappuccino of shellfish and champagne foam; the silky mousse had a positive flavour of langoustine and lobster. For main course came a real highlight: a particularly tender, aged Ayrshire fillet of beef resting on a bed of spinach and a pool of superb demi-glace reduction of the cooking juices. The beef was exceptionally good, and the spinach just about perfect. The epic cheese board featured very fine St Felician and Epoisses. Pre-dessert was an old Square classic: sugar beignet with vanilla yoghurt and a passion fruit and mango coulis and mandarin mousse. Irish coffee baba managed a reasonably moist baba and an intensely flavoured espresso crème brulée topped with Drambuie ice cream, and a good cocoa and vanilla trifle. The superb wine list, is the passionate hobby of owner Nigel Platts-Martin, a man with a nose for the finest burgundy and champagne from the best growers. Alsace has a whole page, Germany, gets two, with the splendid Egon Müller Scharzhofberger Kabinett 1998 at £45, a good buy. Australia has a host of different vintages of Grange.
Chef/s: Philip Howard. **Open:** Mon to Fri L 12 to 2.45, all week D 6.30 to 10.45 (10 Sun). **Closed:** 25 Dec, 1 Jan, L bank hols. **Meals:** Set D £65. **Service:** 12.5% (optional). **Details:** Cards accepted 75 seats. Air-con. No music. No mobile phones. Wheelchair access. Children allowed.

Average price

The average price listed in main-entry reviews denotes the price of a three-course meal, without wine.

Sumosan

Intimate modern Japanese
26b Albemarle Street, W1S 4HY
Tel no: (020) 7495 5999
www.sumosan.com
⊖ Green Park
Japanese | £50
Cooking score: 4

V

More intimate than other restaurants operating at this level, such as Nobu and Zuma, Sumosan attracts a well-heeled European crowd who like to eat late: things don't really get into full swing here until after 9pm. As at many modern Japanese restaurants, there's little that's authentically oriental about many of the dishes, so you'll find roasted leg of wild rabbit in girolle mushroom sauce sitting next to chicken yakitori and, this being Mayfair, high-end ingredients such as wagyu beef and poached oysters with foie gras and sea urchin. Some very creative sushi rolls are a highlight of a meal here, including the Albemarle, a textural treat glistening with flying fish roe and filled with a crunchy mix of salmon, avocado and chunks of tempura batter. Various set menus make choosing easier and, priced between £60 and £80, indicate how much going à la carte is likely to cost; a surprise, then, to find a truly excellent value set lunch menu. House wines are £20 on a global list that isn't as expensive as you might expect. Alternatively, a lengthy selection of saké merits investigation.

Chef/s: Bubker Belkheit. **Open:** Mon to Fri L 12 to 3, all week D 6 to 11.30 (10.30 Sun). **Closed:** Christmas, bank hols. **Meals:** Set L £22.50. **Service:** 15%. **Details:** Cards accepted. 150 seats. Air-con. Separate bar. No mobile phones. Wheelchair access. Music. Children allowed.

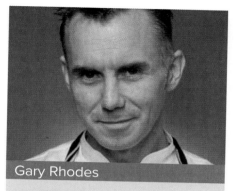

Gary Rhodes

Why did you become a chef?
Cooking from the age of 13 became a necessity at home. However, it was also a complete obsession and one which I still have today – 30 years later!

Who was your main inspiration?
Without doubt, the godfathers of our culinary world – Albert and Michel Roux.

Where do you eat out?
Le Gavroche and The Waterside Inn, but I'm also a big fan of Chris Galvin's, and my local Chinese restaurant, Xi'ans, as well as one of the best Indians in London – The Painted Heron on Cheyne Walk.

Where do you source your ingredients?
We always endeavour to take advantage of great British produce, but also utilise many flavours from all over the world.

Do you have a favourite local recipe?
I love supporting Kent, as I've lived there for many years, so the perfect Kentish apple pie would always be a winner, with lashings of custard or cream.

If you could only eat one more thing, what would it be?
The largest bowl of braised oxtails and creamy mashed potatoes.

What's your proudest achievement?
Being awarded an OBE; it's something you just don't ever dream of receiving.

Tamarind

Basement restaurant with lofty notions
20 Queen Street, W1J 5PR
Tel no: (020) 7629 3561
www.tamarindrestaurant.com
⊖ Green Park
Indian | £47
Cooking score: 4

♀ V

Hopes rarely rise when descending to a basement restaurant, but from the charming greeting at street level to the sight of the smart and classy dining room below it's clear that Tamarind is in the premier league of London restaurants. Well-spaced tables fill a room decorated in warm sandy colours, with cleverly placed mirrors creating a sense of space, despite the lack of windows. Poppadoms with a superior range of chutneys foster high expectations, which are more than matched by a palate-awakening starter such as a cold salad of spicy minced prawns with peppers, pomegranate, coriander and ground spices with mixed leaves. The north-west Indian influence of cooking in the tandoor means that due prominence is given to a range of fragrant kebabs, such as supreme of corn-fed chicken marinated with yoghurt, cream cheese and saffron. Otherwise, main courses might include vibrantly flavoured tiger prawns tossed in a spicy gravy of browned onions, tomatoes and ginger with a blend of Chettinaad spices. House vin de pays d'Oc is £16.50.
Chef/s: Alfred Prasad. **Open:** Sun to Fri L 12 to 2.45, all week D 6 to 11.30. **Closed:** L bank hols.
Meals: alc (main courses £10.50 to £26). Set L £21.50, Set D £52 to £72. **Service:** 12.5% (optional).
Details: Cards accepted. 85 seats. Air-con. Music. Children allowed.

Theo Randall at the InterContinental

Sublime Italian cooking
InterContinental London Hotel, 1 Hamilton Place, W1J 7QY
Tel no: (020) 7318 8747
www.theorandall.com
⊖ Hyde Park Corner
Italian | £41
Cooking score: 6

♀ V

Theo Randall's decision to up-sticks from the River Café and move to the InterContinental Hotel was one of most-awaited openings of 2007. Initially, the choice for showcasing his inimitable talent appeared a strange one. The decoration of the ground-floor dining room is of the kind favoured by most modern business hotels – but what the space lacks in soul, it makes up for with high comfort-levels. And Randall's cooking certainly manages to encapsulate what makes Italian food so special. 'Incredible' fresh crab made an impressive opener at inspection, with herb aïoli and garlic-brushed bruschetta ably demonstrating the virtue of simplicity. A sureness of touch with richer dishes coaxed astonishing depth of flavour out of cappelletti stuffed with slow-cooked veal, artichoke and pancetta, and main courses never missed a beat. A fleshy sea bass (roasted in the wood-fired oven), partnered with contrasting red and yellow peppers delivered 'flavours finely balanced on a tightrope', while meat was treated with equal respect and came in the form of a meltingly tender slow-cooked shoulder of lamb with wet polenta. Among well-reported desserts have been chocolate and hazelnut ice cream, and soft chocolate cake with mascarpone cream. Early reports have commented on the cost of it all, but the lunch menu provides exemplary cooking without denting the wallet. However, there is much vacillation over the wine list, which is eclectic in style but seemingly out of kilter with the culinary aspirations, and ultimately let down by over-zealous pricing. House wine is £16.

Chef/s: Theo Randall. Open: all week L 12 to 3, D 6 to 11.15. Meals: Set L £21 (2 courses) to £25. Service: 12.5%. Details: Cards accepted. 100 seats. Air-con. Separate bar. Wheelchair access. Music. Children's portions.

Umu

Expensive but authentic Japanese cooking
14-16 Bruton Place, W1J 6LX
Tel no: (020) 7499 8881
www.umurestaurant.com
Japanese | £55
Cooking score: 5

Tucked down a quiet Mayfair side street, the discreet frontage is easily missed; inside, the contemporary, pared-down interior exudes an air of exclusivity, not dissimilar to a private members' club. Welcome to Britain's first Kyoto-style restaurant, headed by Ichiro Kubota who has brought his native city's own venerable culinary tradition and a stream of authentic Japanese ingredients with him. It all comes at a price. A range of fixed-price kaiseki menus – which may be taken with pre-selected sakes or wines – starts at expensive, rising to the special Kyoto sushi kaiseki menu for which the old maxim applies – if you have to ask the price you can't afford it; or you might just choose to graze through the carte. Not all dishes impress at these prices, but standouts have included sweet shrimp with sake jelly, fried oysters with lemon vinaigrette, chives and ginger, an alluring clear soup with grilled sea bass, marinated grilled salmon with yuzu citrus-flavoured soy sauce, and the famed wagyu beef in hoba leaf with seasonal vegetables. Chilled green tea soup with pumpkin ice cream is an interesting way to finish. Sake is a speciality, at all levels of age and weight, but there is also a long French-dominated wine list. Pricing is unrestrained and the number of bottles under £25 is statistically insignificant.
Chef/s: Ichiro Kubota. Open: Mon to Fri L 12 to 2.30, Mon to Sat D 6 to 11. Closed: Christmas, 30 July to 14 Aug, bank hols. Meals: alc (main courses £8 to £45). Set L £22 to £44, Set D £60 to £165 (inc wine). Service: 12.5% (optional). Details: Cards accepted. 60 seats. Air-con. Wheelchair access. Music.

Wild Honey

A balance of skill, imagination and value
12 St George Street, W1S 2FB
Tel no: (020) 7758 9160
www.wildhoneyrestaurant.co.uk
⊖ Bond Street
Modern British
Cooking score: 6

With its Georgian front and clubby interior of oak paneling, polished boards and banquette seating, Wild Honey feels as if it has operating from this Mayfair site for decades. This latest opening by Anthony Demetre and Will Smith extends the Arbutus formula (see entry) and is, in one reporter s opinion, a real treat . The menu moves from day to day and although in many ways it shows the inclinations of simple British cooking, its real loyalty is to be reassuringly cosmopolitan red mullet with vegetable à la greque, and braised shoulder of hare with soft polenta and parmesan among starters, for example. The results can be brilliant, full blooded and sensual: glazed salsify and roast quince enriching a main course of wild duck or intensely flavoured roast Buccleuch beef perfectly partnered by baked onion and autumn vegetable purée. From the excellent value-for-money £15.50 lunch, reporters have praised a deliciously meaty mouthful of tête-de-veau (with sauce gribiche), unctious long-cooked shortrib of beef, and an authentic floating island . As at Arbutus (see entry), the wine list has been skillfully assembled and offers great value, starting at £12.50; most bottles are also available in 250ml carafes.
Chef/s: Colin Kelly. Open: all week L 12 to 3, D 6 to 10.30 (9.30 Sun). Meals: alc (main courses £14.95 to £17.95). Set L £15.50, pre-theatre (6-7pm) £17.50. Service: 12.5% (optional). Details: Cards accepted. 65 seats. Air-con. No music. Children's portions. Children allowed.

Wiltons

Antique eatiere with an English ethos
55 Jermyn Street, SW1Y 6LX
Tel no: (020) 7629 9955
www.wiltons.co.uk
⊖ Green Park
British | £50
Cooking score: 4

V

One of the capital's oldest restaurants and one of its best-known, Wilton's is a restaurant of the old school, discreetly opulent and offering a clubby Edwardian ambience and old-fashioned solicitous service at immaculately set tables. As a refuge from the modern world it could hardly be bettered. Just like the surroundings, the classic menu is steeped in tradition and remains little-changed, specialising in fish and game and keeping well at bay the whims and vagaries of fad and fashion. This is the place to come for avocado with crab, potted shrimps, lobster bisque and a plate of oysters for starters. Equally time-honoured main dishes include simple grills, from fillet steak to lamb cutlets, baked Dover sole, poached or grilled fish – may be wild turbot or halibut – and daily dishes like Irish stew, roast rack of lamb, and braised ox tongue with Madeira sauce. It also takes its savouries seriously, serving anchovies on toast as an alternative to apple and rhubarb crumble. Prices on the far-reaching wine list are high, with little under £30, although ten are served by the glass from £6.50.
Chef/s: Jerome Ponchelle. **Open:** Mon to Fri L 12 to 2.30, D 6 to 10.30. **Closed:** Christmas, bank hols. **Meals:** Set D £50. **Service:** 12.5%. **Details:** Cards accepted. 90 seats. Air-con. No music. No mobile phones. Wheelchair access. Jacket and tie required. Children's portions.

Wolseley

A dazzling setting for all-day dining
160 Piccadilly, W1J 9EB
Tel no: (020) 7499 6996
www.thewolseley.com
⊖ Green Park
Global | £36
Cooking score: 3

This art deco beauty – once a car showroom – makes a spectacular setting for Chris Corbin and Jeremy King's take on continental café culture. From the suits in for a Full English at 7am to the post-theatre crowd still teeming in after 11pm, there is no typical Wolseley customer: think tourists, children, celebs, businessmen, ladies who lunch or couples. Given that up to 1000 people pour through the door each day, the service remains remarkably consistent. The menu is an 'all things to everyone' selection from around the globe. There are 'kaffeehaus' classics – sachertorte or the always-reliable wiener Holstein; French brasserie favourites – steak tartare or choucroute alsacienne; even some American options – salt beef on rye or a hamburger; and don't forget the lovely afternoon tea. The all-European wine list (with all but the reserve selection available by the glass), begins at £16.
Chef/s: Julian O'Neill. **Open:** Mon to Fri 7am to 12am, 8am to 12am Sat, 8am to 11am Sun. **Closed:** D 24-25 Dec and 31 Dec-1 Jan. August Bank Holiday. **Meals:** alc (main courses £9.75 to £23).. **Service:** 12.5% (optional). **Details:** Cards accepted. 140 seats. Air-con. Separate bar. No music. Wheelchair access. Children allowed.

ALSO RECOMMENDED

▲ Aubaine

4 Heddon Street, W1B 4BS
Tel no: (020) 7440 2510
www.aubaine.co.uk
⊖ Piccadilly Circus

Old Paris comes to Mayfair in the shape of this fashion-conscious boulangerie-cum-bar-cum-brasserie. The whole set-up is spread over two floors and customers can call in for drinks, order bread and pastries to take out, or enjoy sit-down meals from the all-day restaurant menu. Dishes are in the classic bourgeois mould of salade niçoise (£5.85), coq au vin (£13.50) and grilled fillet of sea bass with carrot mousseline and orange vinaigrette, followed by crème brûlée or lemon tart. Great-value 'petit déjeuner' snacks from £2.50. Wines from £16.50 (£4.50 a glass). Open Mon to Sat. Aubaine's elder brother is at 262 Brompton Road, London SW3 2AS.

▲ Chor Bizarre

16 Albemarle Street, W1H 4HW
Tel no: (020) 7629 9802
www.chorbizarrerestaurant.com
⊖ Green Park

Eternally romantic, Chor Bizarre, the London branch of New Delhi's most innovative and popular restaurant continues to enchant diners with meat and vegetarian dishes from all over India. It also introduces Tak-A-Tak Tawa (street) cooking and typical, authentic 'bazaar' fare. A far cry from Brick Lane's traditional fare, Chor Bizarre invites you to sample the real India and matches three wines to every dish. Try the dakshni crab cakes with salad and coconut chutney (£7) or kaleji tak-a-tak – chicken liver with coriander masala (£6.50). For a tandoori mix, order the sampler (£22) or for one spectacular dish with a difference, choose the chicken chettinad, cooked in a hot sauce with pepper, aniseed and curry leaves (£13). Side dishes include peshwari naan with rich dry fruits (£4) and pudina paratha – tandoori bread topped with dried mint (£3). Well-chosen wines from £17. Downstairs is Chai Bazaar, an Indian tea bar. Closed Sun L.

▲ Momo

25 Heddon Street, W1B 4BH
Tel no: (020) 7434 4040
www.momoresto.com
⊖ Piccadilly Circus

Momo does not trade in the Morocco of street food; rather, the evocatively decorated dining room recalls the expensive riad restaurants of Marrakech and draws a similarly well-heeled international crowd to its party atmosphere. The cooking is mostly made up of large portions of well-spiced, traditional Moroccan dishes – pastilla of pigeon (£10) followed by lamb tagine (£17.50) – plus 'modern Maghrebine cuisine' in which there's a fainter scent of north Africa, say veal cutlet with saffron baby fennel, spinach and wild mushrooms (£12). DJs rock the kasbah in basement bar Kemia or, for something more sedate, there's Mô, a tea room-cum-gift shop next door. House wine is £18.

▲ Rasa W1

6 Dering Street, W1S 1AD
Tel no: (020) 7629 1346
⊖ Bond Street

West End outpost of a mini-chain of Indian restaurants, tucked behind New Bond Street and a popular choice among lunchtime shoppers keen to sample the delights of regional Keralan cuisine. It's famed for its crunchy pre-meal snacks (£4), including murukku, and home-made pickles, and starters like chana masala (5.25). Main courses take in authentic vegetarian dishes ranging from thakkali curry (£6.25) to masala dosa (£9.95), and a range of meat and seafood dishes, perhaps calicut chicken korma (£6.95), and koyilandi konju masala (prawns cooked in ginger, curry leaves and onions; £12.95). Wines from £11.95.

▲ Yatra

34 Dover Street, W1S 4NF
Tel no: (020) 7493 0200
www.yatra.co.uk
⊖ Green Park

The décor in this popular Mayfair restaurant is contemporary, with warm spice colours of red and gold reflecting the flavour of the food, which is a mix of modern and traditional Indian dishes. Starters like spiced tilapia with balsamic tomatoes or sheekh kebab (spiced minced lamb moulded on skewers and grilled) with mint chutney precede main attractions such as the Anglo-Indian dish, railway lamb, tandoori salmon or rogan josh. At least two main courses are tailored to vegetarians, but they could also make a meal from imaginative side dishes like baby aubergines in tamarind and sesame sauce or fried okra with coriander. Early diners may migrate to the basement Bollywood bar, which serves up Indipop, Bhangra and similar sounds along with exotic cocktails.

▲ Yoshino
3 Piccadilly Place, W1J 0DB
Tel no: (020) 7287 6622
www.yoshino.net
⊖ Piccadilly Circus

The menu changes daily as only the freshest fish is served at this simple Japanese restaurant off Piccadilly. The formula remains the same however: sushi, sashimi, grilled or fried fish and side dishes like edamame (green soy beans) and homemade tofu. Rice and miso soup are provided with all set meals. Bento boxes can be as basic as deep-fried fish with omelette and pickle (£5.80), or a more elaborate combination including sashini, tofu, pickle and edamame (£9.80). Sashini and nigiri sushi are also available by the piece from £2, or you can go for a trio of sushi rolls from £2.95. Evenings bring wider choice. Finish with tofu ice cream or green tea sorbet. Closed Sundays.

READERS RECOMMEND
The Café at Sotheby's
British
3435 New Bond Street, W1A 2AA
Tel no: (020) 7293 5077
www.sothebys.com
'You have to try the lobster club sandwich'

Cecconi's
Italian
5a Burlington Gardens, W1X 1LE
Tel no: (020) 7434 1500
www.cecconis.co.uk
'Popular with shoppers and celebrities alike...'

Cocoon
Asian fusion
65 Regent Street, W1B 4EA
Tel no: (020) 7494 7600
www.cocoon-restaurants.com
'Sleek Asian cooking on Regent Street'

Kai Mayfair
Chinese
65 South Audley Street, W1K 2QU
Tel no: (020) 7493 8988
www.kaimayfair.co.uk
'Ostentatious food that comes at a price'

Mosaico
Italian
13 Albemarle Street, W1S 4HJ
Tel no: (020) 7409 1011
www.mosaico-restaurant.co.uk
'Italian restaurant with a neighbourhood feel'

Rose Bakery
Modern European
17-18 Dover Street, W1S 4LT
Tel no: (020) 7518 0680
www.doverstreetmarket.com
'Informal surroundings for a fresh lunch'

Sartoria
Italian
20 Saville Row, W1S 3PR
Tel no: (020) 7534 7070
www.danddlondon.com/restaurants/sartoria
'Focused and innovative Italian food'

Please send us your feedback

To register your opinion about any restaurant listed in the Guide, or a new restaurant that you wish to bring to our attention, please visit the web address at the bottom of the page. Your feedback informs the content of the book and will be used to compile next year's reviews.

Oxford Circus

The Landau
Elegant hotel dining
Langham Hotel, 1 Portland Place, W1B 1JA
Tel no: (020) 7636 1000
www.thelandau.com
⊖ Oxford Circus
Modern European | £47
Cooking score: 4

Andrew Turner is a chef with a track record of good London hotel openings at 1880 at the Bentley Kempinski, and prior to that at Browns. Now he s starring at the Landau, the Langham Hotel s stylishly revamped restaurant. His food takes a broadly European perspective, with grazing menus a trademark (and representing a good way of sampling the range), and an à la carte that offers a well balanced, simply dressed salad of truffles and artichokes with quail eggs, or pumpkin soup with ceps and more quail egg as openers. Main dishes are mostly classics with a modern touch: Dover sole meunière with onions three ways, balsamic, parsley and purple potatoes, for example, or Gloucester Old Spot pork, honey-glazed parsnips, pickled cabbage and star anise. Desserts such as Granny Smith apple millefeuille and sherbet with chocolate oil are followed by good coffee and chocolates and service is generally praised. The wine list is extensive without being intimidating, covering a wide range of countries and including good New World growers such as Ridge. Prices start from £22.
Chef/s: Andrew Turner. Open: all week, L 12.30 to 2.30, D 5.30 to 11 (10 Sun). Meals: alc (main courses £9.50 to £30). Set L £20 (2 courses) to £32.50, pre theatre £20 (2 courses) to £27.50. Service: 12.5% (optional). Details: Cards accepted. 100 seats. Air-con. Separate bar. Wheelchair access. Music. Children allowed.

ALSO RECOMMENDED

▲ Carluccio's Caffé
8 Market Place, W1W 8AG
Tel no: (020) 7636 2228
www.carluccios.com
⊖ Oxford Circus

Opened in 1991, and bustling and popular since day one, Antonio Carluccio's flagship continues to thrive, serving up simple, traditional Italian cooking in a friendly and lively environment. Choose from a selection of breads and pastries (from £1.30 for focaccia) and order antipasta massimo for two (£9.95). Calamari fritti (£5.95) is fresh and crispy with lemon and green leaves. Tortellini filled with ham and served with a cream sauce (£6.75) might be among main courses, as should sea bass with tomato salsa and sautéed potatoes (£11.75). Finish with the likes of tiramisu (£4.50) or affogato (ice cream with an espresso or liqueur poured over the top, £3.95 to £6.50). A decent Italian wine list starts at £11.25 Open all week.

Piccadilly

Bentley's
A revitalised seafood institution
11-15 Swallow Street, W1R 7HD
Tel no: (020) 7734 4756
www.bentleysoysterbarandgrill.co.uk
⊖ Piccadilly Circus
Seafood | £43
Cooking score: 5

Richard Corrigan can do creative fine-dining (see Lindsay House) but he's also got a respect for good old-fashioned classics. His venture at this refurbished Piccadilly seafood institution is the perfect showcase for the latter. Upstairs, the various clubby yet comfortable dining rooms look chic in blue and white with handsome navy chairs and dark wooden flooring. Ordering classics is a good strategy: Dover sole meunière, shellfish cocktail or beef tartare never fail. But dishes like tiger prawns with chickpeas and olive oil or an Asian-inspired lobster with chilli, garlic, and coriander show Corrigan is not afraid to introduce some diverse international notes. Impeccably fresh seafood is Bentley's raison d'être, but there's no shame in hitting the meat entrées. The glorious mixed grill (sausage, beef sirloin, pork belly and lamb chop) and steamed Elwy Valley Lamb Pudding are hardly second best. Puddings are of the 'proper' variety: apple tart, Valrhona chocolate pot or bread-and-butter pudding. For a less buttoned-up experience, head for the jolly crustacea bar downstairs – fun even for solo diners. Grab a stool at the white marble bar and get to work on a plate of plump native oysters or Frank Hederman's smoked salmon over a glass of Ruinart and a chat with one of the friendly oyster shuckers. The strong wine list makes proceedings even more diverting: from only £14.95, there's a super range – heavy on the seafood-friendly whites and sherries too – with a slew available by the glass to maximise tasting opportunities.

Chef/s: Brendan Fyldes. **Open:** all week 12-11 (10 Sunday). **Meals:** alc (main courses £17.50 to £38). **Service:** 12.5% (optional). **Details:** Cards accepted. 120 seats. Air-con. Separate bar. No music. Wheelchair access. Music. Children's portions.

Mint Leaf
Indian food goes untamed
Suffolk Place, SW1Y 4HX
Tel no: (020) 7930 9020
www.mintleafrestaurant.com
⊖ Piccadilly Circus
Indian | £52
Cooking score: 4

 V

In the evenings, this restaurant can feel like one hell of a party, prompting a reader to proclaim that it's 'worth going for the experience'. DJs are often booked and the atmosphere sometimes veers towards a club, as opposed to a restaurant. The interior is stunning, the design of this impressively sized subterranean space simply outstanding. An elevated catwalk connects the entire space, and walnut louvres are cleverly positioned to sub-divide the room into intimate sections. The menu is kept sensibly short, segregated into grilled, roasted or steamed dishes and curries. Unlike the design, the cooking has not been gentrified for Western palates; lightly battered crab claws, teased into life with coriander and chilli, were 'like some exquisite finger food'. A mixed tandoori grill included 'delectable' grouper fish as well as 'tender' lamb cutlets. A curry of smoked aubergine with green pea played nicely against the delicate flavour of cumin. Naan bread is outstanding, but skip desserts, a mango cheesecake was decidedly ho-hum, and service can be out of step with the sleek design. The wine list, commencing from £19, works hard to match the style of food, and there are some classy Burgundies and clarets.

Chef/s: Ajay Chopra. **Open:** Mon to Fri L 12 to 3, Mon to Sun D 5.30 to 11. **Meals:** alc (main course £11 to £26). **Service:** 12.5% (optional). **Details:** Cards accepted. 200 seats. Air-con. Separate bar. Wheelchair access. Music.

St Alban
A modern Mediterranean outlook
Rex House, 4-12 Lower Regent Street, SW1Y 4PE
Tel no: (020) 7499 8558
www.stalban.net
⊖ Piccadilly Circus
Modern European | £42
New Chef

V

This newcomer started life in November 2006, the latest venture from Chris Corbin and Jeremy King, who could have easily repeated the formula of their previous successes – latterly at The Wolseley (see entry) Instead they have deviated from the script, admirably refusing to be typecast. St Alban is set on the ground floor of an anonymous office block, boasting a contemporary and slightly edgy design, while the cooking shows affinity to the Mediterranean. Inside, the spacious dining room may suffer from a lowish ceiling but is smartly furnished with curvy tomato red and green banquettes, while 'take it or leave it', larger-than-life etchings of household items cover all the windows. The room can feel a little 'corporate' and lacks intimacy at times, but the food is superb. The kitchen cooks with distinction, utilising superior produce and keeping a tight rein on seasoning to deliver sophisticated dishes. Flavours are finely balanced, as demonstrated by a main course of flawless slow-roasted Norfolk pig served with Spanish marrow and perfect crackling, a blueberry soufflé dessert was worth the 20-minute wait. Service, from the well-groomed team, is affable and solicitous. The well-considered wine list is full of interesting options, with Italy, Spain and Portugal taking centre stage, while gentle mark-up encourages exploration. Prices start from £15.50.

Chef/s: Dave Osborne. **Open:** all week 12 to 3, 5.30 to midnight. **Closed:** Dec 24 D, 25, 26, 31 D, 1 Jan Aug bank hol. **Meals:** alc (main courses £8.25 to £29.50). **Service:** 12.5%. **Details:** Cards accepted. 140 seats. Air-con. Separate bar. No music. Wheelchair access.

ALSO RECOMMENDED

▲ Veeraswamy

99-101 Regent Street, W1R 8RS
Tel no: (020) 7734 1401
www.veeraswamy.com
⊖ Piccadilly Circus

Big picture windows overlook the West End, offering a view that, by night, rivals the splendid interior of this elegant Indian restaurant. Veeraswamy has a notable pedigree, having been established over 80 years ago. Like many modern 80-year-olds, it has chosen glitz over gravitas, however, with vibrant colours, sparkling chandeliers and rich furnishings creating a sense of occasion. The menu offers all the standards, like rogan josh and chicken tikka, but there are surprises too in the form of coastal specialities such as sea bream paturi and a Malabar lobster curry. Prices are in keeping with the location, but a range of set meals (particularly the lunches and pre- and post-theatre suppers at £16.50) are perfect for the impecunious. The serious wine list starts at £18.50.

■ Soho
Alastair Little
Top-quality ingredients and modern flair
49 Frith Street, W1D 4SG
Tel no: (020) 7734 5183
⊖ Tottenham Court Road
Modern European | £37
Cooking score: 2

At one time, this compact Soho restaurant stood at the forefront of a culinary trend, where chef Alastair Little was one of the first to introduce modern European cooking to the UK. It is many years since Little's departure and Juliet Peston has taken command in the kitchen. The décor is looking more than a little tired around the edges these days and casually attired waiting staff add to a general lack of crispness, though they deal efficiently with a full dining room. One set menu (at £40 for three courses) at dinner, proffers some high points, but also a few inconsistencies. Highlights at inspection included a top-quality, tender chicken breast on a bed of leeks, mash, wood sorrel and morel sauce, and a decent asparagus and wild mushroom risotto with a seasonal salad. Well-presented desserts – an intensely flavoured baked chocolate mousse with Irish coffee liégeois, and pannacotta with rhubarb and pistachio praline – were spot on. The wine list opens at £18.50.

Chef/s: Juliet Peston. **Open:** Mon to Fri L 12 to 3; Mon to Sat D 6 to 11.30. **Closed:** bank hols. **Meals:** Set L £33, Set D £38. **Service:** not inc. **Details:** Cards accepted. 60 seats. Air-con. No music. Jacket and tie required. Children's portions.

Andrew Edmunds

Long-standing Soho favourite
44 Lexington Street, W1F OLP
Tel no: (020) 7437 5708
⊖ Oxford Circus
Modern British | £25
Cooking score: 3

Antiquarian print dealer and wine-buff
Andrew Edmunds' eponymous restaurant in
the backstreets of Soho has a loyal following.
There's a distinct touch of the Dickensian
about the dark, candle-lit interior. Cramped
pew-style seating and tables both upstairs and
down are covered in paper cloths; seasonal
flowers adorn the tables, but while the
basement dining room is a touch gloomy,
upstairs offers prime viewing of the passing
pedestrians outside. Food is rustic both
in flavour and presentation, but has a lightness
of touch and a strong emphasis on seasonality.
A beef fillet and ginger salad with peanuts,
cucumber and bean sprouts, for example, was
fresh and clean-tasting at inspection. A
flavorsome pan-fried tuna with arborio
puttanesca and tomato and chilli salsa
followed, with dessert a crumbly brown bread
ice-cream, an original Victorian recipe. It is,
however, the predominately old world wine
list – virtually no other alcohol is on offer –
that is the talking point. Edmunds' love of
wine is evident in the exhaustive selection of
punctually cellared, reasonably priced
vintages that include a detailed sweet wine list.
A blackboard menu of wine specials often
features unusual and boutique wines. House
wine starts at around £11. Service is as quirky
and unpretentious as this little gem of a
restaurant.
Chef/s: Rebecca St John Cooper. **Open:** all week
12.30 to 3, 6 to 10.45. **Closed:** Easter, Aug bank hol,
Dec 23 to Jan 2. **Meals:** alc (main courses £12 to
£17). **Service:** 12.5% (optional). **Details:** Cards
accepted. 50 seats. 4 seats outside. Air-con. No
music. No mobile phones. Children allowed.

Arbutus

Sophisticated cooking continues to excite
63-64 Frith Street, W1D 3JW
Tel no: (020) 7734 4545
www.arbutusrestaurant.co.uk
⊖ Tottenham Court Road
Modern British | £35
Cooking score: 6

Arbutus embodies everything you could wish
for in a modern bistro – the cooking is
sophisticated, the prices no higher than the
nearby tourist traps and it is the perfect
antithesis to some of the needlessly
complicated dishes in town. Anthony
Demetre's menu takes in half a dozen dishes
per course, punctuated with superior
ingredients – wild halibut, organic beef – and
the cooking style is unpretentious, not bloated
by appetizers or pre-desserts. Start with
smoked eel paired with beetroot and given a
touch of extravagance by horseradish cream,
the flavours are clear and concise. Meat dishes
can be memorable, especially a short rib of
beef accompanied by English snails, which
will have you mopping up the remnants. The
kitchen seems able to keep flavours separate
and eloquent, the star at inspection, a poached
sea bass served with crushed Jersey Royals and
parsley vinaigrette, was brought to life by a
sublime matelote sauce. Momentum is not lost
at the dessert stage with rice pudding mousse
served with Alphonso mango 'a marriage
made in heaven', albeit only a short one given
the fruit's notoriously short season. Warm
chocolate soup with caramelised milk ice
cream 'will guarantee sighs of satisfaction', too.
Service has improved, showing willingness to
explain the dishes and to make sure your meal
is an enjoyable one. The wine list, which starts
at £12.50, has always been an interesting one,
and helpfully most are also available in 250ml
carafes. The team at Arbutus has also opened a
second restaurant in Mayfair. Wild Honey is
located in the former Drones Club site, at 12 St
George Street, W1. Tel (020) 7758 9160.
Chef/s: Anthony Demetre. **Open:** Mon to Sat 12 to
2.30, 5 to 11, Sun 12.30 to 3.00, 5.30 to 9.30.
Closed: 25 and 26 Dec, 1 Jan. **Meals:** alc (main
courses £12.50 to £15.50). Set L £15.50, Set D

£17.50. **Service:** 12.5%. **Details:** Cards accepted. 75 seats. Air-con. Separate bar. No music. Wheelchair access. Children's portions.

Bar Shu

Fiery and uncompromising Szechuan cooking
28 Frith Street, W1D 5LF
Tel no: (020) 7287 8822
⊖ **Leicester Square**
Chinese | £35
Cooking score: 4

Bar Shu stands alone against the uniformity of restaurants in London's Chinatown nearby. You won't find any traces of crispy aromatic duck on the extensive menu and unsurprisingly most of the customers are oriental. The interior 'seems tame enough', with well-appointed dining rooms adorned with rich wood carvings and sturdy dark wooden furniture. The Szechuan cooking here remains the 'real deal' and is ruthlessly authentic, none more so than a blisteringly rich braised beef paired with superbly textured but rarely seen, dried, wild bamboo shoots (although some dishes have been removed due to difficulties in sourcing the ingredients from Chengdu). Bean curd, normally so mild mannered, arrives in puckered 'bear's paw form with a splendid spicy sauce, and assorted offal with duck's blood can still guarantee a 'sortie into your senses'. Portions are preposterously large, but save room for the unusual desserts such as deep-fried sweet potato ingots filled with sweet red bean paste. The willing service team is on hand to guide people through the impenetrable menu with its helpful illustrations. The lengthy wine list starts from £14, but it is not easy to find anything to match the fiery nature of the dishes.
Chef/s: Fu Wenhong. **Open:** all week 12 to 11.30. **Closed:** 25 and 26 Dec. **Meals:** alc (main courses £7 to £68). Set L £19.50 to £22.50, Set D £22.50 to £24.50 (all min 2). **Service:** 12.5% (included). **Details:** Cards accepted. 150 seats. Air-con. Wheelchair access. Music.

Barrafina

Queue for the best tapas in town
54 Frith Street, W1D 4SL
Tel no: (020) 7813 8016
www.barrafina.co.uk
⊖ **Tottenham Court Road**
Spanish | £28
Cooking score: 4

V

There's no doubt that Sam and Eddie Hart's homage to Barcelona's premier tapas bar, Cal Pep, is quite the hippest thing in Frith Street these days. Unlike their tapas restaurant Fino (see entry), it's all rollickingly informal, from the mirrored and marbled interior to the no-booking system, but nonetheless runs like a well-oiled machine thanks to excellent staff and fast-paced chefs cooking in full view behind the counter. Queuing is not necessarily de rigueur for the 23 bar stools – if you get your timing right – but it is worth the wait and you can order drinks and nibble such things as pimientos de padron while doing so. The simple and uncluttered presentation of the dishes highlights the sourcing of materials. Ingredients are all – sweet shavings of Jabugo ham, gambas al ajillo, simply grilled quail with aioli, chorizo perfectly partnered by watercress , or a mini cooked-to-order tortilla– but while the core of the menu doesn't change, daily specials keep regulars interested, whether it's grilled langoustine or a plate of crisp-skinned, succulent suckling pig. Bread is excellent and Santiago tart for dessert is also worth a punt. But note, portions can be small, neighbouring dishes tempting, and the bill quickly inflated. The short all-Spanish wine list opens at £15.
Chef/s: Nieves Barragan. **Open:** Mon to Sat 12 to 3, 5 to 11. **Closed:** Christmas, Bank hols. **Service:** 12.5%. **Details:** Cards accepted. 23 seats. 10 seats outside. Air-con. No music. Music.

Gay Hussar

The obvious choice for hungry Hungarians
2 Greek Street, W1D 4NB
Tel no: (020) 7437 0973
www.gayhussar.co.uk
⊖ Tottenham Court Road
Eastern European | £28
Cooking score: 1

V

This legendary restaurant has a cosy, old-fashioned feel, its dark, wood-panelled walls covered with caricatures of the leading lights in Westminster's political world. The Hungarian menu (with English translation) is heavily meat-orientated but includes some fish and vegetarian options. A fish terrine flanked by cucumber salad and delicious beetroot sauce and Bulgár saláta provided a light start to an inspection meal. Main courses are predominantly more robust – goulashes, pancakes and meat dishes. Kacsa sült is a huge leg portion of roasted duck served with apple sauce, red cabbage and potatoes, and leek and potato cake accompanies grilled sea bass. Finish with somloi galuska – a rum-soaked sponge filled with walnuts and coated with piped cream and chocolate sauce. House wine is £14.25.
Chef/s: Carlos Mendoca. **Open:** Mon to Sat 12.15 to 2.30, 5.30 to 10.45. **Closed:** Bank hols. **Meals:** alc D (main courses £9.50 to £16.50). Set L £16.50 (2 courses) to £18.50. **Service:** 12.5% (optional). **Details:** Cards accepted. 70 seats. Air-con. Wheelchair access. Music. Children's portions.

L'Escargot, Ground Floor

Urban brasserie with dependable cooking
48 Greek Street, W1D 4EF
Tel no: (020) 7439 7474
www.lescargotrestaurant.co.uk
⊖ Leicester Square
French | £32
Cooking score: 3

This long-running restaurant, a Soho institution, was the first to serve the 'slow-mo' molluscan in the country. Inside, the alluring dining room is a showcase for artwork from the likes of Miro and Chagall, which can be admired against a backdrop of cut-glass mirrors and Art Nouveau lamps. In recent times L'Escargot has become less of a destination restaurant – the Franglais menu can appear outmoded and lacking in sparkle, the cooking 'seemingly lacking excitement' and service occasionally 'patchy and uncommunicative'. Nonetheless, the cooking under the helm of Simon Jones is far from complacent, although at inspection a tian of crab with shrimps and avocado was somewhat clouded by a gummy citrus mayonnaise. Reliable technique came to the fore, however, with a pork fillet, tantalisingly succulent, boldly served on the safe side of pink, and flattered by a silky 'au poivre' sauce, as well as a textbook blackberry soufflé with Bramley apple sorbet. Pricing is even-handed, with particular praise for the lunch and pre-theatre menu. Recent reports indicate that the ground floor brasserie can be more rewarding than the upstairs Picasso room. Wines start at £16.
Chef/s: Simon Jones. **Open:** Mon to Fri L 12 to 2.15, Mon to Sat D 6 (5.30 Sat) to 11.30. **Closed:** D 25 and 26 Dec, 1 Jan. **Meals:** alc (main courses £12.50 to £15). Set L and D (not after 7) £15 (2 courses) to £18. **Service:** 12.5%. **Details:** Cards accepted. 70 seats. Air-con. Music.

Lindsay House

A fine showcase for Irish cooking
21 Romilly Street, W1D 5AF
Tel no: (020) 7439 0450
www.lindsayhouse.co.uk
⊖ Leicester Square
Modern European | £55
Cooking score: 6

 V

Rather quaintly, you have to ring a doorbell to enter this townhouse restaurant. Dining itself takes place on two separate floors; the ground floor is the epitome of calm, exuding a warm glow, with green flourishes from the floral wallpaper to the carpets enhanced by some striking artwork. At inspection, a first course of duck served five ways included the gizzards and a croûton of its own liver, every component working like clever little soundbites. Not to be outdone, a roasted fillet of sea bass found empathy with caramelised endives, potato blinis and some lardoons. Flavours were clear and concise; sauces made only the briefest of appearances so as not to overshadow the ingredients. Flaky plum tart with pain d'épices served with vanilla ice cream provided a fitting finale. The standard of craftsmanship was high (an appetiser of salmon fishcake with tomato relish, and a pre-dessert of apple granita with buttermilk were both excellent) but the cooking lacked that little bit of sparkle – Richard Corrigan may not be as peripatetic as some of his peers, but his absence was nonetheless felt at inspection. Service lagged a few steps behind the cooking. The outstanding wine list, full of intrigue, was arranged in an idiosyncratic manner, mostly by weight, followed by sections devoted to Pinot Noir, Bordeaux, Italy and Iberia, and one for 'rare and forgotten grapes', such as Vin Jaune, Gringet and Provignage. Lovers of dessert wines will be impressed. Prices start from £12.50 but there is plenty of choice between £20 and £40.

Chef/s: Richard Corrigan. **Open:** Mon to Fri L 12 to 2.30, Mon to Sat D 6 to 11. **Closed:** Christmas. **Meals:** Set L £27 to £56, Set D £56 to £68. **Service:** 12.5% (optional). **Details:** Cards accepted. 55 seats. Air-con. No music. Wheelchair access. Children's portions.

Red Fort

Long-standing, modern Indian restaurant
77 Dean Street, W1D 3SH
Tel no: (020) 7437 2525/2115
www.redfort.co.uk
⊖ Tottenham Court Road
Indian | £35
Cooking score: 3

V

One of Amin Ali's earliest ventures into the world of contemporary Indian cuisine, the Red Fort has reinvented itself over the years and currently looks in good shape. Below stairs is Akbar (a groovy evening venue for drinks and snacks), while the main dining

room is sleek, cool and unashamedly plush. The kitchen's focus is the cuisine of Lucknow and Hyderabad, although it makes impressive use of native British produce from Devon lamb to Scottish lobsters (perhaps cooked with saffron and garlic). Seafood is a strength and the menu also lists monkfish tikka, spicy kingfish flavoured with curry leaves, and 'smoked' chunks of dorade with mint, garlic and green chillies. Elsewhere, corn-fed chicken breast might appear might appear in a creamed tomato and dill sauce or with brown onions, coriander and red chillies. Among the vegetables, look for kaddu channa (white pumpkin and Bengal chick peas) or the five-lentil panchrangi dhal. Desserts cover everything from Alphonso mango kulfi to chocolate fondant with pistachio ice cream. House wines are £22 (£6 a glass).

Open: Mon to Fri L 12 to 2.15, all week D 5.45 to 11.15 (5.30 to 10.30 Sun). **Meals:** alc (main courses £12.50 to £30). Set L £12 (2 courses) to £25, Set D 5.45 to 7 £16 (2 courses) to £45. **Service:** 12.5% (optional). **Details:** Cards accepted. 77 seats. Air-con. Wheelchair access. Music.

Yauatcha

Fashionable next-generation dim sum
15-17 Broadwick Street, W1F ODL
Tel no: (020) 7494 8888
⊖ Tottenham Court Road
Chinese | £28
Cooking score: 4

V

Alan Yau's trendy Soho dim sum and tea parlour is a far remove from the standard trolley and tea Chinatown joint in every way, including price. But what you get is a stylish venue, and glamour in spades. There's substance as well as style, thanks to exquisitely executed dim sum – asparagus cheung fun; sparkling scallop shumai, and well-made venison puffs – while at the upper end of the menu, you'll find luxury ingredients like Dover sole or Wagyu beef. Four years on, Yauatcha's still packing in a trendy crowd meaning even late afternoon tables are hard to get. The draconian reservation system doesn't ensure seamless service, however; long waiting times and speedy turnaround occasionally raise hackles. The street-level pastel, white and neon all-day parlour – once just for tea and beautiful cakes – is now used in addition to the large shared tables in the moodier ambience of the basement restaurant proper. The wine list (from £23) is a whistle-stop world tour of old and new that leans sensibly towards white to aid food matching. Tea-lovers will thrill to the lengthy, largely Chinese, tea list. NB As we went to press, Alan Yau sold Yauatcha to Tasameem. However, initial indications suggest that standards will stay the same. Reports please.

Chef/s: Cheong Wah Soon. **Open:** Mon to Fri 12 to 3, 5.30 to 11.45, Sat and Sun 11.45 to 11.45 (10.30 Sun). **Meals:** alc (main courses £3.50 to £38). **Service:** 13%. **Details:** Cards accepted. 110 seats.

ALSO RECOMMENDED
▲ Chowki
2-3 Denman Street, W1D 7HA
Tel no: (020) 7439 1330
www.chowki.com
⊖ Piccadilly Circus

Cheerful, busy, and inexpensive Indian diner off Piccadilly Circus where customers sit at traditional wooden tables ('chowki') and choose from monthly changing menus that draw on regional recipes. The northwest Frontier could supply chargrilled fish skewers (£3.95), chicken and turnip cooked in mustard oil (£9.95) recalls Lucknow, while Goa brings a yam and black gram curry (£7.95) to the table. Three-course regional feasts are £12.95; house wines from £10.95. Open all week.

▲ Chuen Cheng Ku
17 Wardour Street, W1V 3HD
Tel no: (020) 7437 1398
www.chuenchengku.co.uk
⊖ Leicester Square

Three storeys of Chinese expertise draw the crowds from Oxford Street and Leicester Square to this long-established Chinatown

haunt. With over 100 dim sum on offer and an extensive menu, choosing something to suit all tastes is relatively easy. From staples such as crispy aromatic duck (£9 to £29.50), via deep-fried prawn dumplings (£4.50), to the tasty seafood and coriander soup (£4.50), starters are varied and interesting. Follow up with fried beef with pickled ginger and pineapple (£7.80). There are various set meals, plus plenty of rice and noodles dishes. Wines from £10.25. Open all week.

▲ Itsu
103 Wardour Street, W1F 0UQ
Tel no: (020) 7479 4790
www.itsu.com
⊖ Tottenham Court Road

Now a familiar name in the capital thanks to its three restaurants and ten shops, Itsu's blend of slick modernity, fresh food and helpful staff is clearly a winning combination. Sit at the kaiten and take your pick from the dishes that pass by – perhaps salmon sushi; crab California roll; chilli crab crystal roll or new-style Asian seared tuna. Alternatively, press your red button to summon a waiter and request made-to-order sashimi, crispy handrolls (perhaps with warm Teriyaki chicken or prawn tempura with salmon). Pudding might be crème brûlée, fresh fruit on white chocolate yogurt, or the Itsu chocolate dessert. Drink-wise, there are cocktails, champagne by the bottle or the glass and wines from £15.95. Open daily. Other branches are situated in Chelsea and Canary Wharf.

▲ Masala Zone
9 Marshall Street, W1F 7ER
Tel no: (020) 7287 9966
⊖ Oxford Circus

Everything about this cheap and cheerfully decorated restaurant encourages a relaxed approach to Indian dining. Starters are based on traditional street food and include puri, bhajia and samosas (all £3.95). Grills, noodles and curries are offered as mains (mostly for between £7 and £8), say lamb curry braised with spinach and garlic or one with fresh vegetables flavoured with green herbs. For a more substantial meal, pick the grand thali: your choice of curry served with the vegetable, potato and dhal of the day with sides of raita, rice and chapatti (approximately £10). House wine is £10.95. Open daily. Additional branches in Islington and Earls Court.

▲ Randall & Aubin

14-16 Brewer Street, W1R 3FS
Tel no: (020) 7287 4447
www.randallandaubin.com
⊖ Piccadilly Circus

Set in one of the racier quarters of Soho, this former butcher's shop has an air of gallic charm. The high stools won't suit everyone (nor will the dance music that kick-starts most evenings) but window seats still remain highly coveted by locals. A rôtisserie offers some diversity in the menu, but the real star of the show is the silver, tiered presentation of fruits de mer (£27 per head). Wines from £13.50. Closed Sun L. A second branch is at 329-331 Fulham Road, SW10; tel: (020) 7823 3515.

▲ La Trouvaille

12A Newburgh Street, W1F 7RR
Tel no: (020) 7287 8488
⊖ Oxford Circus

An inventive take on classic French bistro cooking is what to expect at this Soho dining room. Start with quail and foie gras terrine, or snails bourguignon, before moving on to pan-fried veal loin with Camargue rice, crayfish and squid ink sauce, or perhaps fillet of Galloway beef with seasonal vegetables, parsley jus and wasabi gratin, with hot chocolate fondant and ginger ice cream to finish. Also available are bar snacks ranging from croque monsieur to onglet steak with French fries and béarnaise. Wines from the south of France are a speciality, starting with vins de pays d'Oc at £13.50. Closed Sat L and Sun.

▲ Vasco & Piero's Pavilion

15 Poland Street, W1F 8QE
Tel no: (020) 7437 8774
www.vascosfood.com
⊖ Oxford Circus

Traditional Umbrian dishes are a speciality of this long-established Italian restaurant. Lunchtime starters at around the £7 mark might include roast beetroot with egg, anchovies and tomatoes, while a typical main is calf's liver and sage with grilled polenta and asparagus. Three courses on the daily-changing evening set (£28) brings watermelon and goat's cheese salad with breast of guineafowl with wild mushrooms and lentils, then Robiola cheesecake or panacotta with strawberries. The mainly Italian wine list starts at £14.50 and includes some interesting regional choices, including an oak-conditioned Chardonnay from Umbria and a Salice Salentino (Riserva) from further south which would go well with one of the more robust offerings, such as lombetto (cured pork loin). Closed Sat L and Sun.

READERS RECOMMEND

Kulu Kulu Sushi

Japanese
76 Brewer Street, W1F 9TX
Tel no: (020) 7734 7316
'Quick-fix quality food'

Mildred's

Vegetarian
45 Lexington Street, W1F 9AN
Tel no: 020 7494 1634
www.mildreds.co.uk
'A fresh and vibrant Soho institution'

Mother Mash

British
26 Ganton Street, W1F 7QZ
Tel no: 020 7494 9644
www.mothermash.co.uk
'Comfort food served in wooden booths'

Seasonal produce by month

January – beetroot, fennel, spinach, chard, oranges, venison, cod, mackerel, scallops.

February – cress, chives, parsley, chicory, shallots, wild rabbit, hare, lemon sole.

March – purple sprouting broccoli, spring onions, halibut, wild salmon and sea trout.

April – morel, tarragon, leeks, Welsh lamb, mullet, first crabs and lobster.

May – first asparagus, sorrel, rhubarb, poussin, spring lobster, haddock, prawns.

June – broad beans, new potatoes, watercress, strawberries, radishes, sardines.

July – peas, runner beans, dill, garlic, raspberries, blueberries, herring.

August – courgettes, peppers, plums, apricots, peaches, grouse, crayfish.

September – calabrese, rocket, wild mushrooms, figs, blackberries, grapes, Kentish cobnuts, wild duck, oysters, mussels.

October – fungi, broccoli, English apples, pears, quinces, walnuts, guinea fowl, squid.

November – squash, parsnips, turnips, celeriac, almonds, sea bream.

December – clementines, curly kale, pumpkin, swede, goose, carp.

So Restaurant
Japanese
3-4 Warwick Street, W1B 5LS
Tel no: (020) 7292 0767
www.sorestaurant.com
'A Japanese restaurant with ambition.'

Zilli Fish
Seafood
36-40 Brewer Street, W1F 9TA
Tel no: (020) 7437 4867
www.zillialdo.com
'Italian seafood with ambition in Soho.'

▌St James's Park
Inn the Park
Fantastic views
St James's Park, SW1A 2BJ
Tel no: (020) 7451 9999
www.innthepark.com
⊖ St James's Park
Modern British | £30
Cooking score: 2

There can be few finer places to lunch on a summer's day than the terrace of Inn the Park, as the swans glide past on the lake of St James's Park and with the grand buildings of Whitehall visible through the swaying trees. Inside, the stripped wood ceiling and floors, full-length windows and angular modern furniture lend an almost Scandinavian feel to this most English of settings which, in the best café tradition, is open all day, from breakfast and elevenses through to lunch, afternoon tea and dinner. Lunch on crab on toast and trout fillet with artichokes and pea shoots, while dinner could be rabbit terrine with baby chard and grain mustard, grilled Herdwick lamb cutlets with a salad of spelt, chicory and grapes and pear and almond tart with vanilla ice cream. Australian house red and white is £14.50 while there are canapés and platters of smoked meat and fish to graze on as accompaniment to a short selection of cocktails.

Chef/s: Oliver Smith. **Open:** all week L 12 to 3 (4 Sat and Sun), D 5 to 10.30. **Meals:** alc (main courses £10.50 to £22.50). Set L Sat and Sun £19.50 (2 courses) to £24.50. Bar menu available 5pm onwards. **Service:** 10% (optional). **Details:** Cards accepted. 100 seats. 70 seats outside. Wheelchair access. Music. Children's portions.

▌Tottenham Court Road
Hakkasan
Resurgent Chinese culinary experience
8 Hanway Place, W1T 1HD
Tel no: (020) 7927 7000
⊖ Tottenham Court Road
Chinese | £70
Cooking score: 6

🍷 V

In the back alley off Tottenham Court Road, slip past sharp-suited greeters and descend down dark green stone stairs lit by red lights to enter a surreal world in blue glass and shiny chrome. This is Alan Yau's cavern of cool, populated by staff dressed in Issey Miyake. The menu is far removed from the typical Cantonese format in nearby Chinatown: a short rack of baby spare ribs, for example, is marinated and tea smoked before being grilled so that the meat falls off gently with a slight push of the chopstick, while soup may be a simple broth with a traditional base of wild mushrooms, bamboo and woodberry, but it is studded with so many pieces of contrasting fungi that it becomes a stunning exploration of textures. The Hong Kong-style Chilean sea bass comes with glistening soft flakes covered with thin slithers of sliced pork, dates and mushrooms, to give a meaty intensity. Elsewhere, morning glory is stir-fried with dried bean curd and chilli, while pork dishes 'are usually the highlight'; worth exploring is Hakka ribs, a new addition to the repertoire, which are marinated in, and braised with, preserved cabbage. For one regular, this is food that brings 'memories of Chinese home cooking, a rare accolade, of beautiful soft textures and a pickled, sweet, sour glow'. With a range of cocktails, single malts and Japanese whiskies, you might almost overlook the opulent wine list. This opens at £28 before rocketing skywards. NB As we went to press, Alan Yau sold Hakkasan to Tasameem. However, initial indications suggest that standards will stay the same. Reports please.
Chef/s: Tong Chee Hwee. **Open:** all week 12 to 3.30 (4.45 Sat and Sun), 6 to 11.30 (12 Wed to Sat). **Closed:** 24 and 25 Dec. **Meals:** alc (main courses £12.50 to £68). Set L £30 to £50, Set D £50 to £70. **Service:** 13%. **Details:** Cards accepted. 200 seats. Air-con. Separate bar. Wheelchair access. Music. Children allowed.

▌Trafalgar Square
The National Dining Rooms
Fine dining and afternoon tea
The Sainsbury Wing, The National Gallery, WC2N 5DN
Tel no: (020) 7747 2525
www.thenationaldiningrooms.co.uk
⊖ Leicester Square
Modern British | £25
Cooking score: 4

 £30

Set within the National Gallery's Sainsbury Wing, the stylish National Dining Rooms boast high ceilings and vast windows framing views over neighbouring Trafalgar Square. Catering to the hungry hordes that descend on the Gallery at all times of the day is no mean feat, but Oliver Peyton's latest venture manages the neat trick of satisfying all appetites, tastes and whims while never losing sight of its goal to champion fine British cooking. Thus visitors can opt for a full meal, afternoon tea (smoked salmon sandwiches, buttermilk scones), or traditional savoury pies and tarts from the bakery; a separate children's menu also gets the thumbs-up. Each month head chef Jesse Dunford Wood offers an interesting regional menu alongside the carte. On a spring lunch it was Suffolk's turn: warm asparagus with a silky chervil butter, steamed skate with buttered cockles, welks and baby leeks and Suffolk Gold cow's milk cheese with apple chutney to finish. A good, varied wine list starts at £15.

Chef/s: Jesse Dunford Wood. **Open:** Mon to Sun, 10 to 5. **Meals:** Set D £24.50 (2 courses) to £29.50. **Service:** optional. **Details:** Cards accepted. 100 seats. Children's portions.

▌Victoria
Thomas Cubitt
Gastropub with grand designs
44 Elizabeth Street, SW1W 9PA
Tel no: 020 7730 6060
www.thethomascubitt.co.uk
⊖ Victoria
Gastropub | £30
Cooking score: 3

Ⴒ

Named after London's famous 19th-century master builder, this chic gastropub is inspired by Regency and Georgian design and draws the young and well-heeled from Belgravia's squares for quality modern European cooking. Expect plenty of chatter and clatter in the buzzy downstairs bar, with its oak floors, open fires and big, roll-back windows that allow drinkers and diners to migrate to pavement tables when the sun shines. Tuck into traditional pub meals here, but head upstairs to the more formal restaurant – white-clad tables, muted colours, quirky *objets d'art* – for a more intimate dining experience. Careful buying of top-notch British produce is evident in starters like seared scallops with spiced sausage and celeriac purée and poached crayfish salad with saffron mayonnaise. Main courses take in 42-day aged Highland Black Angus sirloin with béarnaise, and Norfolk pork belly with braised black pudding stuffed trotter and white bean and apple purée. Desserts may include chocolate pot with summer berry salad and pistachio biscuits. Wines from £14.
Chef/s: Phillip Wilson. **Open:** Mon to Fri L 12 to 3, Mon to Sat D 6 to 11.. **Closed:** Christmas and New Year. **Meals:** Main courses £16 to £22. **Service:** 12.5%. **Details:** Cards accepted. 60 seats. Air-con. Separate bar. Music. Children's portions.

ALSO RECOMMENDED
▲ Ebury Wine Bar
139 Ebury Street, SW1W 9QU
Tel no: (020) 7730 5447
www.eburywinebar.co.uk
⊖ Victoria

This long-standing wine bar (here for 40 years) offers a varied menu of Brit/Med influences to accompany an exciting wine list. Starters run to seared scallops with courgette blinis (£9.75) or Parmesan and herb-crusted sardines with tomato salad (£5.50). Steak and lamb grills are available from £16.50 or try a pavé of salmon with roasted fennel and tomatoes (£12.95). Finish with chocolate and black cherry truffle cake (£5.50). The extensive wine list starts at £12.80. Closed Sun L.

▲ Mango Tree
46 Grosvenor Place, SW1X 7EQ
Tel no: (020) 7823 1888
www.mangotree.org.uk
⊖ Victoria

Sophisticated Thai restaurant, a sibling to Awana (see entry), serving elegant 'exquisitely presented' dishes. The repertoire ranges from scallops with a garlic and sweet basil crust (£8) and seared tuna salad with dried chilli and lemongrass (£6.80) to main course slow-roasted pork belly with Chinese kale and an orange and chilli glaze (£15.50), and lobster pad thai with spicy sauce, bean sprouts and cashews wrapped in a pancake (£23.50). House wine is £19. Open daily.

READERS RECOMMEND
Boisdale
British
15 Eccleston Street, SW1W 9LX
Tel no: (020) 7730 6922
www.boisdale.co.uk
'Scottish fare that takes the high road...'

Westminster

Bank Westminster

Lively, contemporary brasserie and bar
45 Buckingham Gate, SW1E 6BS
Tel no: (020) 7379 9797 (centralised number)
www.bankrestaurants.com
⊖ St James's Park
Modern European | £43
Cooking score: 3

V

Pass one of the longest bars in town – the Zander Bar – to reach Bank's airy, modern conservatory-style dining room, situated at the rear of the Crown Plaza Hotel. Its huge glass windows overlook a grand, flowery Victorian courtyard – quite a draw for fair-weather dining. The food is as cosmopolitan as the surroundings, the kitchen's modern brasserie style playing to the gallery with a something-for-everyone approach. The lengthy repertoire puts classics with dishes with modern spin, say cod and chips with mushy peas and tartare sauce alongside Szechuan peppered tuna and wok-fried Asian greens. On the meaty side, classics win supremacy, perhaps grilled ribeye with béarnaise, or maybe Gloucestershire Old Spot sausages served with creamed mash and onion sauce. Finish with a chocolate fondant teamed with pistachio ice cream, or the ubiquitous sticky toffee pudding and butterscotch. The international wine list offers a lively selection, with strength in Bordeaux and Burgundy but sees other regions stand their ground too, with prices starting out at £14.50.
Chef/s: Gavin Maguire. **Open:** Mon to Fri L 12 to 2.45, Mon to Sat D 5.30 to 11. **Closed:** Sundays, bank hols, 25, 26 Dec, 1 Jan.. **Meals:** alc (main courses £12.40 to £22.50). **Service:** 12.5% (optional). **Details:** Cards accepted. 230 seats. Air-con. Separate bar. No music. No mobile phones. Wheelchair access. Children's portions. Children allowed.

Cinnamon Club

Governing Indian gourmet
Old Westminster Library, Great Smith Street, SW1P 3BU
Tel no: (020) 7222 2555
www.cinnamonclub.com
⊖ Westminster
Indian | £41
Cooking score: 4

V

The twenty-first century role of the former Westminster Library (a fine Grade II listed building) is as the host to a top-drawer Indian restaurant. The Cinnamon Club keeps its heritage alive with a classy décor that blends old books, leather banquettes and white-clothed tables with splashes of India. The large airy bar and the modern English club feel to the dining room draw the suits from the nearby Houses of Parliament, as does the inventive Indian menu – the cooking is as far from curry-house as you can get. Expect a modern take on traditional dishes, with unusual ingredients and big flavours evident in such main dishes as smoked rack of lamb with Rajasthani corn sauce, seared rump of water buffalo with Goan spices, and Cumbrian milk-fed goat cooked three ways. Appetisers take in Bombay spiced vegetables with cumin pao, and baked chicken with cracked pepper and thyme, while the pudding choice extends to ginger toffee pudding and semolina halwa with caramelised pineapple. The international wine list complements the food, starting at £18 for house selections.
Chef/s: Vivek Singh. **Open:** Mon to Fri L 12 to 2.45, Mon to Sat D 6 to 10.45.. **Closed:** 26 Dec, 1 Jan, bank hols. **Meals:** alc (main courses £11 to £29). Set L and D before 7 £19 (2 courses) to £22.
Service: 12.5%. **Details:** Cards accepted. 150 seats. Air-con. No music.

Cooking score

A score of 1 is a significant achievement. The score in any review is based on several meals, incorporating feedback from both our readers and inspectors. As a rough guide, 1 denotes capable cooking with some inconsistencies, rising steadily through different levels of technical expertise, until the scores between 6 and 10 indicate exemplary skills, along with innovation, artistry and ambition. If there is a new chef, we don't score the restaurant for the first year of entry. For further details, please see the scoring section in the introduction to the Guide.

Rex Whistler Restaurant at Tate Britain

Up-market eating for art lovers
Millbank, SW1P 4RG
Tel no: (020) 7887 8825
www.tate.org.uk/eatinganddrinking
⊖ Pimlico
British | £30
Cooking score: 2

This classic dining room with soaring columns, white tablecloths and a famed Rex Whistler mural takes its artistic surroundings seriously. Knowledgeable staff glide across the parquet floor to deliver Richard Oxley's faithfully British menu to a mature clientele. Choose from starters such as lamb's kidney Turbigo on toasted sour dough or pickled mackerel with shaved fennel, lemon and salted capers. Brunch–type dishes include salmon, haddock and new potatoes with a poached duck egg and hollandaise, or archetypal fish and chips served in a stiff batter. Desserts include a rather boozy chocolate and amaretti tart served with clotted cream or an elderflower sorbet. But the real talking point is the award–winning wine list compiled by sommelier Hamish Anderson. Presented in an educational folder, it includes a huge selection of New and Old World wines broken down into regions. House wine starts at £15.
Chef/s: Richard Oxley. **Open:** all week L only 11.30am to 3pm. **Closed:** 24, 25, 26 Dec. **Meals:** alc (main courses £14.95). **Service:** 12.5% (optional). **Details:** Cards accepted. 90 seats. 20 seats outside. Air-con. No music. Wheelchair access. Children's portions.

READERS RECOMMEND

Pomegranates
Global
94 Grosvenor Road, SW1V 3LF
Tel no: (020) 7828 6560
'Old world charm'

Quirinale
Italian
1 Great Peter Street, SW1P 3LL
Tel no: (020) 7222 7080
www.quirinale.co.uk
'The place for political power lunches'

NORTH

Archway, Belsize Park, Camden,
Crouch End, Euston, Finchley,
Golders Green, Hampstead , Highbury,
Highgate, Islington, Kensal Green,
King's Cross, Primrose Hill, Queen's Park,
Stoke Newington, Swiss Cottage,
Walthamstow, Willesden

Archway

READERS RECOMMEND
del Parc
Spanish
167 Junction Road, N19 5PZ
Tel no: (020) 7281 5684
'Service can be slow, but the tapas is fantastic'

Belsize Park

XO

Slick, modern pan-Asian restaurant
29 Belsize Lane, NW3 5AS
Tel no: (020) 7433 0888
www.rickerrestaurants.com
⊖ Belsize Park
Asian fusion | £25
Cooking score: 2

🍷 V

The latest outpost of Will Ricker's pan-Asian empire, XO – named after a Chinese pork and dried shrimp sauce – dutifully mimics the successful high-fashion formula of its sister restaurants: Notting Hill, E&O and Chelsea's Eight over Eight (see entries). Dark wood, white tables and strategically angled look-at-me mirrors make for a slick, minimalist dining room. The menu has a good selection of dim sum, Asian salads, tempura, futo maki rolls and sashimi, and dishes tried at inspection included 'refreshing' salmon and green papaya betel leaves, a soft-shell crab maki roll, and a whole sea bass 'flaky and fresh' that walked a fine line between chilli, sweet and savoury. The wine list stays true to the restaurant's pan-Asian roots, with plenty of aromatic grape varietals and an emphasis on New World wines. House wines start at £13. Given that Belsize Park is strangely devoid of decent upmarket restaurants, it's no surprise XO has been welcomed by affluent locals when it opened in early 2007. But while XO has shaken the foundations of Belsize Park's frumpy dining scene, it unfortunately lacks the sassy edge of its sister restaurants.

Tom Parker Bowles

Where do you eat out?
Blueprint Café, Locanda Locatelli, Scotts, Caprice, Greens, Rivington Grill, Kiasu, Que Tre, The Fat Badger, St John, Royal China, Bar Shu, Chisou, Inahao and Assagi.

Who's your favourite chef?
Jeremy Lee or Rowley Leigh.

What's your favourite cookery book?
Food in England by Dorothy Hartley, *Thai Food* by David Thompson, *The Prawn Cocktail Years* by Simon Hopkinson and Lindsey Bareham and *Modern Cookery* by Eliza Acton

What's the best dish you've ever eaten?
Veal sweetbreads stuffed with truffle at Le Grand Vefour in Paris or a bowl of buffalo pho soup in a small roadside stall just outside Luang Prabang in Laos.

What's your guilty food pleasure?
McDonalds cheeseburger.

If you could only eat one more thing, what would it be?
Colchester No 2 native oysters.

What's your favourite wine?
1982 Leoville Barton.

Who would your ideal dinner guests be?
I suppose I should be learned and say Proust, Gandhi or Voltaire. But in truth, it's my wife and friends.

Chef/s: John Higginson. Open: all week L 12 to 3, D from 6. Meals: Set D £29 to £49 (private dining room). Service: 12.5%. Details: Cards accepted. 90 seats. Air-con. Separate bar. Wheelchair access. Music. Children's portions.

Camden

ALSO RECOMMENDED
▲ Gilgamesh

The Stables, Chalk Farm Road, NW1 8AH
Tel no: (020) 7482 5757
www.gilgameshbar.com
⊖ Chalk Farm

Named after an ancient Mesopotamian hero, Gilgamesh is a vast and lavishly decorated restaurant in the heart of Camden. The interior replicates that of a palace built in Babylonian times, combining the history with contemporary and modern art, so the hand-carved Indian furnishings, Middle Eastern bas reliefs and ambient Arabesque music are impressively over the top. Ian Pengelly's menu trawls through Thailand, Hong Kong and Japan for inspiration, so expect a dim sum, a team of sushi chefs preparing sashimi (£4 to £14) and nagiri dishes (£3.60 to £6.20), tempura dishes such as lemon sole with ponzu (£16), and speciality main courses like beef rending (£14). Wines from £18. Open Mon to Sun, 11 to late.

READERS RECOMMEND
Asakusa

Japanese
265 Eversholt Street, NW1 1BA
Tel no: (020) 7388 8533
'Affordable Japanese fare lands in a Camden basement'

Also recommended

An 'also recommended' entry is not a full entry, but is provisionally suggested as an alternative to main entries.

Crouch End

ALSO RECOMMENDED
▲ Khoai Cafe

6 Topsfield Parade, N8 8PR
Tel no: (020) 8341 2120
⊖ Finsbury Park

A small, friendly local restaurant and a good place to introduce yourself to Vietnamese food. The restaurant is basic (think pine décor), but scrupulously clean. Starters are the standard fare: spring rolls, satay and the like, but the summer rolls are particularly fresh and fragrant. The Pho (noodle soup) is outstanding and excellent value at around £. Main courses are the usual choice of beef, chicken, prawn and tofu in various sauces (tamarind is of particular note), along with a variety of noodle dishes. It is best to stick to the local (imported) beers, but the restaurant also has a passable wine list. House offerings start at £10. The staff are friendly, but this is a popular place with the locals, so expect to wait for a table at the weekend. Open daily, L 12 to 3.30 D 5.30 to 11.30.

Euston

Mestizo

A ray of Mexican sunshine
103 Hampstead Road, NW1 3EL
Tel no: (020) 7387 4064
www.mestizomx.com
⊖ Warren Street
Mexican | £30
Cooking score: 2

An unassuming entrance on the Hampstead Road opens onto a dining scene as hot and lively as Mestizo's own green 'tomatillo' salsa. In two short years this authentic cuisine has gathered something of a following – delegates from the Mexican Embassy were spotted lunching eagerly at inspection, it wasn't their first visit either. Newcomers might wish to explore Mexico's vibrant flavours through the tapas-style 'antojitos' menu. Dishes like flauta (crispy chicken-stuffed tortillas topped with sour cream and piquant green salsa), panucho (refried beans and pork on soft tortillas), and jaladas (cream cheese-stuffed jalapeño peppers), deliver complexity, texture and a sheer flavour explosion seldom found on the capital's Mexican scene. From the main menu, traditional chocolate-based mole sauce enlivens poussin or pork cutlets, while hot stone bowls sizzle with chicken, beef and cheese. Turn the heat up even higher with fiery tequilas, at £4.40 a glass.

Chef/s: Dalcy Aguilera and Miguel Bennetts. **Open:** Mon to Wed 12 to 12, Thu to Sat 12 to 1, Sun 12 to 4, 5 to 11. **Closed:** 25 Dec, bank hol Mons. **Meals:** alc (main courses £9.50 to £18.50. **Service:** not inc. **Details:** Cards accepted. 80 seats. Air-con. Wheelchair access. Music. Children allowed.

ALSO RECOMMENDED

▲ Diwana Bhel Poori

121 Drummond Street, NW1 2HL
Tel no: (020) 7387 5556
⊖ Euston

For southern-Indian vegetarian food, the two adjoining eateries that make Diwana have been the pick of the crop for more than 30 years. Choose from nine coconut-laden 'dosas of the coral coasts. Bombay-style dishes include aloo papri chat, bhel puri, and dahi vada (all £3). For a main course try sag aloo, a vegetable curry and puris, or dosai pancakes served with chutney and sambhar (£5.95). The lunchtime buffet is good value at £6.50 for all you can eat. The restaurant is unlicensed, so BYO. Open all week.

READERS RECOMMEND

Snazz Sichuan

Chinese
37 Chalton Street, NW1 1JD
Tel no: 020 7388 0808
www.newchinaclub.co.uk
'Exhuberent and unapologetic Chinese food'

Two Brothers

Deluxe fish and chips
297303 Regents Park Road, N3 1DP
Tel no: (020) 8346 0469
⊖ Finchley Central
Seafood | £30
Cooking score: 1

The Manzi brothers' policy of not taking bookings does not deter people from this renowned fish and chip shop and it's not unusual during busy periods to see the queue stretching round the block. The light and welcoming dining room appeals to families with children and couples alike, and the service is quick without being hurried, but it's the food that's the main draw. Starters include excellent Arbroath smokies, jellied eels and rock oysters, while a good selection of fish, from battered cod and haddock to trout, plaice and sea bass make up the main courses, which are served with chips. Sides such as mushy peas are also available, but the homemade tartare sauce left much to be desired. Puddings are fun and hearty – the knickerbocker glory and the rhubarb strudel did not disappoint. Two Brothers is probably the only fish shop where the owners also produce their own wine, which starts at £11.10 a bottle.

Chef/s: Leon and Tony Manzi. **Open:** Tue to Sat 12 to 2.30pm, 5.30 to 10.15pm. **Closed:** bank hol Mon. **Meals:** alc (main courses £9 to £18.50). **Service:** not inc. **Details:** Cards accepted. 90 seats. Air-con. Music. Children's portions. Children allowed.

ALSO RECOMMENDED

▲ Rani

7 Long Lane, N3 2PR
Tel no: (020) 8349 4386
www.raniuk.com

A gleamingly spick-and-span Indian restaurant offering a varied menu of traditional home-style vegetarian cooking based on the region of Kathiawar in Gujerat. Among the cold starters are bhel poori (£4.20) and chola papri chat (£4.10), while hot options include mixed bhajias (£3.80) and bhakervelli (spiced vegetables served with date chutney; £4). Speciality main courses range from chana (chick peas cooked with onions, tomato and tamarind; £5.10) to bhindi (deep-fried okra delicately spiced and cooked with onions; £6). All-in-one set meals offer good value. Drink lassi, falooda or wine from £10.

▌Golders Green

Café Japan
Animated sushi joint
626 Finchley Road, NW11 7RR
Tel no: (020) 8455 6854
⊖ **Golders Green**
Japanese | £22
Cooking score: 4

£30

Simple, unaffected charm and good-value food bring the crowds to Koichi Konnai's animated Japanese eating house on Finchley Road. Queues regularly form outside, but there's a rapid turnover in the canteen-style dining room with its buzzy counter and rows of lacquered tables. Top-drawer, ultra-fresh sushi is the restaurant's trump card and the range of species is extensive, taking in octopus, sea urchin, flying fish roe and razor shells in addition to the more familiar tuna, eel and sea bass. 'Delux' sets are a good way of sampling the range and chirashi specialities (sliced fish on sushi rice) are also worth noting. Beyond raw fish, the kitchen delivers familiar cooked specialities such as salmon teriyaki, grilled eel and salt-grilled yellowtail neck. To finish, opt for one of the ice creams or try dorayaki (Japanese pancakes filled with sweet red bean paste). Wines are limited to white or red at £8.50 (£2.50 a glass), otherwise drink plum wine, saké, beer or green tea. Note that it's cash only at lunch.
Chef/s: Koichi Konnai. **Open:** Sat and Sun L 12 to 2, Wed to Sun D 6 to 10 (9.30 Sun). **Closed:** 3 weeks Aug Meals: alc (main courses £4.50 to £20). Set L £8.50 (2 courses), Set D £12 (2 courses) to £18. **Service:** not inc. **Details:** Cards accepted. 39 seats. Air-con. Music.

Philpott's Mezzaluna
Neighbourhood Italian doesn't skimp on portions
424 Finchley Road, NW2 2HY
Tel no: (020) 7794 0455
www.philpotts-mezzaluna.com
Italian | £42
Cooking score: 4

V

This is what is meant by a neighbourhood restaurant, a convivial, welcoming place that has a good local following, and looks after its customers well with unfashionably large portions of Italian-influenced food. Seared calf's tongue makes a diverting opener, garnished with celeriac and grape salsa, while a spring dinner menu featured grilled asparagus with olive oil, balsamic, pine-nuts and shaved Parmesan. You might opt for an intermediate pasta course in the Italian way – perhaps fusilli with mushrooms – or else just steam straight into the main courses, where involtini of pesto-crusted plaice, or hearty bollito misto, await. If you get to the finishing line with room left, there's mango ice-cream with poached berries, or chocolate tart, in store. The wine list does a commendably thorough job in Italy, sourcing wines from all regions of the boot, in amongst offerings from other countries. The bidding opens at £14 (with glasses from £3.50).
Chef/s: David Philpott. **Open:** Tue to Fri and Sun L 12 to 2.30 (3 Sun), Tue to Sun D 7 to 11. **Closed:** Christmas and New Year's Day. **Meals:** Set L £17 (2 courses) to £20, Set D £24.50 (2 courses) to £29.50. **Service:** 12.5% (optional). **Details:** Cards accepted. 60 seats. 10 seats outside. Air-con. Wheelchair access. Music. Children's portions.

▌Hampstead

READERS RECOMMEND
Spaniard's Inn
Gastropub
Hampstead Lane, NW3 7JJ
Tel no: (020) 8731 6571
'Hearty Sunday roasts on the edge of the Heath

Highbury

ALSO RECOMMENDED
▲ Il Bacio

178184 Blackstock Road, N5 1HA
Tel no: (020) 7226 3339
www.ilbaciohighbury.co.uk
⊖ Highbury and Islington

This informal Italian is part of a (very small) chain of restaurants but don't hold that against it. Staff are ultra-friendly, making a welcoming place for both families and Italian football fans to gather. The cuisine is mainly Sardinian. Try the Crespolina Bacio (spinach and ricotta pancake) to start, or the minestrone soup if you're particularly ravenous (it's huge). For mains, there is an extensive list of pasta dishes (£6-£10) with a choice selection of meat and fish dishes (£10 -£14). The ravioli zola (ricotta ravioli, cherry tomatoes and rocket) is surprisingly light and yet spicy. Seafood pastas are presented on huge dishes with what looks like the cast of '20,000 Leagues Under the Sea' nestled appetisingly under unfeasibly large portions of pasta. The pizzas (£6 -£9) are mammoth, so either share one or get the staff to pack up the leftovers for breakfast. Open every evening and some lunchtimes.

Highgate
The Bull

Comfort cooking in Highgate
13 North Hill, N6 4AB
Tel no: (0845) 456 5033
www.inthebull.biz
⊖ Highgate
French | £32
Cooking score: 2

'The Bull' achieves a stylish informality that embraces the service as much as the food, a formula that attracts full houses. Much is made of the careful sourcing of ingredients with reassuring specifics such as Loch Fyne smoked salmon, Goosnargh chicken or Elwy lamb. Imaginative daring, which often works, takes dishes way beyond the meat and two veg

approach; smoked haddock gets welsh rarebit crust and leeks and bacon, scallops have cauliflower fritters and almonds and sultanas and bass meets potatoes with porcini, créme fraîche and onion gravy. Buttermilk pudding or apple tart and roast rhubarb exemplify simpler desserts – you can even have tea and homemade biscuits. Wines, and beers, come from all over and show discrimination; a few are available by the glass and bottles start at £13.50

Chef/s: Jeremy Hollingsworth. Open: Tue to Sun L 12 to 2.30, all week D 6 to 10.30. Meals: alc (main courses £13.50 to £24.50). Set L £14.95 (2 courses) to £17.95. Service: 12.5% (optional). Details: Cards accepted. 70 seats. Air-con. Wheelchair access. Music. Children's portions. Car parking.

The Parsee

Popular Indian regional fare
34 Highgate Hill, N19 5NL
Tel no: (020) 7272 9091
www.the-parsee.com
⊖ Archway
Indian | £23
Cooking score: 2

V £30

Opposite the Whittington Hospital, in an area of north London more famous for its late-night kebab shops than good restaurants, this modern, sparsely decorated dining room is something of a surprise. A sibling of Café Spice Namaste in the City, it specialises in the cuisine of India's Parsee community which, in its liberal use of herbs and low-fat cooking methods, bears the hallmarks of its Persian heritage. The richness of pan-fried chicken livers is balanced with a masala of cumin, coriander, garlic and ginger, with roti on the side to mop up the offal juices. A main course arrives as a plate of steamed rice accompanied by two gleamingly white bowls, one containing a moreish and deeply flavoured dhal, the other a colourful jostle of good-sized prawns cooked with red onions, red masala, tamarind and jaggery. Other dishes that display a similarly satisfying balance of flavour include fried potato cakes filled with curried

beef mince, peas and coriander and served with a cinnamon-flavoured tomato gravy. Staff are kind and welcoming. House wine is £13.90.
Chef/s: Cyrus Todiwala. **Open:** Mon to Sat D only 6 to 10.40. **Closed:** 25 Dec to 1 Jan, bank hols. **Meals:** alc (main courses £10 to £13). Set D £25 to £30. **Service:** 10% (optional). **Details:** Cards accepted. 50 seats. Air-con. Wheelchair access. Music.

Islington

Almeida

Theatre crowds meet French tapas
30 Almeida Street, N1 1AD
Tel no: (020) 7354 4777
www.conran.com
⊖ **Highbury and Islington**
French | £40
Cooking score: 4

Almeida functions both as a civilised Islington local and a convenient pit-stop for the Almeida Theatre opposite. It's a smart-casual sort of place, where large, well-spaced tables are set in a stylish dining room decorated in neutral tones, with an open kitchen at one end and a sunken bar area to one side. Cooking from a set-price menu mixes trad French bistro with sunnier Mediterranean dishes, so that you might construct a meal from escargots, oysters or terrine de foie gras followed by honey-glazed breast of duck or a rib-eye steak with mustard crust, or you could equally go for a salad of seared tuna, chervil and parsley followed by poached sea bass with mussels and saffron velouté. Sweet and savoury trolleys bearing charcuterie and tarts appear at the beginning and end of meals, and there is a cheeseboard and classic puddings such as crème brûleé. The food is soundly prepared: a splendid main course of spit-roast rack of pork with ceps and Madeira jus impressed on a recent inspection. The succulent meat edged with a ruff of terrific crackling and set off by the musky mushrooms. A lengthy wine list is particularly strong on Languedoc-Roussillon and south-

western France and offers around 15 bottles by the glass or pot lyonnais. House wine is £15.95.
Chef/s: Alan Jones. **Open:** Mon to Sat 12 to 2.30, 5.30 to 10.45, Sun 1 to 9. **Closed:** Christmas, Easter Mon. **Meals:** alc (main courses £12.50 to £25). Set L and D 5.30 to 7 £14.50 (2 courses) to £17.50. Bar tapas menu available. **Service:** 12.5% (optional). **Details:** Cards accepted. 100 seats. Air-con. No music. Wheelchair access.

The House

A cut above your average gastropub
63-69 Canonbury Road, N1 2DG
Tel no: (020) 7704 7410
www.inthehouse.biz
⊖ **Highbury and Islington**
Modern European | £30
Cooking score: 2

Pre-gentrification, this was a rough Islington pub. How times have changed. Although a sign swinging outside suggests that The House is your typical tarted-up gastropub, it's a little more polished than that: a smart-ish bar and restaurant where dinner might be preceded by a mojito and concluded with an espresso martini. The menu, however, is gastropub through and through, offering a mix of hearty Sunday lunch-style dishes interspersed with shafts of Mediterranean sunlight. So devilled kidneys and ceps on toasted brioche with smoked bacon, might be followed by shepherd's pie or, for more gloss, sea bass with braised fennel and a ragout of borlotti beans and baby onions. Finish, perhaps, with banoffee pie or British cheeses from La Fromagerie up the road in Highbury. The wine list has been assembled with humour and passion with house French £13.50. Another break from the norm: there's a weekend breakfast sourced from the local farmers' market.
Chef/s: Rob Arnott. **Open:** Tue to Sun L 12 to 2.30 (3.30 Sat and Sun), all week D 6 (6.30 Sat and Sun) to 10.30. **Closed:** Christmas. **Meals:** alc (main courses £9.50 to £22.50). Set L Tue to Fri £14.95 (2

Best for breakfast

The most important meal of the day.

If another hurried piece of toast and marmalade at home has lost its appeal, consider stepping out good and early, and letting someone else scramble the eggs and grind the coffee-beans.

The Wolseley

The Wolseley on Piccadilly may be one of the few places open in these parts at 7am, when eggs Benedict, smoked salmon, or prunes with orange and ginger might set you up for a hard day's aspirational shopping.

Smith's

The breakfasts at Smith's in Smithfield Market await to sustain Londoners (as well as market porters) with proper porridge, doorstop bacon butties, and mugs of tea to put hairs on your chest.

Roast

Market breakfasting is also on offer in the breathlessly trendy Borough Market in the form of Roast. Opening at 7am weekdays and 8am Saturdays, it offers bacon and egg butties, or scrambled eggs with smoked trout.

Aubaine

A brasserie, bar and boulangerie all in one, Aubaine aims to brings a petit morceau of Paris to Mayfair. Is there any better way to start the day than with a flaky, buttery croissant and soul-stirring coffee?

Automat

You might not expect to find a trad American diner in Mayfair, but Automat looks the part, and feels the part too. Breakfasts cater for the Stateside appetite. Eggs Benedict and home fries, buttermilk pancakes with maple syrup, ham muffins with hash browns and more all feature.

The Tavern at the Bleeding Heart

Open for business from 7.30 on weekdays, fortifying City types for the day ahead with freshly baked croissants, proper orange juice, and full English fry-ups featuring fine Suffolk bacon.

High Road Brasserie

Homely menus at this Chiswick brasserie take in eggs Florentine, smoked salmon bagels and porridge with sultanas and muscovado sugar. A range of fruit smoothies completes the picture.

Fifteen

Breakfast the Jamie Oliver way. 'Pukkola' muesli based on rolled oats, a breakfast 'Bling' deal of smoked salmon with scrambled eggs on sourdough, or bubble and squeak with baked beans are the order of the morning.

Bryn Williams   Odette's

Why did you become a chef?
Seeing the process of bread being made hooked me from that day on.

Who do you most admire amongst today's chefs?
Michel Roux Jnr.

Where do you eat out?
Mostly London because of its great variety, but I love the odd trip to Paris.

Who is your favourite producer?
Rhug Estate Organic Farm, North Wales. Top Class producer.

Whats your favourite cookery book?
Michel Roux, Le Gavroche Cook Book.

What's the best dish you've ever eaten?
My mam's Sunday Dinner.

What's your guilty food pleasure?
My guilty pleasure has to be crisps.

Whats the hardest thing about running a restaurant?
The long hours and a pressurised environment.

courses) to £17.95. **Service:** 12.5% (optional). **Details:** Cards accepted. 40 seats. Wheelchair access. Music. Children's portions.

Metrogusto
Fine food with a fiery Silician streak
13 Theberton Street, N1 0QY
Tel no: (020) 7226 9400
www.metrogusto.co.uk
⊖ Angel
Italian | £32
Cooking score: 3

🍷 🍶 **V**

High ceilings, white walls covered with bright and bold contemporary paintings, and chunky furnishings set the cool, idiosyncratic scene at this modern Italian restaurant off Upper Street. Cooking is described as 'progressive Italian' with an emphasis on regional foods although there is a definite Sicilian slant to the menu, which is laid out in traditional style with risottos and pastas following starters like Sicilian mussel soup with garlic bruschetta, or sea bream carpaccio with grilled fennel. Main courses range from grilled lamb cutlets with red wine and peach sauce and steak with apple and gorgonzola sauce to lemon sole fillets with roasted pepper coulis. Desserts take in the trendy (poached pear with pecorino ice cream) and the traditional (pannacotta with caramelised lime sauce). The all-Italian wine list concentrates on good producers, with around 15 by the glass from £4.50 and bottles starting at £15.50.
Chef/s: Antonio Di Salvo. **Open:** Sat and Sun L 12 to 2.30 (3 Sun), all week D 6.30 to 10.30 (11 Sat, 10 Sun). **Closed:** Christmas to New Year. **Meals:** Set L and D £14.50 (2 courses) to £19.50. **Service:** 12.5% (optional). **Details:** Cards accepted. 60 seats. 10 seats outside. Air-con. Separate bar. Wheelchair access. Music. Children's portions.

Morgan M

Entente cordiale in Islington
489 Liverpool Road, N7 8NS
Tel no: (020) 7609 3560
www.morganm.com
⊖ **Highbury and Islington**
French | £39
Cooking score: 5

V

A recent makeover has helped this modest, corner dining room to project a warmer outlook, with plush burgundy walls and oak panelling accented by the chef's own paintings. Well-spaced tables highlight the modest but comforting appeal of the place. New cutlery and crockery add lustre, too, and the repertoire now includes two multi-course menus, one catering for vegetarians, along with an increased selection of French farm cheeses. What hasn't changed are the glowing reports with consistent applause for the very high quality food and polished service. While the cooking can appear conventional, Morgan Meunier's distinctive flair elevates it to a high standard. First to arrive at inspection, for example, was a 'delightful' amuse bouche of beetroot soup with Roquefort foam. Next, a ravioli of Burgundian snails in Chablis, served with poached garlic, followed by a main course of grilled Anjou squab pigeon, parsnip purée and braised pear, then a pre-dessert of rice pudding wrapped in orange tuile with a strawberry sorbet and raspberry coulis. But the highlight of the meal was the 'superb' warm strawberry tarte with fresh basil and olive oil ice cream, which had to be ordered at the start of the meal. The Francocentric wine list has also been improved, with some fine older vintages, and starts at the foothills of £15 and climbs to a pinnacle of £1,200 for a Château Pétrus 1983.
Chef/s: Morgan Meunier and Sylvain Soulard. **Open:** Wed to Fri and Sun L 12 to 2, Tue to Sat D 7 to 10. **Closed:** 23 to 30 Dec. **Meals:** Tasting menu £45. **Service:** 12.5%. **Details:** Cards accepted. 48 seats. Air-con. Wheelchair access. Children's portions.

Ottolenghi

Bold fresh flavours
287 Upper Street, N1 2TZ
Tel no: (020) 7288 1454
www.ottolenghi.co.uk
⊖ **Highbury and Islington**
Global | £23
Cooking score: 3

V

Queues often stretch out of this inventive café/deli at weekends, but this isn't a chore – it's an opportunity to eye up the fresh salads, breads and cakes on display in the shop (takeaway if you don't fancy the wait). The minimalist dining area at the back takes in two long refectory tables with tight-packed chairs as well as cramped tables for two. Not a place for a lingering meal, then, but the food aims high nevertheless with the cooking taking inspiration from all over. Inspection was in time for a breakfast dish (served until 1pm) of perfect poached eggs and spinach, homemade muffin and blood orange mayo, while rare roast beef with mixed herbs and mustard yoghurt sauce, from the lunch menu, came with two highly imaginative salads noted for 'big, bold, fresh flavours', the pick being roasted aubergine with chilli garlic yoghurt, pistachios, preserved lemon and parsley. There's more ambition at dinner with dishes served starter-size – three per person is recommended – and quail baked on cedar wood with pomelo and coriander salad and tamarind relish is a typical choice. Desserts from a selection on display have included an intensely rich chocolate fondant cake. The breads are first class, and service is swift and efficient. The short wine list opens at £13.50.
Chef/s: Tricia Jadoonanan and Ramael Scully. **Open:** Mon to Sat 12 to 10.00, Sun 9 to 7. **Closed:** 25, 26 Dec, 1 Jan. **Meals:** alc D (main courses £6.00 to £9.50). Set L £8.50 to £13.50. **Service:** not inc. **Details:** Cards accepted. 45 seats. 5 seats outside. Air-con. Wheelchair access. Music. Children allowed.

Rooburoo

Inventive, all-day modern Indian
21 Chapel Market, N1 9EZ
Tel no: (020) 7278 8100
www.rooburoo.com
⊖ Angel
Indian | £15
Cooking score: 3

V

Down-at-heel Chapel Market is an unlikely setting for this restaurant, given the pie'n'mash or greasy spoon offerings nearby. The clean, cream walls and wooden tables set the scene for some of the freshest home style Indian cooking a Brick-Lane-weary London has seen for a long time. The conservatively priced menu takes inspiration from across the sub continent, hamming up the Indian love affair for an all-day snacking culture. Choose from small dishes such as flavoursome gram flour pancakes with chicken for a purse-friendly £2.75. Main courses for under £10 are chosen from the comically named 'rooburoast' or 'rooby murray' sections. Fresh tuna bhuna was flawless, perfumed with ginger and garam masala and finished with crunchy green beans. Other dishes include monk fish tikka or lamb chops with lemon juice and herbs. Desserts include gajjar halwa (Indian carrot cake) or sweet baked Indian yoghurt. Background music flits between modern tabla and Bollywood style drum and bass, while service is snappy but falls on the right side of casual. A cursory wine list features just four red and four white starting at £11.95.

Chef/s: Michael Tarat. **Open:** all week 12pm to 11pm (D 6pm to 11pm Mon). **Closed:** n/a. **Meals:** alc (main courses £5.75 to £9.95). **Service:** 12.5% optional. **Details:** Cards accepted. 60 seats. 8 seats outside. Air-con. Wheelchair access. Music. Children's portions.

ALSO RECOMMENDED

▲ The Albion

10 Thornhill Road, N1 1HW
Tel no: (020) 7607 7450
www.the-albion.co.uk
⊖ Angel

Given the location of this pub, it's a wonder that it wasn't revamped years ago. A tattered old-man's boozer has been transformed into an elegant series of dining rooms, with a sophisticated garden that can seat over 100 Islingtonites at a time. Another Mark Hix-influenced menu offers a selection of well-executed dishes, such as broad bean and smoked ham-knuckle soup at £6; mains include roast mackerel with a gooseberry and fennel compote, and slow-roast Gloucester Old Spot with herb mash, both at £11. A sense of humour prevails, as news reaches us that diners in the garden were presented with sombreros on a particularly sunny Sunday afternoon. However, the party atmosphere means that weekends are best avoided if you have a tendency towards the quiet life. House wines start at £12.95. Reader reports please.

READERS RECOMMEND

Afghan Kitchen

Afghani
35 Islington Green, N1 8DU
Tel no: (020) 7359 8019
'Memorable food in stark surroundings'

Marquess Tavern

Gastropub
32 Canonbury Street, N1 2TB
Tel no: (020) 7354 2975
www.marquesstavern.co.uk
'A gastropub with grand designs.'

▌Kensal Green

READERS RECOMMEND

Paradise by way of Kensal Green

Gastropub
19 Kilburn Lane, W10 4AE
Tel no: (020) 8969 0098
'The forbidden fruit of London gastropubs...'

William IV

Modern British
786 Harrow Road, NW10 5JX
Tel no: (020) 8969 5944
www.elparadorlondon.com
'Excellent tapas in the garden'

▌King's Cross

Acorn House

Eco-evangelists with a missionary zeal
69 Swinton Street, WC1X 9NT
Tel no: 020 7812 1842
www.acornhouserestaurant.com
⊖ King's Cross
Modern British | £32
Cooking score: 2

Acorn House is the eco-friendly creation of ex-Fifteen chef Arthur Potts Dawson and manager James Grainger-Smith. The restaurant sits on a corner plot on a busy junction in the lower reaches of Kings Cross, an area in the throws of transformation, due to the impending arrival of Eurostar. The design is utilitarian and contemporary, with lime-green chairs, neat dark wooden tables and wooden banquettes (which can get uncomfortable after a while). The menu is well-formed, divided into soups, salads, cured meats, pastas and main courses. Our inspection comprised of earthy dishes such as Jerusalem artichoke and chestnut soup, along with a main course of roast shoulder of mutton with mint and quince. However, a venison taglietelle dish was fairly sloppy, causing one reader to raise an eyebrow towards the training kitchen. A poached rhubarb and custard dessert with sable stars was similarly disappointing. However, it is fair to say that Acorn House may well prove to be a seminal venture in the world of catering; an early adopter of standards that will undoubtedly become the norm. The concept is as sustainable as the restaurant's intentions, but the relentless brow-beating about the ethics of the operation can become a little wearing. (Packet of seeds for you, sir? Biofuel cab, madam?). A tidy wine list includes some English offerings, with prices starting at £13.
Chef/s: Arthur Potts Dawson. **Open:** B 8 to 11; L 12 to 3; D 6 to 10.30. **Meals:** Main courses, £12.50 to £18.50. **Service:** 12.5%. **Details:** Cards accepted. 50 seats. Wheelchair access. Music. Children allowed.

Konstam at the Prince Albert

Seasonal food sourced within the M25
2 Acton Street, WC1X 9NA
Tel no: (020) 7833 5040
www.konstam.co.uk
⊖ King's Cross
Modern British | £26
Cooking score: 3
 £30

Starting in the inauspicious surroundings of King's Cross, Oliver Rowe, chef-patron of Konstam, had a mission. Not only did he elevate the humblest of eateries, the café, into a place where imaginative food could be bought at a reasonable price, but he sourced ingredients from local producers too. This quest and preparations for the ambitious Konstam at the Prince Albert were chronicled in *The Urban Chef*, the BBC2 documentary that made Rowe's name. The remarkable transformation of the Prince Albert is only apparent to diners once through the doors. It is now one of the most original dining rooms around. The menu is also a definite cut above; essentially Anglo-French, it is at turns both traditional and playful. Classic pork rillettes might come with pickled cauliflower and herb salad. Mains generally include a choice of fish (the grilled Mersea brill with tarragon salad was excellent on a recent visit) and game. Puddings have a distinctly British feel, with gooseberries and Earl Grey tea featuring. A compact, well-chosen wine list includes English choices as well as continental offerings, is strong on dessert wines and complimented by a selection of beers and a wonderful cider. Konstam at the Prince Albert could be dismissed as modish, but that would be unfair. The quality of the ingredients, subtle invention of the menu, good-natured service and solidity of the cooking set this establishment apart and make it somewhere to seek out. House wines start at £14.

Chef/s: Oliver Rowe. **Open:** L Mon to Fri, 12.30 to 3, D Mon to Sat, 6.30 to 10.30. **Closed:** Christmas and New Year. **Meals:** alc (main courses from £12 to £16). **Details:** Cards accepted. 50 seats. No music. Wheelchair access. Children allowed.

READERS RECOMMEND

Camino

Spanish
3 Varnishers Yard, N1 9FD
Tel no: (020) 7841 7331
www.barcamino.com
'Modern influences in a converted warehouse'

Primrose Hill

★ BEST VEGETARIAN RESTAURANT ★

Manna

A vegetarian trail-blazer
4 Erskine Road, NW3 3AJ
Tel no: (020) 7722 8028
www.manna-veg.com
⊖ Chalk Farm
Vegetarian | £26
Cooking score: 2

V

Heaven-sent to north London's vegan and vegetarian constituency, Manna, founded in the 1960s, describes itself as 'Britain's first vegetarian restaurant'. Its food draws intricate flavours from around the world, resulting in a restaurant that meat eaters will happily flock to. A recently revamped menu offers thai tempeh falafel balls flavoured with lemongrass and galangal to start a starburst of flavour followed by a baby vegetable & apricot tagine.

Top this off with a homel,y yet exotic, tibetan goji berry rice pudding brulée, with ginger & nutmeg cream for dessert. Much of the food is organic and the menu also accommodates those with a gluten allergy. House wines start at £11.75.

Chef/s: Matthew Kay. **Open:** Daily, 6.30 to 11. Sun L, 12.30 to 3. **Closed:** Christmas and New Year. **Meals:** Mains £9 to £13. **Service:** 12.5%. **Details:** Cards accepted. 50 seats. Air-con. Separate bar. Wheelchair access. Music. Children's portions.

Odette's

Rejuvenated stalwart
130 Regents Park Rd, NW1 8XL
Tel no: (020) 7586 8569
www.odettesprimrosehill.com
⊖ Chalk Farm
Modern European | £40
Cooking score: 5

🍷 **V**

When the denizens of Primrose Hill heard Bryn Williams was the new chef at their beloved Odette's, they breathed a sigh of relief. The determined young Welshman shot to fame on the *Great British Menu* last year, when he punched above his weight and won the fish course for the Queen's 80th birthday banquet. At Odette's, he showcases the accomplished cooking skills that led to the breakthrough in his career – 'it's a dining experience not to be missed'. The décor is classic with modern undertones. White tablecloths, white painted brick and bright yellow chairs clash loudly with brown patterned wallpaper and blue carpet. But what the 'bijou' dining room lacks in harmony, the food makes up for in taste and presentation: delicate pan-fried foie gras 'rich and soft', perfectly paired with the earthy flavours of beetroot, for example, and seared blue fin tuna with a smear of avocado purée and fresh radish and apple salad. Mains include a roasted wild sea trout with a pea and mint purée, and braised shoulder of Elwy Valley lamb with pine nuts and courgette, while Valrhona chocolate fondant with milk ice cream for dessert, was pronounced 'exquisite' at inspection. Service is highly polished. The wine is a Francophile's dream, starting with house wines at £23. NB As we went to press, rumours were circulating that Bryn Williams was looking to acquire another restaurant site, to be called 'Bryn's'. Reports please.

Chef/s: Bryn Williams. **Open:** Tues to Sun 12 to 2.30 (Sat to 3, Sun to 3.30), Tues to Sat 6.30 to 10.30. **Closed:** Christmas. **Meals:** Set L and D £23.95 (3 courses). **Service:** 12.5% (optional). **Details:** Cards accepted. 55 seats. 12 seats outside. Air-con. Separate bar. No mobile phones. Wheelchair access. Music. Children's portions.

■ Queen's Park

READERS RECOMMEND
Salusbury
Gastropub
50-52 Salusbury Road, NW6 6NN
Tel no: (020) 7328 3286
'Imaginative cooking with an Italian theme'

■ Stoke Newington

Rasa
Keralan restaurant curries favour with veggies
55 Stoke Newington Church Street, N16 0AR
Tel no: (020) 7249 0344
www.rasarestaurants.com
⊖ Finsbury Park
Indian | £24
Cooking score: 2

V

This is the original vegetarian Keralan restaurant in the Rasa chain. The staff are all Keralan, exuding enthusiasm and charm, always ready to describe a dish in heartfelt detail as if they'd watched their mothers making it. 'The Kerala Feast' (£16 per person) allows the chef to present a well-balanced selection, starting with the unmissable crunchy fried nibbles served with six different fresh chutneys including sweet garlic spiked with fenugreek. An array of vibrant curries will follow, such as mango and plantains in gently spiced yoghurt, savoy cabbage thoran with freshly grated coconut, plus tamarind rice and fresh parathas. An 'auspicious rice

pudding' is a delicately perfumed finale. House wine is £11.95. Other branches are based in Bond Street, Fitzrovia, Euston, King's Cross and Newcastle.

Chef/s: Rajan Karattil. **Open:** Sat and Sun L 12 to 3, all week D 6 to 10.45 (11.45 Fri and Sat). **Closed:** 24 to 26 Dec, 1 Jan. **Meals:** alc (main courses £3.50 to £5.95). Set L and D £16. **Service:** 12.5% (optional). **Details:** Cards accepted. 64 seats. Air-con. Wheelchair access. Music.

ALSO RECOMMENDED

▲ Istanbul Iskembecisi
9 Stoke Newington Road, N16 8BH
Tel no: (020) 7254 7291
www.istanbuliskembecisi.co.uk
⊖ Highbury and Islington

For Turkish food in informal surroundings, this family-run restaurant is worth considering. The menu is appealing, combining staple dishes of the generic Middle Eastern restaurant with more unusual Anatolian fare. Hot and cold mezzes range from hummus (£3) to Albanian-style liver with onions (£3.50). Main dishes such as baked diced lamb on white sauce and aubergine purée (£8.50) are to be had alongside stews and fish (£8 to £11). House wine is £10. Open daily.

READERS RECOMMEND
Mangal Ocakbasi
Turkish
4 Stoke Newington Road, N16 8BH
Tel no: (020) 7254 7888
www.mangal2.com
'Meats cooked on an open charcoal grill'

The Three Crowns
Gastropub
175 Stoke Newington High Street, N16 0LH
Tel no: (020) 7241 5511
'Rejuvenated pub with a Mediterranean menu'

▌Swiss Cottage
Bradleys

Anglo-French menu in North London
25 Winchester Road, NW3 3NR
Tel no: (020) 7722 3457
⊖ Swiss Cottage
French | £33
Cooking score: 3

🍾

Handy for the cultural buzz generated by Hampstead Theatre, Bradley's is a fine neighbourhood restaurant. Stepping up to the mark for the Swiss Cottage set, it deals in straightforward Anglo-French cooking with an appreciable degree of polish. Crab ravioli with broad beans, spinach and a tomato and saffron sauce was a typical spring starter, and sat alongside a wealth of other seafood options, such as red mullet niçoise, fried scallops or Rossmore oysters. Main courses haul in fish from the Cornish day-boats, together with well-judged meat dishes like Barbary duck breast with turnip gratin, or Dales lamb with boulangère potatoes and creamed flageolets. A cornucopia of ice creams and sorbets pours forth to garnish desserts such as hot lemon and raspberry soufflé with raspberry ripple ice cream, or passion-fruit bavarois with fresh pineapple and a coconut sorbet. The wine list is a model of what a small restaurant can achieve when it puts its mind to it. Arranged by style, concisely annotated, and packed with great producers, it genuinely tries to offer something for everyone. Wine per glass starts at £3.50, bottles at £13.
Chef/s: Simon Bradley. **Open:** Tue to Sun L 12 to 3, Tue to Sat D 6 to 11. **Closed:** Christmas, bank hols. **Meals:** alc £12.00 to £17.95 (main courses). Set L Tue to Sat £10.95 (2 courses) to £14.95. **Service:** 12.5% (optional). **Details:** Cards accepted. 60 seats. Air-con. No mobile phones. Wheelchair access. Music. Children's portions.

Singapore Garden

Far-East flavour in Swiss Cottage
83-83A Fairfax Road, NW6 4DY
Tel no: (020) 7328 5314
www.singaporegarden.co.uk
⊖ Swiss Cottage
Asian | £30
Cooking score: 2

V

Stylish floor-to-ceiling glass and tables laid with pristine white cloths and fresh roses lend an elegant, contemporary feel to this Swiss Cottage dining room. It is a popular spot for families at weekends, drawn by the friendly service and authentic Singaporean cooking. Familiar favourites include starters of charcoal-grilled satay beef, or chicken in filo pastry 'money bags' with a chilli dip. The rest of the long-ish menu is divided into sections, such as fish and seafood – where you'll find claypot prawns and scallops with glass noodles, or pan-fried mackerel in spicy samba sauce – while chicken, duck and pork dishes stretch to braised pig's trotters infused with five-spice, and a page of Singapore and Malaysian specialities features squid in prawn chilli paste with crunchy sugar snap peas. Finish perhaps with soya beancurd with palm sugar. House selections from £15 open an uncomplicated wine list.
Chef/s: Mr Kok Sum Toh. **Open:** all week L 12 to 3 (5.30 Sun), D 6 to 11 (11.30 Sun). **Closed:** 4 days Christmas. **Meals:** alc (main courses £6 to £29). Set D £23.50 to £38.50. **Service:** 12.5% (optional). **Details:** Cards accepted. 85 seats. Air-con. Wheelchair access. Music. Children allowed.

▌Walthamstow

READERS RECOMMEND
Trattoria La Ruga
Italian
59 Orford Road, E17 9NJ
Tel no: (020) 8520 5008
'An oasis for intelligent Italian cooking'

Child-friendly dining

Taking the kids out for a meal shouldn't mean limiting your options. These days, more and more establishments are opening their doors to youngsters.

'Children allowed' doesn't always mean 'children welcome' – just ask any parent who has ever struggled to find somewhere to park their pushchair. The following restaurants get the thumbs up for food, attitude and ambience.

The River Café

Rose Gray and Ruthie Rogers' seminal River Café is a serious restaurant with a wonderfully relaxed attitude to children. The impeccably sourced ingredients may be served with a steep price tag, but portions are generous enough for youngsters to share a forkful or two of your starter, before enjoying their own kiddie-sized main.

Leon

Allegra McEvedy's likeable, healthy fast-food chain rates highly for its fresh, seasonal organic fare. Ribs, falafel and meatballs come in kid-friendly, bite-sized portions. Restaurants are bright and spacious and the plastic cutlery and paper food boxes make it a doddle for kids to feed themselves.

High Road Brasserie

Nick Jones' popular and buzzy brasserie boasts a gargantuan menu that succeeds in being all things to all diners – kids included. There's a bespoke 'little people' menu (think mini sausages and mash, organic chicken and broccoli or homemade fish fingers), and added attractions of colouring in and crayons.

Carluccio's

Antonio Carluccio's successful chain of cafés is spacious, welcoming and well-equipped for little ones (puzzles and colouring-in

books keep them entertained while you finish your cappuccino). Children can create their own pasta and sauce combinations from the kids' menu, which also features bread-crumbed chicken and mini house gelati.

National Dining Rooms, National Gallery

A smart dining room, café and bakery rolled into one, Oliver Peyton's paean to modern British dining manages the neat trick of catering to all crowds, at all times of the day. The Dining Rooms offer an à la carte menu with a separate children's section (boiled egg with soldiers, chicken drumsticks) alongside plenty of other child (and adult) friendly options.

Willesden

Sushi-Say

Unpretentious sushi house
33B Walm Lane, NW2 5SH
Tel no: (020) 8459 2971
⊖ Willesden Green
Japanese | £31
Cooking score: 3

V

Katsuhara Shimizu's likeable Japanese eating house fizzes with enthusiasm since the dining room has been remodeled. Natural colours blend with modern clean lines, counter seating and tables are simply laid and there's an appealing warm ambience. Eating options on a long, user-friendly menu range widely from sushi and sashimi to combinations of vegetables, meat or fish, which may be fried, boiled, grilled or served in soup. Plenty of set meals for one person at lunch and dinner make ordering easy (teriyaki, sushi and sashimi lunches, for example, all come with rice, pickles and miso soup). Familiar appetizers, from edamame beans to gyoza dumplings (filled with minced pork and vegetables) start the ball rolling, and grilled black cod with salt is a fine main course. Meals end simply with fresh fruit or ice cream – which can include wasabi and red bean flavours. House wine is £12, otherwise choose from a comprehensive list of cold sake – 'the best fit for Japanese food' – or hot sake for traditionalists, alongside beer and tea.

Chef/s: Katsuharu Shimizu. **Open:** Tue to Sun L 12 to 2 (1 to 3 Sat, Sun) D 6.30 to 10 (6 to 10.30 Sat, 6 to 10 Sun). **Closed:** Christmas, Easter, Summer (2 weeks), bank hols. **Meals:** Set L £9 (3 courses) to £15, Set D £21 (3 courses) to £35. **Service:** not inc. **Details:** Cards accepted. 40 seats. Air-con. No music. Wheelchair access. Children allowed.

Which? Campaigns

To find out more about Which? food and drink campaigns, please visit:
www.which.co.uk

EAST

Bethnal Green, Canary Wharf, City,
Clerkenwell, Hackney,
Hoxton: see Shoreditch, Limehouse,
Shoreditch, Spitalfields, Tower Hill,
Wapping, Whitechapel

▌Bethnal Green

Green & Red
Welcoming and chilled-out atmosphere
51 Bethnal Green Road, E1 6LA
Tel no: (020) 7749 9670
www.greenred.co.uk
⊖ Liverpool Street
Mexican | £25
Cooking score: 3

V

Green and Red is inspired by the cantinas and regional specialties of Jalisco – the home of tequila – so you know what to drink. It's an easygoing place. Starters such as chorizo con papas, with shallots, potatoes and coriander are served in traditional eathernware pots, while mains might include the popular carne asada (chargrilled, aged ribeye with chipotle salsa and spring onions) or slow-roasted pork belly and ribs with pasilla chilli and orange salt. Watermelon served with crushed piquin chilli and lime is a refreshing way to finish, but churros served with a thick spiced hot chocolate dipping sauce are recommended, too. Young staff are friendly, passionate and knowledgeable about the food and drinks. South American wines start at £12.50 and there's a great range of cocktails.
Chef/s: Alberto Figueroa. **Open:** Sat and Sun L 12 to 5, all week D 6 to 11. **Closed:** 25 to 30 Dec. **Meals:** alc (main courses L £4.50 to £6.50, D £9.50 to £14.50). Bar menu available. **Service:** 12.5% (optional). **Details:** Cards accepted. 65 seats. 15 seats outside. Air-con. Wheelchair access. Music.

Les Trois Garçons
High-end dining in camp surrounds
56 Redchurch Street, E2 7DP
Tel no: (020) 7012 1234
www.lestroisgarcons.com
⊖ Liverpool Street
French | £35
Cooking score: 3

Set in a drab and down-at-heel part of town Les Trois Garçons positively shrieks its high-end credentials, with alluring torches flickering over its entrance and, inside, an outrageously camp décor of stuffed pitbulls decked out in fairy wings and giraffes swathed in jewels. Among such outlandish surrounds, you might fear garish offerings on the menu, but happily the kitchen has resisted the obvious temptation. Start with a 'tremendously smooth and richly flavoured' sweet potato and ginger velouté served with just the right amount of gnocchi and poured at the table 'with a delicate flourish'. For mains, try wild Scottish lobster on squid ink linguini with celeriac purée and lobster foam, while the 'wonderfully rich' dessert trio of chocolate opera, Marquise and Valrhona chocolate profiterole with vanilla ice cream is strongly recommended. Whispers of snooty staff seem unkind; at inspection service was charming and slick, if perhaps just a little too efficient during the first early evening weekend sitting. The wine list is predominantly French and prices are stiff, starting at £19.
Chef/s: Jerome Henry, Yuka Aoyama & Erol Defoe. **Open:** all week D 7-9.30. **Closed:** Christmas, bank hols. **Meals:** alc (main courses £17.50-£34.00) Set D £24 (2 courses) £28 (3 courses). **Service:** 12.5% (optional). **Details:** Cards accepted. 180 seats. Air-con. Music. Children allowed.

▌Canary Wharf

Gun
A gastropub loaded with French method
27 Coldharbour, E14 9NS
Tel no: (020) 7515 5222
www.thegundocklands.com
Gastropub | £35
Cooking score: 3

Smack beside the Thames in the heart of the Docklands, a stone's throw from Canary Wharf, the Gun is a rejuvenated eighteenth-century dockers' pub with cracking views from it smart decked terrace across the Thames to the Millennium Dome. Tom and Ed Martin, who also own the White Swan and Empress of India (see entries), have painstakingly restored this once burnt-out boozer to make a classy drinking and dining venue. There's a splendid traditional bar with reclaimed oak floors, a smattering of maritime artefacts and a dining area with white-clad tables, as well as a couple of snugs and private dining rooms. Versatile menus combine modern British pub food with French brasserie cooking, say, pea and mint soup or seared scallops with pancetta, polenta with black olive sauce, and pan-fried gilt head bream with oxtail ravioli or lamb rump with white bean purée and morel jus. The list of desserts may take in warm chocolate fondant with camomile tea ice cream. The wine list, arranged stylistically, is comprehensive but pricey, although Spanish wines kick off at £13. **Chef/s:** Scott Wade. **Open:** Mon to Fri 12 to 3, 6 to 10.30, Sat and Sun 10.30 to 4.30, 6 to 10.30 (9.30 Sun). **Closed:** 26 Dec. **Meals:** alc (main courses £11 to £21). Bar menu available. **Service:** 12.5% (optional). **Details:** Cards accepted. 85 seats. Air-con. Wheelchair access. Music. Children's portions.

Plateau

The place to dock for good French food
Canada Place, Canary Wharf, E14 5ER
Tel no: (020) 7715 7100
www.conran.com/eat
⊖ **Canary Wharf**
French | £43
Cooking score: 3

In the heart of Canary Wharf, on the fourth-floor of a striking steel and glass building with stunning views over Canada Square, this stylish and informal restaurant draws the suits for accomplished modern French cooking. The two contemporary dining areas are separated by a semi-open kitchen, there are floor-to-ceiling windows, and immaculately laid marble-topped tables. The seasonally changing menu may kick off with black truffle gnocchi with white pepper sauce, goat's cheese fondue with baby beetroot, or a plate of Falmouth Bat native oysters. Mains favour fish from Billingsgate, perhaps spice-crusted cod with curried artichoke and tamarind sauce or line caught sea bass à la plancha with mushroom broth. Carnivores are not forgotten, there may be roast pheasant with

braised red cabbage and wild rice, or beef fillet the celeriac and pear purée and remoulade. Puddings have included roasted fig with mulled wine jelly and ginger ice cream. Expect a simpler menu in the Bar & Grill and summer barbeques on the terrace. The well-constructed wine list opens at £21
Chef/s: Tim Tolley. **Open:** Mon to Fri L 12 to 3, Mon to Sat D 6 to 10.30. **Closed:** Christmas, Easter, bank hols. **Meals:** alc (main courses £17 to £27.50). Set D £24.75 to £48. Bar and Grill menus available. **Service:** 12.5% (optional). **Details:** Cards accepted. 124 seats. Air-con. No music. Wheelchair access.

Ubon by Nobu

High-impact Japanese cuisine
34 Westferry Circus, E14 8RR
Tel no: (020) 7719 7800
www.noburestaurants.com
⊖ **Canary Wharf**
Japanese | £48
Cooking score: 5

Ring the bell at the iron gates, journey through the landscaped gardens of the Four Seasons Hotel, then take the lift to the fourth floor. It is a tortuous trek but, once inside the über-cool dining room, all is dramatically revealed. Like its siblings, Nobu at Hyde Park Corner and Nobu Berkeley St (see entries), this is a restaurant fuelled by celebrity glamour. As with its near namesakes, the food is a curious symbiosis of Japanese cuisine old and new with some South American influences. Many dishes are common to all three establishments – the yellowtail sashimi with jalapeño and ponzu sauce, the much-vaunted black cod in sticky sweet miso, the toro tartar with caviar, and more besides. Raw fish is of dazzling freshness, whether it is high-art sushi or more modern inventions like 'new style' tofu and tomato sashimi. Cooked dishes set out to dazzle the senses and presentation is eye-poppingly sharp: there is beauty to behold in everything from the oysters in filo with five sauces to lobster salad with spicy lemon dressing. Various forms of ceviche and Anti-Cucho Peruvian-style grills represent the Latin American constituency, while the specials list extends to asparagus with egg sauce and salmon roe, sea urchin tempura and even Dover sole with black bean sauce. Wagyu beef is sold in 50 gram portions. Desserts aim for full-on sensual impact, as in apricot and jasmine soup with peanut crumble and Nobu beer ice cream. Speciality sakes and champagnes claim pole position on the exclusive wine list, which promises quality at a price: bottles start at £27, selections by the glass from £7.

Chef/s: Mark Edwards. **Open:** Mon to Fri L 12 to 2, Mon to Sat D 6 to 10. **Closed:** bank hols. **Meals:** alc (main courses £5.50 to £29.50). Set L £45 to £55, Set D £70 to £90. **Service:** 15% (optional). **Details:** Cards accepted. 120 seats. Air-con. Wheelchair access. Music. Car parking.

▌City

Bonds

Light-handed contemporary cooking
Threadneedle Hotel, 5 Threadneedle Street, EC2R 8AY
Tel no: (020) 7657 8088
www.theetoncollection.com
⊖ Bank
Modern European | £45
Cooking score: 6

🍶 ⌁

Formerly the HQ of Citibank, the Threadneedle Hotel is another of those lordly, moneyed transformations much favoured by savvy developers in the Square Mile. Bonds occupies the old banking hall, an imposing high-ceilinged room with plushness and gravitas aplenty, but some light relief provided by contemporary murals and vases of greenery. The refined setting is perfectly in tune with Barry Tonks's modern French and European-biased menus, which might open with Dorset Bay crab, pea and pistachio bavarois with pink grapefruit jelly or chicken liver and foie gras parfait with quince purée and pain d'epice mousse. Main courses suggest that the kitchen is eager to cast its net wide for top-drawer ingredients: Label Rouge 'poulet fermier' is roasted and served with wild garlic

leaves, gnocchi, morel and Madeira juice, lamb comes from the Elwey Valley and fillet of line-caught sea bass could be accompanied by borlotti bean and basil minestrone; also look for the slow-cooked Baillet mountain pork with spring vegetables. After that, consider sharing a textbook tarte Tatin with Calvados crème fraîche or investigate the exotic possibilities of coconut rice pudding with Alphonso mango and sesame seed 'dentelle'. France and the rest of Europe are at the forefront of the heavyweight wine list, which brings together a classy assortment of oenophilic tipples, big-name superstar labels and tantalising options to match the food. Prices are in keeping with the location, although the page of house selections (from £5.75 a glass) should prevent the bill from spiralling skywards.

Chef/s: Barry Tonks. **Open:** All week B 6:30am to 10:30am (7.30 to 11 Sat and Sun). Mon to Fri L 12pm to 2.30pm, D 6pm to 10pm. **Closed:** 24 Dec to 3 Jan, bank hols. **Meals:** alc main courses £15 to £24. Set L £14.50 (2 courses) to £19.50.. **Service:** 12.5% (optional). **Details:** Cards accepted. 80 seats. Air-con. Separate bar. Wheelchair access. Music. Children allowed.

Club Gascon

Perfect showcase for southern-French cooking
57 West Smithfield, EC1A 9DS
Tel no: (020) 7796 0600
www.clubgascon.com
⊖ Farringdon
French | £48
Cooking score: 6

🍶 V

For ten years Club Gasgon has stood beside St Bartholomew's Priory Church in Smithfield Square, yet Pascal Aussignac's cooking still feels as original and exciting as it did when it first opened. The dining room exudes conviviality, exotic flower displays enliven the marble walls and close-together tables, and service is 'charming and sure-footed'. Aussignac's grazing menu has strong roots in southwest France (from where many of the high class ingredients are sourced), and is

Bjorn van der Horst La Noisette

Why did you become a chef?
Life's circumstances really, but I also find profound joy in pleasing others, teaching and training.

Which of today's chefs do you admire?
Alain Passard and Alain Ducasse for very different reasons. The first for passion and elegance, the latter for leadership and business sense.

What's the best dish you've ever eaten?
I had a Zarzuela sort of Catalan-style bouillabaisse in a village called Cadaques just north of Barcelona once. One of those magical moments when everything was just right. The food, the company and the setting. It doesn't happen often, but when it does even a New York slice could be the best thing in the world and rival any top restaurant.

What's your guilty food pleasure?
Overstuffed bagels.

Who is your favourite producer?
Mother nature.

Which are your proudest achievements?
Seeing the chefs that have worked with me grow and prosper. Two chefs in New York now own their own restaurants.

What's coming up next for you?
Peace. I think I've finally found myself.

divided into sections such as 'la route du sel' or 'les paturages' and so on, with centre stage reserved for items based on foie gras. Even those with high expectations find them fulfilled by the innovative style: superbly balanced morels and broad bean 'ragout' paired unusually with aromatic rice crispies, a pressed duck foie gras with king crab and hot tomato – 'a clever marriage of contrasting flavours and textures' – a thought-provoking glazed black cod served with verijuice, crunchy grapes and pomegranate. Timing is good, textures carefully considered and there is an appealing simplicity to much of the cooking, including, at inspection, a Charolais beef fillet with creamy morels. Among desserts a marinated rhubarb, partnered with an exceptional champagne sorbet and rose Chantilly has proved a perfect finish. The wine list, extending over 25 pages, starts from £18 (£5 per glass), and provides a roll call of the best makers from south-west France. Champagne and Bordeaux do feature but this is a place to sample wines from Irouleguy, Cahors, Madiran, Languedoc, Roussillon and Provence.

Chef/s: Pascal Aussignac. **Open:** Mon to Fri L 12 to 2, Mon to Sat D 7 to 10.30. **Closed:** bank hols. **Meals:** Set L and D £42 and £60. **Service:** 12.5% (optional). **Details:** Cards accepted. 45 seats. Air-con. Wheelchair access. Music. Children's portions. Children allowed.

Comptoir Gascon
Gutsy French cooking
61-63 Charterhouse Street, EC1M 6HJ
Tel no: (020) 7608 0851
www.clubgascon.com
♦ Farringdon
French | £27
Cooking score: 4

V

Pleasingly, Comptoir Gascon continues to be a beacon of *cuisine terrior* and the laid back ambience of this deli-cum-bistro has a sense of *la bonne vie* about it with helpful service full of Gallic charm. The cooking, hailing from southwest France, is as gutsy as the interior (think rough walls and simple wooden furniture) and hard to ignore on the menu is a plate of piggy treats, featuring various parts of the porker. Duck, too, is celebrated, appearing in various guises from Gascony pie to the 'wicked' confit *a la diable*, and its fat is used to cook the irresistible fries. Veal comes in the form of the loin, head and deep-fried brains – the richness tamed by French cornichon to balance the flavours. Nor is seasonality ignored, a plate of white asparagus bolstered by basquaise (red pepper) dressing is a lighter option. Large portions mean that it's tempting to skip dessert, but the lemon tart is worth leaving room for 'prior to Herculean strength coffee'. It's all resolutely regional, right down to the wines, which start at £14.

Chef/s: Julien Carlon. **Open:** Tue to Sat 12 to 2, 7 to 10. **Closed:** Christmas to New Year. **Meals:** alc (main courses £8.50 to £13.50). **Service:** 12.5% (optional). **Details:** Cards accepted. 30 seats. Air-con. Wheelchair access. Music.

Le Coq d'Argent
Rooftop dining in the City
No. 1 Poultry, EC2R 8EJ
Tel no: (020) 7395 5000
www.coqdargent.co.uk
⊖ Bank
French | £47
Cooking score: 1

Two express lifts whisk diners from street level to this rooftop restaurant where there's a wow factor about the setting and the option of alfresco eating in fine weather increases the attraction. The predominance of wood, stone, steel and glass gives a masculine city edge, softened only by the roof terrace greenery. At inspection, a dish of thyme roasted stone bass fillet with white bean casserole and caper dressing demonstrated that the kitchen knows how to treat fish, while six roast salt marsh lamb cutlets (served with creamed ratatouille pesto, black olives and rosemary jus) were tender, tasty and served perfectly pink'. Highlight, though, was a warm bitter chocolate fondant exposing a rich runny middle, and a classic tarte Tatin served with the

'smoothest' calvados ice-cream. The star attraction, however, is the good value and extensive wine list with something for all pockets; house wines start at £15.

Chef/s: Mickael Weiss. **Open:** Mon to Fri L 11.30 to 3.00, D 6 to 10. Sat D only 6 to 10. Sun L only 12 to 3. **Meals:** alc D (main courses £18.50 to £25). Set L and D £24.00 (2 courses) to £28.50 (3 courses). **Service:** 12.5% (optional). **Details:** Cards accepted. 150 seats. 56 seats outside. Air-con. Music.

The Don
Versatile and intelligent destination diner
The Courtyard, 20 St Swithin's Lane, EC4N 8AD
Tel no: (020) 7626 2606
www.thedonrestaurant.co.uk
⊖ Bank
Modern European | £45
Cooking score: 2

Named after the Sandeman Port 'Don' whose cellars occupied the premises for over 170 years, this chic City restaurant is set in a courtyard, like its sister restaurant Bleeding Heart (see entry). The striking very twenty-first century dining room is the setting for some refined modern European cooking that makes sound use of luxury and more humble ingredients. The shortish carte may open with baked scallops with asparagus, tomato and lime sauce, go on to main courses of roast duck with confit leg and glazed root vegetables, and finish with tarte Tatin of pineapple and black pepper with rhubarb ice cream. The bistro has a separate menu promising more straightforward dishes. Wines are given star treatment here, with big names peppered throughout the 50-page list. There are also plenty of more modest bottles, with eight house wines from the proprietor's own Trinity Hill wines (from £16.95).

Chef/s: Matt Burns. **Open:** Mon to Fri 12 to 3, 6 to 10.30. **Closed:** bank hols. **Meals:** alc (main courses £13 to £25). **Details:** Cards accepted. 120 seats. Air-con. No music. Wheelchair access.

The Fox Public House

City gastropub open for week-day dining
28 Paul Street, EC2A 4LB
Tel no: (020) 7729 5708
www.thefoxpublichouse.com
⊖ **Old Street**
Gastropub | £25
Cooking score: 3

V

As former chef at The Eagle – London's original gastropub – and author of two defining cookbooks on gastropub cooking, Australian Trish Hilferty knows a thing or two about the genre. The Fox, too, has won plaudits for its simple, rustic cooking that puts the emphasis on seasonality and provenance. Away from the boisterous bar, the upstairs dining room is surprisingly dark, its chandeliers, wax-splattered candelabras and gloomy wood interior oddly reminiscent of a nineteenth-century Gothic novel. The set menu keeps things simple with a choice of five or so starters and mains. Descriptions are straight to the point and avoid the need to scream their sourcing credentials: a starter of smoked mackerel with pickled beetroot was exactly that – a great tranche of meaty fish unapologetically unadorned. Roast onglet with terrific fat chips and pungent aïoli was gargantuan in size and packed a great big meaty punch. Desserts reinforce the simplicity of approach and might include buttermilk pudding with poached rhubarb. A good, varied wine list starts at £13.50, with around half available by the glass.
Chef/s: Araldo de Vitas. **Open:** Mon to Fri 12 to 3pm, 6.30 to 11pm. **Meals:** Set L and D £16.50 (2 courses) to £21.50. Bar L menu available. **Service:** 12.5% (included). **Details:** Cards accepted. 35 seats. 25 seats outside. Separate bar. No music. Children allowed.

Refettorio at The Crowne Plaza Hotel

An Italian yardstick for the City
19 New Bridge Street, EC4V 6DB
Tel no: (020) 7438 8052
www.refettorio.com
⊖ **Blackfriars**
Italian | £37
Cooking score: 2

 V

The minimalist interior of this darkly stylish dining room is somewhat disarming given the no-holds barred approach to the cooking, which is firmly Italian. The kitchen knows its techniques. Star attractions are the convivium selections of cheeses and cold meats designed for shared eating and the fresh, homemade pasta. Fish and meat are cooked with precision and excellent timing, say a first course of ox tongue with honey potato bread, served with marinated button onions, and Ligurain style halibut with grass peas and mild vinegar dressing. Sweet ricotta cheesecake with candied fruits is a good way to finish. Champagne apart, wines are a cleverly succinct range of entirely Italian bottles. Considering its location, prices start fairly modestly – a decent range of by-the-glass is available, and bottles open at £15, but extravagant tastes are well looked after, with top-end Chianti and Piemontese Nebbioli.
Chef/s: Mattia Camorani. **Open:** Mon to Fri L 12 t 2.30, Mon to Sat D 6 to 10.30 (10 Fri and Sat). **Closed:** Christmas, bank hols. **Meals:** alc (main courses £16 to £22) Set L and D £45 to £65. **Service:** 12.5% (optional). **Details:** Cards accepted 80 seats. Air-con. Separate bar. Wheelchair acces Children's portions.

Rhodes Twenty Four

Quality cooking and capital views
Tower 42, 25 Old Broad Street, EC2N 1HQ
Tel no: (020) 7877 7703
www.rhodes24.co.uk
⊖ **Liverpool Street**
Modern British | £41
Cooking score: 5

Once the escalators, lifts, security passes and air-port style checkpoints have been negotiated, diners are relieved to find that the designer of the high-flying Rhodes 24 has sensibly decided not to compete with the stunning views over London. Apart from a 'minimum of obligatory modern art', there's nothing to detract from the view through curving windows. Space between tables is perfect for private deal making and service is discreet and considerate. You might think Adam Gray had his work cut out to match the cooking to theses rarefied surroundings, but reporters remain convinced that his interpretation of Gary Rhodes' colloquial English-style is much more than just surface gloss. There is real invention, for one thing: successful dishes have included potted duck with foie gras terrine and burnt orange salad, buttered organic salmon with smoked bacon and oyster champ, and a roasted partridge, which arrived medium-rare with a gamey undertone, served with an outstanding buttered-bacon cabbage and caramelised turnips. While a finger is kept firmly on the pulse of today's taste for robust combinations, desserts are almost nostalgic, with steamed potted dick with honey ice cream and warm custard, raspberry Bakewell tart with raspberry ripple ice cream, and bread and butter pudding among the repertoire of heritage puddings. The imaginative wine list opens at £22, but don't waste time sniffing for bargains, as mark-ups reflect the City location. **Chef/s:** Adam Gray. **Open:** Mon to Fri 12 to 2.30, 6 to 9. **Closed:** Christmas, bank hols. **Meals:** alc (main courses £17.50 to £25). **Service:** 12.5% (optional). **Details:** Cards accepted. 75 seats. Air-con. Wheelchair access. Music.

Saki Bar and Food Emporium

Sublime sushi in a stylish setting
4 West Smithfield, EC1A 9JX
Tel no: (020) 7489 7033
www.saki-food.com
⊖ **Farringdon**
Japanese | £29
Cooking score: 3

 V £30

The Saki food complex is divided into deli, bar and restaurant. The smart and stylish restaurant is in the basement, the concept based on the Kaiseki idea of ordering a number of courses made up of small dishes with the menu divided into categories such as nimono (braised), mushimono (steamed) and oshokuji ('carb-up' dishes). It is a nice idea but 'putting a meal together becomes rather complex'. At inspection, a platter of assorted sushi was outstanding, and brought the likes of mackerel, scallop and sea bass nigiri. Other stand-out dishes included a wispy light lobster tempura, and kakuni, a meltingly tender braised pork dish. There's an impressive list of sake and wines, starting at the £15 mark, and you can also order wine and sake sets to match the 'pricey' tasting menus, which start at £40 for six courses. Service is well-meaning. **Chef/s:** Hiroyuki Saotome. **Open:** Mon to Fri, L 12 to 2.30, Mon to Sat D 6 to 10.30. **Closed:** bank hols. **Meals:** alc (main courses £6.20 to £18.50). Set D £40. **Service:** 12.5% (optional). **Details:** Cards accepted. 100 seats. Air-con. Separate bar. Wheelchair access. Music. Children allowed.

Searcy's

A fitting pit-stop for arts lovers
Level 2, Barbican Centre, Silk Street, EC2Y 8DS
Tel no: (020) 7588 3008
www.barbican.org.uk
⊖ **Barbican**
British | £30
Cooking score: 2

V

Situated on the second level of the Barbican Centre, Searcy's affords good views of this historic part of London, perhaps best enjoyed on a summer evening before taking in a play. Jane Collins offers a pre- and post-theatre menu, as well as the main carte, and it's all up-to-the-minute cooking that piles on the style. Stone bass accompanied by Jerusalem artichoke, fennel and broad beans is a typically robust main course, while meat eaters might be drawn to rosemaried Welsh lamb with spring greens, onion purée and sweetbread croquettes. Precede these dishes with salt cod ravioli, or a plate of Italian cured meats with pickles and truffled pecorino and, if time permits, conclude proceedings with ricotta and ginger tart, served with figs and 'honey crunch'. The single-page wine list offers a good mixture, with prices from £16.60, or £4.25 a glass.

Chef/s: Quentin Fitch. **Open:** Mon to Sat, 10 to 10.30 (Sat from 5). **Meals:** alc (main courses £14.50 to £24.50). Set D £24.50 (2 courses) to £28.50. **Service:** 12.5%. **Details:** Cards accepted. 120 seats. Air-con. Separate bar. No mobile phones. Wheelchair access. Music. Children's portions.

ALSO RECOMMENDED
▲ Mehek
45 London Wall, EC2M 5TE
Tel no: (020) 7588 5043
www.mehek.co.uk
⊖ Moorgate

This upmarket Indian restaurant in the heart of the City aims to make an impact with lavishly theatrical décor. The kitchen similarly hopes to impress with a menu that is broad in scope, dipping into the different regions of the Subcontinent for inspiration. King prawn puri (£5.70) lines up alongside sheek kebab (£3.70) and malai chops (£5.90) among starters, while a wide choice of main courses encompass tandoor-cooked spiced squab (£12.90), tender, cinnamon-infused lamb shank (£12.50) as well as familiar curry-house favourites such as chicken korma (£7.90). Traditional Indian desserts to finish and house wines from £15.

▲ Moshi Moshi
Unit 24, Liverpool Street Station, Broadgate, EC2M 7QH
Tel no: (020) 7247 3227
⊖ Liverpool Street

The conveyor belt defines proceedings in th elite mini-chain of casual Japanese eating places. The original kaiten kitchen in the U is still regarded as the best and the setting is unique – high above Liverpool Street's platforms with views of trains coming and going. Sit at the counter and take your pick from colour-coded plates (£1.20 to £3.50) they pass by; choose from a range of sushi s (nigiri sushi; 10.50, temaki; £8.40, sashimi; £13), or opt for a hot seasonal dish, say, salmon teriyaki (£9), or the tempura selecti (£8.50). Sake is £6 a flask and house wine i £13.80. Closed Sat and Sun.

READERS RECOMMEND
Café du Marche
French
22 Charterhouse Square, EC1M 6AH
Tel no: (020) 7608 1609
www.cafedumarche.co.uk
'Three French restaurants under one roof'

Carnevale
Vegetarian
135 Whitecross Street, EC1 8JL
Tel no: (020) 7250 3452
www.carnevalerestaurant.co.uk
'Tiny, but charming; a gem in the City'

Northbank
Modern British
Millennium Bridge, One Paul's Walk, EC4V 3Ql
Tel no: (020) 7329 9299
www.northbankrestaurant.com
'A fine view with a patriotic menu'

Farmers' markets

'We grow it. We sell it.' That's the ethos behind the burgeoning phenomenon of farmers' markets.

Food markets provide a shop window to the countryside, which is a vital asset for Londoners in particular. Since everything is grown, reared, raised, baked or produced by the person actually selling the stuff, no middlemen are involved: freshness is guaranteed. As a rule, farms must be within 100 miles of the M25 – although many are much closer than that. Overseeing the whole movement is the National Farmers' Retail & Markets Association (FARMA), which assesses and certifies individual producers (visit: www.farmersmarkets.net for more information).

By its nature much of the produce on offer is organic or free-range: rare-breed pork, lamb and beef, geese, chickens and turkeys, venison, pheasants and other game, not to mention all manner of vegetables and fruit (often unusual varieties) depending on the season. You will also find pies and pickles, cakes and cheeses, freshly grown herbs, even oysters and smoked fish in some places.

Champions of cause are fervently campaigning for weekly markets in every major shopping centre in the capital: they can help revitalise urban neighbourhoods and they are a way of generating real local enthusiasm for local produce. Demand from shoppers is certainly rising and there are currently around 30 sites in London – although many of these are still quite modest, intermittent affairs.

Here is a list of the largest and most regular outlets: for more detailed information visit the London Farmers' Markets website at: www.lfm.org.uk.

Acton: High Street/King Street. Sat, 9am-1pm
Blackheath: Railway Station car park. Sun, 10am-2pm
Clapham: Bonneville Primary School, Bonneville Gardens. Sun, 10am-2pm
Ealing: Leeland Road, West Ealing. Sat, 9am-1pm
Finchley Road: O2 Centre car park. Wed, 10am-3pm
Islington: William Tyndale School, Upper Street. Sun, 10am-2pm
Marylebone: Cramer Street car park, off Marylebone High Street. Sun, 10am-2pm
Notting Hill: Kensington Church Street (car park behind Waterstones). Sat, 9am-1pm
Peckham: Peckham Square, High Street. Sun, 9.30-1.30pm
Pimlico Road: Orange Square. Sat, 9am-1pm
Queens Park: Salusbury Primary School, Salusbury Road. Sun, 10am-2pm
Stoke Newington: William Patten School, Stoke Newington Church Street. Sat, 10am-2.30pm
Walthamstow: Selbourne Walk Shopping Centre, Town Square. Sun, 10am-2pm

The Fox and Anchor

Gastropub
115 Charterhouse Street, EC1M 6AA
Tel no: (020) 7253 5075
www.foxandanchor.co.uk
'Smart pub grub in smart, refurbished setting'

The Place Below

Vegetarian
St Mary-le-Bow Church, Cheapside, EC2V 6AU
Tel no: 020 7329 0789
www.theplacebelow.co.uk
'Menu changes daily, with seasonal ingredients'

▌Clerkenwell

Ambassador

Confident, competent cooking stands out
55 Exmouth Market, EC1R 4QL
Tel no: 020 7837 0009
www.theambassadorcafe.co.uk
⊖ Farringdon
Modern British | £26
Cooking score: 2

V

The Ambassador has made a fine job of the open house concept. It's unpretentious, informal, welcoming – all the things that mark out neighbourhood success stories – with smart, well-executed dishes from the kitchen and equally smart service out front. The seasonal menu is both elegant and comforting: the freshness of sea bream ceviche is perfectly accented with a celery and cucumber purée and pickled cucumber, rabbit loin comes with Alsatian bacon and a fresh burst of early summer pea purée, and pork belly is rendered of fat but not of juicy tenderness, and brightened with the flavours of orange and lovage. An adult chocolate pudding with marmalade ice cream is refreshingly bitter. The good wine list is comprehensive and comprises an eclectic mixture of Old and New World (from £14.50), with a wide selection available in carafes (from £9) or by the glass.

Chef/s: Tobias Jilsmark. **Open:** Mon to Fri 9am to 11pm, Sat 11am to 11pm, Sun 11am to 4pm. **Closed:** 24 December to 2 January. **Meals:** alc (main courses from £10 to £14). Set L £12.50 to £16. **Details:** Cards accepted. 60 seats. 25 seats outside. Air-con. Separate bar. Wheelchair access. Music. Children's portions.

Bleeding Heart

A favourite for Francophile diners
The Cellars, Bleeding Heart Yard, Greville Street, EC1N 8SJ
Tel no: (020) 7242 8238
www.bleedingheart.co.uk
⊖ Farringdon
French | £32
Cooking score: 2

The address is so named after a seventeenth-century *belle dame* who was rather gruesomely dismembered here by one of her rejected lovers. There is an inn and an informal bistro in the vicinity now, with a smart, ambitious French restaurant in the basement. Here, Christophe Fabre took over in 2007, but maintains the tone set by his predecessor. The bilingual menus deal in salmon confit with black olive coulis and cherry tomatoes, or venison fillet with cabbage and bacon in bitter chocolate sauce. Not all is textbook French, as is attested by a starter that dresses seared tuna salad with rice wine, soy and ginger, but terrine of foie gras with homemade brioche will reorientate you, as will desserts such as hazelnut praline with raspberry coulis or tarte au citron. The proprietors own the Trinity Hill vineyard in Hawkes Bay, New Zealand, so the list isn't as Francocentric as you may be expecting. Indeed, its broad and generous compass makes for fine worldwide drinking. New Zealand prices start at £16.95, or £4.50 a glass, for the Trinity Hill Sauvignon.

Chef/s: Peter Reffell. **Open:** Mon to Fri 12 to 2.30, 6 to 10.30. **Closed:** bank hols. **Meals:** alc (main courses £12.45 to £22.95). **Service:** 12.5%. **Details:** Cards accepted. 150 seats. 30 seats outside. Air-con. Separate bar. No music.

Clerkenwell Dining Room

Bank on culinary dexterity
69-73 St John Street, EC1M 4AN
Tel no: (020) 7253 9000
www.theclerkenwell.com
⊖ Farringdon
Modern British | £32
Cooking score: 3

Andrew Thompson's confident modern British cooking sets this quietly civilised restaurant apart from its nearby rivals in trendy Clerkenwell – despite its unpromising location on the ground floor of an office block. The modern, simply decorated dining room with parquet flooring and cream and blue colour scheme is an elegant and comfortable space, while the kitchen delivers gutsy, bold dishes that are big on flavour through good handling of great raw ingredients. Expect starters in the modern vein, perhaps oxtail ravioli with red wine jus, ballotine of foie gras with fig jam, Muscat jelly and toasted brioche, or squid with polenta and spicy tomato and pepper sauce. Well-constructed main courses extend to pork belly with scallops, celeriac purée and walnut salsa, or perhaps sea bream accompanied with steamed mussels and orange velouté. Finish with hot chocolate fondant with black forest ice cream, poached pear tart with blackberry sorbet, or a selection of British and French farmhouse cheeses. The well-chosen wine list favours Europe over the New World, with prices from £15.
Chef/s: Daniel Groom. **Open:** Mon to Fri 12 to 2.30, Mon to Fri D 6 to 10.30 (Sat 7 to 11). **Meals:** Set L and D £37.50. **Service:** 12.5% (optional). **Details:** Cards accepted. 110 seats. Air-con. Wheelchair access. Music. Children's portions. Children allowed.

Coach and Horses

British cooking in a no-nonsense setting
26-28 Ray Street, EC1R 3DJ
Tel no: (020) 7278 8990
www.thecoachandhorses.com
⊖ Farringdon
Gastropub | £30
New Chef

The Coach and Horses is a no-frills pub that's deservedly popular with locals. The separate dining room can feel somewhat spartan but is run by friendly and knowledgeable staff and the kitchen knows how to treat high quality British ingredients. The techniques and presentation on display are simple but effective. To start, there is smoked mackerel from Mersea Island with a light but potent horseradish cream and chicory, or a salad of beetroot with fresh goat's curd and peppery watercress. A crisp potato cake filled with blue cheese is served with a poached duck egg, and leg of rabbit is roasted with tarragon. The real treats are on the dessert menu: rhubarb queen of puddings 'stickily sweet', served with a 'spectacular' marmalade ice cream and thick wedges of toasted brioche. There's a basic but tempting bar menu and an interesting wine list. House wine is £12.50.
Chef/s: Nick Leonard. **Open:** Mon to Fri L 12 to 3, Sat D 6 to 10, Sun 12 to 3.. **Closed:** 24 Dec to 2 Jan, bank hols. **Meals:** alc (main courses £10 to £14.50).. **Service:** 12.5%. **Details:** Cards accepted. 60 seats. Wheelchair access. Music. Children's portions. Children allowed.

Eagle

Pioneering Farringdon gastropub
159 Farringdon Road, EC1R 3AL
Tel no: (020) 7837 1353
⊖ Farringdon
Gastropub | £26
Cooking score: 2

V £30

Michael Belben's ground-breaking East London gastropub virtually defined the genre and it continues on its merry way, serving food and drink in a bare-boarded room with deconstructed, mismatched furniture and abundant greenery. The short menu is chalked on a board above the bar and it comprises around a dozen dishes with no conventional distinctions between 'starters' and 'mains'. Here you will find spring vegetable minestrone and Kirkham's Lancashire cheese with pickles sharing the bill with full-blooded dishes like Venetian-style calf's liver with onions, red wine vinegar, parsley and toast or roast pollack with purple sprouting broccoli, anchovy, chilli and aïoli. Bifeana (marinated rump steak sandwich) has been on the menu since the very beginning, likewise pasties de nata (Portuguese custard tarts). A modest choice of tapas is also available. Beer drinkers get their fill and everything on the minimal wine list is available by the glass. Bottle prices start at £11.75.

Chef/s: Ed Mottershaw. **Open:** all week L 12.30 to 3 (3.30 Sat and Sun), Mon to Sat D 6.30 to 10.30. **Closed:** 1 week Christmas, bank hols. **Meals:** alc (main courses £8.50 to £18.00). **Service:** not inc. **Details:** Cards accepted. 65 seats. 24 seats outside. Wheelchair access. Music. Children's portions.

Flâneur

Accomplished deli dining
41 Farringdon Road, EC1M 3JB
Tel no: (020) 7404 4422
www.flaneur.com
⊖ Farringdon
French | £24
Cooking score: 2

⏣ **V**

This hybrid deli/restaurant is almost a foodie theme park. Oversized chairs (à la Mad Hatter's tea party) and blond wood barrel-like light fittings add to the surreal feeling of dining while surrounded by floor-to-ceiling racks of interesting food. The daily changing menu includes charcuterie, cured fish platters, and salads such as watercress, pear, almond and Roquefort. Mains take in pan-fried mackerel with smoked paprika, garlic and parsley, and a 'gutsy' fish stew, the accompanying rouille 'luxuriously flavoured with saffron'. Puddings

are predominantly cakes – many displayed in the deli section. A hazelnut chocolate tart, for example, comes with sweet, crisp pastry. The wine list is largely French but includes some New World names, with bottles from £13 and a good selection available by the glass from £4.

Chef/s: Simon Phelan. **Open:** 8am to 11. **Closed:** 25 Dec to 2 Jan. **Meals:** Set menu 2 courses £19.50, 3 courses £24.50. **Service:** 12.5% (optional). **Details:** Cards accepted. 72 seats. 9 seats outside. Air-con. No music. Wheelchair access. Children's portions. Children allowed.

Medcalf

Straightforward subtle cooking
40 Exmouth Market, EC1R 4QE
Tel no: (020) 7833 3533
www.medcalfbar.co.uk
⊖ Farringdon
Modern British | £30
Cooking score: 4

Don t be fooled by the scruffy décor of wobbly chairs and scuffed tables – Medcalf serves simple and well-prepared cooking with a strong British flavour and an eye for the seasons; appropriate for premises that used to house a butcher s. And while it might blur the line between bar and restaurant, its cool and casual vibe suits its buzzy Exmouth Market surrounds to a tee. Starters range from duck and pork rillette, say, or salt cod fish cakes with poached egg, to salads such as smoked chicken and bacon, while watercress is a popular accompaniment, typical of the gutsy nature of much of the menu: a winter main course might be game pie with celeriac purée and brussel tops. But the kitchen is capable of subtlety, too: the same menu could deliver sweet seared scallops with tomato and saffron vinaigrette, for instance, and Barbary duck breast served alongside roasted sweet potato purée and tomato and cardamon jus. British cheeses with oatcakes and chutney lead the dessert list, and there s chocolate fondant with raspberry ripple ice cream or pear and frangipane tart. Roasts of rib of beef and leg of lamb are served at Sunday lunch, followed by treacle tart. House white is £13.50 on the short Franco-Spanish wine list, and there are interesting beers, such as the sour cherry-flavoured Liefmans Kriek from Belgium. **Chef/s:** Brent Taylor. **Open:** all week L 12 to 3 (4 Sat and Sun), D 6 to 10. **Closed:** bank hols, 25 Dec to 2 Jan. **Meals:** alc (main courses £10 to £14). **Service:** 12.5%. **Details:** Cards accepted. 60 seats. 20 seats outside. Air-con. Wheelchair access. Music. Children allowed.

Moro

Buzzy, relaxed hotspot
34-36 Exmouth Market, EC1R 4QE
Tel no: (020) 7833 8336
www.moro.co.uk
⊖ **Farringdon**
Spanish | £27
Cooking score: 4

V

More than a decade since it first opened, Moro still rocks, continuing to draw a savvy cosmopolitan crowd who crank up the decibels at this Exmouth Market champion. The laid-back, no-frills, open-plan space comes with few decorative flourishes and something of a canteen buzz, its hard surfaces doing battle with the sounds and aromas of an open-to-view kitchen, chatter from the long zinc-topped bar (where tapas is served throughout the day) and the hubbub of an upbeat dining room. Polished floorboards, serried ranks of informally set, closely packed tables, plain walls and round pillars all have their say too. But it is Sam and Sam Clarks' cuisine that really plays to the gallery. Its blend of Spanish and Moorish influences comes full of interest and big on flavour, though not without a few lapses. Driven by well-sourced produce and unfussy execution, the kitchen's wood-fired oven or charcoal grill inspires many dishes on the weekly changing menu. Take wood-roasted Middlewhite pork teamed with chard, new potatoes and romesco aïoli, or perhaps charcoal-grilled grey mullet served with lemon and bay butter and a broad bean, tomato and grilled red onion salad. To finish, perhaps the yoghurt cake with pistachios and

pomegranates might catch the eye, while the wine list is a resolutely Spanish-bias affair, headed by an impressive line up of sherries and house wine from £12.50. **Chef/s:** Sam and Sam Clark. **Open:** Mon to Sat L 12.30 to 2.30, D 7 to 10.30. **Meals:** alc (main courses £14.50 to £17). Tapas menu available. **Service:** not inc. **Details:** Cards accepted. 96 seats. 12 seats outside. Air-con. No music. Wheelchair access. Children's portions.

St John

Nose-to-tail dining
26 St John Street, EC1M 4AY
Tel no: (020) 7251 0848
www.stjohnrestaurant.com
⊖ **Farringdon**
British | £30
Cooking score: 6

V

Terse, sometimes eccentric descriptions make the twice-daily changing menu at St John a fun read: snails and oak leaf or brill, bread and green sauce, for example, are as described, but the results are magic: dazzling produce – often British – resplendently unadorned. Chef Fergus Henderson's 'nose-to-tail' culinary philosophy sees offal figure high, an approach that certainly appeals to the hardcore, dare we say macho, foodie. But it would be a shame not to sample, say, ox heart and celeriac, chitterlings and chips, or the signature bone marrow and parsley salad. Excellent game, rare breed meats, and lesser-spotted cuts (Bath chaps, spleen etc) – all entirely in keeping for an establishment on Smithfield Meat Market's doorstep – are popular choices, but don't ignore the 'softer' options of seafood or salads. Old-fashioned puds like rhubarb trifle or burnt cream make a fitting climax. St John has legion admirers, but one reader (and self-confessed fan) reports disappointedly this year of 'brusque service' and second-best menu substitutions, bewailing the high price charged for 'a small piece of meat with some lukewarm beetroot'. Though portions aren't usually ungenerous, the line between no-frills presentation and parsimony might be too fine for some. Similar caveats should be raised about the décor; to some the former smokehouse's white walls and floors, and its schoolroom chairs will be the height of cool; to others it will be plain spartan. Wine on the all-French list starts at £15. Note that there's also a friendly bar and excellent in-house bakery.

Chef/s: Fergus Henderson and Trevor Gulliver. **Open:** Mon to Fri L 12 to 3, Mon to Sat D 6 to 11. **Closed:** Christmas, Easter. **Meals:** alc (main courses £12.50 to £21.50). **Service:** not inc. **Details:** Cards accepted. 105 seats. Air-con. No music. No mobile phones.

ALSO RECOMMENDED

▲ Little Bay

171 Farringdon Road, EC1R 3AL
Tel no: (020) 7278 1234
www.little-bay.co.uk
⊖ Farringdon

Modern bistro-style food at low prices is the defining feature of this unpretentious restaurant on the edge of an increasingly fashionable part of London. A flat price for each course rises by a pound or two after 7pm, so starters become £2.95, main courses £7.95 and desserts £2.95. Imagination has not been entirely constrained by the budget, alongside familiar starters such as mussels marinière, expect duck, figs and cranberry terrine and salmon fillet served with spicy coconut potatoes, with pears in red wine with vanilla pannacotta for dessert. Roasts every Sunday. Other branches now operate across London in Battersea, Kilburn and Fulham. House wine £10.90. Open daily.

READERS RECOMMEND

Pho

Vietnamese
86 St John Street, EC1M 4EH
Tel no: (020) 7253 7624
'A plethora of flavours; a real gem'

St Germain

French
89 Turnmill Street, EC1M 5QU
Tel no: 020 7336 0949
www.stgermain.info
'Classic French comfort food'

■ Hackney

Empress of India

Outstanding addition to the Hackney scene
130 Lauriston Road, E9 7LH
Tel no: (020) 8533 5123
www.theempressofindia.com
⊖ Mile End
Gastropub | £26
New Chef

£30

Close to Victoria Park, this is not a tandoori but a smart new brasserie from Tom and Ed Martin (see entries for the Gun and White Swan) – reincarnated from a former existence as a florist and nightclub. In twenty-first-century 'gastro' style, the restaurant, all wood floors and cream fabric blinds, elides into the long zinc bar cooled by vast brass fans above. Menu choices are sensibly selective and simple, ingredients are excellent – including breads, unsalted butter and proper espresso. Starters range from Vichysoisse with soft boiled quail egg and battered monkfish with aïoli; lunchtime specials span old Irish favourites like boiled gammon with colcannon and parsley sauce, to fish and chips with minted purée. At dinner Cornish fish stew with samphire or roast suckling pig raises the kitchen's game. Cooking is very competent. The attractive wine list trawls the world from classic champagnes and burgundies to the stars of southern Italy, Iberia and the New World. A fine choice of wines by the glass from £3.30; bottles from £14.00

Chef/s: Kane Planken. **Open:** L Mon to Fri 12 to 2.30 (Sat all day), D 7 to 10 (Sat 10.30). **Closed:** Christmas, Boxing day. **Meals:** alc main courses

£9.50 to £22.50. **Service:** 12.5%. **Details:** Cards accepted. 60 seats. 24 seats outside. Air-con. Wheelchair access. Music. Children's portions.

READERS RECOMMEND

Buen Ayre

Argentinian
Broadway Market, E8 4QJ
Tel no: (020) 7275 9900
www.buenayre.co.uk
'Scintillating steak house in Hackney'

Hoxton: see Shoreditch

Limehouse

The Narrow

Ramsay's take on a British pub
44 Narrow Street, E14 8DP
Tel no: 020 7592 7950
www.gordonramsay.com
⊖ Limehouse
Gastropub | £23
Cooking score: 3
£30

Currently vying with the Ivy as London's hardest to book restaurant, Gordon Ramsay's first pub venture occupies a pretty Edwardian dockmaster's house overlooking the Thames. It's a good-looking pub, a useful venue for the local community of yuppies – decent pubs, or restaurants for that matter, not being thick on the ground in Limehouse. The spacious riverside terrace pulls the fair-weather drinking crowd from the large, basic bar, while pub classics such as ploughman's, sausage roll with HP sauce, or half a pint of prawns are among the offerings for anyone who gets peckish. Those lucky enough to have secured a reservation, head for the pretty, raftered dining room – the diminutive size explains the pressure on tables – for some robust, unfussy cooking of regional British food. At inspection that included potted Morecambe Bay shrimps, tasty, tender, braised Gloucester pig cheeks served with a pile of mashed neeps, and a very rich baked custard with Goosnargh cakes. Service is exemplary – the right mix of casual and on-the-ball – and reasonable prices extend to the wine list, where house French kicks off at £13.50. Good range of real ales and bottled beers, too.
Chef/s: John Colllin. **Open:** Mon to Fri L 11.30 to 3, D 6 to 10; Sat. 12 to 10; Sun, 12 to 9. **Meals:** Main courses £9 to £14.50. **Service:** 12.5%. **Details:** Cards accepted. 32 seats. 100 seats outside. Separate bar. Wheelchair access. Music. Children allowed. Car parking.

READERS RECOMMEND

The Grapes

Seafood
76 Narrow Street, E14 8BP
Tel no: 020 7987 4396
'Fresh fish in a Dickensian setting'

Shoreditch

Bacchus

Global gastronomy lands in Hoxton
177 Hoxton Street, N1 6PJ
Tel no: (020) 7613 0477
www.bacchus-restaurant.co.uk
⊖ Old Street
Modern European | 40
Cooking score: 6
V

Bacchus may be the god of wine but here in Hoxton he's also the deity of ambrosial food realised in the sublime cooking of Nuno Mendes. A widely travelled Portuguese chef, Nuno worked at El Bulli in Spain and Jean-Georges in New York before settling in London by way of Tokyo. His truly original touch combines the subtlest flavours of East and West, underpinned by a mastery of sous-vide, low temperature cooking techniques. To get a glimpse, the express lunch menu (Monday – Friday) is a good intro at £22. At dinner,the six-course tasting menu rises to a wholly different level. An appetiser of the most intensely flavoured sea-green English pea purée with hazelnut crumble and Enoki

mushrooms is an indelible memory, so too the sous-vide pork jowl which is brilliantly partnered by langoustine and slivers of black radish. A great fish dish of obviously both Japanese and Iberian influence is the warm cod with 'paella paint' (squid ink?), tomato hearts, wafer-thin potatoes and garlic. Or as thoughts turn to red wine, the slow-cooked lamb shoulder with fragrant kappa curry leaf and goat's cheese is inspired by the chef's spell in Thailand. Finally, some heavenly desserts particularly those showing a mastery of sweet and savoury tastes, as in a classic financier cake flavoured with black olive, served with roasted pear ice cream, fig purée and pine nuts reduced in milk and cream. Wines are suitably Bacchanalian: seriously good reds and whites by the glass from £5, and a deftly selective range of classic and new wave wines by the bottle, strongest for quality and value in Italy and Spain: the Clos de Torribas, Penedes, Crianza 2003 is a snip at £21 – for something special, the Hamilton Russell Chardonnay 2005 from South Africa (£40) is exceptional. Great informal atmosphere in this uncluttered make-over from a Victorian pub – linen jackets and jeans *de rigueur,* and charming staff who are knowledgeable and watchful.
Chef/s: Nuno Mendes. **Open:** all week 6 to 12.
Meals: Set D £30 (6 courses) to £40 (9 courses).
Service: 12.5%. **Details:** Cards accepted. 50 seats.
Air-con. No mobile phones. Wheelchair access.
Music. Children's portions. Children allowed.

Eyre Brothers

For elaborate Iberian, go East
70 Leonard Street, EC2A 4QX
Tel no: (020) 7613 5346
www.eyrebrothers.co.uk
⊖ Old Street
Mediterranean | £52
Cooking score: 2

In an edgy but trendy corner of Shoreditch, this light, buzzy room with friendly, likeable staff points to an impressive start from the brothers who brought us The Eagle. This is, however, a step up from gastropub ambitions.

On the menu could be white bean and pancetta soup to start, a 'finely executed' grilled veal chop, or 'three enormous and delicious' tiger prawns for mains, with montada of raspberries making a simple but 'stunning end'. The wine list is a relative bargain and Iberia happily dominates. There are several considered choices by the glass starting at £3.75, and for the more discerning there are informed additions from France and Argentina. An outstanding white Rioja 2001 seemed a steal at £24. Not surprisingly, the list is also strong in the sherry and port departments, again with a number available by the glass.
Chef/s: David Eyre and João Cleto. **Open:** Mon to Fri L 12 to 3, Mon to Sat D 6 to 11 (6.30 Sat). **Closed:** bank hols, Christmas, New Year. **Meals:** alc (main courses from £10 to £21). **Service:** 12.5% (optional). **Details:** Cards accepted. 75 seats. Air-con. Separate bar. Wheelchair access. Music. Children allowed.

Fifteen

Jamie O's bright take on Italian cooking
15 Westland Place, N1 7LP
Tel no: (0871) 330 1515
www.fifteenrestaurant.com
⊖ Old Street
Italian | £60
Cooking score: 3

The urban warehouse setting is as bright and breezy as Jamie Oliver's TV persona. On the ground floor is an all-day trattoria where you can pop in for coffee, or tuck into the likes of linguine alla carbonara or rib eye with porcini butter. The main dining room is below. Here the menu makes a virtue of simplicity, offering prosciutto with Italian black figs and leaves, and even pasta dishes can be as straightforward as ravioli of Scotch beef in a light marjoram broth. An occasional braise, such as 12-hour cooked rare-breed pork with fresh cannelloni beans in a light tomato sauce takes its place alongside the principle cooking techniques: pan-frying (scallops wrapped in pancetta) and chargrilling (leg of lamb). To finish there may also be chocolate and orange parfait, while

Rooms with a view

There's nothing like a view to add the final flourish to an outstanding meal.

Le Coq D'Argent

Renowned for its top-of-the-world roof garden, which has panoramic views over the Square Mile and the City skyline.

Galvin at Windows

Arguably the last word in 'fine dining with a view', Chris Galvin's reincarnation of the 28th floor of the London Hilton oozes big-city glamour. You can even peek into Her Majesty's backyard.

Inn the Park

An elegant construction of wood and glass by the lakefront in one of London's most beautiful parks – no wonder this is a dream ticket for al fresco eating with views for free.

National Portrait Gallery

A feast for the eyes, whether you are perusing the celebrated canvases or chilling out in the family-friendly rooftop restaurant overlooking Trafalgar Square.

Oxo Tower

Take the lift to the eighth floor of the Tower, which rises like a beacon above the South Bank. The restaurant provides A-list chic at high altitude.

Plateau

High on the fourth floor of the Canada Square building, this dazzling, futuristic glass structure has the bonus of great views across the lawns and sculptures of Canada Square.

Le Pont de la Tour

A glamorous riverside rendezvous 'par excellence'. The best views of Tower Bridge are from the waterfront terrace; at night, watch the fairy lights twinkle along this sought-after stretch of the Thames.

Roast

The razzamatazz of Borough Market is one of the absorbing delights visible from the windows of this new champion in the British food renaissance.

Rhodes 24

You need a head for heights if you want to sample the food in Gary Rhodes' venue on the 24th floor of the old Nat West building. Drink in expansive, jaw-dropping views from the restaurant's curving windows.

Skylon

The punning title refers to the iconic 1951 sculpture that was a star attraction outside the old Royal Festival Hall. Level 3 has been transformed. Its floor-to-ceiling windows are tailor-made for Thames-watchers.

Send your reviews to: www.which.co.uk/gfgfeedback

'good service' creates 'a fantastic eating experience'. The wine list is a global, but pricey affair – bottles open at £21 – but there's fair choice by the glass from £6.

Chef/s: Andrew Parkinson. **Open:** trattoria all week L 12 to 3, D 6 to 10 (5.30 to 9.30 Sun); restaurant all week L 12 to 2.30, D 6.30 to 9.30. **Meals:** trattoria alc (main courses £15 to £18); restaurant alc L (main courses £17.50 to £23.50). Set D £60. **Service:** 12.5% (optional). **Details:** Cards accepted. 65 seats. Air-con. Wheelchair access. Music. Children's portions.

Great Eastern Dining Room

Gastronomic survey of a continent
54-56 Great Eastern Street, EC2A 3QR
Tel no: (020) 7613 4545
www.greateasterndining.co.uk
⊖ **Old Street**
Asian | £43
Cooking score: 3

The Hoxton outpost of Will Rickers's ever-expanding pan-Asian empire offers a buzzing introduction to the genre. The dining room is achingly hip, the atmosphere, convivial. The menu certainly adds to the feeling that this is group meal territory rather than dinner for two, but staff are friendly and keen to help those less familiar with the myriad choices. A selection of dim sum hits the ground running, being fresh and impressive, while a red curry comes deeply flavoured with beautifully tender beef, and salt and pepper squid is 'cooked perfectly'. The pan-Asian staple dessert of chocolate fondant with green tea ice cream rounds things off nicely. The wine list is fashionable, as you might expect, with some unusual selections such as Grüner Veltliner featured, and a wide selection of wines by the glass starting at £3 (£13 a bottle), as well a serious cocktail list.

Open: Mon to Fri L 12 to 3pm, Mon to Sat D 6.30 to 11pm. **Meals:** alc (main courses £7 to £19.50). Set L and D £22.50 (2 courses) to £45. Bar menu available. **Service:** 12.5% (optional). **Details:** Cards accepted. 65 seats. Air-con. Separate bar.

Rivington Grill

No-frills British cooking
28-30 Rivington Street, EC2A 3DZ
Tel no: (020) 7729 7053
www.rivingtongrill.co.uk
⊖ **Old Street**
Modern British | £31
Cooking score: 3

From the Caprice Holdings stable, the Rivington comes tucked away in a one-time warehouse-style building in upbeat Shoreditch. A large bar, whitewashed walls and stripped-wood floors create an easy-going mood, while off to one side, the dining area is bright and well set out. The relaxed, buzzy, unbuttoned mood is picked up by the menu's theme; no frills, back-to-basics British cooking driven by quality seasonal produce. Think fish fingers and chips, lamb chop with bubble and squeak, or perhaps roast pork served with 'crisp' crackling and a 'tangy' apple sauce. There is no over complication or pretension here, just admirably straightforward, honest flavours. Desserts are equally comforting, perhaps a treacle tart or 'rich' chocolate moouse, and, while wines may nudge toward the expensive side, they kick off at a pocket-friendly £15 before plateauing off at £85. (There is also a Rivington sibling in Greenwich.)

Chef/s: Simon Wadham. **Open:** Mon to Fri, L 12 to 3, Mon to Sun D 6.30 to 11 (10.30 Sun). **Meals:** alc main courses £9.75 to £27.50. **Service:** optional. **Details:** Cards accepted. 120 seats. Air-con. No music.

	Symbols
🛏	Accommodation is available.
£30	Three courses for less than £30.
V	More than five vegetarian dishes.
♀	Free glass of wine voucher scheme.
🍷	Notable wine list.

★ BEST BUDGET RESTAURANT ★

Viet Grill
Astonishing value
58 Kingsland Road, E2 8DP
Tel no: (020) 7739 6686
www.vietgrill.co.uk
⊖ Old Street
Vietnamese | £15
Cooking score: 2

V

Before we begin, this restaurant is not situated
in the most salubrious part of town (think
more urban grime, less Hoxton glamour), but
it is certainly worth the expedition to extreme
northern climes. A sleek, bright room defies
all the canteen stereotypes often associated
with Vietnamese dining. Decadent birdcages
hang in draped windows and dark wood is
offset with patterned wallpapers. At
inspection, a mango, chilli and calamari salad
was absolutely outstanding. Summer rolls
were fresh and fragrant – it's hard to believe
that you're eating £3 plates at this level.
Dishes with names such as 'feudal roasted
beef' and 'stuffed swimming crabs' entice and
delight in equal measure. Other successful
mains included a duck curry with lemongrass
and coconut milk; the gloriously tender meat
falling off the bone. On a pedantic note, red
wine is served in comedy half-bottle glasses
(rectified with a standard white wine glass
upon request). The service is offhand, but
efficient. Mind you, it's easy to forgive them
for having bunked off charm school at these
prices.
Chef/s: Vinh Vu. Open: Mon to Thu, L 12 to 3 D 5.30
to 11, Fri and Sat L 12 to 3 D 5.30 to 11.30, Sun 12 to
10.30. Closed: Christmas. Meals: Mains £4 to £12.
One-dish meal £6.. Service: 10%. Details: Cards
accepted. 80 seats. Air-con. Music. Children
allowed.

ALSO RECOMMENDED
▲ Cru
2-4 Rufus Street, N1 6PE
Tel no: (020) 7729 5252
www.cru.uk.com
⊖ Old Street

Located in a warehouse, this eaterie is also
home to the White Cube Gallery, but it's
brunch that sees the Hoxton folk flocking in at
weekends – try porridge with bananas and
maple syrup (£4.50), or kippers with roasted
potatoes and spinach (£6.75). At other times
the restaurant serves starters of panfried
scallops with tomato and chilli (£8.50), with
mains ranging from Buccleuch ribeye steak
(£16), via burger with chips (£11.75) to a
shared platter such as pork cassoulet with
seasonal roast (£39 for two). Finish with
marzipan pannacotta with lavender biscuits
(£5.50). The bar downstairs is a welcome stop
for tapas and a beer. Wines from £15. Closed
Mon.

READERS RECOMMEND
Brickhouse
Modern European
Old Truman Brewery, 152c Brick Lane, E1 6RU
Tel no: (020) 7247 0005
www.thebrickhouse.co.uk
'Fine dining with cabaret to boot'

Cay Tre
Vietnamese
301 Old Street, EC1V 9LA
Tel no: (020) 7729 8662
www.vietnamesekitchen.co.uk
'Vietnamese food prepared with gusto'

Hoxton Apprentice
Modern British
16 Hoxton Square, N1 6NT
Tel no: (020) 7749 2828
www.hoxtonapprentice.com
'Training restaurant in a Victorian building'

Pinchito Tapas

Spanish
32 Featherstone Street, EC1Y 8QX
Tel no: (020) 7490 0121
'Hip tapas restaurant on Old Street.'

▌Spitalfields

Canteen

Market setting for modern Brit classics
2 Crispin Place, E1 6DW
Tel no: (0845) 686 1122
www.canteen.co.uk
⊖ **Liverpool Street**
Modern British | £25
Cooking score: 3

There's something of the American artist
Edward Hopper about the long stretch of plate
glass through which you can see plainly laid
out wood tables and booth seating – the style
echoing the clean lines of 1930s American
diners. But there's not a burger in sight. Right
in the heart of Spitalfields Market, Canteen is
one of those places that has creatively
redefined what we expect of eating out. It's
open all day for a flexible menu of modern
Brit classics at great prices – no wonder there
are queues at weekends. Eggs Benedict with
'perfect, rich hollandaise' from the all-day
breakfast menu vies for attention with potted
duck with piccalilli, and potted shrimps on
the starters list. Gammon with plain boiled
potatoes and parsley sauce is a well-praised
main, or you could opt for the meat pie of the
day. Deliberately saving room for dessert
rewards with an apple crumble with
'amazingly rich, creamy vanilla flecked
custard'. Service is on the ball, and a sound
choice of wines by the glass opens a decent
selection that's almost evenly divided between
France and the rest of the world. Prices
from £12. A second branch of Canteen is to be
found at the Royal Festival Hall on the
Southbank, with a third opening planned
shortly.

Chef/s: Cass Titcombe. **Open:** all week 11 (9 Sat and
Sun) to 11. **Closed:** 25 and 26 Dec. **Meals:** alc (main
courses £7 to £12.50). **Service:** 12.5% (optional).
Details: Cards accepted. 50 seats. Air-con. No
music. Wheelchair access. Children's portions.

St John Bread & Wine

The upper crust of British dining
94-96 Commercial Street, E1 6LZ
Tel no: (020) 7251 0848
www.stjohnbreadandwine.com
⊖ **Liverpool Street**
Modern British | £30
Cooking score: 3

A spinoff of the original St John (see entry
above), this venue is a bakery, wine shop and
deli, as well as somewhere to eat, just opposite
Spitalfields market. The atmosphere is as
casual as at its elder sibling, and the British
food will warm the cockles of your heart.
Smoked sprats and horseradish is a good way
to start, or you might take the plunge and go
for the potted squirrel (no, really). As the
evening draws on, main dishes come into play,
perhaps beef forerib with celeriac and
mustard, or black bream with cabbage. You
might opt to wait 15 minutes at the end of it
all, while the kitchen rustles you up a plate of
madeleines (sold by the dozen or half-dozen,
like oysters), or there are baked egg custard, or
rhubarb fool, on offer. Cheeses are great too.
Nothing could be more British than an all-
French wine list, and here is one, starting with
vins de pays at £15.20, and motoring up to a
1992 premier cru Puligny-Montrachet
at £110.

Chef/s: James Lowe. **Open:** all week Mon to Thu
9am to 11pm (10am to 11pm Sat, 10am to 6pm Sun).
Closed: Christmas and Easter. **Meals:** alc (main
courses £13 to £14.30). **Service:** not inc.
Details: Cards accepted. 56 seats. Air-con. No
music.

ALSO RECOMMENDED

▲ Leon
3 Crispin Place, E1 6DW
Tel no: 020 7247 4369
www.leonrestaurants.co.uk
⊖ Liverpool Street

Spitalfields outpost for this likeable mini-chain of central London eateries (also at Carnaby Street, The Strand, Brompton Road and Ludgate Circus), which offer Allegra McEvedy's appealing, fresh take on fast food. With a mix of North African and Mediterranean ideas, the predominantly repertoire offers healthy, seasonal dishes that make good use of organic and free-range ingredients. Call in for power smoothies, organic porridge (£2) or a bacon sandwich (£2.40) for breakfast, savour Moroccan meatballs (£5.50), flatbread wraps, or a grilled chicken salad (£5.50) at lunch, while evening grazing and sharing menus take in hot mezzes (£1.50-£4.30) and daily specials like green pea curry and chicken tagine (£4.90).

Tower Hill

Café Spice Namaste
A sweep of opulent Asian flavours
16 Prescot Street, E1 8AZ
Tel no: (020) 7488 9242
www.cafespice.co.uk
⊖ Tower Hill
Indian | £45
Cooking score: 2

V

Cyrus Todiwala's modern, vibrant pan-Asian cuisine is as fresh as ever. Start with beetroot and coconut samosa or cholya prawn chappati (a Nepalese-style dish of diced prawns with chopped shallots, ginger, chilli and tomato in a chapatti coated with date and tamarind chutney then pan-grilled). Main courses include a lengthy selection from the tandoor – from familiar chicken tikka to chargrilled marinated king prawns with garlic pulao and light, green coconut curry, and numerous vegetarian dishes – perhaps paneer tikka sagwala or water chestnut and sweetcorn masala. Wines start at £15.50.
Chef/s: Cyrus Todiwala. Open: Mon to Fri L 12 to 3, Mon to Sat D 6.15 to 10.30. Closed: 25 Dec to 1 Jan, bank hols. Meals: alc (main courses £12.50 to £18.50). Service: 12.5% (optional). Details: Cards accepted. 140 seats. 80 seats outside. Air-con. Wheelchair access. Music. Children's portions. Children allowed.

Wapping

Wapping Food
Ultra-hip culinary powerhouse
Wapping Hydraulic Power Station, E1W 3ST
Tel no: (020) 7680 2080
www.thewappingproject.com
⊖ Wapping
Modern European | £29
Cooking score: 3

♀

Housed in a former hydraulic power station, Wapping Food is one impressive-looking restaurant, in a cavernous space where changing art installations are also on show. The menu offers a sprightly mix of Italian, Spanish, and Pacific Rim influences, delivering fresh, zingy flavours in unaffected, easy-to-like combinations. Buffalo mozzarella with anchovies, fennel, chilli, and garlic, or seared scallops, chickpeas, and aubergine, and chargrilled Welsh Black sirloin, parsnip purée and roast garlic, are typical. If you're amenable to something a bit different, the all-Australian wine list (from £16) is real delight; if you're not, you might get short shrift.
Chef/s: Cameron Emirali. Open: Mon to Sat 12 to 11 (from 10 Sat), Sun 10 to 6. Closed: Christmas and Bank Holidays. Meals: Set L and D £45.
Service: 12.5%. Details: Cards accepted. 150 seats. 35 seats outside. Air-con. Separate bar. No mobile phones. Wheelchair access. Music. Children allowed. Car parking.

Whitechapel

ALSO RECOMMENDED
▲ Kasturi

57 Aldgate High Street, EC3N 1AL
Tel no: (020) 7480 7402 / (020) 7481 0048
www.kasturi-restaurant.co.uk
⊖ Aldgate

Don't be put off by the the definition of
'kasturi' as a strong-smelling secretion found
in rare musk deer; a glance at the menu reveals
appetising Indian specialities from the
northwest of India. Ginger-flavoured lamb
chops (£5.50) and main courses such as mild
chicken and cashew curry flavoured with
saffron (£8.95) and knuckles of lamb cooked
with cardamom (£9.95) are typical.
Vegetarians are well served by a broad
selection – baby aubergine with peanut and
poppy seeds (£3.95), for example – with
chicken tikka massala (£8.95) and chicken or
lamb Madras or vindaloo (£7.95). House wine
is £13.95. Closed Sun.

SOUTH

Balham, Battersea, Bermondsey,
Blackheath, Borough: see London Bridge,
Clapham, Dulwich, Greenwich, Kennington,
London Bridge, Putney, South Bank,
Southwark, Tooting, Vauxhall, Waterloo,
Wimbledon

Balham

Amici

Family-friendly Italian venue
35 Bellevue Road, SW17 7EF
Tel no: (020) 8672 5888
www.amiciitalian.co.uk
Italian | £27
Cooking score: 2

V

Celebrated gastro-diva Valentina Harris lends her considerable experience to this sociable 'bar and Italian kitchen' overlooking Wandsworth Common. Amici lives up to its 'friendly' name and it regularly plays to full houses. Crowds congregate under the shade of olive trees when the weather is kind; at other times, the spacious dining room provides an animated setting for robust food with sound credentials. The menu opens with starters like fennel and lemon soup with gremolata or octopus terrine, ahead of salmon baked 'in cartoccio' with dry Vermouth, basil and mint butter or corn-fed chicken breast with roast pepper gratin, pine nut and Vin Santo jus. Desserts are Italian standards such as tiramisu, sgroppino and coffee pannacotta with zabaglione. The drinks list is packed with glamorous cocktails, with support provided by some keenly priced Italian wines. House selections start at £13 a bottle (£9.25 for a 50cl 'pot', £3.50 a glass).
Chef/s: Paolo Zanca. **Open:** Mon to Fri 12 to 3, 6 to 10.30, Sat and Sun 11 to 4, 6 to 10.30 (9.30 Sun). **Closed:** 25 and 26 Dec. **Meals:** alc (main courses £8.50 to £15). **Service:** 12.5% (optional). **Details:** Cards accepted. 40 seats. Air-con. Music. Children's portions.

Please send us your feedback

To register your opinion about any restaurant listed in the Guide, or a new restaurant that you wish to bring to our attention, please visit the web address at the bottom of the page. Your feedback informs the content of the book and will be used to compile next year's reviews.

Chez Bruce

Exquisite Anglo-French cooking
2 Bellevue Road, SW17 7EG
Tel no: (020) 8672 0114
www.chezbruce.co.uk
⊖ Balham
Modern European | £45
Cooking score: 6

Bruce Poole's eponymous restaurant is a shining beacon of excellence in south-west London. The restaurant has its drawbacks: the room is cramped, particularly in the evening, with too many tables squashed into a small space; the chairs are uncomfortable and the decibel levels are brasserie-like – this is not a restaurant of hushed appreciation. However, the Guide's post bag is bursting with praise from appreciative diners. Poole's style of cooking marries classical French technique with the very best that the larder of England and Europe has to offer, be they pigs trotters or truffles. At a recent dinner, an elegant and restrained starter of English asparagus cooked just-so and enlivened by the addition of Joselito ham and parmesan was surprisingly overshadowed by a really gutsy melange of chicken wings, duck hearts and snails with parsley purée. Main courses which followed included an old-fashioned blanquette of pork, given the necessary lift with a pungent choucroute and a perfectly cooked roast cod with olive oil mash, served with grilled, marinated mediterranean vegetables. The prix-fixe menu formula makes a necessity of the dessert course and from a classic crème brûlée to a more adventurous millefeuille of pistachio and valrhona chocolates served with griottine cherries, they're exemplary. And so to the wine list: as befits the restaurant's status, the cellar is magnificent, with a huge global wine list touching top Meursaults and Bordeaux grands crus as well as magnificent Australian and American offerings. But where the menu pricing may look very reasonable, the wines seem rather more expensive, though the paucity of wines by the glass is relieved by a generous selection by the half bottle.

Chef/s: Bruce Poole and Matthew Christmas. **Open:** Mon to Fri 12 to 2, 6.30 to 10.30, Sat 12.30 to 2.30, 6.30 to 10.30, Sun 12.30 to 3, 7 to 10. **Closed:** 24 to 26 Dec, 1 Jan. **Meals:** Set L Mon to Fri £23.50, Set L Sat £27.50, Set L Sun £32.50, Set D £37.50. **Service:** 12.5% (optional). **Details:** Cards accepted. 75 seats. Air-con. No music. Wheelchair access. Children's portions.

READERS RECOMMEND

Gurkhas Diner
Nepalese
1 The Boulevard, Balham High Road, SW17 7BW
Tel no: (020) 8675 1188
www.gurkhasdiner.co.uk
'Try the chuli dishes, cooked over charcoal'

Harrison's
French
15-19 Bedford Hill, SW12 9EX
Tel no: 020 8675 6900
www.harrisonsbalham.co.uk
'Kid-friendly outpost for the Soho House group'

Lamberts
Modern British
2 Station Parade, SW12 9AZ
Tel no: 020 8675 2233
www.lambertsrestaurant.com
'Legendary Sunday roasts and kid-friendly too'

Polish White Eagle Club
Polish
211 Balham High Road, SW17 7BQ
Tel no: (020) 8672 1723
www.whiteeagleclub.co.uk
'Try the pierogi and herring platters'

Readers recommend

A 'readers recommend' review is a genuine quote from a report sent in by one of our readers. We intend to follow up these suggestions throughout the year to come.

▮ Battersea

Greyhound
Destination restaurant disguised as a pub
136 Battersea High Street, SW11 3JR
Tel no: (020) 7978 7021
www.thegreyhoundatbattersea.co.uk
Modern European | £44
Cooking score: 3

Holding onto its credentials as a public house by virtue of the big, open bar area at the front of the premises, The Greyhound leaves the awkwardly shaped extension at the rear to discerning diners. Best use is made of the space, with colour and clever lighting creating a certain uniformity, wallpaper and plants carving out more intimate spaces, the kitchen just visible at the end. Alessio Brusardin took over the stoves in March and has adjusted the menu to fit his style, but the ambition and intricacy of the dishes remain intact as does the gargantuan size of the portions: a starter of panfried scallops produces four fat, beautifully cooked bivalves divided by wafer thin croutons, served on brunoise cut peppers and a thick gaspacho sauce; a dish of black pork loin served fashionably pink arrives with accompanying pork belly and black pudding as well as sweet potato & spinach. Quality is high, but some of the combinations, like duck breast interlaced with foie gras are too rich for all but the most hardy. Quirky puddings like passionfruit tiramisu and chocolate tortellini with black pepper ice cream are worth a look, but more important is the huge wine list. Wine is proprietor Mark Van Der Goot's passion and the wine list is encyclopaedic in length and global in concept, and starting at £3.10 for a decent sized glass of something drinkable, very affordable.
Chef/s: Diego Sales. **Open:** Tue to Sun L 12 to 3, Tue to Sat D 7 to 10.30. **Closed:** Christmas and New Year. **Service:** 12.5%. **Details:** Cards accepted. 34 seats. 20 seats outside. Separate bar. Wheelchair access. Music. Children allowed.

Ransome's Dock

Assured cooking beside the Thames
35-37 Parkgate Road, SW11 4NP
Tel no: (020) 7223 1611
www.ransomesdock.co.uk
⊖ South Kensington
Modern European | £33
Cooking score: 4

A fine-weather riverside terrace overlooking the old docks between Albert and Battersea Bridges is one of the major draws at Martin and Vanessa Lam's enduring neighbourhood restaurant. The kitchen is known for its loyalty to regional British produce, although most of its culinary inspiration comes from across the Channel. Warm Lincolnshire smoked-eel fillets are served with buckwheat pancakes and crème fraîche, Devon-reared Creedy Carver duck breast might appear with apple sauce, red cabbage and fondant potato, while noisettes of Rhug Estate organic lamb could be accompanied by a thyme and Syrah sauce. Daily fish specials are also worth noting: sea bass with asparagus, pea and broad bean risotto or medallions of monkfish with creamy lobster sauce and pennette, for example. Rhubarb fool is English nostalgia at its best; otherwise the kitchen roams around for prune and Armagnac soufflé (a fixture dessert) and labneh (strained yoghurt) with mango in orange blossom syrup. Saturday brunch attracts crowds of weekend tourists and chillout locals, while the style-conscious global wine list provides something to suit most palates and preferences. Top-notch labels from California, France and Italy grab the attention, along with expertly chosen 'Ransome's Dock Selections' from £13.95 a bottle. The list also provides some fine drinking by the glass (from £4).
Chef/s: Martin and Vanessa Lam. **Open:** all week 12 to 5 (3.30 Sun), Mon to Sat D 6 to 11. **Closed:** Christmas, 1 Jan and Aug bank hol. **Meals:** alc (exc Sat and Sun L; main courses £7.25 to £21.50). Set L £15 (2 courses). **Service:** 12.5% (optional).

Details: Cards accepted. 56 seats. 24 seats outside. No mobile phones. Wheelchair access. Music. Children's portions. Car parking.

★ BEST VALUE RESTAURANT ★

Tom Ilic

Imaginative, gutsy, big on flavour cooking
123 Queenstown Road, SW8 3RH
Tel no: 020 7622 0555
www.tomilic.com
Modern British | £25
Cooking score: 4

There s no doubt that Tom Ilic s eponymous restaurant looks and feels more like a neighbourhood bistro than a serious restaurant. The plain double dining room with its bare tables and homely pot plants would not necessarily lead one to expect this standard of cooking, but in bringing together the best ingredients in the daily market and combining them on a menu that is short, imaginative and very reasonably priced, serious intent is apparent. Tom Ilic has, after several false steps, set up on his own in familiar territory (Ilic was a chef here a decade ago, when the premises were known as the Stepping Stone) and is happily belting out his brand of imaginative, gutsy, big on flavour cooking. He flaunts his passion for meat cookery with starters such as braised pig s cheeks and chorizo with garlic and parsley mash and mains of slow-cooked beef with roasted bone marrow, caramelized root vegetables and garlic bread. But equally well considered have been fish dishes like the hand-picked crab tortellini with shellfish nage and seared mackerel with horseradish soufflé that opened a good value Sunday lunch in early January. That meal went on to deliver with deceptive and effortless flair rump of lamb with perfect mash and spinach, a belting squab pithivier with savoy cabbage and lentil cream, and ended with a quite outstanding sticky toffee pudding the best I have ever had . The manageable wine list is helpfully categorised by style. Prices start at £13.

Chef/s: Tom Ilic. **Open:** Wed to Fri and Sun L 12 to 2.30 (3.30 Sun), D Tue to Sat 6 to 10.30. **Closed:** 25 to 29 Dec. **Meals:** alc (main courses £9.75 to £13.50). Set lunch £12.50 (2 courses). Set Sun lunch £14.50 (2 courses). **Service:** not inc. **Details:** Cards accepted. 55 seats. Wheelchair access. Music. Children's portions. Children allowed.

ALSO RECOMMENDED
▲ Butcher and Grill
3941 Parkgate Road, SW11 4NP
Tel no: (020) 7924 3999
www.thebutcherandgrill.com

Bullishly carnivorous in style, this Battersea young-blood combines a butcher's shop and deli with a laid-back bar and child-friendly restaurant. Meat from the owners' farm dominates proceedings, with everything from grilled steaks and new season's lamb cutlets (£19) to burgers and bespoke sausages. Alternatively, opt for the fish of the day or a main course like salt-and-pepper duck breast with crushed Jersey Royals and sweet black bacon sauce. Start with duck rillettes (£6) or tea-smoked quail with steamed aubergine salad, and finish with profiteroles or poached peaches and elderflower sorbet (£5). Keenly priced modern wines from £13.50 (£3.50 a glass). Open Mon to Sat 12 to 3.30 and 6 to 11, Sun 12 to 4.30

▌Bermondsey
Delfina
Inventive cooking and an art gallery
50 Bermondsey Street, SE1 3UD
Tel no: (020) 7357 0244
www.delfina.org.uk
⊖ London Bridge
Global | £41
Cooking score: 4

A converted, one-time chocolate factory provides the colourful space for this Bermondsey restaurant-cum-art gallery. The vast white-walled, high-ceilinged, ground-floor (with artists' studios above) is a bright affair, with plenty of light from windows and skylight and large blocks of colour from modern art. Floors are honey-coloured wooden boards and the furniture is fittingly modern and stylish, with well-spaced tables decked out with lime-green tops. Opening times may be limited (lunchtimes and Friday evenings) but invention abounds, the ambitious modern approach peppered with some unusual ingredients and combinations. Take aubergine, cherry tomato, red onions and a mint-parsley salad with tahini dressing as the accompaniment for a main-course of chargrilled, smoked, paprika-marinated lamb, or maybe ginger-braised Puy lentils and roasted beetroot alongside pan-fried calf's liver. Desserts continue the theme, with a chocolate malva pudding teamed with frangelico ice cream, while the compact but interesting wine list is also a global affair, with prices setting out at £13.50 to plateau at £58, and there are plenty on offer by glass too.
Chef/s: Maria Elia. **Open:** Mon to Fri L 12 to 3, Fri D 7 to 10. **Closed:** 23 Dec to 2 Jan. **Meals:** alc (main courses £10 to £14). **Service:** 12.5% (optional). **Details:** Cards accepted. 140 seats. Wheelchair access. Music.

Le Pont de la Tour
Stunning river views
36d Shad Thames, SE1 2YE
Tel no: (020) 7403 8403
www.conran.com
⊖ Tower Hill
French | £35
Cooking score: 3

🍷 V

Panoramic views of Tower Bridge and the London skyline will always come with a hefty price tag. Le Pont de la Tour certainly isn't cheap, but it manages to deliver the goods with enough finesse and old-fashioned elegance to warrant the bill. Pale yellow walls, white tablecloths and bow-tied waiters add to the French-style setting. The carpeted restaurant has an air of occasion, while the adjoining brasserie with its seafood bar is more of a relaxed, noisy affair. Accomplished French cooking with a British twist completes the

continental experience. Starters included a fishy crab, tomato and avocado tian, or guinea fowl tortellini with wild mushroom and tarragon. Mains extend from poached skate, black rice and sauce vierge, to calf's liver, pomme purée and sauce diable. Finish off with a signature dessert of champagne jelly, berries and crème Chantilly. The hefty 80-page wine list dedicates 22 pages to French varieties, but also takes in small wine-producing countries such as Slovenia and England (a lone Chapel Down Reserve is listed here). It notably features a good selection of rare and exceptional wines, some available in larger formats, such as jeroboams and imperials. Or, if you're budgeting, you could pick up a decent bottle starting at around £19.
Chef/s: James Walker. **Open:** all week 12 to 3, 6 to 11. Brasserie open all day at the weekends. **Meals:** alc D (main courses £17 to £26.50). Set L £30. Bar/grill menu available. **Service:** 12.5% (optional). **Details:** Cards accepted. 100 seats. 72 seats outside. Separate bar. Wheelchair access. Music. Children's portions.

Tentazioni
Modern cooking in an amiable atmosphere
Lloyds Wharf, 2 Mill Street, SE1 2BD
Tel no: (020) 7237 1100
www.tentazioni.co.uk
⊖ London Bridge
Italian | £38
Cooking score: 3
V

Riccardo Giacomini's narrow warehouse restaurant close to Tower Bridge is a likeable place, from the modern paintings on vibrantly coloured walls via the amiable atmosphere to the modern Italian menu. The food may lack a little refinement, but that directness is part of its appeal. The repertoire opens with the likes of goat's cheese and roasted tomato ravioli with pesto sauce, and risotto matecato with foie gras, duck confit and port sauce. Among main courses, fine materials are evident in a robust dish of basil-roasted cod steak served with ratatouille wrapped in a puff pastry and a pepper sauce, while sound technique has

produced a tender mint-crusted rack of lamb with potato timbale and button onions. Meals might end with wild berry pannacotta or a classic tiramisu. In addition, vegetarians are well catered for, and a five course 'degustazione' menu gives an edited version of the à la carte. A diverse bunch of Italian wines make up the intelligent list. In general, mark-ups are reasonable with a house selection opening at £15.
Chef/s: Riccardo Giacomini. **Open:** Tue to Fri 12 to 2.45, Mon to Sat D 6.30 to 10.45. **Closed:** bank hols. **Meals:** Set D £40 (5 courses). **Service:** 12.5%. **Details:** Cards accepted. 65 seats. Air-con. No music. Wheelchair access. Music. Children's portions.

ALSO RECOMMENDED
▲ Arancia
52 Southwark Park Road, SE16 3RS
Tel no: (020) 7394 1751
www.arancia-uk.co.uk
⊖ Bermondsey

Locals show loyalty to Arancia (Italian for orange) for good reason – and its worth knowing about if you are in the neighbourhood. It has a warm décor, a busy atmosphere and a menu that changes weekly. Dishes such as rosemary-stuffed sardines (£4.75), home-made pumpkin gnocchi (£8.80) or delicate fishcakes with green bean salad and pesto (£8.80) can be followed by the likes of belly pork with borlotti beans (£9.75) and a range of desserts such as the popular and rich chocolate semifreddo (just £3) or Italian cheeses (£4.75). Italian wines from £10.50. Closed Sun and Mon.

▲ Village East
171-173 Bermondsey Street, SE1 3UW
Tel no: 020 7357 6082
www.villageeast.co.uk
⊖ London Bridge

This restaurant is the second outlet from the team behind the Garrison gastropub up the road. The warehouse-style conversion is well-suited to the local creative set, featuring a mezzanine and a private dining room. Starters included a parfait of foie gras with pear and tomato chutney at £7.50, and the star of the main courses is undoubtedly Chateaubriand with green beans and château potatoes (to share, £34.80). One report remarked on 'surly service' and our inspector was given a slightly patronising introduction to the grape varieties on the wine list. However, the general vibe is open and relaxed, much like the clientele. House wines start at £14. Open all week.

READERS RECOMMEND

The Garrison
Gastropub
99-101 Bermondsey Street, SE1 3XB
Tel no: 0207 089 9355
www.thegarrison.co.uk
'A fortress for fine gastropub fare.'

Blackheath

Chapter Two
Good value contemporary restaurant
43-45 Montpelier Vale, SE3 0TJ
Tel no: (020) 8333 2666
www.chaptersrestaurants.co.uk
Modern European | £38
Cooking score: 4

The younger sibling of Chapter One (see entry, Farnborough, Kent) is set over two floors, the light and airy ground floor giving way to a larger, dramatically dark basement. Regulars are effusive in their praise, delighted with 'outstanding' cooking 'at prices you couldn't hope to imagine in the centre of the capital'. The set menu (which varies in price, but not content, between lunch and dinner) is comforting and modern. Trevor Tobin keeps the kitchen pretty well to a seasonal rhythm, in early June, for example, offering a salad of Kentish asparagus (with sweet and sour onions and sauce mousseline), and pea velouté with crushed peas and deep-fried haddock. Among main courses you might expect skate accompanied by oxtail ragu, beetroot, spinach and cauliflower purée , or braised shoulder of English lamb with spring vegetables, white

bean purée and jus gras. To finish, go for mille-feuille of coconut pancake served with poached yellow peaches and nutmeg ice cream, or baked vanilla yoghurt with iced rhubarb crumble and citrus rum baba. A selection of eight wines by the glass, £4.15 to £4.75, is available from a pleasingly varied list starting at £16.
Chef/s: Trevor Tobin. **Open:** all week 12 to 2.30, 6.30 to 10.30. **Closed:** 2 to 5 Jan. **Meals:** Set L £15.95 (2 courses) to £19.95, Set D Sun to Thur £18.45 (2 courses) to £23.50, Set D Fri and Sat £24.50. **Service:** 12.5% (optional). **Details:** Cards accepted. 75 seats. Air-con. No music. Wheelchair access.

Borough: see London Bridge

Clapham

Trinity Restaurant
New restaurant with serious ambition
4 The Polygon, Clapham Old Town, SW4 0JG
Tel no: (020) 7622 1199
www.trinityrestaurant.co.uk
⊖ Clapham Common
Modern European | £33
Cooking score: 2

Chef-proprietor Adam Byatt's return to Clapham, where he first made his mark with the fondly remembered Thyme, has been greeted with almost universal delight. Rather than re-introducing haute grazing, whch was Thyme's trademark, dining is now strictly à la carte. Byatt is capable of good things: his charcuterie is impeccable and the choice of whole joints for sharing at Sunday lunch (prior booking by previous Thursday required) suggests Byatt's fondness for meat is worth bearing in mind when ordering. Yet, though the menu invariably reads enticingly and ticks all the right fashionable boxes with its choice of modish ingredients and techniques, inspection found perfect balance is not always struck within the dishes. The highlight was a simple escabeche of mullet with saffron aïoli and basil from the light lunch menu, which had vibrant, well-judged flavour. Desserts mask beautiful ingredients such as Alphonso mango by playing too hard with myriad mousse and ice shots. The thoughtful, if relatively highly priced, wine list opens at £16.50.

Chef/s: Adam Byatt. **Open:** L Tue to Sun 12.30 to 2.30, D Mon to Sun from 6.30. **Closed:** L Mon. **Meals:** alc main courses £15 to £25. **Service:** optional. **Details:** Cards accepted. 60 seats. Air-con. Separate bar. Wheelchair access. Children allowed.

Tsunami

Reliable Japanese cooking
5-7 Voltaire Road, SW4 6DQ
Tel no: (020) 7978 1610
www.tsunamirestaurant.co.uk
⊖ **Clapham North**
Japanese | £34
Cooking score: 2

Sitting cheek-by-jowl with Clapham's railway sidings, this well-liked restaurant does good business with its unflashy Japanese cooking. Appetisers and sharing plates head the lengthy menu: enjoy a succession of appealing, freshly prepared items including chicken and cabbage gyoza dumplings or Nobu-inspired yellowtail sashimi with jalapeño in yuzu ponzu sauce. Moving on there are oysters every which way (try the 'shooter' with sake, ponzu, momiji oroshi, quail egg and scallion), salads and tempura (including mixed vegetarian versions with sweet potato, lotus root and shiitake mushrooms). Main courses and specials feature 'toban' claypots as well as chargrilled lamb with wasabi pepper sauce and hira unagi (grilled marinated eel). Sushi appears traditionally at the end of the menu, with nigiri and hand rolls involving everything from sea urchin to salmon skin. Beers and cocktails figure on the drinks list, along with assorted wines from £12 (£3.75 a glass).

Chef/s: Ken Sam. **Open:** Mon to Fri 6 to 11, Sat 12.30 to 11, Sun 1 to 9. **Closed:** 3 days Christmas, 31 Dec, 1 Jan. **Meals:** alc (main courses £6.50 to £16.50). **Service:** 12.5% (optional). **Details:** Cards accepted. 100 seats. Air-con. No music. Children's portions.

READERS RECOMMEND

Santa Maria del Sur

Argentinian
129 Queenstown Road, SW8 3RH
Tel no: (020) 7622 2088
www.santamariadelsur.co.uk
'A first-rate steak house'

▋ Dulwich

Franklins

Friendly one-time pub
157 Lordship Lane, SE22 8HX
Tel no: (020) 8299 9598
www.franklinsrestaurant.com
British | £38
Cooking score: 2

♟

On a busy East Dulwich thoroughfare the blue-tiled frontage picks this buzzy, unbuttoned neighbourhood brasserie-cum-bar out from the crowd. Run the gauntlet of the bar to reach the airy dining room beyond, which is decked out with darkwood chairs, white paper-clad tables and bare-brick walls hung with large mirrors. The kitchen deals in carefully sourced seasonal produce (and some lesser-used ingredients) delivering a plain, unfussy, traditional style, its earthiness perfectly echoing the surroundings. Take chitterlings with chicory and snails as an opener, for instance, or tripe, saffron and mash, with Old Spot pork belly, beetroot and dandelion to follow. Puddings hit a homely nod too, with maybe Eton Mess, a chocolate pot, or strawberry tart to further strain the waistband. Menus come short on adjectives but not on flavour, with the carte backed by value fixed-price lunch, while the compact wine list has France in ascendancy and opens at £12.50.

Chef/s: Philip Greene. **Open:** all week 12 to 12. **Closed:** 25 and 26 Dec, 1 Jan. **Meals:** Set L and D Mon to Fri £11.50 (2 courses) to £15. Bar menu available. **Service:** not inc. **Details:** Cards accepted. 60 seats. 20 seats outside. Air-con. Separate bar. No mobile phones. Wheelchair access. Music. Children's portions.

The Green

A versatile and lively brasserie
58-60 East Dulwich Road, SE22 9AX
Tel no: (020) 7732 7575
www.greenbar.co.uk
Modern European | £30
Cooking score: 2

'Friendly, welcoming and contemporary' is how this Dulwich eaterie styles itself, a multi-mode establishment that functions as a bar, café and brasserie-style dining room, with a touch of modern art gallery thrown in for good measure. Eclectic cooking takes in everything from salmon, ginger and coriander fishcakes to glazed foie gras with black pudding, apple sauce and toasted brioche to start, followed by fillet of beef with red wine sauce, Cajun chicken Caesar salad, or pan-fried sea bass with sorrel and watercress sauce. Live jazz every Thursday evening adds to the buzz, and there's also a monthly opera night. House red and white at £10.50 a bottle, £4.25 a glass, open a straightforward, value-conscious wine list.

Chef/s: Damien Gillespie. **Open:** all week 9 to 11.30pm. **Closed:** 1 Jan. **Meals:** Set L £11.95. **Service:** 10% (optional). **Details:** Cards accepted. 120 seats. 35 seats outside. Separate bar. Wheelchair access. Music. Children's portions.

Which? Campaigns

To find out more about Which? food and drink campaigns, please visit:
www.which.co.uk

ALSO RECOMMENDED
▲ Le Chardon

65 Lordship Lane, SE22 8EP
Tel no: (020) 8299 1921
www.lechardon.co.uk

Occupying a listed Victorian building with decorative thistle tiles, Le Chardon offers an authentic French bistro experience. The wide-ranging menu takes in starters of snails in garlic butter, moules mariniere, and fishcakes with sweet chilli sauce, as well as classic cheese-topped French onion soup. Meat main courses might feature lamb shank with lemon and mint couscous, while fish dishes typically include roast sea bass with grilled fennel and an orange and lemon dressing. An open patio to the rear allows for alfresco dining. Wines are mostly French, as you'd expect, with house red and white at £10.95 a bottle, £3.85 a glass.

▌Greenwich
Inside

Local eaterie with big ideas
19 Greenwich South Street, SE10 8NW
Tel no: (020) 8265 5060
www.insiderestaurant.co.uk
Modern European | £38
Cooking score: 1

♀

Close to Greenwich station, this converted former shop is the kind of friendly restaurant every neighbourhood should have. Simple décor and a lively atmosphere provide the ideal setting for some inventive modern cooking. An international outlook brings starters ranging from lobster and salmon cannelloni with broad beans, tomato and basil, to five-spice chicken, coriander and coconut spring rolls, while mains take in seared Moroccan-spiced salmon with lemon couscous, and roast chump of lamb with Puy lentils, red cabbage, roast parsnips and rosemary jus. Spiced chocolate tart with roast almond ice cream is among original dessert ideas. Eight wines by the glass from £3.25 open an international list with house French red and white at £11.95.

Best neighbourhood deli's

London's deli's are many and varied. They might stock speciality groceries, make you a sandwich NYC-style, sell you a home-made pork pie to take home for dinner, or have tables tucked away for sipping tea and nibbling on freshly baked delicacies.

Daylesford Organic
44B Pimlico Road, SW1W 8LP
A beautifully appointed shop with a sumptuous deli counter selling irresistible (though pricey) produce.

Panzer's 13-19 Circus Road,
St John's Wood, NW8 6PB
A north-west London institution, Panzer's sells produce from all over Europe.

Tavola 155 Westbourne Grove,
Notting Hill, W11 2RS
Alistair Little's Italian deli is deservedly popular with locals.

Manicomio 85 Duke of York Square,
Chelsea, SW3 4LY
Deli-restaurant selling tempting, hard-to-find Italian goods in a light, airy setting.

Polsmak 9 Balls Pond Road, N1 4BW
A little corner of Poland in Dalston.

I Camisa & Sons
61 Old Compton Street, W1D 6HS
The original London deli, still selling a vast range of dried pastas and fine Italian produce.

A Gold 42 Brushfield Street, E1 6AG
Traditional British food shop in an old Spitalfields milliners.

Trinity Stores
5&6 Balham Station Road, SW12 9SG
An enticing range of mostly British and French produce and organic vegetables.

Olga Stores
30 Penton Street, Islington, N1 9PS
Much-loved deli with an encyclopedic range of Italian store cupboard items.

Megan's Deli 571 King's Road, SW6 3EB
Plush, well stocked and efficient Fulham deli with adjoining garden café serving freshly baked cakes, sandwiches and antipasti.

Send your reviews to: www.which.co.uk/gfgfeedback

Chef/s: Guy Awford and Brian Sargeant. Open: Tue to Sun L 12 to 2.30, Tue to Sat D 6.30 to 11. Closed: Christmas. Meals: alc (main courses £11.95 to £17.95). Set L £11.95 (2 courses) to £15.95, Set D £15.95 (2 courses) to £19.95. Service: not inc. Details: Cards accepted. 36 seats. Air-con. Wheelchair access. Music. Children's portions.

Kennington

ALSO RECOMMENDED
▲ Lobster Pot
3 Kennington Lane, SE11 4RG
Tel no: (020) 7582 5556
www.lobsterpotrestaurant.co.uk
⊖ Kennington

Ring a doorbell to gain admittance to a tiny dining room hung with nautical knick-knacks where seagulls cry on the sound system. It sounds like the height of naff but somehow the effect is charming rather than kitsch. The menu is predominantly old-fashioned French, lightened by a few more modern dishes: gratinated oysters with a champagne sauce might be followed by grilled fillet of tuna with a tomato, garlic, chilli and coriander sauce, or, of course, lobster every which way. Grilled fillet of beef with green peppercorn sauce is one of five or so meat mains – while classic desserts include crêpes. A short wine list leans towards whites from Burgundy and the Loire; house wine is £12 a bottle. Note that between 8 and 10pm there is a minimum spend of £23 per person.

London Bridge
Champor-Champor
Riotous décor and bold Asian cooking
62-64 Weston Street, SE1 3QJ
Tel no: (020) 7403 4600
www.champor-champor.com
⊖ London Bridge
Malaysian | £43
Cooking score: 3

The name roughly translates as 'mix and match', which applies equally to the food and the décor in this idiosyncratic restaurant. Diners sit in what looks like an anthropologist's den stuffed with tribal masks carvings, a portly Buddha and other weird ethnic artefacts. The food is dubbed 'creative Malay-Asian': traditional village (kampong) cooking is the jumping-off point, but influences and ingredients are garnered from the Far East and beyond. Crabmeat and Asian chive toast with yellow pickled water chestnuts could open proceedings, alongside braised ostrich sausages in Szechuan pepper and miso. Next comes a palate-cleansing 'inter-course' granita before stir-fried kangaroo fillet in chilli oil, petai (an exotic legume) and egg noodles or cassava, ginko nut and preserved Chinese plum tagine with garlic shoot pilau and parsnip crisps. Desserts are equally riotous concoctions like green tea jelly topped with coconut custard, warm pineapple and brandy pajery. The drinks list includes Asian-Pacific beers and spirits, plus a neat selection of global wines with bottles from unlikely sources including Georgia. Prices start at £14.
Chef/s: Adu Amran Hassan. Open: Mon to Sat D only 6.15 to 10.15. Closed: 6 days Christmas, 4 days Easter, bank hols. Meals: Set D £23.50 (2 courses) to £27.90 (3 courses) Tasting £42.50.
Service: 12.5%. Details: Cards accepted. 38 seats. Air-con. Wheelchair access. Music. Children allowed

	Symbols
	Accommodation is available.
	Three courses for less than £30.
V	More than five vegetarian dishes.
♀	Free glass of wine voucher scheme.
	Notable wine list.

Magdalen

Lively newcomer showcasing honest British cooking
152 Tooley Street, SE1 2TU
Tel no: (020) 7403 1342
www.magdalenrestaurant.co.uk
⊖ **London Bridge**
British | £28
Cooking score: 4

James and Emma Faulks have transformed this double-decker restaurant just a short walk from London Bridge station. The atmosphere is informal, staff are charming and the food is straightforward, displaying a fondness for robust, hearty dishes as well as a strict regard for seasonality and for top quality produce. Dishes are simply described on the daily changing menu and the geographical provenance of dishes is easy to spot: potted Devon crab, roast pheasant with braised red cabbage, chestnuts and bacon, and treacle sponge pudding and custard fly the flag for England. But there are dishes in the modern vein too, say hot foie gras and caramelised blood orange, or fried squid with tartare sauce. Cooking tends toward the unadorned (or plain , if you will), so among main courses might be ox cheek braised in red wine, tomatoes and olives, or smoked haddock, leeks, poached egg and butter sauce. French toast, marmalade and vanilla ice cream has been a successful dessert. The French leaning wine list opens at £13.50.
Chef/s: James Faulks. **Open:** Mon to Fri 12 to 2.30, Mon to Sat 6.30 to 10.30. **Closed:** 23 Dec to 3 Jan. **Meals:** alc (main meals £14.50 to £16). **Service:** not

inc. **Details:** Cards accepted. 85 seats. Air-con. Separate bar. Wheelchair access. Music. Children allowed.

★ BEST FOR BREAKFAST ★

Roast

Fine dining in the middle of the market
Floral Hall, Borough Market, Stoney Street, SE1 1TL
Tel no: (020) 7940 1300
www.roast-restaurant.com
⊖ **London Bridge**
Modern British | £33
Cooking score: 4

Stylish and sassy, this modern British restaurant commands absorbing views of Borough Market, the railway line and the dome of St Paul's beyond. The buzz in the market outside is reflected by the kitchen's enthusiasm for well-sourced British ingredients. It's a versatile space – come for a relaxed brunch and enjoy a tattie scone with field mushrooms and Ayrshire bacon or the (recommended) full Borough cooked breakfast. From 11am you can savour more extensive all-day dining, featuring such home-grown delights as cold Yorkshire Dales beef, black pudding hash or grilled mackerel. And just to show how unstuffy Roast is, they'll cheerfully offer you your favourite British condiments, too, like Marmite on your toast, Coleman's with your sausages — even Bird's Custard if you follow the dessert route. Dinner takes itself more seriously (and at £22 for a 10oz rump, so it should). The latter was cooked beautifully, dripping in horseradish and mustard butter; grilled spring lamb chops with pease pudding and mint sauce were also a success. Starters on this packed spring evening included dressed Dorset crab with pickled cucumber and smoked haddock fishcake with rocket and lemon balm. Roast's wine list is by no means a snip (house starts at £18) but the global selection is interesting and around 15 are offered by the glass. Ask for a window table when you book.

Cass Titcombe | **Canteen**

Why did you become a chef?
I was encouraged to cook from an early age by my parents, we lived in a smallholdings in the Welsh mountains, where we produced or collected a lot of the food we ate.

Who do you most admire amongst today's chefs?
Fergus Henderson, Richard Corrigan and Mark Hix.

Where do you eat out?
Depending on my mood, Pied-à-Terre or Scotts for a special occasion. Côte in Wimbledon is really good and the Lahore Kebab House in Whitechapel is fantastic for Indian food.

What do you cook at home?
Lots of fish or simple Italian or Asian food when I am with my kids.

What's your favourite cookery book?
Alistair Little's Keep It Simple.

What's your guilty food pleasure?
Fried chicken.

If you could only eat one more thing, what would it be?
Fried Gamberetti at Hotel Carasco, Lipari in the Aeolian islands.

Chef/s: Lawrence Keogh. **Open:** Sun to Fri L 12 to 2.30pm (4pm Sun), Mon to Sat D 5.30 to 10.30pm **Meals:** alc (main courses £13.50 to £25). Set L £18 (2 courses) to £21. Set D (exc 6.45 to 9) £18 (2 courses) to £21. Breakfast and bar menus available. **Service:** 12.5% (optional). **Details:** Cards accepted 110 seats. Air-con. Wheelchair access. Music. Children's portions.

Tapas Brindisa
Outstanding tapas in packed surroundings
18-20 Southwark Street, SE1 1TJ
Tel no: (020) 7357 8880
www.brindisa.com
⊖ Borough
Spanish | £25
Cooking score: 3

V

This extremely convivial tapas restaurant on the edge of Borough Market is run by the renowned Spanish produce supplier Brindisa. Located in a potato warehouse, the curved building with its floor-to-ceiling windows, concrete floors and tightly packed bare wooden tables make for a light and airy dining room that becomes pleasantly boisterous during peak service. A changing menu features a superb choice of hot and cold tapas, that can either be eaten in the restaurant or standing at the bar. Choose from a selection of regional charcuterie, including Teruel serrano ham or salchichon de vich, a traditional Catalan recipe. Hot tapas include pungent prawns cooked in olive oil, garlic and chilli, or more adventurous dishes such as pan-fried sea bass with beetroot, orange and red onion salad. The exclusively Spanish wine list includes a fine selection of sherries and cava. Choose a bottle of house white Verdejo for £16, or a house Tempranillo for £13.20.
Chef/s: José Manuel Pizarro. **Open:** Mon to Thurs 11 to 11, Fri to Sat L 12 to 4, D 5.30 to 11. **Closed:** Christmas, bank hol Mon. **Meals:** alc (tapas £3 to £8). **Service:** 12.5% (optional). **Details:** Cards accepted. 40 seats. 9 seats outside. Air-con. Separate bar. Wheelchair access. Music.

READERS RECOMMEND
Shipp's Tea Rooms
Café
4 Park Street, SE1 9AB
Tel no: (020) 7407 2692
www.shippstearooms.info
'One of the warmest welcomes in town'

Wright Bros Oyster Bar
Seafood
11 Stoney Street, SE1 9AD
Tel no: (020) 7403 9554
www.wrightbros.eu.com
'Fresh produce, straight from Borough Market'

█ Putney
Emile's
An enduring favourite
96-98 Felsham Road, SW15 1DQ
Tel no: (020) 8789 3323
www.emilesrestaurant.co.uk
⊖ Putney Bridge
Modern British | £24.50
Cooking score: 1

A well-known feature in the smart, sleepy streets of Putney, Emile's has been keeping the locals well-fed with its world-influenced, British based food for years. But as fashions move on, Emile's seems stuck in a timewarp and there are signs of fatigue. The furnishings are tired, the menu less exciting than it once appeared and the kitchen cooking by numbers instead of flair. Stick to the less adventurous dishes for the best results: a starter of Keens cheddar soufflé with a white wine beurre blanc was fine, but the Szechuan fillet of pork with Thai noodles that followed was less successful, delivering gloopy noodles and a withered accompanying salad. The wine list is a much happier experience and great value with house wine at under £12 a bottle and most of the eclectic selection offered under £20.
Chef/s: Andrew Sherlock and Matthew Johnson. Open: Mon to Sat D only 7.30 to 11. Closed: Christmas, bank hols. Meals: Set D £21.50 (2 courses) to £24.50. Service: not inc. Details: Cards accepted. 100 seats. Wheelchair access. Music. Children allowed.

Enoteca Turi
A truly epic wine list
28 Putney High Street, SW15 1SQ
Tel no: (020) 8785 4449
⊖ Putney Bridge
Italian | £35
New Chef
🍾 V

The fashion of modern Italian cooking with its lightness of touch, deconstruction and simplification of classical dishes has certainly touched this smartish Italian, but the basis of the menu here is still rooted in regional Italy, with the use of really good raw ingredients and plenty of long, slow cooking when appropriate. A starter of antipasto Pugliese with roasted vegetables and a rich, flavoursome fava bean purée has all the beauty and colour of the former and makes a great contrast to the full old-fashioned potency of a ragu d'agnello served with papardelle. The cooking's perfectly competent, but what makes this restaurant really special is the wine list. Proprietor Giuseppe Turi has a passion for Italian wines and his 300-strong list, fully annotated and very fairly priced list is an education in itself. Wines start at £3.75 and each dish on the menu has its own recommendation, but if diners wish to make their own choice, the staff are only too happy to help.
Chef/s: Roger Serjent. Open: Mon to Sat 12 to 2.30, 7 to 11. Closed: bank hols. Meals: Set L £14.50 (2 courses) to £17.50. Service: 12.5% (optional). Details: Cards accepted. 85 seats. Air-con. Wheelchair access. Music. Children's portions. Children allowed.

Phoenix

A magnet for well-heeled locals
162-164 Lower Richmond Road, SW15 1LY
Tel no: (020) 8780 3131
⊖ Putney Bridge
Italian | £30
Cooking score: 4

V

The Phoenix is a comfortable place to sit, with its generous tables, high ceilings and interesting modern-art collection indoors, but on warm days and especially warm evenings, most people want a table in the romantic, fairylit garden. Roger Brooks's Anglo-Italian menu has plenty to please, from potted shrimps to a fresh, seasonal broad bean, rocket and mint salad with pecorino to start and the likes of slow roast pork belly with beetroot and grilled halibut, sauce vierge to follow. Portions are generous, cooked with total competence and flair and served with grace by a team of cheerful, patient staff. The wine list is an eclectic affair, though there's plenty from Italy, including a decent prosecco and Vin Santo for those wanting to keep to the Italian theme, and at 11.95 for house wine to £60 for an Amarone Classico, fairly good value.
Chef/s: Roger Brooks. **Open:** all week 12.30 to 2.30 (3 Sun), 7 to 11 (10 Sun). **Closed:** 3 days Christmas. **Meals:** alc (main courses £11.50 to £17.50). Set L Mon to Sat £13.50 (2 courses) to £15.50, Set L Sun £19.50, Set D Sun to Thur £15.50 (2 courses) to £17.50. **Service:** 12.5% (optional). **Details:** Cards accepted. 100 seats. Air-con. Wheelchair access. Music. Children's portions.

ALSO RECOMMENDED

▲ L'Auberge

22 Upper Richmond Road, SW15 2RX
Tel no: (020) 8874 3593
www.ardillys.com
⊖ East Putney

An intimate, much-loved asset to the local community, Pascal Ardilly's Putney restaurant serves classic French dishes. Start with frogs' legs with garlic purée and parsley jus (£6.25)

or gratin of queen scallops (£7.90). Follow with pan-fried calf's liver with shallots and raspberry vinegar (£14.95) or grilled shark steak and hot tomato sauce (£14.95). Desserts are a must so save room for the lemon chocolate tart (£4.20). French wines from £12. Open Tue to Sat D only.

▮ South Bank

Oxo Tower

Perennial chic at high altitude
Oxo Tower Wharf, Barge House Street, SE1 9PH
Tel no: (020) 7803 3888
⊖ Blackfriars
Modern British | £64
Cooking score: 4

Ownership by Harvey Nichols ensures this eighth-floor dining room remains perennially chic, though it's arguably what's outside – a smashing view of St Paul's, the City skyline and the Thames – that's the main attraction, and a pre-dinner drink on the terrace is one of the capital's ultimate alfresco experiences. The high-rise location is matched by some very steep pricing, but the quality of cooking is generally sound and, although the menu is inevitably peppered with foie gras and lobster for corporate expense accounters, you'll also find creative, up-to-date assemblies such as tuna tartare with an enoki mushroom salad and a cucumber and lemon salsa followed by wild Scottish salmon with fennel gnocchi and baby vegetables. Gutsier tastes might be accommodated by roast fillet of beef with cep purée, oxtail and a truffle cream bon-bon. Finish with a spin on a classic dessert: lemon balm pannacotta with mango trifle, say. A shorter, less expensive menu is offered at lunch, while the next-door brasserie serves cheaper food (much of it with an Asian/Italian slant) in funkier surrounds. The 25-page wine list is a comprehensive tour of the world's major growing areas, with a strong selection of Champagne, Bordeaux and Burgundy underlining Oxo's celebration credentials. Elsewhere there's something for every budget, including house French for £16.50 and 20 by the glass.

Chef/s: Jeremy Bloor. **Open:** Restaurant Mon to Sat 12 to 2.30, 6 to 11, Sun 12 to 3, 6.30 to 10; Brasserie all week 12 to 3.15 (2.45 Sun), 5.30 to 11 (6 to 10.30 Sun). **Meals:** Restaurant alc D (main courses £16.50 to £25). Set L £33.50 to £35, Set D £33.50 to £70; Brasserie alc (main courses £14 to £18). Set pre-theatre D £16.50 (2 courses) to £21.50.
Service: 12.5% (optional). **Details:** Cards accepted. 80 seats. Air-con. No mobile phones. Wheelchair access. Music. Children's portions.

Skylon

Capturing the spirit of the Festival of Britain
Belvedere Road, SE1 8XX
Tel no: (020) 7654 7800
www.danddlondon.com/restaurants/skylon
⊖ Waterloo
Modern British | £39
Cooking score: 2

The reworking of the interior of this restaurant on level 3 of the Royal Festival Hall is 'a brilliant job', the vast space houses a bar, grill and restaurant with floor to ceiling windows providing a panoramic river and cityscape. In the kitchen, Helen Puolakka keeps an eye on London fashion, the broad British brush strokes augmented by contemporary combinations like carpaccio of scallops with liquorice vinaigrette and dried cranberries. Bold combinations are favoured at main course caramelised pork belly and butter poached lobster, say or braised ox cheek served with truffled pommes purée but when tried at an inspection lunch, both dishes were found to require more attention to detail. Indeed, disappointments have been reported elsewhere, and prices are high for one and all. The smartly assembled wine list spans various styles and budgets, and starts at £15. A section devoted to rare wines from the 1950s is, unsurprisingly, at prices as elevated as this restaurant.
Chef/s: Helena Puolakka. **Open:** all week, L 12 to 2.30, D 5.30 to 10.45 (bar 11am to 1am). **Meals:** Set L £19.51 (2 courses) to £24.50. Set L & D £29.50 (2 courses) to £34.50. Pre & post theatre £24.50 (2 courses) to £29.50. **Service:** 12.5%. **Details:** Cards accepted. 92 seats. Air-con. Separate bar. Wheelchair access.

ALSO RECOMMENDED

▲ Mezzanine

National Theatre, SE1 9PX
Tel no: (020) 7452 3600
⊖ Waterloo

Buzzy eaterie attached to the National Theatre, popular for its stunning view across the River Thames and good value pre-show set deals (two-courses 19.95), so arrive early to bag a window seat or a table on the terrace. The post-show carte offers similar dishes along the lines of salad of wild rabbit and chorizo with broad bean hummus (£7), herb-crusted baked Pollack with spinach, tomato and saffron (£10.50), rump of lamb with roasted Mediterranean vegetables and basil (£12.95), with rhubarb and custard brûlée among the desserts. Wines from £13.25. Open Mon-Sat D and Sun L only.

READERS RECOMMEND

Benugo at the BFI

Modern European
Belvedere Road, SE1 8XT
Tel no: (020) 7401 9000
www.benugo.com
'Super-stylish restaurant and bar'

Canteen

Modern British
Royal Festival Hall, Belvedere Rd, SE1 8XX
Tel no: 0845 686 1122
www.canteen.co.uk
'A worthy sibling to the Spitalfields branch.'

Southwark

READERS RECOMMEND
Cafe One Seven One
Modern British
Jerwood Space, 171 Union Street, SE1 0LN
Tel no: 020 7654 0100
'Great-value food in modern gallery space'

The Table
Global
83 Southwark Street, SE1 0HX
Tel no: 020 7401 2760
www.thetablecafe.com
'Friendly canteen at an architects' practice'

Tooting

Kastoori
Gujarati food with African influences
188 Upper Tooting Road, SW17 7EJ
Tel no: (020) 8767 7027
⊖ Tooting Broadway
Gujarati | £21
Cooking score: 3

V

Dinesh and Manoj Thanki have been plying their trade in Tooting since 1987 and have made Kastoori a favourite destination for skilfully spiced Gujarati vegetarian food. Their restaurant is bright and cheerfully decorated, with Hindu sculptures adding an extra touch of exoticism. The family hails from the temperate region of Katia Wahd (the only part of the Sub-continent where tomatoes grow naturally) and also spent many years in Uganda. Both influences shine through on their menu, which moves from mainstay appetisers like samosas, bhel puris and dosas to intriguing vegetable curries and specials. The kitchen makes good use of aduki beans, cassava root, karela (bitter gourd) and other exotica: in particular, look for matoki (a green banana curry), kasodi (sweetcorn cooked in coconut milk with peanut sauce) and the family's 'sensational Euro-veg special' involving everything from leeks to rhubarb. Desserts are traditional stalwarts like shrikhand, ras malai and khir (rice pudding 'like granny never made it'). House wine is £9.95.
Chef/s: Manoj Thanki. **Open:** Wed to Sun L 12.30 to 2.30, all week D 6 to 10.30. **Closed:** 25 and 26 Dec. **Meals:** alc (main courses £4.75 to £6.25). **Service:** not inc. **Details:** Cards accepted. 82 seats. Air-con. Wheelchair access. Music. Children's portions. Children allowed.

Radha Krishna Bhavan
Authentic Keralan food
86 Tooting High Street, SW17 0RN
Tel no: (020) 8682 0969
www.mcdosa.com
⊖ Tooting Broadway
Indian | £24
Cooking score: 1

V

A life-size, traditional Kathakali statue and huge murals evoking the palm-fronded beaches of Kerala set the mood in this colourfully bedecked restaurant. The menu has its share of kurmas, dhansaks and other curry house stand-bys, but the real highlights are the specialities from the owner's beloved South Indian province. Skilfully prepared starters almost steal the show, especially the range of dosas with vegetable sambar and coconut chutney, uthappam (India's answer to a pizza, studded with chillies and tomatoes) and Mysore bonda (deep-fried spiced lentil and potato balls). The kitchen also focuses on exotic Cochin specialities such as lamb fry masala and kappa meen masala (boiled, spiced tapioca served with fish curry). Among the vegetable-based dishes look for avial and kalan (sweet mango and yam with coconut, yogurt and green chillies) or dry-cooked beetroot thoran. Drink lassi, juice or beer; workaday wines from £9.95.
Chef/s: Mr Terab Ali. **Open:** all week 12 to 3, 6 to 11 (12 Fri and Sat). **Closed:** 25 and 26 Dec. **Meals:** alc (main courses £4.50 to £7). **Service:** 10%. **Details:** Cards accepted. 50 seats. Air-con. No music. Wheelchair access. Music. Children's portions. Children allowed.

Rick's Café

Modern European
122 Mitcham Road, SW17 9NH
Tel no: (020) 8767 5219
'A well-kept secret for Tooting locals'

▌Vauxhall

ALSO RECOMMENDED
▲ Rebato's

169 South Lambeth Road, SW8 1XW
Tel no: (020) 7735 6388
www.rebatos.com
⊖ Vauxhall

Step into Rebato's and you step back into the 1970s as little has changed over the years at this traditional and much-loved tapas bar. In the dimly lit dark wood and tiled-front bar, tuck into some classic tapas dishes – boquerones (anchovies in olive oil and garlic), deep-fried squid, grilled sardines. More substantial traditional Spanish dishes are served in the light-filled formal dining room out back. Feast on fish soup Cantabrica (£4.95), chargrilled lamb cutlets served with garlic mayonnaise (£11.95) and finish with crème caramel (£3.95) from the trolley. Good value set lunch menus, cheerful, professional service and Spanish house wines from £10.50. Closed Sat L and Sun.

▌Waterloo

Anchor & Hope

An urban gastropub
36 The Cut, SE1 8LP
Tel no: (020) 7928 9898
⊖ Southwark
British | £26
Cooking score: 4

You have to hand it to the team at the Anchor and Hope; this place is still on fire, as hot – nay, hotter – than it was when it opened four years ago: 'on a midweek lunch we had no choice but to perch at the bar'. It remains a credit to the word 'gastropub' as you'd expect of St John and Eagle alums: open kitchen, battered and bruised décor, and dressed-down service, yet it proves the formula isn't bankrupt. Flavours are unapologetically full-on. Snail, bacon, and laverbread on duck fat toast was a rich start, mains get even richer, in the form of a chicken, ham and morel gratin or slow-cooked Hereford beef, dripping potatoes and grass, with flourless chocolate cake to finish. It's worth spending a little extra on your wine choice (and not only for the sake of an upgrade to 'proper' glasses from the wretched thimble-sized tumblers): it's a well-chosen Francophile list, from £10 to just £65, with a few intriguing choices from elsewhere in Europe. Reservations are only taken for Sunday L. A new brasserie, Great Queen Street (see entry), is set for similar popularity levels.

Chef/s: Jonathon Jones. **Open:** 11am to 11pm.
Closed: Mon L, Sun D, Christmas, 2 weeks August.
Meals: alc (main courses £6 to £16). Set L Sun £30.
Details: Cards accepted. 40 seats. 24 seats outside.
Wheelchair access. Music.

Baltic

Ultra-hip Eastern European restaurant
74 Blackfriars Road, SE1 8HA
Tel no: (020) 7928 1111
www.balticrestaurant.co.uk
⊖ Southwark
Eastern European | £35
Cooking score: 3

Opposite Southwark tube station, and within ambling distance of Tate Modern, Baltic combines a deeply cool and strikingly minimalist bar serving trendy vodkas, with a sumptuous airy dining space, all muted colours, modern art and mood lighting, and housed within an eighteenth-century building. The theme of the food is Eastern European, the enticing menu taking in dishes familiar to the countries between the Baltic and the Black Sea, but mixed with modern British ideas. Start with Siberian Pelmeni – small beef and pork dumplings – barley and bacon soup, or pig trotter croquettes with pickled saffron cucumber salad. Then tuck into beef stroganoff with sour cream and pickles, roast pork shank with braised sauerkraut and bacon, or a less obvious Baltic dish like roast cod with lemon dumplings. Puddings extend to Ukranian rhum baba, and white chocolate cheesecake. House vins de pays at £13 kick off the wine list.

Chef/s: Peter Repinski. **Open:** all week 12 to 3, 6 to 11.15. **Closed:** 1 Jan. **Meals:** alc (main courses £10.50 to £18.50). **Set L and D** 6 to 7 £11.50 (2 courses) to £13.50. **Service:** 12.5% (optional). **Details:** Cards accepted. 100 seats. Wheelchair access. Music. Children's portions.

RSJ

Sturdy restaurant with sound technique
33 Coin Street, SE1 9NR
Tel no: (020) 7928 4554
www.rsj.uk.com
⊖ **Waterloo**
French | £43
Cooking score: 3

This reliable, imaginative place, a stone's throw from the Old and Young Vics and the Southbank is as robustly unsusceptible to fashion as the steel joist it's named after. Clean minimalism and with everything from decent napkins and glasses to knowledgeable service done properly and without fuss, ensures RSJ's enduring and wide appeal. Sound francophile techniques emphasise the flavours of the ingredients straightforwardly: a smooth soup with beetroot and tomato finely balanced; accurately grilled salmon; classic puddings including excellent ice creams, epitomise the approach. Set two or three dish meals offering real choice are especially good value. A marvellous obsession with bottles from the Loire, virtually to the exclusion of all else, French or otherwise, makes doubters of the quality and range of wines offered from Muscadet to the Nivernais think twice. A wonderful stack of sweeties and halves completes the picture.

Chef/s: Ian Stabler. **Open:** Mon to Fri L 12 to 2.30, Mon to Sat D 5.30 to 11. **Meals:** alc (main courses £13 to £18). **Set L and D** £15.95 (2 courses) to £17.95. **Service:** 12.5% (optional). **Details:** Cards accepted. 90 seats. Air-con. No music. Children's portions.

Wimbledon

Côte

Elegant bistro in a village setting
8 High Street, Wimbledon Village, W19 5DX
Tel no: (020) 8947 7100
www.cote-restaurants.co.uk
⊖ **Wimbledon**
French | £20
Cooking score: 2

Wimbledon has been crying out for this place; a restaurant with all the elegance of a classic Parisian bistro and an informal, vibrant atmosphere. The décor is traditional, with dark wood tables and tall mirrors creating an inviting space. The menu veers towards Provençale cooking, with specialities including pissaladière, a traditional flatbread from Nice, served with caramelised onions and anchovies. At inspection, a starter of Bayonne ham with a celeriac remoulade was small but perfectly formed; a decent horseradish kick complemented the meat well. For mains, a blue steak was requested and served impeccably, while the mash accompanying a crisp duck confit was absolutely exquisite. At dessert, a chocolate pot was served in a tiny espresso cup. At first, this seemed like a paltry offering, but was in fact an intense hit of deep, dark chocolate. To eat more than a mouthful would have been sheer gluttony. The cheese platter was similarly minute three thumb-size pieces but was served at the right temperature and well selected. Service is slightly erratic, but charming all the same. For a more casual dining experience, ask to sit in the booths towards the front of the restaurant, but for group/occasion dining, head for the more formal tables towards the rear. The restaurant was packed when we inspected, so expect to book ahead for weekends. House wines start

Green cuisine

Organic and sustainable dining is undoubtedly the way forward in London.

Konstam at the Prince Albert

Fronted by Oliver Rowe, this is a thoroughly laudable and successful attempt to bring seasonal dining to a stressed-out city crowd.

Acorn House

Dedication to the eco-friendly cause doesn't come much more passionate; an imaginative, forward-thinking establishment.

Leon

Allegra McEvedy's mini-chain of central London eateries bring a no-nonsense sensibility to cooking for urban types.

Manna

Manna claims to have been the first to have brought veggie and vegan cookery to London in the 1960s, and is still going strong.

The Gate

The Gate in Hammersmith is run by two brothers, who draw on their complex ethnic roots to provide a vibrant, inspiring menu.

Bumpkin

With a repertoire of Fairtrade and traceable food, Bumpkin brings a taste of country living to the denizens of Westbourne Park.

Nayaab

Offering subcontinental classics that are low in fat, free of colouring and produced from organic ingredients, with fresh herbs and spices.

Café Spice Namaste

Organic ingredients and careful sourcing have won this restaurant two Environmental Best Practice awards.

Chez Lindsay

Authentic Breton cuisine is the draw here, and the menu mainstays are the organic buckwheat pancakes.

Flâneur

An eclectic range of quality produce from near and far in a deli on Farringdon Road. Expect hormone-free meats, conscientiously produced fruit and vegetables, and organic wines among the fare.

at: £12.95. NB As we went to press, news reached us that a new branch of Côte is set to open in Soho. Reports please.

Open: Mon to Fri 12 to 11, Sat 9.30 to 11, Sun 9.30 to 10.30. **Closed:** Christmas Day. **Meals:** Set menu £9.95 (two courses) to £11.95. **Service:** 12.5%. **Details:** Cards accepted. 90 seats. 8 seats outside. Air-con. Wheelchair access. Music. Children allowed.

Light House Restaurant

Wimbledon's culinary bright light
75-77 Ridgway, SW19 4ST
Tel no: (020) 8944 6338
www.lighthousewimbledon.com
⊖ Wimbledon
Modern European | £32
Cooking score: 3

♀

Enormous windows let the light flood into this bright and breezy contemporary-styled neighbourhood restaurant, the pale wood floors and modern art-adorned walls adding to the airy and cheerful atmosphere. Informal and helpful service contributes to a laid-back feel that seems to suit the sunny food. There's a strong Italian influence to the menu, although dishes trawl all over the Mediterranean shores and further afield to Asia for inspiration, ensuring that there's something to please all tastes. Ingredients are confidently handled and dishes are rustic with robust flavours allowed to shine through. Devilled lambs' kidneys with pancetta and field mushrooms on toast, or seared scallops with Jerusalem artichoke puree and morcilla could be a good way to start, then follow with calf's liver accompanied by potato gnocchi, gorgonzola, roast sweet potato and crispy sage. Alternatively, opt for fish, perhaps pan-fried sea bass with carrot and ginger purée, bok choi and oyster mushrooms. Round off with white chocolate parfait with strawberry sorbet, or treacle tart. The wine list (house starts at £13.50) has a good selection by the glass and is well-judged, if not great value.

Chef/s: Chris Casey. **Open:** all week L 12 to 2.30 (3 Sun), Mon to Sat D 6.30 to 10.30. **Closed:** Christmas. **Meals:** alc (main courses £11.50 to

Cooking score

A score of 1 is a significant achievement. The score in any review is based on several meals, incorporating feedback from both our readers and inspectors. As a rough guide, 1 denotes capable cooking with some inconsistencies, rising steadily through different levels of technical expertise, until the scores between 6 and 10 indicate exemplary skills, along with innovation, artistry and ambition. If there is a new chef, we don't score the restaurant for the first year of entry. For further details, please see the scoring section in the introduction to the Guide.

£17.50). Set L £14.50 (2 courses) to £17, Set D £14.50 (2 courses) to £18. **Service:** 12.5% (optional). **Details:** Cards accepted. 75 seats. 15 seats outside. Air-con. Wheelchair access. Music. Children's portions.

ALSO RECOMMENDED

▲ Earl Spencer

260-262 Merton Road, SW18 5JL
Tel no: (020) 8870 9244
www.theearlspencer.co.uk
⊖ Southfields

This lively gastropub comes with a winter log fire and three cask-conditioned ales. Service is good 'once you have ordered and paid at the bar', and the menu changes daily. Start with grilled sardines and saffron potatoes (£6.50), or spinach and feta filo pastries with mint yoghurt (£5.50). For mains consider La Garbure smoked sausage, ham and white bean casserole (£10) or an above-average beer-battered whiting and cuttlefish with chips and minted peas (£10.50). Finish with sticky ginger pudding (£5) or apricot and frangipane tart with crème anglaise (£5). Wines start at £11. Open all week.

WEST

Bayswater, Chelsea, Chiswick, Earl's Court,
Fulham, Hammersmith, Kensington,
Notting Hill, Paddington ,
Shepherd's Bush, South Kensington,
Westbourne Grove, Westbourne Park

Bayswater

ALSO RECOMMENDED
▲ Kiasu
48 Queensway, W2 3RY
Tel no: 020 7727 8810
www.kiasu.co.uk
⊖ Bayswater

Kiasu, a quintessential term in Singapore translates to 'fear of being second best', aptly describes the competitive spirit of this most successful Tiger economy. This newcomer, in a tightly packed space, resembles many simple cafes in South-East Asia. Blue/mauve walls with various connotations of the Kiasu theme help to brighten up the room. Service is cheery and fleet-footed. The restaurant has been a hit, thanks in part to the generous portions and reasonable prices. On a hot and humid evening, the bustling atmosphere can trick you into thinking that you are near the Equator. The menu features an extensive repertoire of street food from the Straits, although the popular Filipino dish of chicken and pork Adobo (£6.60) makes an appearance. Satay (£5.80) is acceptable, Penang style char kway teow (£6.50) (stir fried with rice noodles with prawns) is authentic. Hokkien mee (£6.70) (prawn and noodle soup) comes with tasty pork ribs. Ice kachang (£4.80) (shaved ice with sweet corn and red aduki beans), is a good way to finish especially on a hot day, or you if you are brave try the infamous durian fruit, used for the ice cream. Wines, starting from £11.50 are inconsequential. Drink Tiger beer or tea tarik (stretched tea) instead.

Please send us your feedback

To register your opinion about any restaurant listed in the Guide, or a new restaurant that you wish to bring to our attention, please visit the web address at the bottom of the page. Your feedback informs the content of the book and will be used to compile next year's reviews.

Chelsea
The Admiral Codrington
Not afraid to experiment
17 Mossop Street, SW3 2LY
Tel no: (020) 7581 0005
www.theadmiralcodrington.com
⊖ South Kensington
Gastropub | £44
Cooking score: 3

V

A blend of country-style décor – fussy floral banquettes and nautical knick-knacks – and well-informed, efficient and friendly staff makes this smart pub restaurant stand out from the crowd. You can't go wrong with the menu, which lists the kind of comfort food everybody likes to eat: fishcakes, roast lamb, roast chicken, steak and chips, and pork belly. There are occasional flourishes of ambition, too: artichoke salad is tossed with dandelion leaves and Valencia almonds, foie gras and chicken liver parfait comes with Vin de Constance jelly, and sausages are made with wagyu beef. Similarly, fluffy, rustic hand-made potato gnocchi is dressed with lusty, full-bodied tomato sauce crammed with sprightly spring vegetables and herbs. Puddings, like rich, dense chocolate and peanut butter parfait with pinot noir-glazed cherries, keep the comfort factor high. A fairly basic list of Old and New World wines starts at £13 a bottle, with around fifteen available by the glass.
Chef/s: Jon Rotheram. **Open:** all week 12 to 2.30 (3.30 Sat, 4.00 Sun), 6.30 to 12 midnight (7 to 10 Sun). **Closed:** Christmas Day, Boxing day. **Meals:** alc (main courses £10.95 to £17.50). Cover £1 at D. Bar L menu available. **Service:** 12.5% (optional).
Details: Cards accepted. 50 seats. Separate bar. No mobile phones. Wheelchair access. Music. Children allowed. Car parking.

Aubergine

Polished French cooking in a Chelsea backwater
11 Park Walk, SW10 0AJ
Tel no: (020) 7352 3449
www.auberginerestaurant.co.uk
⊖ **South Kensington**
French | £65
Cooking score: 5

🍾 V

Little seems to change at this genteel Chelsea venue, which is discreetly tucked away in the affluent environs of SW10. William Drabble continues to deliver deft, technically skilled dishes from the bedrock of the modern repertoire and polished French cooking remains the order of the day. Diners can expect a generous smattering of luxury ingredients, from starters of sautéed foie gras served with figs in red wine and gingerbread crisps to poached lobster tail, which keeps company with a warm salad of asparagus, morels, artichokes and truffled potatoes. Frog's legs and a galette of pig's head (albeit with roasted langoustines) help to restore the earthy balance, while dishes such as chump of Lune Valley spring lamb with Provençal vegetables and rosemary jus suggest that the kitchen is happy to stay in the mainstream. Tradition also rules when it comes to classically inclined desserts such as apricot soufflé with dark chocolate sauce or caramelised apple with roasted almond ice cream. Almost everything here is ever-so-French, apart from the intriguing choice of world beers that is now a feature of the place. The lengthy wine list is a Francophile's dream, with stellar selections from the big-name regions backed up by serious contenders from the Italian new wave and California. Prices may seem financially challenging, but there are some attractive bargains to be had – especially from Southwest France. House selections start at £17.
Chef/s: William Drabble. **Open:** Mon to Fri L 12 to 2.30, Mon to Sat D 7 to 11. **Meals:** Set L £34 (inc wine), Set D £64 to £77. **Service:** 12.5% (optional).

Details: Cards accepted. 60 seats. Air-con. No music. No mobile phones. Wheelchair access. Children allowed.

Awana

A keystone of Malaysian cooking
85 Sloane Avenue, SW3 3DX
Tel no: (020) 7584 8880
www.awana.co.uk
Malaysian | £62
Cooking score: 1

 V

The décor in Awana's long, rectangular dining room is inspired by the traditional Malaysian teak houses – all dark wood, glass screens and leather furnishings. The name means 'in the clouds' in Malay and the restaurant is under the same ownership as the Mango Tree (see entry). Typically, begin with a roti canai (flat bread) appetiser red curry sauce, move on to an assorted seafood satay starter, or, perhaps spicy crab and potato cakes with asian celery and coriander. High-quality ingredients are evident in the main courses, which take in a cumin-spiced curried lamb shank with pumpkin, sweet potato and lemongrass, whole grilled sea bass served with lime and lemongrass butter, and a good choice of stir-fries. The wine list has some exciting bottles, although mark-ups are a touch on the high side, with prices starting at £19.
Chef/s: Lee Chin Soon. **Open:** all week 12 to 3, 6 to 11.30. **Meals:** alc (main courses £9.50 to £24). Set L £12.80 (2 courses) to £15, Set D £36. Bar menu available. **Service:** 12.5% (optional). **Details:** Cards accepted. 80 seats. Air-con. Wheelchair access. Music. Jacket and tie required. Children's portions.

Le Colombier

Patriotic neighbourhood bistro
145 Dovehouse Street, SW3 6LB
Tel no: (020) 7351 1155
www.lecolombier-sw3.co.uk
⊖ South Kensington
French | £28
Cooking score: 2

The 'entente' is decidedly 'cordiale' in Didier Garnier's dyed-in-the-wool Chelsea bistro, which is brimful of Gallic bonhomie. Blue and white colours set the tone in the opened-out dining room, which is a classic mix of wide floorboards, etched windows and Art Deco wall lights; a terrace out front attracts fair-weather crowds. No-nonsense French bistro food with a few Mediterranean flourishes is the kitchen's stock in trade, and the menu skips its way through potted goose rillettes, garlicky snails in puff pastry, veal kidneys with Dijon mustard sauce and fillet of wild sea bass with olive oil and lemon. Straightforward grills are a fixture, while desserts don't stray far from the realms of crêpes Suzette and crème brûlée. Frances rules emphatically on the big-hearted wine list, with bottle prices starting at £19.
Chef/s: Phillipe Tamet. Open: all week L 12 to 3. Meals: alc (main courses £13.50 to £23). Set L £16.50 (2 courses), Set L Sun £19. Service: 12.5% (optional). Details: Cards accepted. 35 seats. 25 seats outside. No music. Wheelchair access. Children allowed.

Eight Over Eight

Fusion meets fashion in this celeb hangout
392 King's Road, SW3 5UZ
Tel no: (020) 7349 9934
www.eightovereight.nu
⊖ Sloane Square
Asian | £48
Cooking score: 2

V

A converted Chelsea theatre pub is the setting for this branch of Will Ricker's in-vogue fusion group. Glitterati, media celebs and star-watchers throng the visually dramatic space, which has been done out with handsome furniture and ersatz oriental trappings. Food provides the accompaniment to serious socialising, and the menu is designed to make things as user-friendly as possible. Dishes are grouped into categories for grazing, and the kitchen delivers vibrant assemblages based on authentic ingredients: a glossary on the menu explains all. Dim sum and salads (duck with watermelon and cashews) share the billing with sushi and sashimi, tempura (soft-shell crab with ponzu and jalapeño), BBQs and curries (roast monkfish with choi sum). Specials such as Shanghai-style whole snapper provide extra choice, while desserts are flights of fancy such as chocolate pudding with green tea ice cream. Exotic cocktails fit the bill, and the wine list is a racy global affair. Prices start at £15 and there are numerous options by the glass.
Chef/s: Grant Bronsden. Open: Mon to Sat L 12 to 3 (4 Sat), all week D 6 to 11. Closed: 23 to 27 Dec, Jan 1 and 2. Meals: alc (main courses £6 to £22). Set L and D £35 to £59. Service: 12.5% (optional). Details: Cards accepted. 95 seats. Air-con. Separate bar. Music. Children allowed.

Gordon Ramsay

An unmissable experience
68-69 Royal Hospital Road, SW3 4HP
Tel no: (020) 7352 4441
www.gordonramsay.com
⊖ Sloane Square
French | £96
Cooking score: 9

Gordon Ramsay is now the proud owner of an international brand, fronting serious top-end restaurants in Dubai, New York and Tokyo (with Paris beckoning) in between hosting TV shows, running marathons and endorsing just about every product under the sun. He is also a consummate restaurateur and Hospital Road remains his treasured London flagship. Thanks to a £1m makeover from David Collins, this must-visit destination has been presented with a new suit of clothes. The result is a dining room that is more restrained than before, with simplified design gestures, predominantly cream and beige colours, long slim mirrors – of course – GR-branded Royal Doulton crockery. This prevailing mood of calm simplicity allows the food to take centre stage, although there is a great deal of subtle orchestration along the way. Much depends on indefatigable maitre d' Jean-Claude Breton, who ensures that service comes complete with exactly the required amount of French polish. All of this comes at a price, although it is worth remembering that the admirable set lunch menu provides a tantalising and affordable glimpse of the kitchen's prowess. The whole culinary set-up is marshalled by executive chef Mark Askew, and regulars reckon that he has raised the bar of late when it comes to presentation: consider a ring of unctuous ballotine of foie gras filled with camomile jelly set alongside a row of baby pickled vegetables, with top-notch rosemary focaccia as an accompaniment. Breathtaking freshness and supremely good raw materials are the kitchen's hallmarks, coupled with 'peerless technique' and dazzling execution: an entrecôte of roast Gressingham duck breast, for example, is artfully arranged with honey-glazed onions and morels, offset by the bitter edge of a chicory tart and tempered with a limpid Madeira juice. Elsewhere, the kitchen works its magic with Northumbrian beef, cooked medium-rare, ringed by kohlrabi and finished with an infusion of root vegetables (which also appears in a cup ready to be drunk). Fish is no less impressive, whether it is a pair of scallops given the thinnest of Parmesan crusts then served with Parmesan velouté and octopus carpaccio or brilliantly timed fillet of line-caught halibut resting on rolls of pappardelle (one tinged green with coriander, the other red with ginger) with passion fruit butter sauce meticulously poured around it. Desserts remain as spectacular as ever: a star turn is Granny Smith parfait with honeycomb, bitter chocolate and Champagne foam – a 'complex labyrinth of sophisticated flavours'. By-pass coffee and you will miss the dramatic entrance of white chocolates filled with strawberry ice cream served in a silver

dish with liquid nitrogen spilling out. Given the levels of expectation that are part and parcel of this rarefied culinary experience, there are bound to be occasional quibbles and lapses. Reporters are bemused by the fact that the kitchen seems unwilling to bake its own bread; some also find the 'wow' factor has faded a little of late, but the consistency of the kitchen still warrants plaudits. The awe-inspiring wine list is a cause for celebration, particularly if price is no option. One eagle-eyed oenophile observed that 'the number of bottles worth more than £10,000 exceeds the options under £20' which says a great deal about the restaurant's priorities. Rarities are sprinkled liberally throughout, with legions of mighty offerings from the classic French regions (as might be expected) but also some dazzling gems from Australia and the USA. The sommelier's advice is exemplary, and there is plenty to enjoy for around £30.
Chef/s: Mark Askew, Clare Smyth. **Open:** Mon to Fri 12 to 2.30, 6.30 to 11. **Meals:** Set L £40 to £110, Set D £85 to £110. **Service:** 12.5% (optional). **Details:** Cards accepted. 44 seats. Air-con. No music. No mobile phones. Wheelchair access. Children's portions.

Rasoi Vineet Bhatia
A domestic approach to Indian cooking
10 Lincoln Street, SW3 2TS
Tel no: (020) 7225 1881
www.vineetbhatia.com
⊖ Sloane Square
Indian | £69
Cooking score: 5

♨ V

If you were looking for the kind of upscale Indian restaurant where you had to ring a doorbell to get in, Chelsea would be a good place to start. Look no further. Vineet Bhatia's singular establishment, not far from Sloane Square, is a little gem. Inside, the Lilliputian scale is compensated by vivid décor and a conservatory roof, and the feeling of domesticity is a world away from the last curry house you visited. As is the cooking. Bhatia brings a new-wave sensibility to dishes such as a wild mushroom starter that is comprised of rice- and lentil-based khichdi, tomato ice-cream, tandoori shiitakes and a mushroom-topped naan dressed in truffle oil. Variations on crab encompass a masala crab cake, crab chutney and a crab and corn samosa. The vibrant, enlivening flavours continue through main courses like shredded duck confit in korma dressing with walnuts, potato, and apricot chutney, or in fish dishes such as herbed sea bass on crushed tandoori potatoes, with crispy okra and coconut sauce. If an agony of indecision overtakes you, there is a bells-and-whistles gourmand option of seven courses. The desserts are just as alluring as the rest, bringing on a samosa of marbled chocolate, chenna (crumbly cheese) and roasted almonds, with Indian tea ice cream. Wines are in keeping with the elevated tone. A generous page of half-bottles opens a list that is high on quality. The centre of gravity is France, and prices are not giveaway, but everything has been chosen with an eye to the food, as it should be. Glass prices start at £5, bottles at £20.

Chef/s: Vineet Bhatia. **Open:** Mon to Fri L 12 to 2.30, Mon to Sat D 6 to 10.45. **Closed:** Christmas. **Meals:** alc (main courses £15 to £39). Set L £24, Set D £75. **Service:** 12.5% (optional). **Details:** Cards accepted. 52 seats. Air-con. No music.

Tom Aikens

Superstar chef comes of age
43 Elystan Street, SW3 3NT
Tel no: (020) 7584 2003
www.tomaikens.co.uk
⊖ South Kensington
French | £59
Cooking score: 8

🍷 **V**

As has been noted before in these pages, Tom Aikens' cooking has become more assured and less showy since his Pied-à-Terre days. The word 'simplicity' is not the first that springs to mind even now, but dishes are not quite as busy as they once were. Perhaps it's the effect of the interior design in this sober-looking restaurant, where even the flowers obey the

Tom Aikens

Why did you become a chef?
I was exposed to fantastic food from an early age, mainly due to my father's trade as a wine merchant.

Who was your main inspiration?
Professionally, David Cavalier and Pierre Koffman helped me become who I am today.

Which of today's chefs do you admire?
Unfortunately, not many of the 'well known' chefs still cook in their kitchens. Admiration though has to go to Michel and Albert Roux, for their dedication and consistency in their commitment to the industry.

Where do you eat out?
Close to home, either the Wolseley or Tom's Kitchen. When I am away, I try to eat at local top restaurants to pick up ideas and trends.

Where do you source your ingredients?
We have a great number of suppliers, but working for Lady Bamford when she was developing Daylesford farm has meant that organic produce has been a firm principle of mine ever since.

What's the best dish you've ever eaten?
A simple, but exquisite, grilled chicken with summer truffles at Eugenie les Bains in South-West France.

If you could only eat one more thing, what would it be?
My brother Rob's freshly baked muffins.

black-and-white colour scheme. On arrival, you are greeted by 'excellent' staff who maintain well-paced service throughout, starting with an initial selection of nibbles, which might include a crisp, intensely flavoured red pepper tuile; a poached quail's egg with a little Jabugo ham and a sliver of truffle; and a milk bottle from which you extract earthy celeriac foam and sweet Sauternes jelly with a long spoon. Fish shines out as fresh and correctly timed, from a starter of cod brandade with poached cod, cauliflower florets, two quail's eggs, a little mint oil and a few pea shoots and nasturtium leaves for colour, to a main course of Dover sole served with very good Jersey Royals, slices of baby cucumber, potato mousse, baby leeks and vichyssoise sauce, topped with a little caviar. Elsewhere, surf and turf combinations come into their own: poached native lobster teamed with virtually transparent ham, a few slices of summer truffle and pleasantly assertive langoustine oil, or a main course of roast pork cutlet and loin of pork with baby squid, a fine 'beignet' of pork meat and a mini lasagne of pork, while excellent caramelised baby onions and pork crackling filled out any missing elements of flavour or texture. One reporter grumbled that you needed a 'mouth like a vacuum cleaner' to successfully slurp a thick pre-dessert of plum jelly, plum foam and vanilla cream through the accompanying straw, but was cheered by the 'magnificent' chocolate fondant that followed it – where, it seems, the effort of restraint finally became too much. That said, the artiness serves well in the 'awe-inspiring' array of 22 petits fours – a gleeful jaunt from beignets and meringues to the playful sweetshop science of test tubes, jelly and lollipops. The wine list is a lengthy tome, presided over by a capable sommelier. It changes frequently but typically offers a smattering of German choices, some prime California and Australian wines, and a good covering of France, which takes in the lesser regions as well as the classics. Mark-ups are moderately stiff but not the worst in London, with the price of a bottle starting at £25.

Chef/s: Tom Aikens. Open: Mon to Fri 12 to 2.30, 6.45 to 11. Closed: 2 weeks Christmas to New Year, last 2 weeks Aug, bank hols. Meals: Set L £29, Set D £60 to £75. Service: 12.5% (optional). Details: Cards accepted. 60 seats. Air-con. No music. No mobile phones. Wheelchair access. Jacket and tie required. Children's portions.

Tom's Kitchen

New opening is drawing the crowds
27 Cale Street, SW3 3QP
Tel no: (020) 7349 0202
www.tomskitchen.co.uk
⊖ Sloane Square
Modern British | £33
Cooking score: 4

This popular, lively and noisy dining room is the creation Tom Aiken who, rather than jump on the bandwagon and open a pub, opened this straightforward brasserie as his second string. It's a very trendy space with a soaring ceiling and neutral colour scheme and, if you're sitting in the right place, an open-to-view kitchen. But plainly laid wooden tables are inches apart, that's if you're not placed at a shared refectory table, and decibel levels are high at peak times. Thankfully, the food makes amends for any aural discomforts. The cooking looks to France for much of the inspiration – celeriac remoulade with Bayonne ham, bouillabaisse, roast rack of lamb with herb crust, mustard mash and confit garlic. An inspection meal found a few dishes requiring more attention to detail, but hits included sour dough bread, leeks with black truffles, lentils, parmesan and meat juices – a straightforward dish that made a big impact due to the quality of the ingredients – and a soup of butternut squash with sage and honey. Seriously good buttery mash accompanied spit-roast chicken with ceps and a side dish of savoy bacon with smoked bacon proved a 'brilliant combination'. Baked Alaska for two was a suitably retro finish. House wine is £13. NB As we went to print, the opening of Tom Aikens new sustainable fish and chip restaurant, 'Tom's Place' had been delayed. The restaurant will be situated at 1 Cale Street, SW3 3QT. Reports please.

Chef/s: Tom Aikens. **Open:** Mon to Fri L 12 to 3 D 6 to 11, Sat B and L 10 to 3, D 6 to 11. Sun 11 to 3 6 to 11. **Closed:** Christmas. **Meals:** alc main courses £12 to £35. **Service:** optional. **Details:** Cards accepted. 70 seats. Separate bar. Wheelchair access. Music. Children allowed.

READERS RECOMMEND

Foxtrot Oscar
Modern British
79 Hospital Road, SW3 4HN
Tel no: (020) 7352 4448
www.gordonramsay.com
'Low-key offering from Ramsay'

Osteria dell'Arancio
Italian
383 Kings' Road, SW10 0LP
Tel no: (020) 7349 8111
'Sound Italian home-style cooking.'

Royal Court Cafe Bar
Modern British
Royal Court Theatre, Sloane Square, SW1W 8AS
Tel no: (020) 7565 5058
www.royalcourttheatre.com
'Recently revamped cultural setting'

Yi-Ban
Chinese
5 The Boulevard, Imperial Road, SW6 2UB
Tel no: (020) 7731 6606
www.yi-ban.com
'Accomplished restaurant with great dim sum.'

▐ Chiswick

Fish Hook
Eclectic seafood in downtown Chiswick
6-8 Elliott Road, W4 1PE
Tel no: (020) 8742 0766
www.fishhook.co.uk
⊖ Turnham Green
Seafood | £32
Cooking score: 2
♀

Michael Nadra's bright, unfussy neighbourhood restaurant plies its trade in a tall Victorian house on one of Chiswick's residential streets. An emphatic piscatorial moniker spells out the kitchen's intentions and allegiances: fish from far and wide is the main business and Nadra rings the changes each day depending on the market. Red mullet might be turned into escabèche with broccoli 'micro leaves' and crostini as accompaniments, while soft shell crabs are given the tempura treatment. Global themes also point up main courses of grilled sea bream with chorizo, peppers and couscous, or monkfish with Alsace bacon, salsa verde and summer-bean salad. Meat fanciers are offered aged, Scotch fillet steak with shiitake mushrooms, while desserts could feature blueberry and almond sponge with Greek yogurt and honey sorbet. Fish-friendly French whites are the pick of the wine list, with prices starting at £10.

Chef/s: Michael Nadra. **Open:** all week L 12-2.30 (3.30 Sat and Sun) D 6 to 10.30 (10 Sun). **Closed:** Christmas. **Meals:** alc (main courses £16) Set L £10 (2 courses) to £13.50. **Service:** 12.5%. **Details:** Cards accepted. 54 seats. Air-con. Wheelchair access. Music. Children allowed.

Sam's Brasserie and Bar

All-singing, all-dancing favourite
11 Barley Mow Passage, W4 4PH
Tel no: (020) 8987 0555
www.samsbrasserie.co.uk
⊖ Turnham Green
Modern European | £29
Cooking score: 4

V

Sam Harrison's lively Chiswick venue aims to be a neighbourhood hot-spot and is big enough for a diverse range of neighbourhood needs, with a large bar and eating area, along with a brasserie on ground-floor and mezzanine levels. It's an infectiously buzzy place, and there is good eating to be had. Pasta dishes in two sizes include orecchiette with courgettes, tomatoes, basil and capers, while starters bring on rare tuna with bean salad, or grey shrimps with endive and bacon. Robust fish main courses take in seared monkfish with parsley mash and caper butter, or there is the tri-nations composition of Italian sausages with bubble and squeak and sauerkraut. Finish with chocolate pithiviers, cooked to order, or blood orange and mango jelly with mint syrup. Wines are a pleasing international jumble, the whites majoring in Sauvignon and Chardonnay, the reds ascending to the full-throttle glory of Penfold's Grange at £165. Prices start at a distinctly gentler £12.50 (£3.50 a glass).
Chef/s: Rufus Wickham. Open: all week 12 to 3 (4 Sat and Sun), 6.30 to 10.30 (10 Sun). Closed: 24-26 Dec. Meals: alc (main courses £8.75 to £17.50). Set L Mon to Fri £11.50 (2 courses) to £15. Set D £13.50 (2 courses). Set D Sun £19.50. Bar menu available. Service: 12.5% (optional). Details: Cards accepted. 100 seats. Air-con. Separate bar. Wheelchair access. Music. Children's portions.

The Devonshire

Ramsay's pub formula rolls on
126 Devonshire Road, W4 2JJ
Tel no: (020) 7592 7962
www.gordonramsay.com
⊖ Turnham Green
Gastropub | £26
Cooking score: 2

The good folk of Chiswick seem to have been spoiled of late, with a host of new openings along the High Street. This time, the Ramsay roadshow rolls into the back streets of town in the form of another gastropub to add to his ever-burgeoning stable. A dark wood, traditional pub has been given a cosmetic overhaul to create a standard bar area with comfy chairs and an austere dining room. High-backed wooden chairs and white linen create an effect that feels slightly too stiff for the food in question. The menu is formulaic, echoing Ramsay's first gastropub outing with The Narrow (see entry). We expect the forthcoming opening of the Warrington in Maida Vale to wheel out more of the same. At inspection, starters included potted Morecambe Bay shrimps with granary toast (the bread being decidedly ordinary) and a home-made pork pie with piccalilli. Stone bass with savoy cabbage, bacon and pickled cockles was well-executed, but very plain. The Hereford beef in ale pie with mash was altogether more succesful, with melt-in-the-mouth pastry and a deep, heart-warming sauce. Desserts are a traditional affair, with the likes of bread and butter pudding with custard making an appearance. To be fair, this is solid cooking using decent ingredients, but the wow factor that Ramsay invites us to expect of him is somehow missing. However, prices reflect the simplicity of the menu and the low-key setting. House wines start at £13.50, rising to £75 for a Chateau Grand Puy Lacoste.

Chef/s: Chris Arkadieff. **Open:** Mon to Fri L 12 to 3, D 6 to 10, Sat and Sun 12 to 10. **Meals:** alc (main courses from £10 to £20). **Service:** 12.5%. **Details:** Cards accepted. 42 seats. Air-con. Separate bar. Wheelchair access. Music. Children allowed.

La Trompette

A buzzing neighbourhood restaurant
5-7 Devonshire Road, W4 2EU
Tel no: (020) 8747 1836
www.latrompette.co.uk
⊖ Turnham Green
French | £35
Cooking score: 6

Don't underestimate this tasteful restaurant on its leafy Chiswick side street. Fans say it's more than just a good local; it's a 'destination restaurant' in its own right. The French-style fixed price (£35 for three courses) approach garners praise, as do the menus that offer an enticing range of seven or so starters, mains and pudds that 'reflect the season'. The cooking is French with a Mediterranean touch; simple dishes with flavours that sing out loud. All our dishes at inspection had an endearingly split personality: a Salad Lyonnaise charmed us with its neat celeriac remoulade, petite croutons and delicate slices of duck breast, then wham!, shards of crisped-up duck skin, hunks of gutsy confit leg meat, and an orange globe of runny poached egg yolk made a mockery of the dish's affectation of refinement. A gilthead bream main course was a dream of soft white flesh and crispy skin, enhanced by subtly lemony gremolata. Puddings showed well too in the form of a Brillat Savarin cheesecake and a Valrhona fondant. The 'fabulous' Cheese board comes at a £5 supplement but certainly warrants it. There's a lot of fun to be had with the wonderful wine list. Vinous thrills abound, starting low (at £16) with wines plucked from all corners of the world including Georgia, Lebanon, Canada and Switzerland.

Chef/s: James Bennington. **Open:** all week L 12 to 2.30, D 6.30 to 10. **Meals:** Set L and D £35. **Service:** 12.5%. **Details:** Cards accepted. 75 seats. 16 seats outside. Air-con. No music. Wheelchair access. Children's portions.

Le Vacherin

Chiswick's Parisienne enclave
76-77 South Parade, W4 5LF
Tel no: (020) 8742 2121
www.levacherin.co.uk
⊖ Turnham Green
French | £31
Cooking score: 4

V

A little dollop of Paris is an unlikely find on a Chiswick thoroughfare, but that is what Chef/Patron Malcolm John has striven to create and the resulting restaurant has the feel of one that has been part of the neighbourhood for years. Locals treat it as a place to sup or to celebrate and the hubbub of happy diners is all pervading. The French, bistro décor, complete with piles of Vacherin cheeses, leaves little room for mistaking the style of the food – escargots, foie gras, truffled, baked Vacherin (in season) abound as do steaks (avec frites), grilled fish and rich, carefully made stews, followed by ile flotante and tarte aux amandes. The menu may seem nostalgic, but John knows what he's about and he cooks well within his limits. A well-annotated all French wine list and friendly, if rather harrassed, service complete the picture. House wines start at £3.50 a glass.

Chef/s: Malcolm John. **Open:** Tue to Sun L 12 to 3, all week D 6 to 10.30. **Closed:** Bank hols. **Meals:** alc (main courses L £10 to £12, D £13 to £19). **Service:** 12.5% (optional). **Details:** Cards accepted. 80 seats. 10 seats outside. Air-con. No music. No mobile phones. Children's portions.

READERS RECOMMEND

Budsara
Thai
99 Chiswick High Road, W4 2ED
Tel no: (020) 8995 5774
'Above-average cooking in a relaxed setting'

High Road Brasserie
French
162 Chiswick High Road, W4 1PR
Tel no: 020 8742 7474
'A fantastic Parisian-style bistro'

Pissarro
Modern European
Corney Reach Way, W4 2UG
Tel no: (020) 8994 3111
www.pissarro.co.uk
'Solid cooking at a waterside location'

Roebuck
Gastropub
122 Chiswick High Road, W4 1PU
Tel no: (020) 8995 4392
'Simple, decent food and good service'

▌Earl's Court

Cambio de Tercio
Clearly proud of its Spanish accent
163 Old Brompton Road, SW5 0LJ
Tel no: (020) 7244 8970
⊖ Gloucester Road
Spanish | £37
Cooking score: 2
🍷

White clothed tables are closely packed and
there are a few pavement tables outside under
an awning for fair weather dining – this
warmly decorated restaurant positively throbs
with activity and is popular with a young
crowd. The cooking is modern Spanish in that
it blends old ideas with new and offers the
menu as a conventional starter/main/dessert
combo or with every dish served tapas style
(where three to four dishes per person is
recommended). An inspection meal found a

few dishes requiring more attention to detail
but hits included 'brilliant' organic sobrasada,
chorizo and El Suspiro goats' cheese
caramelised served on toast, a well-judged
plate of garlic prawns with baby chillies and
lemon oil, deep-fried squid with ink and
garlic mayonnaise, and arroz negro with baby
squid and cockles. Desserts lack lustre –
although chocolate fondant has impressed –
and service, though good, can be rushed. An
impressive range of sherries proudly heads up a
patriotic modern wine list and mark-ups are
not greedy.
Chef/s: Alberto Criado. Open: all week 12.15 to
2.30, 6.45 to 11.30. Closed: 2 weeks at Christmas.
Meals: alc (main courses £14 to £17). Service: not
inc. Details: Cards accepted. 45 seats. Air-con.
Music.

Lou Pescadou
Friendly venue for French seafood
241 Old Brompton Road, SW5 9HP
Tel no: (020) 7370 1057
⊖ Earls Court
Seafood | £45
Cooking score: 3

V

This glass-fronted French seafood outfit,
pitched up on a stretch of the Old Brompton
Road, is something of a neighborhood
favourite with the Earl s Court crowd. The
very friendly, relaxed, laid-back Gallic service
is beloved by most, though others may find it a
tad over-familiar, but all agree that seafood is
the main player. Inside follows a marine
theme, with light walls donned with naïve
paintings of French quayside scenes and
seafaring paraphernalia. Tables come with blue
cloths (what else) and accompanying wicker
café-style chairs, while floors are decked out
with russet-coloured titles. Mixed seafood
platters catch the eye, but the crowd-pleasing
menu takes in all things piscine (and a handful
of non-fish options too). Think clams served
with a thyme and cream sauce, perhaps
followed by Sole meunière, and, to finish,
classic apple tart flambéed with Calvados all
archetypal Gallic fare you might eat over the

Channel. The wine list is understandable fish-friendly and mostly French, with prices setting out at £12.20

Chef/s: Laurent David. **Open:** all week 12 to 3, 7 (6.30 Sat and Sun) to 12. **Meals:** alc (main courses £13.50 to £18). Set L Mon to Fri £10.90, Set L Sat and Sun £14.50, Set D Sat 6.30 to 7.45 and Sun £14.50. **Service:** 15% (optional). **Details:** Cards accepted. 15 seats. No music. Wheelchair access. Children's portions.

READERS RECOMMEND
Veggie Vegan
Vegetarian
222 North End Road, W14 9NU
Tel no: (020) 7381 2322
www.222veggievegan.com
'Eco-friendly vegan food'

Fulham
Blue Elephant
Flamboyant Thai cooking
3-6 Fulham Broadway, SW6 1AA
Tel no: (020) 7385 6595
www.blueelephant.com
⊖ Fulham Broadway
Thai | £45
Cooking score: 1

Part of an international chain that spreads from Brussels to Bangkok, the Blue Elephant offers a tourist's-eye-view of the Thai experience. Its dazzling interior comes complete with luxuriant, sub-tropical foliage, exotic flora, carp ponds and a sumptuous bar designed to resemble a royal barge. The kitchen deals in extravagant tours through the repertoire, with classics such as fishcakes and roast duck curry, lining up beside stir-fried crocodile with chilli, basil and palm hearts, or poached lobster 'swimming in a sea of vegetables, ginger and perfumed mushrooms'. Seared foie gras with tamarind sauce adds a touch of fusion, while desserts explore the native by-ways with jasmine cakes, steamed banana pudding and Thai mango with sticky rice. Sunday brunch is a lavish

family affair. The wine list has a broad span and matches the incisive flavours of the food. Prices start at £17 (£5 a glass).

Chef/s: Sompong Sae-Jew. **Open:** Mon to Fri 12 to 2.30, (Sun 12 to 3.30), all week 7 to 12 (to 10.30 Sun). **Closed:** 4 days Christmas. **Meals:** alc (main courses £11 to £28). Set L Mon to Fri £10 (2 courses) Set D £35 to £53 (3 courses). **Service:** 12.5% (optional). **Details:** Cards accepted. 300 seats. Air-con. Wheelchair access. Music. Children allowed.

Chutney Mary
Respectable food and cosseting service
535 King's Road, SW10 0SZ
Tel no: (020) 7351 3113
www.realindianfood.com
⊖ Fulham Broadway
Indian | £44
New Chef

V

The scale of the dining room is impressive, it's smartly furnished and there's a conservatory filled with large plants creating a 'seductive enviroment'. An army of good-natured staff is on hand to ensure that all your creature comforts are catered for, making it feel as if you are a resident of a deluxe hotel not in an upmarket Indian restaurant on the King's Road. Not surprisingly, all this pampering comes at a high price, but judging by reporters enthusiastic comments, the standard of cooking has improved this year with the kitchen succeeding in its aim to provide refined, modern Indian cooking. At inspection chicken tikka was 'superb', made a bit more special by judicious seasoning. It was followed by a deeply flavoured, slow-cooked lamb osso bucco and carefully cooked bhindi dopiaza. Leave room for above average desserts, in particular a tasting plate with seasonal Alphonso mango used for the sorbet and kulfi, or try the crumbly rhubarb tart. The wine list is assembled with care to match the style of food, and starts from £17.25.

Chef/s: Siddhart Krishna. **Open:** Fri to Sun L 12.30 to 2.30 (3 Sun), all week D 6.30 to 11.30 (10.30 Sun). **Meals:** Set D £45. **Service:** 12.5% (optional). **Details:** Cards accepted. 110 seats. Air-con. Wheelchair access. Music. Children allowed.

Deep
Stylish seafood by the Thames
The Boulevard, Imperial Wharf, SW6 2UB
Tel no: (020) 7736 3337
www.deeplondon.co.uk
⊖ Fulham Broadway
Seafood | £49
Cooking score: 4

Its location in the swanky new Thames-side development of Imperial Wharf may be a tad off-the-beaten track, but it certainly rewards with modern curb appeal and impressive seafood. Huge glass windows embrace the large, ultra-cool, minimalist space, perhaps recognisable to some as the venue for 'The F-Word' and 'The Great British Menu'. An open kitchen and sushi cabinet catch the eye, as do the side and front terraces for alfresco drinks or dining – both with glimpses of the Thames. The cooking suits the venue; equally clean cut and classy. Well-sourced produce, with seafood taking centre stage, cuts a tilt towards its Swedish owner's roots, while offering the occasional nod to carnivores. Take 'ocean fresh' steamed halibut topped with egg, prawns and horseradish in warm butter, or perhaps braised shoulder of lamb 'escargot' served with wild garlic and tomato. Save room for a 'cracking' chocolate fondant dessert with warm cherries and almond cream. The drinks list comes with a fine selection of aquavits and fashionable globetrotting wines varietally laid out, though with little under £20 but house South African at £14.75.
Chef/s: Christian and Kerstin Sandefeldt. **Open:** Tue to Fri and Sun L 12 to 3, Tue to Sat D 7 to 11. **Meals:** alc (main courses £13 to £22). Set L £15.50 (2 courses) to £19.50. Cover £1.. **Service:** 12.5% (optional). **Details:** Cards accepted. 40 seats. Air-con. Wheelchair access. Music.

READERS RECOMMEND

Mao Tai
Asian
58 New Kings Road, SW6 4LS
Tel no: (020) 7731 2520
www.maotai.co.uk
'A gastronomic survey of Asia in Fulham'

▌Hammersmith

★ BEST GASTROPUB ★

Carpenter's Arms
Great local with good food
91 Black Lion Lane, W6 9BG
Tel no: 020 8741 8386
⊖ Stamford Brook
Gastropub | £25
Cooking score: 2

The corner-sited pub may look traditional from the outside, but the uncomplicated single bar room with its plain wood floor and junk shop tables and chairs bears the hallmark of a modern-day gastro-pub. The menu changes daily, delivering refreshingly robust and uncomplicated creations, classic British dishes with the odd nod towards France and Italy. Potted shrimps and roast bone marrow share the stage with a whole roast poussin or roast halibut served with pig's trotter, carrots and grain mustard, and the roll-call of dishes reporters recommend include gutsy peppered venison Barnsley chop (served with roast swede and steeped raisins) and oxtail, pearl onion and parsnip pie. The style of cooking is light and its simplicity and clear flavours reflect prime materials treated confidently. Desserts range from poire belle Hélène to pumpkin Bakewell with candied sage, Valrhona and mascarpone. The food represents good value for money – and so do the wines, which start at £13.50.
Chef/s: Paul Adams. **Open:** Mon to Sat L 12 to 3, D to 10, Sun L 12.30 to 4, D 7.30 to 9. **Meals:** alc (main courses from £10.25 to £16.50). **Service:** 12.5% (optional). **Details:** Cards accepted. 35 seats. 20 seats outside. Music. Children's portions. Children allowed.

Chez Kristof

french food from a winning formula
11 Hammersmith Grove, W6 0NQ
tel no: (020) 8741 1177
www.chezkristof.co.uk
➔ Hammersmith
French | £31
cooking score: 3

Having brought hearty Eastern European cooking to Southwark (Baltic, see entry), Jan Woroneicki now offers unpretentious, straightforward French regional cooking at his bustling brasserie. Peruse the flexible, seasonally changing menus over crudités at the bar, then tuck into some robust and gutsy dishes at closely spaced tables in the light and airy dining room, or dine alfresco under the front canopy when the sun shines. Start with devilled lambs' kidneys, sautéed prawns with white wine, parsley and garlic, or a plate of charcuterie, then follow with steamed hake with clams and peas, confit duck with potato and turnips, or braised shoulder of lamb with broad beans and garlic. Leave room for a classic apple tarte Tatin or rice pudding with caramelised oranges. Wines are all French, with prices to suit every budget and a good showing of top-value regional wines. Prices open at £14.

chef/s: Jan Woroneicki. Open: all week 12 to 3 (4 Sat/Sun), 6 to 11.15 (10.30 Sun). Meals: alc (main courses £12.50 to £16.50). Set L and D before 7pm £12 (2 courses) to £15. Service: 12.5%. Details: Cards accepted. 85 seats. Wheelchair access. Music. Children's portions.

River Café

fresh and thoughtful Italian cooking
Thames Wharf, Rainville Road, W6 9HA
tel no: (020) 7386 4200
www.rivercafe.co.uk
➔ Hammersmith
Italian | £65
cooking score: 6

There is no end of opinion about the River Café and not all of it good. It is famously difficult to get a booking, and it is awkward to get to. The tables and chairs are squashed in together and eaves-dropping on one's neighbour is not so much a party game as a necessity given that the volume of noise is so great that it's often easier to hear your neighbour than your companion. Beyond that, there is the annoying demand on diners that comes with time slot dining and the eye-watering, seemingly unjustifiable prices. But once settled in, the brilliance of the place becomes clear. The daily changing menu is entirely seasonal, celebrating all that's good in England and Italy when treated with an Italianate hand – a spring dinner saw deep-fried anchovies as an antipasto, with a dish of fresh bright-green tagliorini served with delicate spring nettles to follow. A sublimely rich stew of veal shin was given vitality and lightness by a generous dosing of lemon zest and new season garlic. A tranche of turbot, on the other hand, makes the most of their searingly hot wood-fired oven, arrivingly perfectly cooked and slighty crispy, the flavours enhanced with the classic Italian combination of lemon, capers, olives and oregano. Portions are enormous but if possible save room for one of their classic Italian puds, including excellent tarts and pannacotta. The entirely Italian wine list (from £18.50 per bottle) is fairly impenetrable to all but the cognoscienti, so the habitually friendly and knowledgeable staff and wine waiters are an added bonus.

chef/s: Rose Gray and Ruth Rogers. Open: all week L 12.30 to 2.15 (2.30 Sat, 12 to 3.30 Sun), D 7 to 9 (9.15 Fri and Sat). Closed: Christmas, bank hols. Meals: alc (main courses £25 to £31). Service: 12.5%. Details: Cards accepted. 110 seats. 90 seats outside. Separate bar. No music. Wheelchair access. Children's portions. Car parking.

Snows on the Green

Chic neighbourhood restaurant
166 Shepherds Bush Road, W6 7PB
Tel no: (020) 7603 2142
www.snowsonthegreen.co.uk
⊖ Hammersmith
Modern European | £30
Cooking score: 4

V

Sebastian Snow has been cooking at this well-liked neighbourhood restaurant on Brook Green (hence the title) since 1990, and continues to deliver carefully crafted, unshowy food in a setting of soft lights, arty photos and considerate table spacings. His signature dish is foie gras with fried egg and balsamic vinegar, which he describes as 'eccentrically eclectic'. Other seasonal ideas are closer to the modern European mainsteam, witness a 'spring green' risotto with peas, broccoli and fava beans, baked fillet of cod with chorizo, clams, wild garlic leaves and leek purée or roast corn-fed chicken breast with asparagus and morels. The Italian old guard also gets a look in with fritto misto, vitello tonnato and osso buco. Desserts put hot treacle tart and steamed chocolate pudding alongside espresso crème caramel with poached fruits, and fans of unpasteurised Italian cheeses won't be disappointed by the selection served with toasted walnut bread and pickled grapes. The wine list offers a broad spread of fine bottles from around the globe. Fourteen are available by the glass, and bottle prices start at £12.50.

Chef/s: Sebastian Snow. Open: Mon to Fri L 12 to 3, Mon to Sat D 6 to 11. Closed: 4 days Christmas, bank hols. Meals: alc (main courses £15 to £17). Set L and D £13.50 (2 courses) to £16.50.. Service: 12.5%. Details: Cards accepted. 80 seats. 10 seats outside. Air-con. No mobile phones. Wheelchair access. Music. Children's portions.

The Gate

Cosmopolitan vegetarian grub
51 Queen Caroline Street, W6 9QL
Tel no: (020) 8748 6932
www.thegate.tv
⊖ Hammersmith
Vegetarian | £34
Cooking score: 2

♀ V

Perennially popular, this vegetarian haven seems to be going from strength to strength. Sit inside the sparsely furnished church or take advantage of the courtyard on sunny days to enjoy the innovative, full flavours that come out of the kitchen. Cooking styles and influences are wide-reaching: a light, creamy courgette and gorgonzola tart sits comfortably alongside a slightly tame Thai salad of green mango and paw-paw and Indo-Iraqi potato cake stuffed with spiced vegetables and served with a sweet tamarind sauce amongst the first courses, whilst a Thai flavoured laksa with pumpkin wontons features alongside simpler pastas and risottos to follow. The kitchen shows real ambition and happily dispels any sandal-wearing 'hippie' notions. A short, but decent, wine list starts at £3.50 a glass.

Chef/s: Marinsz Wegrodski. Open: Mon to Fri L 12 to 2.45, Mon to Sat D 6 to 10.45. Closed: 23 Dec to Jan. Meals: Set L and D £18.50 (two courses) to £2. Service: 12.5%. Details: Cards accepted. 60 seats. 40 seats outside. Air-con. Music. Children's portions.

READERS RECOMMEND

Agni

Indian
169 King Street, W6 0QU
Tel no: 020 8846 9191
www.agnirestaurant.com
'Genuine home-style cooking'

Bianco Nero
Italian
206 Hammersmith Road, W6 7DP
Tel no: (020) 8748 0212
www.biancorerestaurants.com
'Sophisticated twists on Italian classics'

Sagar
Indian
157 King Street, W6 9JT
Tel no: (020) 8741 8563
'Vegetarian food without compromise'

Tosa
Japanese
332 King Street, W6 0RR
Tel no: (020) 8748 0002
'Authentic Japanese food with friendly staff'

▌Kensington

11 Abingdon Road
Relaxed and informal atmosphere
11-13 Abingdon Road, W8 6AH
Tel no: (020) 7937 0120
⊖ High Street Kensington
Modern European | £31
Cooking score: 3

Tucked away down a little street off High Street Kensington, this light, simply decorated neighbourhood restaurant continues to prosper. It's owned by Rebecca Mascarenhas, who also operates Sonny's and the Pheonix (see entries). Young, friendly and casually dressed staff deliver three kinds of bread, including cinnamon, to the table, which precede soundly cooked modern European dishes. First-class materials underpin the operation, from starters of chargrilled sardines with lemon couscous and Sicilian dressing, or smoked eel with horseradish crème fraîche to successful main courses, like roast veal shin with spinach, artichokes, peas and gremolata, or seared skate wing on crushed potatoes with brown shrimps and capers. Finish with artisan cheeses

or apricot and almond tart. The global wine list is compact but knowledgable, and starts at £12.75 for French house selections.
Chef/s: David Stafford. Open: all week 12 to 2.30, 6.30 to 11. Closed: bank hols. Meals: alc (main courses £11.50 to £17.50). Set L £13.50, Set D £17.50.. Service: 12.5% (optional). Details: Cards accepted. 80 seats.

Popeseye
Uncompromising steak house
108 Blythe Road, W14 0HD
Tel no: (020) 7610 4578
www.popeseye.com
⊖ Kensington (Olympia)
British | £45
Cooking score: 1

If steak is your thing, this no-nonsense west London eatery will be just the ticket, its sole raison d'être being a celebration of prime grass-fed Aberdeen Angus beef from the Highlands, hung for a minimum of two weeks to ensure maximum flavour and tenderness. Occupying a corner site, the simply decorated dining room opts for modern prints on plain white walls, bare floorboards and tartan tablecloths, with the grill open to view in the corner. The menu takes an equally uncomplicated approach, listing a choice of popeseye (rump), sirloin or fillet, in cuts from 6oz up to 30oz, all served with chips, plus salad as an optional extra. And that's it. No vegetarian options, nor starters, and to finish there's a perfunctory choice of desserts or cheeses. But when the steak's this good, who's complaining? Wines focus on vintage clarets, with basic house red at £11.50.
Chef/s: Ian Hutchison. Open: Mon to Sat D only 6.45 to 10.30. Meals: alc (main courses £10 to £45.50). Service: 12.5% (optional). Details: Cash only. 32 seats. Air-con. Wheelchair access. Music. Children's portions.

Also recommended

An 'also recommended' entry is not a full entry, but is provisionally suggested as an alternative to main entries.

Timo

Made by Italians, for Italians...
343 Kensington High Street, W8 6NW
Tel no: (020) 7603 3888
⊖ High Street Kensington
Italian | £52
Cooking score: 2

V

It's reassuring when Italian restaurants are frequented by Italians; Timo is one such so the rest of us might be wise to take the hint. Each dish receives a useful translation, necessary since much will be unfamiliar. Wild boar with fresh broad beans, raviolini filled with braised guinea fowl with beetroot butter and thyme are not run of the mill. Dishes that look like old friends have a twist; asparagus with poached egg is topped with pancetta and a mustard dressing. Vigorous combinations such as monkfish with cream of pumpkin or bass with runner beans and dill show a kitchen in touch with imaginative, pragmatic, peasant cooking. Desserts touch standard territory, with tiramisu, a range of *sorbetti della casa* and panacotta scented with espresso. Wines, start at £16, proceed to astonishing heights and are exclusively Italian; there's a coda of a dozen or so grappa.
Chef/s: Franco Gatti. Open: Sun to Fri L 12 to 2.30, all week D 7 to 11. Meals: alc D (main courses £13.50 to £19.50). Set L £14.50 (2 courses) to £21.50. Service: 12.5% (optional). Details: Cards accepted. 119 seats. 4 seats outside. Air-con. Wheelchair access. Music. Children's portions.

Zaika

Excellent tasting menu
1 Kensington High Street, W8 5NP
Tel no: (020) 7795 6533
www.zaika-restaurant.co.uk
⊖ High Street Kensington
Indian | £34
Cooking score: 3

V

Zaika translates as sophisticated flavours and this is the driving force behind a menu that is a vivid take on the Europe-meets-West theme.

But is this acclaimed contemporary Indian, once seen as daring and cutting edge, now in the danger of resting on its laurels? Opinion is divided, with some delighted by the whole operation, while others ask 'if it is time to overhaul the menu?' But there is still talent in the kitchen – puff pastry-crusted biryani, prolific use of curry leaves, several interpretations of single ingredients (like lamb or chicken) on the same plate, use of classic Gujarati and south Indian snacks as garnish and, of course, the chocolate samosas. The combining of old and new, with traditional dishes alongside original creations, has considerable appeal and the six-course tasting menu is a good introduction. The earthy-hued former bank building opposite Kensington Gardens is kitted out with ornate screens and stone carvings and continues to be a warm, pleasant place. A carefully chosen drinks list features spice-friendly wines from around the world, tropical fruit cocktails and spirits.
Chef/s: Sanjay Dwivedi. Open: Sun to Fri L 12 to 2.45, all week D 6 to 10.45 (9.45 Sun). Closed: 25 and 26 Dec, 1 Jan. Meals: alc (main courses £14 to £19). Set L £15 (2 courses) to £19, Set D £38 to £88 (inc wine). Bar menu available. Service: 12.5% (optional). Details: Cards accepted. 80 seats. Air-con. Separate bar. Wheelchair access. Music.

ALSO RECOMMENDED

▲ Cumberland Arms

29 North End Road, W14 8SZ
Tel no: (020) 7371 6806
www.thecumberlandarmspub.co.uk
⊖ Kensington (Olympia)

The Mediterranean dominates the menu at this understated, well-worn dining pub. To start, try the antipasti – chicken liver purée on crostini with fried onions, pan-roast sea bass fillet with chicory, or a tomato, wild rocket and Parmesan frittata (£7). Mains might include grilled skewered marlin and tiger prawns with lemon rice, mint and sultanas (£12.50), and Tuscan lamb casserole (£11). For something different try the pheasant and merguez tagine with quince and saffron.

Finish with apple and cinnamon crumble with cream (£4). Wines from £10.50. Open all week.

READERS RECOMMEND

Brunello

Italian
60 Hyde Park Gate, SW7 5BB
Tel no: 020 7636 9709
www.brunellorestaurants.com
'Assured regional cooking'

Kensington Square Kitchen

British
9 Kensington Square, W8 5EP
Tel no: (020) 7938 2598
www.kensingtonsquarekitchen.co.uk
'No-frills comfort cooking in Kensington.'

Nyonya

Malaysian
2A Kensington Park Road, W11 3BU
Tel no: (020) 7243 1800
www.nyonya.co.uk
'Affordable cuisine'

▌Notting Hill

Ark

An intimate Italian establishment
122 Palace Gardens Terrace, W8 4RT
Tel no: (020) 7229 4024
www.ark-restaurant.com
⊖ Notting Hill Gate
Italian | £33
Cooking score: 2

V

Generous portions and well-cooked, traditional dishes sum up the food at this neighbourhood favourite. A balsamic jus with pan-fried calf's liver and grilled figs, for example, is one of the few concessions to trendy cooking. Meals start with a homemade unsalted foccacia, ultra-thin grassini and pesto, and there is a good selection of home-made pastas, sorbets and ice creams. Main courses can include grilled yellow-fin tuna

with salsa verde or lamb rump with canellini beans. Desserts have a retro feel with favourites such as raspberry fool with home-made lady-fingers. The long, narrow room, with its taupe walls, dim wall lighting and tealights, can be cozy and intimate, but has felt 'flat' with too many empty tables. The front terrace is inviting, but remember buses, cars and taxis pass a few feet away. Wines start at £4.75 with bottles from £15.
Chef/s: Alberto Comai. **Open:** Tue to Sat L 12 to 3, Mon to Sat D 6.30 to 11. **Closed:** Sundays, bank hols. **Meals:** Set L £28.50, Set D £32.20. **Service:** 12.5%. **Details:** Cards accepted. 48 seats. 13 seats outside. Air-con. Separate bar. Music. Children allowed.

Assaggi

Simple and authentic
39 Chepstow Place, W2 4TS
Tel no: (020) 7792 5501
⊖ Notting Hill Gate
Italian | £58
Cooking score: 4

In a terrace of large white houses, oddly situated above a perfectly ordinary pub, this boldly decorated restaurant has a rustic style of Southern-Italian cooking. It is lively and always full: book well in advance. The short menu is in Italian, but cheerful staff are ready with translations. A meal might start with grilled vegetables marinated in olive oil and herbs, or tartare of tuna, take in ravioli stuffed with ricotta as a pasta dish, then go on to simple main courses such as grilled sea bass, fritto misto, or fillet of pork with black truffle, with side dishes of new potatoes cooked with garlic, rosemary and tomatoes, with rucola and basil. The humble materials are sound as a bell. Flourless chocolate cake is a perfect way to finish. Some 30 Italian wines are fairly pricey, starting with Sardinian red and white at £21.95 or £5 by the glass.
Chef/s: Nino Sassu. **Open:** Mon to Fri 12.30 (1 Sat) to 2.30, 7.30 to 11. **Closed:** 2 weeks Christmas, bank hols. **Meals:** alc (main courses £17.50 to £20).

Allegra McEvedy **Leon**

Why did you become a chef?
I went into it because I was attracted by the food, excitement and creativity.

Which of today's chefs do you admire?
I admire nearly every chef out there, out of respect for the sheer graft it takes to succeed in our business.

Where do you source your ingredients?
At Leon we put a lot of time and resources into our suppliers; all our meat is free-range and British, all our fish is sustainable.

Who is your favourite producer?
Lloyd Maunder – our chicken people in Devon.

What's the best dish you've ever eaten?
Nova Scotia lobster poached in butter at Thomas Keller's restaurant in NYC.

What's your guilty food pleasure?
Haribo Tangfastics – the sour mix!

What's the hardest thing about running a restaurant?
Keeping on top of the training. The team are everything: the more love you give them, the better and happier they are.

Which achievement are you most proud of?
Not having spent any time in jail. Or when my Colour Cookbook won International Chef's and Restaurants' Book of the Year.

Service: not inc. **Details:** Cards accepted. 35 seats. Air-con. No music. Children's portions. Children allowed.

Bumpkin
Country life imported to the city
209 Westbourne Park Road, W11 1EA
Tel no: 020 7243 9818
www.bumpkinuk.com
⊖ **Westbourne Park**
British | £35
Cooking score: 2

With a pastoral design taking in olive-green walls and floral wallpaper, tan leather chairs and satin pink blinds, this sprawling former pub is intended 'for city folk who like a little country living'. But any notion of a bucolic experience is short lived; the noise level generated by the well-heeled diners can reach fever pitch at peak times. The open-plan kitchen cooks in the British idiom with top-notch produce shining through in an appealing starter of seared tuna carpaccio with wild rocket, spiced up by lemon, capers and chili again, and in a juicy pork chop with cider and tarragon. Proper Bramley apple crumble with custard is a satisfying end. It's fun and relaxing, children are actively encouraged, and the service team is jovial and energetic. Wines start from £14, with 20 by the glass kicking off at £3.50, although 1997 Mersault, Coche Dury (£240) is not something you will see in a country inn outside W11. Whisky covers an entire page with some rarities such as a Springbank 1968 36 year at £392 a bottle or £28 for a 50ml shot.
Chef/s: Oliver Prince. **Open:** Tue to Fri 12 to 3 (11 to 3.30 Sat, 12.15 to 3.30 Sun), 6 to midnight (10.30 Sun). **Meals:** alc (main courses £12 to £16), Set L £22.50 (2 courses) on Sun. **Service:** 12.5% (included). **Details:** Cards accepted. 110 seats. 4 seats outside. Air-con. Wheelchair access. Music. Children's portions.

Clarke's

Where simplicity meets style
124 Kensington Church Street, W8 4BH
Tel no: (020) 7221 9225
www.sallyclarke.com
⊖ **Notting Hill Gate**
British | £52
Cooking score: 4

After 24 years, Sally Clarke's vibrant, exciting and very delicious food continues to enthral at her eponymous restaurant, which is set amid the antique shops of Church Street. Eating takes place on two levels, a small ground floor area and the much more relaxing, low-lit basement room with its open-plan kitchen. She has waivered little from her tried and tested formula: using impeccable, seasonal ingredients to produce simple but perfectly executed dishes. The only change in recent years is that she now offers a choice of dishes in the evening, and it is no longer necessary to have all four courses. Lunch is a selection of four starters, three main courses, and either cheese or a couple of puddings, and dishes are priced individually. Dinner often kicks off with a salad – perhaps peas, grilled spring onions and pea shoots with San Daniele ham and a crème fraîche dressing. To follow, there may be chargrilled Angus ribeye with parsley, lemon and garlic butter and hand-cut chips, or halibut baked 'en papillotte' with Jersey Royals, shallots and tarragon and served with roasted fennel and beetroot. First-class cheeses with oatmeal biscuits precede imaginative desserts: say, warm-baked cherry soufflé pancake with bay-leaf ice cream. The wine list is a pick and mix of good and prestigious bottles from around the globe. Prices climb steeply from the £15 starting point.
Chef/s: Sally Clarke. **Open:** Mon to Sat L 12.30 (11 Sat brunch) to 2, Tue to Sat D 7 to 10. **Closed:** 23 Dec to 5 Jan. **Meals:** alc L (main courses £14 to £16). Set D £43.25 to £49.50. **Service:** net prices. **Details:** Cards accepted. 80 seats. Air-con. No music. No mobile phones. Wheelchair access.

e&o

Stylish pan-Asian dining
14 Blenheim Crescent, W11 1NN
Tel no: (020) 7229 5454
www.eando.nu
⊖ **Ladbroke Grove**
Asian fusion | £30
Cooking score: 3

V

A chic but sparse dining room forms the backdrop to this stylish pan-Asian eaterie from the Ricker stable. Slick but friendly staff serve a trendy, buzzy crowd at night and a laidback mix of families (children are welcome) and lunching groups during the day. The handy glossary helps navigate a menu built on plenty of choice. Sharing is de rigueur, recommended as a means of ensuring maximum coverage of the delicately flavoured dim sum – delicate prawn and chive dumplings, say, or baby pork spare ribs dressed in a sticky black bean sauce with fiery red chillies and generous flecks of ginger. Any sushi and sashimi worth its wasabi should be well presented, but e&o's excels, with beautifully presented asparagus and avocado maki, and excellent seared tuna. Or try lamb redang curry with sweet potato or whole barbecued shredded duck. Traditional sweets get a Thai twist in the shape of ta koh pannacotta, but a chocolate fondue may prove hard to resist. A good, varied wine list opens with modest vin de pays at £13.50.
Chef/s: Simon Treadway. **Open:** all week 12 to 3 (12 to 4 Sat, 12.30 to 4 Sun), 6 to 11 (10.30 Sun). **Closed:** 25, 26 Dec, August bank hol. **Meals:** alc (main courses £5.50 to £21.50). **Service:** 12.5% (optional). **Details:** Cards accepted. 84 seats. 20 seats outside. Air-con. Separate bar. Wheelchair access. Music. Children allowed.

Geales

Posh fish and chips
2 Farmer Street, W8 7SN
Tel no: (020) 7727 7528
www.geales.com
⊖ Notting Hill Gate
Seafood | £30
Cooking score: 1

It calls itself a neighbourhood fish and chip restaurant, but smart leather chairs and pristine cloth-clad tables (despite being crammed together) suggest there's more on offer than a quick fish supper. This legendary fish and chip shop (established in 1939) has been given a major revamp by new owners Mark Fuller and Garry Hollihead; even the menu has been overhauled, with starters such as dressed-crab and prawn cocktail marked by stylish presentation as strictly Notting Hill. Similarly, mains range from fish and leek pie to a token meaty sirloin steak with sauce béarnaise. Haddock was deliciously moist and concealed in super-crunchy batter, and although the accompanying chips and mushy peas are by separate price and order, the former delivered 'crunch then fluffiness', the latter 'bite and flavour'. Finish with jam roly-poly or rice pudding with strawberries. A glass of Sauvignon Grenache is £3.95. Bottles start at £12.95.
Chef/s: Gary Hollihead. **Open:** Tue to Sat L 12 to 2.30, D 6 to 11; Sun D 6 to 10.30. **Closed:** Mon lunch. **Meals:** alc main courses £9 to 16. **Service:** optional. **Details:** Cards accepted. 60 seats. 16 seats outside. Air-con. Wheelchair access. Children allowed.

Hereford Road

A showcase for great British produce
3 Hereford Road, W2 4AB
Tel no: 020 7727 1144
www.herefordroad.org
⊖ Bayswater
British | £30
Cooking score: 4

The robust, simple British food pioneered by Fergus Henderson at St John should come as no surprise to diners at this former butcher s

shop. Tom Pemberton has worked in both St John restaurants and is simply doing what he does best in this, his own venture. While there is innovation rather than complexity, what catches the eye is the sheer common sense of the menu. Here is a kitchen prepared to produce the perfect lamb broth. Here is a kitchen not afraid to offer a whole crab on its daily menu or show no qualms at serving things like ox liver and heart. The ingredients are, of course, first class, which means dishes such as fresh grilled anchovies, braised duck leg with turnip, or onglet, chips and aïoli speak for themselves. The kitchen is also faithful to some old-fashioned dishes such as devilled kidneys or braised beef and carrots with desserts continuing the traditional tone with rice pudding and sticky date pudding. The value is good. The décor is simple. House wine is £13.
Chef/s: Tom Pemberton. **Open:** All week L 12 to 3, D 6 to 10.30 (10 Sun). **Meals:** alc (main courses from £9 to £15). **Service:** not inc. **Details:** Cards accepted. 70 seats. Air-con. No music. Children's portions. Children allowed.

Kensington Place

Modern British food in a buzzy space
201-209 Kensington Church Street, W8 7LX
Tel no: (020) 7727 3184
www.egami.co.uk
⊖ Notting Hill Gate
Modern British | £39
New Chef

 V

Rowley Leigh, the man whose name is inextricably bound up with this seminal restaurant, has moved on (to Les Café des Anglais in Bayswater, see entry) and, just as we went to press, has his replacement. All eyes are now on new chef Henry Vigar, whose Mediterranean-influenced menu certainly reads well, seemingly hitting just the right notes, so reports please. Expect the likes of Cornish crab lasagne, followed by grilled red mullet with braised beef, gnocchi and carrot and caper emulsion, or tartiflette reblochon, potato, bacon, caramelised onions served

Sunday roasts

The well-rendered Sunday roast- all crisped fat and rustling potatoes – signifies the best of traditional British cooking.

If you're going to eschew your family dining room on a Sunday and pay to sit in someone else's, it's got to be good; luckily London can deliver.

Grill at the Dorchester

A roast tastes most British eaten from a straight-backed chair. Rack of pork and roast rib of Aberdeen Angus are on offer.

Anchor & Hope

This gastropub serves a simple, set lunch. Starters might feature smoked herrings, followed by roast beef with a beetroot salad and chocolate pots to finish.

Roast

Every day is roast meat day at Borough Market's Floral Hall. The menu here encompasses game in season as well as daily roasts at solid-to-hefty prices.

Wolseley

Though it's styled on a continental cafe, Sundays see roast beef and Yorkshire pudding satisfying regulars and tourists alike.

Lundum's

For something different – though still with roast meat at its heart – try the Sunday buffet at South Kensington's airy Danish restaurant. 'Det kolde bord' is indeed a cold board of fresh and variously cured fish, hams, salamis, meatballs and pate, with a Danish-style pork rib roast.

Tom's Kitchen

Tom Aiken's second, more casual venue calls its Sunday offering 'brunch', but among the eggs Benedict are classic beef, chicken and pork roasts using thoughtfully-selected meat. It's not a serene option – the modern space is noisy and tables are at close quarters – but it's got a buzzing atmosphere.

Franklins

The house style of this comfortable East Dulwich favourite (with another branch in Kennington) is big-flavoured British cooking, with the odd throwback ingredient. It lends itself well to Sunday lunch, when a roast rump of beef with all the trimmings is on offer on the seasonally-changing menu.

ahead of côte du boeuf (for two), or roasted saddle of rabbit with morcilla and apple and white bean ragout. Desserts run to blueberry clafoutis with almond ice cream or rum baba with roasted pineapple and caramelised banana. The choice of wines complements the food, the large selection (including 35 by glass) from quality winemakers across the globe, and offering a good choice under £20.
Chef/s: Henry Vigar. **Open:** all week 12 to 3.30, 6.30 to 11.15 (11.45 Fri and Sat, 10.15 Sun). **Meals:** alc (main courses £15.50 to £24.50). Set L Mon to Sat £19.50, Set L Sun £24.50, Set D Mon to Fri £24.50 to £39.50 (with glass of wine). **Service:** 12.5% (optional). **Details:** Cards accepted. 140 seats. Air-con. No music. Wheelchair access. Children's portions.

Le Café Anglais

Inspired by a famous Parisian brasserie
8 Porchester Gardens, W2 4DB
Tel no: 020 7221 1415
www.lecafeanglais.co.uk
⊖ Bayswater
French | £40
Cooking score: 5

Swagger and cool on the second floor of Whiteley's Shopping Centre, where Rowley Leigh has opened his 140-seater homage to a Parisian brasserie. The room is handsome, huge windows with latticed panes give plenty of light, there are big tarnished mirrors, vast light fittings, comfortable banquettes. The atmosphere crackles. Polished service takes an interest. On view in the open kitchen is a huge rotisserie rotating chickens (offered whole, half, breast, or leg), game, lamb, rib of beef (served for two with bone marrow, shallots and red wine). From the various sections of the menu there are some very good things to eat indeed, on one table there may be fish pie, at another, oeuf en gelée, while hors d'oeuvres of Parmesan custard with anchovy toasts and a first course pike boudin with fines herbes and beurre blanc have been described as 'sublime'. A lunch special of confit of duck with bubble and squeak and spiced clementines was 'a nice old favourite well done'. Desserts such as a

'deeply comforting' queen of puddings and bitter chocolate soufflé with pistachio ice cream are followed by good coffee. Prices star at £15 on the mainly French wine list and climb quickly, but there are plenty of option by the glass or 250ml carafe.
Chef/s: Rowley Leigh, Colin Westall. **Open:** All wee L 12 to 3.30, D 6.30 to 11 (10 Sun). **Meals:** alc (mai courses £11 to £18). Set lunch (Mon to Fri) £16.50 (courses). **Service:** 12.5% (optional). **Details:** Card accepted. Air-con. No music. Wheelchair access. Children allowed.

Notting Hill Brasserie

A reassuringly local clientele
92 Kensington Park Road, W11 2PN
Tel no: (020) 7229 4481
⊖ Notting Hill Gate
Modern European | £59
Cooking score: 4

The term 'brasserie' rather underplays the strikingly lit, enticing interior, where high-ceilinged dining rooms have intricate cornic work, well-spaced tables and impressive flora displays, and there's a jazz quartet in the front bar. Former sous chef, Karl Burdock, now heads the kitchen, but the broadly contemporary menu with Mediterranean influences remains the same. Among starters offers well-reported cannelloni of lobster and prawns served with a cep purée and a 'frothed up', nicely balanced shellfish velouté, and a single scallop classically paired with cauliflower purée but with the addition of chorizo, squid, black pudding and potato. Among meat main courses chateaubriand 'w of good quality and was correctly cooked in salt crust' and came with béarnaise sauce and large chips. A typical fish dish was well-time halibut with a sauce of morels, peas and broa beans. Amaretto cheesecake with a vanilla cake and cherry cream made a happy ending. The wine list of 70 bins is roughly half Frenc with the rest given to a reasonably imaginativ choice from around the globe. House wine is £15 and there's plenty of choice in the £25 t £40 range.

Chef/s: Mark Jankel. Open: all week L 12 to 3.30, Mon to Sat D 7 to 11. Closed: Christmas. Meals: alc D (main courses £19 to £24.50). Set L Mon to Sat £14.50 (2 courses) to £19.50, Set L Sun £25 (2 courses) to £30. Bar menu available. Service: 12.5% (optional). Details: Cards accepted. 110 seats. Air-con. Wheelchair access. Music. Children's portions.

ALSO RECOMMENDED

▲ Electric Brasserie

191 Portobello Road, W11 2ED
Tel no: (020) 7908 9696
www.electricbrasserie.com
⊖ Notting Hill Gate

Part of the Electric Cinema complex, this trendy bar/brasserie is lively on weekends, when the breakfast menu pulls crowds to munch on grilled sausage sandwich (£6), pancakes with blueberry compote (£7) or the deluxe hunger buster of smoked haddock, mushrooms, poached egg and hollandaise (£7.50) at the communal tables and benches. Elsewhere, brunch brings beef bourguignon (£12.50) and lobster and chips (£28), while for dinner there could be roast duck (£14.50). Small plates, sandwiches, burgers and salads are also available, as is a host of seafood (half-dozen oysters £9). Finish with white chocolate crème brûlée, or Sussex pond pudding (all £6). An international wine list starts at £3.75 per glass. Open all week.

READERS RECOMMEND

Crescent House

Gastropub
47 Tavistock Crescent, W11 1AD
Tel no: (020) 7727 9250
www.crescenthouse.uk.com
'A gastropub with a split personality.'

Fat Badger

Gastropub
310 Portobello Road, W10 5TA
Tel no: (020) 8969 4500
www.thefatbadger.com
'Modern menu and friendly service'

■ Paddington

Pearl Liang

Style and substance
8 Sheldon Square, W2 6EZ
Tel no: (020) 7289 7000
www.pearlliang.co.uk
⊖ Paddington
Chinese | £31
Cooking score: 2

'A dead ringer for Hakkasan' mused one who managed to find this promising newcomer, tucked into the pedestrianised Paddington Central complex (do get directions). It's certainly drawing the crowds, including a fair proportion from the Chinese community, with a mix of fair pricing and stylish design, despite being in a 'culinary dead spot'. The spacious bar and dining room is expensively and attractively decorated with funky low chairs in pink fabric, dashes of mauve, with an outsized abacus and the flowery mural. Unlike the décor, the menu is rather more mainstream, based primarily on Cantonese cooking, although you can get lobster with belacan – a hot shrimp paste from Malaysia. But it's dim sum that steals the show, notably, at inspection, a dazzling zucchini and prawn dumpling. Deep-fried soft-shell crab has also been singled out for praise, and fried sweet black sesame ball is a popular way to end. The service team, dressed in modish black, is cordial and attentive. Wines are hastily assembled, and start from £13.40.
Chef/s: Paul Ngo. Open: all week 12 to 11. Closed: 25 and 26 Dec. Meals: alc (main courses £6.80 to £24). Set Menus £20 to £65. Service: 12% (included). Details: Cards accepted. 150 seats. Air-con. Separate bar. Wheelchair access. Music.

Yakitoria

Slick, canal-side modern dining
25 Sheldon Square, W2 6EY
Tel no: 020 3214 3000
www.yakitoria.co.uk
⊖ **Paddington**
Japanese | £35
New Chef

♀ V

Forget the Hogwart Express from platform nine and three-quarters at King's Cross – the real magic is happening behind platform eight at Paddington Station. Yakitoria is flying the flag for exceptional contemporary Japanese cuisine, set amongst the new glass and steel structures of the Paddington basin redevelopment. Once you've managed to actually find the restaurant (take the ramp beside platform eight then hang a left along the canal) you're greeted with plenty of high-fashion, clean lines in an industrial setting. The airy L-shaped restaurant offers a calming water view, with a slick bar set back from the main room. An extensive menu includes the usual suspects like sushi and maki handrolls, modern fusion dishes, and some unexpected surprises. Push the boat out and try quail confit with wasabi ponzu, or green tea smoked rack of lamb with cucumber and bonito salad. Small dishes might include tamgo, fatty tuna or sea urchin nigiri, or sushi pancake with soy jelly and wasabi foam. An inventive cocktail list features Oriental-style cocktails with storybook names such as Tokyo Beauty, White Siberian, and Madame Butterfly. The well-chosen wine list includes some unusual labels starting from £16, and an ample selection of sake and plum wines.

Chef/s: Lin Pattamavong. Open: Mon to Fri L 12 to 3 Mon to Sat D 6 to 11,. Closed: 25, 26 Dec, 1 Jan. Meals: Set L and D £25 to £40. Service: 12.5%. Details: Cards accepted. 100 seats. 40 seats outside. Air-con. Separate bar. Wheelchair access. Music. Children allowed.

READERS RECOMMEND

Fontana

Middle Eastern
10 Craven Terrace, W2 3QD
Tel no: 020 8892 5417
'Above-average Lebanese cooking'

Frontline

British
13 Norfolk Place, W2 1QJ
Tel no: (020) 7479 8960
www.frontlineclub.com
'Dependable cuisine in a war reporters' club'

▮ Shepherd's Bush

Adams Café

Arabic offerings
77 Askew Road, W12 9AH
Tel no: (020) 8743 0572
⊖ **Ravenscourt Park**
Moroccan | £25
Cooking score: 3

V

'Very good North-African cooking, excellent service, incredible value for money' wrote one delighted reader after a visit to this long-established café whose revamped evening menu skips effortlessly from simple grilled meat and fish options, to earthy, aromatic tagines. Among the starters are fish soup, grilled spicy lamb sausages, pastilla (Moroccan sweet chicken, almond and filo pastry pie), and chorba (a spicy Tunisian vegetable, lamb and pasta soup). Follow with one of seven different tagines (perhaps monkfish, tomatoes, peppers, saffron potatoes and coriander), a whole grilled sea bass with French fries and tastira sauce, or one of the kitchen's legendary couscous dishes. Desserts include tartelette au citron, an orange fruit salad with dates, cinnamon and orange blossom water, and crêpe berbère (a Moroccan-style pancake with a honey sauce). You can bring your own bottle (corkage is £3 per bottle) or order from the short, inexpensive wine list which opens at £9.

Chef/s: Sofiene Chahed. **Open:** Mon to Sat D only 7 to 11. **Closed:** Christmas to New Year, bank hol Mon. **Meals:** Set D £11.50 (1 course) to £16.95 (3 courses). **Service:** 12.5%. **Details:** Cards accepted. 60 seats. Wheelchair access. Music.

Anglesea Arms

Perennially popular gastropub
35 Wingate Road, W6 0UR
Tel no: (020) 8749 1291
⊖ Ravenscourt Park
Gastropub | £25
New Chef

The Anglesea is all distressed wooden floors, exposed brickwork and battered furniture – the kind of enticing establishment that's cosy in winter and bright in summer. Drinkers sit on homely sofas by the bar (or under parasols out front in sunny weather). The open-plan kitchen bats well above its average for a gastropub and service is generally very well judged. Starters might be a fluffy twice-baked goat's cheese soufflé, while a spring Sunday lunch included plaice cooked just-so and complemented by brown shrimp, cucumber and new potatoes dressed in dill and crème fraîche. A standout was a generous portion of tremendous roast pork belly with perfectly crisp crackling, silky mash, sweet roasted apples and purple sprouting broccoli. Desserts might be chocolate mocha tart or strawberry cheesecake. A decent and varied sheet of wines starts at £12.50, with a good clutch available by the glass (from £3). You can't book at this neighbourhood favourite so arrive promptly.
Chef/s: Dion Scott. **Open:** Mon to Sat 11-11, Sun 12-10.30. **Closed:** Christmas. **Meals:** alc (main courses from £11 to £15). **Service:** not inc. **Details:** Cards accepted. 38 seats. 25 seats outside. Air-con. No music. Wheelchair access. Children's portions. Children allowed.

Brackenbury

Simple elegant fare
129-131 Brackenbury Road, W6 0BQ
Tel no: (020) 8748 0107
www.thebrackenbury.co.uk
⊖ Hammersmith
Modern European | £30
Cooking score: 4

An 'oasis in the heart of a tranquil village' is how one reader described this upbeat neighbourhood fixture, just a few minutes' away from the bustle of the Goldhawk Road. With soft lighting, mushroom-coloured walls, polished dark-wood tables, upholstered high-backed chairs and surprisingly comfy cushioned banquettes, the atmosphere and staffing is warm and welcoming. The sensibly compact, regularly changing menu is driven by quality seasonal produce, and, with a new chef onboard, comes intelligently less complicated than its predecessor. Take starters such as asparagus served with poached egg and lemon butter, or razor clams with lemon, garlic and parsley, their success a testament to accomplished simplicity. Mains like slow-roasted duck teamed with a rösti, braised endive and an orange sauce continue the theme, while 'attractively presented' desserts like a 'light, moist' chocolate cake with fresh cherries and fior de latte (vanilla ice cream to you and me) and 'exceptionally good' coffee round things off in style. A varied international wine list starts at £12.95 with plenty to choose from under £20, and wines by glass from £3.50.
Chef/s: Matt Cranston. **Open:** Mon to Sat 12 (10 Sat) to 3, 6.30 to 10.45. Sun 10 to 3.30. **Closed:** Sunday Evenings. **Meals:** Set L Mon to Fri £12.50 (2 courses) to £14.50. Set D £15 to £18. **Service:** 12.5% (optional). **Details:** Cards accepted. 60 seats. 20 seats outside. Air-con. Separate bar. Music. Children's portions. Children allowed.

Send your reviews to: www.which.co.uk/gfgfeedback

READERS RECOMMEND

Blah Blah Blah

Vegetarian
78 Goldhawk Road, W12 8HA
Tel no: 020 8746 1337
'Inventive vegetarian offerings and BYO'

▌South Kensington

Bibendum

A balance of elegance and informality
Michelin House, 81 Fulham Road, SW3 6RD
Tel no: (020) 7581 5817
www.bibendum.co.uk
⊖ South Kensington
Modern British | £44
Cooking score: 4

Bibendum's great quality is the light – day or night –and the integrated Michelin-contoured design makes it a compelling and gratifying space, well suited to the food's reassuring foundation of approachable, unfussy modern British and French dishes. Materials and treatments are impressively varied; start with ,perhaps, a warm salad of smoked eel, Jersey Royals and crisp pancetta and watercress velouté. At inspection a sauté of rabbit with new season garlic, basil and white wine was 'wonderfully tender and well-flavoured', its counterpart, a slow-cooked, crisp pork belly with caramelised onions, apple sage and calvados sauce 'succulent and with a sweet earthiness'. Desserts such as chocolate tart with chocolate malt ice cream show 'lightness of touch in the kitchen'. Wines may be a tad expensive but the extensive global list is worth exploring. There's a decent choice of half bottles under £20 and well-chosen offerings by the glass. But it's the house wines that stand out and a lot of care has been taken in choosing an extensive selection mostly under £25.
Chef/s: Matthew Harris. **Open:** all week 12 to 2.30 (12.30 to 3 Sat and Sun), 7 to 11 (10.30 Sun). **Meals:** alc D (main courses £16.50 to £26). Set L £24 (2 courses) to £28.50 (3 courses). **Service:** 12.5% (optional). **Details:** Cards accepted.

80 seats. Air-con. Separate bar. No music. No mobile phones. Wheelchair access. Children's portions. Children allowed.

L'Etranger

Ambitious fusion of French and Japanese cuisine
36 Gloucester Road, SW7 4QT
Tel no: (020) 7584 1118
www.circagroupltd.co.uk
⊖ Gloucester Road
Modern European | £56
Cooking score: 2

Muted grey and aubergine colours mark out the interior of this smartly attired Kensington restaurant. It may be French by name, but the 'strangeness' of the menu often befuddles first-timers. A few Gallic fixtures such as Charolais beef tartare or confit shoulder of Pyrénean lamb with grilled aubergine remain, although a tide of Japanese-influenced fusion has overrun just about everything else: even roast duck and orange is tweaked with white miso paste. Elsewhere, Chilean sea bass is served with black bean sauce and green tea soba noodles, while lime leaves and 'mi sancho' pepper are used to flavour-enhance roast Côte de Veau 'Blonde Aquitaine'. Desserts go with the flow, offering Nashi pear tarte Tatin as well as mango soufflé with yuzu and tofu sorbet. The deeply serious wine list majors in Burgundy and the rest of the world receives exhaustive coverage (sake included). A cut-price selection is offered at lunchtime and everything can be purchased from the adjacent wine shop. Prices start at £22 and there are plentiful options available by the glass.
Chef/s: Jerome Tauvron. **Open:** Mon to Fri L 12 to 3 (Sun 3 to 6), all week D 6 to 11 (10 Sun). **Closed:** 23 to 27 Dec. **Meals:** alc (main courses L £16.50 to £29, D £16.50 to £49). Sun brunch £16.50 (2 courses) to £19.50. **Service:** 12.5% (optional). **Details:** Cards accepted. 75 seats. Air-con. Music. Children's portions. Children allowed.

Lundum's

Modern take on Danish cooking
119 Old Brompton Road, SW7 3RN
Tel no: (020) 7373 7774
www.lundums.com
⊖ Gloucester Road
Scandinavian | £55
Cooking score: 3

London's 'only Danish restaurant' takes place behind a delightful terracotta Edwardian façade, reflected inside in nostalgic Danish design; afficianados of minimal Scandinavian will be disappointed. Many ingredients are sourced from northern Denmark so Aquavit served with marinated herrings is no surprise. But these are set alongside more modern takes on tradition; gravad lax with a mustard-dill foam or roast-cured duck with white asparagus and oyster mushrooms bring the worthiness of Denmark bang up to date in reliably stylish manner. Try Sunday lunch, drifting on into the afternoon starting with herrings with egg and caviar and a lavish buffet of north sea fish, meatballs and pig in many transformations. Puddings command respect and pleasure as does the wine list, a range of classic Europeans; prices start at £18.50 but rise inexorably including the best of Piedmont, Medoc and Rioja.

Chef/s: Kay Lundum and Torben Lining. Open: all week L 12 to 4, Mon to Sat D 6 to 11. Closed: 22 Dec to 4 Jan. Meals: alc Mon to Sat (main courses L £13 to £18.50, D £14.50 to £28). Set L Mon to Sat £13.50 (2 courses) to £16.50, Sun buffet brunch £21.50, Set D £19.50 (2 courses) to £24.50. Service: 13.5% (optional). Details: Cards accepted. 80 seats. 28 seats outside. Air-con. Wheelchair access. Music.

▎Westbourne Grove

READERS RECOMMEND

Urban Turban
Indian
98 Westbourne Grove
Tel no: (020) 7243 4200
W2 5RU
'Tapas-style dishes from an acclaimed chef'

▎Westbourne Park

Ledbury
European master settling into its niche
127 Ledbury Road, W11 2AQ
Tel no: (020) 7792 9090
www.theledbury.com
⊖ Westbourne Park
Modern European | £44
Cooking score: 6

🍷 V

Tucked away in a quiet corner of Westbourne Grove, the Ledbury is an oasis of calm civility amid the bustle of W11. It's a high-ceilinged dining-room with a diverting black-beaded chandelier and, although the floor is uncarpeted, it somehow doesn't get too rackety. The fixed-price menus offer a broad spectrum of culinary thinking, from some once off-beat ideas that have become established fixtures (scallops roasted in liquorice is a stayer), to simply conceived, but skilfully rendered, pasta dishes. A pasta option might be tender ravioli of chicken and morels, in a white asparagus fondue with caramelised onion, a dish that was well-delivered at inspection, gaining extra depth from its frothy Parmesan velouté. Crab with green asparagus (it was spring, after all) came with a perfectly apposite citrus dressing combining pink grapefruit and pomelo. Pigeon has always impressed as a main course, and was good again, the various bits treated separately and sensitively, the breast resting on soft spinach, the legs properly timed, and the various accoutrements including a sausage of the offals and the liver presented on a skewer. Artichoke purée and a tarte fine of ceps added to the sense of occasion. Fish is handled with equal confidence, as witness the monkfish roasted in rosemary that came with the cheek meat schnitzel-battered and truffled. Only a slightly underwhelming sauce of mushrooms and capers, not quite achieving the intensity of the rest, fell a little short here. Cheeses offer a wide, mostly French selection, some being in better nick than others on inspection night, but desserts inspire unalloyed respect, in the form of a complex citrus terrine with a trio of rhubarb and vanilla beignets, a Sauternes anglaise and rocket-fuelled passion-fruit sorbet. The wine list is substantial, and very well compiled. There are no fewer than 15 German wines, good Italian choices, and gems from Burgundy and Alsace. Six reds and six whites come by the glass. Bottles prices start comfortably north of £20.

Chef/s: Brett Graham. **Open:** all week 12 to 2.45, 6.30 to 10.30. **Closed:** 24 and 25 Dec, 1 Jan, Aug bank hol. **Meals:** Set L Mon to Sat £24.50 (2 courses) to £55, Set L Sun £30 to £55, Set D £45 to £55. **Service:** 12.5% (optional). **Details:** Cards accepted. 64 seats. Air-con. No music. No mobile phones. Wheelchair access.

ALSO RECOMMENDED

▲ Cow Dining Room

89 Westbourne Park Road, W2 5QH
Tel no: (020) 7221 0021
www.thecowlondon.co.uk
⊖ Royal Oak

The Saloon Bar downstairs is quite often packed, with everyone supping Guinness and slurping on Irish rock oysters (£7.75 a dozen). Upstairs, the dining room offers a simple but tasty menu of dishers such as foie gras, lentil and French bean salad (£7.50) or smoked eel with potato salad and bacon (£9). Mains include roast halibut with leeks, laverbread toasts and an orange butter sauce (£16.50), and loin of rabbit with black pudding, fennel and celeriac (£18.50). There's a popular weekend brunch and and wines from £13.75. Dining room open Sat and Sun L and all week D.

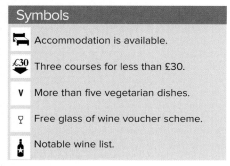

Symbols	
🛏	Accommodation is available.
£30 ⬇	Three courses for less than £30.
V	More than five vegetarian dishes.
♀	Free glass of wine voucher scheme.
🍾	Notable wine list.

GREATER
LONDON

▌Barnes

Sonny's

A well-established consistent local
94 Church Road, SW13 0DQ
Tel no: (020) 8748 0393
www.sonnys.co.uk
⊖ Hammersmith
Modern European | £30
Cooking score: 3

Part of the neighbourhood for long enough that locals cannot imagine life without it, Sonny's is the epitome of a good London 'village' restaurant. Its well-heeled clientele are not short of choice for decent dining, but Sonny's has won their loyalty – half the customers are regular enough to be known by name; those who are not are welcomed with equal politeness and ushered into the reassuringly unchanging, comfortabe and relaxed dining room. The menu is a seasonal affair featuring modern classics; a fragrant broad bean and thyme soup and a generous plate of zesty endive & smoked trout salad were both winners from a list of seven starters; a a terrific, hearty chunk of monkfish with a rich borlotti bean stew to follow outshone a more pedestrian duck leg with new season turnips. Typical modern British puddings: tarte Tatin and lemon tart are worth saving room for. To accompany, there's an eclectic wine list ranging from £3.50 for a glass of house white to £100 Corton Charlemagne, but there's plenty in between, and the staff are confident and knowledgable enough to recommend unusual but clever pairings.
Chef/s: Ed Wilson. **Open:** all week L 12 to 2.30, Mon to Sat D 7 to 11. **Closed:** bank hols. **Meals:** alc (main courses £11.50 to £16.50). Set L Mon to Sat £15.50 (2 courses) to £17.50, Set D Mon to Thur £18.50 (2 courses) to £21.50.. **Service:** 12.5% (optional). **Details:** Cards accepted. 100 seats. Air-con. No music. Wheelchair access. Children's portions.

▌Bushey Heath

READERS RECOMMEND
ChikaYan
Chinese
27-29 High Road, WD23 1EE
Tel no: 020 8950 4886
www.chikayan.co.uk
'Fresh dim sum and subtle flavours'

▌Crystal Palace

Numidie
Laid-back dining
48 Westow Hill, SE19 1RX
Tel no: (020) 8766 6166
www.numidie.co.uk
Mediterranean | £21
Cooking score: 2

With a name that harks back to ancient Algeria and a room filled with an eclectic mix of old mirrors, stone floor tiles and traditional wooden chairs, you would expect a menu boasting a range of North African dishes, but there's a much wider feel to the food. Alongside merguez in harissa and vegetable tagine, there might be courgette and Roquefort fritter with black cherry sauce as well as bouillabaisse. Sadly, some of the Mediterranean dishes try too hard and tend to disappoint. The Algerian couscous and slow-cooked lamb, on the other hand, are more reliable and should not be missed. From the short list of desserts, stuffed pear with almond, pistachio and yoghurt has distinct flavours and wonderful textures. Service is delightful and the wine list offers good value with several wines by the glass and plenty of interest under £20.
Chef/s: Serge Ismail. **Open:** Tue to Sat 6 to 10.30, Sun 12 to 10.30pm. **Closed:** 25, 26 Dec. **Meals:** Set L and D Tue to Thur £13. **Service:** not inc. **Details:** Cards accepted. 35 seats. Air-con. Separate bar. Wheelchair access. Music. Children's portions.

Ealing

Ealing Park Tavern

Victorian gastropub with friendly staff
222 South Ealing Road, W5 4RL
Tel no: (020) 8758 1879
⊖ South Ealing
Gastropub | £30
Cooking score: 2

A thoroughly modern gastropub, the Ealing Park Tavern is as much a drop-in drinking establishment as a destination local restaurant. The kitchen is an open-plan affair, lively and animated, offering an attractively simple, daily changing, market-led menu, with light salad based starters and heavier mains of seared calf's liver with trimmings or fillet of mullet with white bean stew and harissa to follow. The cooking is surprisingly good – a chargrilled chilli squid salad was punchy but not overwhelming; a plump and tender roast chicken breast given a richness from its accompaniment of tomatoes, sultanas, pinenuts and citrus dressing. However, one reader felt that the 'raft of garnishes' was excessive. Puddings; sticky toffee pudding, poached pear, apple and rhubarb pancake are an Anglophile's dream but, given the portion sizes, possibly surplus to requirements. House wines start at £3.25 a glass.
Chef/s: John O'Riordan. **Open:** Tue to Sun L 12 to 3 (3.45 Sun), all week D 6 to 10 (9 Sun). **Closed:** 25 Dec to 1 Jan. **Meals:** alc (main courses £9 to £16). Bar tapas menu available Thur to Sat D.
Service: not inc. **Details:** Cards accepted. 75 seats. 40 seats outside. No music. Children allowed.

READERS RECOMMEND

Monty's

Nepalese
54 Northfield Avenue, W13 9RR
Tel no: 020 8567 6281
www.montys-restaurant.com
'Speedy food and generous portions'

East Sheen

La Saveur

A short menu of French classics
201 Upper Richmond Road, SW14 8QT
Tel no: 020 8876 0644
www.brula.co.uk
French | £25
Cooking score: 1

♀ **V** £30

This latest restaurant from the Lawrence Hartley/Bruce Duckett partnership (see entries for Brula Bistro and La Buvette) sees an expansion into Sheen. The long, narrow site lacks the quirkiness of their other restaurants but they make the most of the space with a lining of smoked mirror along the full length of the dining room proper, lending an illusion of airiness and space and the big wooden bar at the front which gives a proper continental feel. The short, very French menu is a parade of all time greatest hits – pâté of foie gras, escargots, onglet steak frites and coquilles St Jacques – all dishes simple enough for the kitchen to be able to cope very well. The equally brief but unashamedly French wine list, with wines by the glass from £3.25 to decent burgundies at £50 a bottle, make it useful whatever the occasion. A well-priced lunch and early evening menu add to the appeal though the breakfast and tea sessions have yet to make a proper impact.
Chef/s: Bruce Duckett and Jamie Russel. **Open:** Tue to Sun 12 to 3, 6 to 10.30. **Closed:** Mondays, 25 Dec, 26 Dec, 1 Jan. **Meals:** Set L £14.50 (3 courses), Set D £17 (3 courses). **Service:** 12.5% (optional). **Details:** Cards accepted. 50 seats. 10 seats outside. Separate bar. No music. No mobile phones. Wheelchair access. Children's portions. Children allowed.

Also recommended

An 'also recommended' entry is not a full entry, but is provisionally suggested as an alternative to main entries.

Edgware

READERS RECOMMEND
Mr Man
Vegetarian
236 Station Road, HA8 7AU
Tel no: (020) 8905 3033
'Vegetarian buffet run by a Chinese family'

Forest Hill

Babur Brasserie
Tradition meets innovatation
119 Brockley Rise, SE23 1JP
Tel no: (020) 8291 2400
www.babur.info
⊖ New Cross Gate
Indian | £25
Cooking score: 2

V

Traditional Indian arts and crafts form the decorative focal points at this long-established venue, set against a backdrop of exposed brick walls and bare, walnut tables. Though the mood is relaxed, the kitchen takes a serious approach, with starters taking in murgh pattice (a Delhi street snack of minced chicken with potato and crispy sev) and tandoor-roasted lamb chops with ginger, alongside modern inventions such as ostrich infused with fenugreek and sandalwood. Main courses are similarly varied, ranging from Parsee chicken with apricots and straw potatoes to pan-fried barbary duck breast with honey and coriander, or red snapper with a Himalayan berry sauce on an Indian version of risotto. Alongside the more familiar side dishes are intriguing creations such as green banana with sweet potato, baby aubergine and shallot. Traditional Indian desserts round off the meal, and wines have been cleverly chosen to match the food, priced from around £13. **Chef/s:** Enam Rahman. **Open:** all week 12 to 2.30, 6.30 to 11.30. **Closed:** 25 and 26 Dec. **Meals:** alc exc Sun L (main courses £9 to £12). Tasting menu £24.95. **Service:** not inc. **Details:** Cards accepted. 72 seats. Air-con. No mobile phones. Wheelchair access. Music. Children's portions. Children allowed.

Harrow

Golden Palace
Authentic Chinese food in an unlikely setting
146-150 Station Road, HA1 2RH
Tel no: (020) 8863 2333
⊖ Harrow-on-the-Hill
Chinese | £23
Cooking score: 2

V

A neighbourhood restaurant with a national reputation, the Golden Palace flies the flag for authentic Chinese food in suburban Harrow. The action takes place in a cheerful dining room where crowds can choose from a long menu based on skilled renditions of the core repertoire. Around 200 dishes are regularly on show, with earthy, peasant-style hotpots such as braised beancurd with shredded pork sharing the limelight with other Cantonese and Peking-style staples ranging from scallops with spicy salt and chilli, or baked lobster with ginger and spring onion, to crispy aromatic duck. Our inspector found service to be laconic at best, obnoxious at worst. On Sundays, all-day dim sum extravaganzas are the star attraction: expect a selection that might range from steamed, stuffed baby squid in shrimp paste to five-spiced pork belly with Chinese turnip. **Chef/s:** Mr G. Ho. **Open:** Mon to Sat 12 (11 bank hols) to 11.30, Sun 11 to 10.30. **Closed:** 25 Dec. **Meals:** alc (main courses £5.50 to £30). Set L and D £16.50 to £24 (all min 2). **Service:** 10%. **Details:** Cards accepted. 160 seats. Air-con. No music. Wheelchair access.

READERS RECOMMEND
Incanto
Italian
41 High Street, HA1 3HT
Tel no: (020) 8426 6767
www.incanto.co.uk
'Local Italian restaurant is on song.'

▮ Kew

Glasshouse

A gastronomic highlight
14 Station Parade, TW9 3PZ
Tel no: (020) 8940 6777
www.glasshouserestaurant.co.uk
⊖ **Kew Gardens**
Modern European | £32
Cooking score: 5

Glasshouse shines literally and metaphorically in this quaint, leafy corner of the world. The awkward, high-ceilinged room is given a smart, understated glamour with an interior of creams, beiges and golds surrounded by huge plate glass walls (retractable in good weather), which enlarge the space with their reflections by use of clever lighting during the evening and flood the room with natural light during the day. The ambiance is pleasant enough but the draw here is the food. Out of the same mould as Chez Bruce in Wandsworth (see entry), Glasshouse serves fine British cooking refined by classical technique, and embracing modern ingredients and flavours. The menu, which is a set price affair, changes every service but never fails to interest. The sweet meatiness of a starter of rare grilled tuna with carrot salad and shrimps is balanced with a gremolata sauce; the richness of a foie gras and chicken-liver parfait is mitigated by a covering of dressed lentils, while a main of roast middlewhite pork with morteau sausage and choucroute is a real restaurant marriage of high art and peasant cookery. The 500-bin strong wine list is an oenophile's delight, but the sommelier seems to find as much pleasure in matching tastes and budgets – house wine starts at £15.
Chef/s: Anthony Boyd. **Open:** all week L 12 to 2.30, D 6.30 to 10.30. **Closed:** 24 to 26 Dec, 1 Jan. **Meals:** Set L Mon to Fri £23.50 (3 courses), Set L Sat £25 (3 courses), Set L Sun £27.50 (3 courses), Set D £35. **Service:** 12.5% (optional). **Details:** Cards accepted. 65 seats. Air-con. No music. No mobile phones. Children's portions.

Ma Cuisine

French nostalgia
9 Station Approach, TW9 3QB
Tel no: (020) 8332 1923
www.macuisinekew.co.uk
⊖ **Kew Gardens**
French | £23
Cooking score: 3

V £30

Expense has been spared on the décor of this French bistro – plastic tablecloths and laminated menus are in evidence, along with cheap banqueting chairs. Yet, somehow, these features enhance the atmosphere. To be fair, the money that Ma Cuisine appears to have saved on interior decoration seems to have been spent on raw ingredients .The restaurant is on the cusp of becoming a chain with an establishment in Twickenham and another opening due in Barnes. The formula at each restaurant is much the same – French bistro classics. Begin with Mediterranean crab soup with rouille or assiettes de charcuterie. Main courses include crisp pork belly with choucroute, moules marinières or steak tartare. Apart from a few blips, everything was well prepared and served quickly (with a smile). House wines start at £12.50.
Chef/s: Tim Francis. **Open:** all week 9 to 3, 6.30 to 10.30 (all day Sat and Sun). **Meals:** alc (main courses £12.50 to £15). Set L £12.95 (2 courses) to £15.50, Set D (exc Sat) £18.50. Light L menu available Sat. **Service:** 10% (optional).
Details: Cards accepted. 60 seats. 20 seats outside. Wheelchair access. Music. Children's portions.

▮ Kingsbury

READERS RECOMMEND

Tandoor

Indian
232-234 Kingsbury Road, NW9 0BH
Tel no: (020) 8205 1450
'A hidden gem of North Indian cooking.'

▋ Kingston-on-Thames

READERS RECOMMEND
Riverside Vegetaria

Vegetarian
62 High Street, KT1 1HN
Tel no: (020) 8546 7992
www.rsveg.plus.com
'Exquisite food and great views'

▋ Richmond

La Buvette

Comfortable and elegant
6 Church Walk, TW9 1SN
Tel no: (020) 8940 6264
www.brula.co.uk
⊖ **Richmond**
French | £27
Cooking score: 3

🍷 **V** ⌑30

Before the entrance is a courtyard filled with tables and a huge canvas parasol, which sets a continental tone for this agreeably appointed French restaurant. Start with a rich, hearty fish soup (with rouille and Gruyère), or a chunky terrine de campagne layered with prunes and served with gherkins and chutney. For mains, the generous steak grillé has been described as 'rare and tender', carré d'agneau roti has 'loads of flavour' and comes with merguez sausage, baby broad beans and harissa, while desserts include a classic crème brûlée and strawberry tart. The exclusively French wine list ranges from £12.75 to £50, with many available by the glass, from £3.25. Under same ownership as Brula Bistrot in Twickenham (see entry).
Chef/s: Buck Carter. **Open:** all week 12 to 3, 6 to 10:30. **Closed:** 25 and 26 Dec, 1 Jan. **Meals:** alc exc Sun L (main courses £10 to £18.75). Set L £14.50, Set D £17.00. **Service:** 12.5% (optional). **Details:** Cards accepted. 40 seats. 30 seats outside. Wheelchair access. Music. Children's portions. Children allowed.

Petersham Nurseries Café

Straight from the kitchen garden
Church Lane, off Petersham Road, TW10 7AG
Tel no: (020) 8605 3627
www.petershamnurseries.com
Modern British | £32
Cooking score: 3

V

The potholed lane and the sleepiness of this pseudo-rural neighbourhood aren't great augurs but any misgivings are quickly dispelled when diners finally arrive at this extraordinary establishment. A working nursery, the restaurant area occupies the back of one glasshouse with a tea and coffee area in another, but the surroundings are more like a Fellini film set than a plant-selling business. The kitchen relies greatly on local producers and farmers as well as its own kitchen garden and though the daily changing menu is brief, offering around five starters and five main courses at the beginning of service, rather less by the end, dishes tend to be inventive and well thought out; a beautifully balanced Thai influenced salad of crab with a light Nam Jim dressing might sit next to lamb served with sprouting broccoli, anchovies and harissa. Choices from the Old-World-led wine list (glasses from £4.50) are limited but there's a relatively wide choice of juices and infusions including a delightful old fashioned home-made Amalfi lemonade. The only drawback is the service which, though charming, is rather inefficient, and the poor parking which at this distance from main transport links is fairly essential.
Chef/s: Skye Gyngell. **Open:** Wed to Sun L only 12.30 to 3. **Meals:** alc (main courses £14 to £24). **Service:** 12.5% (optional). **Details:** Cards accepted. 80 seats. No music. Car parking.

Average price

The average price listed in main-entry reviews denotes the price of a three-course meal, without wine.

Restaurant at the Petersham Hotel

Fine food matched by superb views
Nightingale Lane, TW10 6UZ
Tel no: (020) 8939 1084
www.petershamhotel.co.uk
⊖ Richmond
Modern British | £34
Cooking score: 4

🛏 V

This Gothic-style hotel, perched on the side of a hill just outside Richmond, is home to a fabulous view of the River Thames, clearly one of the main draws to this many-windowed venue. The food produced by Alex Bentley and his team is equally impressive. Probably best described as modern British but with evident influences from classic French cooking, starters include the likes of split-pea soup with the unusual addition of deep-fried cubes of feta; brown shrimp cocktail on rocket and little gem with Marie Rose sauce; and terrine of foie gras and green peppercorns. Great care is taken with presentation, illustrated in a colourful main course of baked sea bass with seaweed on saffron-scented celeriac mash, accompanied by sauce vierge and slithers of courgette. The kitchen's expertise in pastry shines through in the desserts, such as pineapple tarte Tatin with coconut sorbet and apple galette with yoghurt and honey ice cream. Wines are mainly French but with a smattering from other European growers and the New World. Prices start at £19.50, £5 for a glass, and half-bottles are plentiful.
Chef/s: Alex Bentley. **Open:** all week 12.15 to 2.45, 7 to 9.45. **Closed:** 25, 26 Dec, 1 Jan. **Meals:** Set L £18.50 (2 courses), Set L Sun £31.50 (3 courses). **Service:** 10% (optional). **Details:** Cards accepted. 70 seats. Air-con. Separate bar. No mobile phones. Wheelchair access. Music. Children's portions. Car parking.

Victoria

Packed gastropub with tapas offerings
10 West Temple Sheen, SW14 7RT
Tel no: (020) 8876 4238
www.thevictoria.net
⊖ Richmond
Gastropub | £32
Cooking score: 2

🍷 🛏

This well-established gastropub has little competition in the smart, sleepy streets of Sheen Common. Securing a table, especially on sunny weekends when its bright white conservatory, garden and children's play area have extra appeal to the well-heeled families of the area, can be very hard. There is plenty to please at other times too: a comfortable bar; a relaxed attitude and an up-to-the-minute fully traceable and seasonal menu featuring excellent tapas (evening only), estofada of squid and morcilla, grilled sea bream with wild garlic mash, sauce ravigote and huge, tender Berkshire-bred Charolais steaks; a decent wine list starts at £13.95. If only the service were a little sharper and the cooking a touch tighter, this would be exemplary.
Chef/s: Stephen Paskins. **Open:** all week L 12 to 2.30 (3 Sat, 8 Sun), Mon to Sat D 7 to 10. **Closed:** Christmas. **Meals:** alc (main courses £9 to £22) Set L £15.95 (2 courses), Set D £17.95 (2 courses). **Service:** 12.5% (optional). **Details:** Cards accepted. 70 seats. 50 seats outside. Separate bar. No mobile phones. Wheelchair access. Children's portions. Car parking.

ALSO RECOMMENDED

▲ Chez Lindsay

11 Hill Rise, TW10 6UQ
Tel no: (020) 8948 7473
www.chezlindsay.co.uk

This is the place to come for authentic Breton cuisine. The organic buckwheat galettes range from those simply filled with cheese (£4.75) to speciality combinations like onion sauce, celery, walnuts and Roquefort sauce (£7.45). Fresh seafood is also something of a speciality or you can choose from enticing salads and 'grand plats' like braised lamb shank with red-wine sauce, gratin dauphinois and seasonal vegetables (£13.75). For desserts there are filled crêpes (from £3.50), ices (£5.50) or crème brûlée (£5.25). The set lunch is two courses for £14.50, dinner £17.50. Breton cider is served in ceramic 'boles' (litre jug £9.95); French wines start from £13.95. Open all week.

READERS RECOMMEND
Pizzeria Rustica
Italian
32 The Quadrant, TW9 1DN
Tel no: (020) 8332 6262
'Authentic pizza in generous portions.'

Southall
Brilliant
Revamped local stalwart
7276 Western Road, UB2 5DZ
Tel no: (020) 8574 1928
www.brilliantrestaurant.com
⊖ Hounslow West
Indian | £25
Cooking score: 3

V £30

After over 30 years, Brilliant continues to accumulate awards and this Guide has long recognised the qualities that set it apart. The main dining room has finally been completely refurbished to include plasma screens showing Bollywood films, and the overall look is 'modern and tasteful'. Details like crisp, vibrantly spiced onion bhaji and 'terrific' romali bread contribute as much to the experience as more substantial dishes. These draw largely from Northern India but aspects of East Africa, as in chicken dishes cooked and served on the bone, reflect the Anand family's journey to Britain via Kenya. Lengthy menus can bring on the unsettling uncertainty, if not plain disbelief, in a kitchen's abililty to deliver. But, here, the sheer size of the restaurant provides assurance that dishes are properly prepared and not the result of a last

minute pick-and-mix operation. Newly introduced 'healthy options' unsurprisingly do not extend to the sweet section that includes kulfi with pistachio and almond. Wines start at £9 but the usual range of beers or one of the several versions of lassi might provide more appropriate accompaniment.
Chef/s: Jasvinderjit Singh. **Open:** Tue to Fri L 12 to 2.30, Tue to Sun D 6 to 11.30. **Closed:** Mondays. **Meals:** alc (main courses £4.50 to £13). Set L and D £17.50. **Service:** not inc. **Details:** Cards accepted. 225 seats. Air-con. Wheelchair access. Music. Children's portions. Children allowed. Car parking.

Madhu's
Excellent service and fantastic fish dishes
39 South Road, UB1 1SW
Tel no: (020) 8574 1897
www.madhusonline.com
Indian | £28
Cooking score: 3

V £30

More than 25-years old, Madhu's popularity is part-founded on impressively professional service, but it's the food that really counts. The care and attention on timing and the retention of texture and distinct flavours across the board is notable. On inspection, well-marinated tandoori salmon allowed 'subtle hints of spice' while preserving excellent texture in the fish. Dishes, drawn from the entire sub-continent and East Africa, are described accurately; 'you get to know the spices in the range of rice preparations'. Several dishes for six people encourage sharing. Vegetarians are looked after with a tantalising range of dishes that go well beyond the usual. For less chilli-rich dishes, wines from £9 are fairly priced and might be worth considering, but beers or lassi would be better matches for the more fiery offerings.
Chef/s: J.P. Singh. **Open:** Wed to Mon L 12.30 to 3.00, Wed to Mon D 6 to 11.30. **Closed:** 25 Dec. **Meals:** alc (main courses £9 to £12).. **Service:** not inc. **Details:** Cards accepted. 104 seats. Air-con. Wheelchair access. Music. Children's portions.

ALSO RECOMMENDED

▲ Gifto's Lahore Karahi

162-164 The Broadway, UB1 1NN
Tel no: (020) 8813 8669
www.gifto.com

This Pakastani restaurant stands out among the throng on Southall's Broadway. Expect crowds, noise and action in the vast ground-floor eating area, and contemporary Pakastani cooking with an authentic punch – it really is the real thing. In the snack department (£1.50 to £3) you will find pani puri, onion bhaji and dahi bhalla (lentil doughnuts with tamarind sauce). Follow with a tandoori dish (from £4.20), or go for a tawa special cooked on a hotplate, perhaps ginger chicken (£7.20) cooked with green chillies and onions, or one of the Lahore dishes – king fish curry (£6.90). Bread and rice dishes are plentiful, while desserts include kheer (rice pudding, £1.80). Unlicensed but bring your own (no corkage). Open all week.

▮ Tottenham Hale

The Lock Dining Bar

Riverside dining
Heron House, Hale Wharf, Ferry Lane, N17 9NF
Tel no: (020) 8885 2829
www.thelockrestaurant.com
⊖ Tottenham Hale
Modern European | £23
Cooking score: 5

♈ V £30

Maybe the 2012 effect is heading up the Lea Valley? The Lock Dining Bar has now established itself in this unlikely industrial riverside location in N17. The gamble by chef Ade Adeshina and partner/front-of-house manager Fabrizio Ruso appears to have paid off. The menu changes with the seasons – it was due to move from winter/spring to spring/summer at inspection. Other changes include a new alfresco seating area, and new furniture for the light, bright, wooden-floored main restaurant. The à la carte treats vegetarians, pescatarians and meat lovers equally, with vegetarian options no afterthought. Meat and fish are sourced as locally as possible. Starters may include pan-fried polenta fritter, baked goat cheese with mushroom tapenade crust, dressed with truffle emulsion. Alternatively, there may be a pan-fried scallop, alongside a perfectly timed mackerel fillet, and a small square of pungent Cheddar cheese pasta bake with a herby tomato sauce. Terrines, pâtés and foie gras often also feature as opening options. Technical skill is demonstrated with a main course dish of well-timed pan-roasted fillet of freshwater pink trout with a garlic and vanilla foam, sautéed potatoes, caramelised onions and warm tomato dressing. Alternatively, there may be roast Barberry duck on a bed of braised cabbage and mushrooms and wine reduction. Desserts do not disappoint, and may include tarte Tatin for sharing. Expect top-notch amuse-bouche – an intense cauliflower soup, for instance – and pre-desserts. Service is efficient, knowledgeable and welcoming. The Lock has a lighter lunch menu and a Sunday lunch menu. The wine list focuses on Italy and France, along with 'the rest'. Sicilian house wines start at a reasonable £13.50, with four red and four white options by the glass from £3.50.
Chef/s: Ade Adeshina. Open: Sun to Fri L 12 to 2, D 6 to 10. Meals: Set L £11 (2 courses) to £15 (Sun only). Service: 10%. Details: Cards accepted. 60 seats. 20 seats outside. Separate bar. Wheelchair access. Music. Children's portions. Car parking.

▮ Twickenham

A Cena

Simple Italian dining in the suburbs
418 Richmond Road, TW1 2EB
Tel no: (020) 8288 0108
www.acena.co.uk
Italian | £45
Cooking score: 2

V

A Cena sits pretty on a row of chichi boutiques at the foot of Richmond Bridge. Candles in bottles illuminate a mismatch of wooden chairs, tables and church pews, suggesting relaxed charm. But the chasm between bench (fixed to the floor) and table (at least a foot away) will have the average-sized customer 'hailing a taxi to get to their plate'. The seasonal menu features beef carpaccio or asparagus with fried egg and Parmesan – safe choices, simply presented and well-executed. Slow-roast rabbit bruschetta or Parmesan frittella catch the more intrepid diner's eye. Main courses tread a well-beaten path: grilled ribeye steak, pan-fried corn-fed chicken or veal chop arrive with mash and seasonal vegetables. Desserts are a lip-smacking dairy-fest: vanilla cheesecake, rhubarb and custard trifle or mocha tartufo with cream. Portions are generous. Service is discreetly attentive. A Merlot Corvina 2006 opens the all-Italian wine list at £13.50.

Chef/s: Nicola Parsons. **Open:** Tue to Sun L 12 to 2.30pm, Tue to Sat D 7 to 10.30pm. **Meals:** alc (main courses L £8 to £15, D £11.50 to £20). Set L Sun £22.50. **Service:** not inc. **Details:** Cards accepted. 55 seats. Air-con. Wheelchair access. Music. Children's portions.

La Brasserie McClements

A renaissance for Twickenham?
2 Whitton Road, TW1 1BJ
Tel no: (020) 8744 9610
www.labrasserietw1.co.uk
French | £33
Cooking score: 4

It's all change again at Brasserie McClements. Having dumbed down from his glory days last year and seemingly put the concept of grand French cooking firmly in the past, John McClements has had a change of heart. The shortened menu is now a set-price affair, with the likes of 'Fantasy of Oysters' (oysters prepared five ways) and assiettes Landaise (a tasting of foie gras and confit duck) offered as two of the five starters. Mains include turbot with lobster, or sausage and veal chop (with sweetbread and loin, little gem and pommes purée). McClements demonstrates his assured technique throughout. The aforementioned turbot was excellent, delivering the great fish cooked perfectly; it was well contrasted with a

Top food websites

Egullet
www.egullet.org
An online culinary society for gourmands, covering all interests and locations.

Chez Pim
www.chezpim.typepad.com
Pim Techamuanvivit blogs on her envy-inspiring, global visits to restaurants.

Chocolate and Zucchini
www.chocolateandzucchini.com
Clotilde Dusoulier has recorded her daily food observations and recipes since 2003.

Noodlepie
www.noodlepie.com
Relocated from Saigon to Toulouse, this blog covers food issues entertainingly.

101 Cookbooks
www.101cookbooks.com
An attempt to cook through every cook-book owned by the author.

Dos Hermanos
www.majbros.blogspot.com
Punchily written and stylishly designed, recording two food lovers' experiences.

Moveable Feast
www.moveable-feast.com
One of the few blogs written by a chef.

The Tracing Paper
www.tracingpaper.org.uk
Discusses local, forgotten foodstuffs such as Jack-by-the-hedge and alexanders.

rich, bean cassoulet. The wine list (starting at £17.50 for house wine) is well chosen, and given the classicism of the food, has a surprisingly broad scope.

Chef/s: John McClements. **Open:** Mon to Sat L 12 to 3, D 7 to 11. **Closed:** 1 Jan. **Meals:** alc (main courses £15 to £25). Set L (exc Sat) £20. Set D £30 (2 courses) to £35. **Service:** 10% (optional). **Details:** Cards accepted. 45 seats. Air-con. Music. Children's portions.

Brula Bistrot
Gallic delight
43 Crown Road, St Margaret's, TW1 3EJ
Tel no: (020) 8892 0602
www.brulabistrot.com
French | £31
Cooking score: 4

A real comfort spot for St Margaret's, Bistrot Brula is reliable, familiar and unchallenging in equal measure. The first of the mini restaurant empire from Bruce Duckett and Laurence Hartley which includes La Saveur in East Sheen and La Buvette in Richmond (see entries), Brula remains the best of the bunch. The cooking has a very French accent, featuring escargots and foie gras as well as onglet steak, grilled fish and confit duck, and the kitchen has a confidence of long practice and competence. The wine list is similarly Gallic but kindly priced, starting at £12.75 and offering plenty of choice by the glass or 50cl pichet. If in a celebratory mood the final bill can stack up, but locals tend to be drawn to the very good value set lunches and early evening dinners.

Chef/s: Bruce Duckett, Toby Williams. **Open:** all week L 12 to 3, D 6 to 10.30. **Closed:** 25 and 26 Dec, 1 Jan,. **Meals:** alc (main courses £11.50 to £18.50). Set L £11 (2 courses) to £13.50. **Service:** 12.5% (optional). **Details:** Cards accepted. 45 seats. 12 seats outside. No music. No mobile phones. Wheelchair access. Children's portions.

Tapas Y Vino
Modern and traditional tapas
111 London Road, TW1 1EE
Tel no: 020 88925417
www.elvinotapas.co.uk
⊖ Twickenham
Spanish | £20
Cooking score: 2
V

John McClements seems to be taking over this corner of Twickenham, but this latest string to his bow takes his cooking out of the grand French tradition and into tapas. He hasn't splashed out on the interior: tables and chairs are basic and the looped Gypsy Kings on the sound system might grate, but the food is fun and relatively cheap. A generous plate of Jabugo is unmissable, but there is plenty else on offer: from clams with chickpeas and chorizo, or perfect deep-fried squid with a properly pungent aïoli, to hare royal, here served as a slice of deep, rich pâté. Portions are small, so multiple ordering is de rigueur, but at £4.50 or less per portion, there is little chance of a massive bill at the end. Fill up on the savouries: desserts are not a strong point and nor, despite its name, is the wine list. Note: no children under 10 after 9pm.

Chef/s: Michael Jackson. **Open:** Mon to Sun, L 12pm to 3pm, D 7pm to 10.30pm. **Closed:** Sun. **Meals:** alc (main courses £12 to 15). **Service:** 10% (optional). **Details:** Cards accepted. 45 seats. Wheelchair access. Music. Children's portions.

READERS RECOMMEND

Tangawizi
Indian
406 Richmond Road, Richmond Bridge, TW1 2EB
Tel no: (020) 8891 3737
'Mixing the familiar with the more ambitious'

Vegetarian options

All of these restaurants have passed the 'Will I enjoy the food if I'm not a veggie?' test, so take your friends with confidence.

The Conservatory, Lanesborough
Executive chef Paul Gayler has a thing about vegetarian food (in a nice way). With parlour palms and tinkling ivories, this is a splendid, unhurried place in which to indulge yourself, knowing you are in safe hands. With notice, they will also devise a menu especially for you.

Eat and Two Veg
If you like fast food, then Eat and Two Veg, an American style diner might float your boat, with mock meats a speciality. The jury is out as to how good it is in a 'Do you like Marmite?' sort of way.

Manna
Recently refurbished, this restaurant remains the trusted, reliable saviour of the veggie community. With starched white cloths on the table, a good wine list and international food, it is the place to take veggie sceptics.

Carnevale
Small but almost perfectly formed. Food is imaginative, but during busy times it feels cramped (because it is!).

Kastoori
Well established authentic Gujarati vegetarian cuisine with interesting African inspirations. If you like it hot, you'll love it.

The Gate
An all-time favourite that serves good food, of that there can be no doubt; but it can feel chilly, being in a converted church hall. Ideal for larger groups.

Blah, Blah, Blah
They don't take credit cards or have a drinks licence, but the food is invariably good and portions generous. Staff can be tetchy.

222 Veggie Vegan
It's tiny and in a run-down part of town. The success is due to the culinary skills of the experienced chef/proprietor Ben. Forget the ambience: the food is fresh and fabulous. Bargain buffet at lunchtime.

Riverside Vegetaria
The food is reliable, it never seems to close and if you get a table by the window, you can watch the watery world go by.

Mr. Man
A Chinese vegetarian family run the Mr Man restaurant, serving a buffet at lunchtime and à la carte in the evening. The mock duck is fantastic. A utilitarian layout with friendly service. No alcohol.

Wembley

READERS RECOMMEND

Alisan
Chinese
The Junction, Engineers Way, HA9 0EG
Tel no: (020) 8903 3888
www.alisan.co.uk
'Great chinese food with a location to match.'

Jeevan
Indian
381 High Road, HA9 6AA
Tel no: 020 8900 0510
'Pleasant tandoori dishes'

Wood Green

Mosaica @ The Factory
Reliable results
Chocolate Factory, Clarendon Road, N22 6XJ
Tel no: (020) 8889 2400
www.mosaicarestaurants.com
⊖ Wood Green
Modern European | £26
Cooking score: 3

V

The former factory has an open kitchen, an
eclectic mix of old tables and chairs, wooden
floors, local artists' work on the walls, and
friendly and welcoming service. After a period
of change in the kitchen and some
inconsistencies, a new chef is now producing
more reliable results. Some Mosaica menu
staples remain, joined by some imaginative
additions. Chilled cucumber soup made a
refreshing opening at inspection, while
charred English asparagus with rocket and
Parmesan shavings was 'simple and just right'.
Pan-fried chicken was well handled with great
flavour, and came set a bed of spinach with
roasted baby potatoes and jus, while roasted
halibut was presented on a bed of good, fresh
pappardelle pasta with an inventive cockle
beurre noisette. Desserts were a notable
highlight, including a lime and lychee
cheesecake with an intense pineapple ice
cream. House wines start from £12, with four
or five choices by the glass from £3.30.
Chef/s: Phil Ducker. **Open:** Tue to Fri and Sun L 12
to 2.30, Tue to Sat D 7 to 9.30. **Closed:** 2 weeks
Christmas. **Meals:** alc (main courses L £5 to £15, D
£10 to £16). **Service:** 10% (optional). **Details:** Cards
accepted. 100 seats. Air-con. Wheelchair access.
Music. Children's portions. Car parking.

INDEX

INDEX BY TUBE | Index

This book couldn't happen without a cast of thousands.
Our thanks are due to the following contributors:

Mrs Sarah Aaronson
Mr Julian Abbotts
Mr V Abraham
Mr Damian Abrahams
Mrs Janet Abrahams
Miss Elaine Ackrill
Miss Victoria Ackroyd
Ms Sarah Adamczuk
Mr Chris Adams
Mr R C Adams
Mr Wayne Adams
Mrs Severine Adams
Mr Colin Addison
Mr Chris Addison
Mr David Adey
Mrs Sarah Adkins
Mr Bernard Ager
Miss L Ainsworth
Mr John Aird
Mr Les Aitkin
Mrs Anita Albone
Mr Ian Aldrich
Mrs Nicky Alexander
Mrs Gillian Alexander-Davis
Miss Kirsty Allan
Mr Robert Allen
Miss Kerry Allen
Miss Maria Aller
Mrs Carolyn Alty
Mr Daniel Ambrosioni
Mrs Karin Ament
Mr William Anderson
Mr Jovan Andjelopolj
Mr Robert Andrew
Mrs Annie Andrews
Mr Igor Andronov
Mr Gavin Ansell
Mr Dyfrig ap Dafydd
Mrs Lorna Appiah
Mr Jonathan Appleby
Mrs Cynthia Archer
Ms Hilary Armstrong
Mr Glen Armstrong
Miss Lorea Arrizabalaga
Mr Alan Arthurs
Mr Paul Ash
Mr Bernard Asher
Mr Kenneth Ashken
Mr Vidal Ashkenazi
Miss Shahida Aslam
Mrs Hannah Aspey
Mrs Dalvinder Assi
Mrs Kathryn Astley
Miss Jeannie Atha
Ms Margaret Atherton
Mr James Aufenast
Mr Nick Avery
Mr Roger Avon
Mr David Avrell
Mrs Janet Awty
Mr Michael Awty
Mrs Christina Bacon
Ms Alexandra Badwi
Mr Robin Baiden
Mrs Elizabeth Baillie
Mr James Baird
Mr Michael Baker
Mr Nick Baldwin
Ms Janet Baldwin
Mrs Carol Ball
Mr John Banks
Mr Raymond Banning
Miss Sally Barber
Mr Andy Barden
Mrs Susan Barham
Mr George Barker
Mr Rebecca Barker
Mr John Barker
Mr Jason Barlow
Mr Ray Barlow
Ms Stella Barnass
Miss Sarah Barnes
Mr Michael Barratt
Mrs Judith Barrett
Mr Barry Barrett
Miss Kathryn Barry
Mrs Jane Barry
Mrs Victoria Bartlett

Ms Mels Barton
Mr John Keith Barton
Miss Sue Bates
Mr John Bates
Mr Conrad Bayliss
Ms Lesley Beach
Ms Carol Beannon
Mr George Beardow
Ms Sarah Beattie
Mr Anthony Beavan
Mr Brian Beaves
Mrs Janet Bebb
Mr Simon Beckett
Mr Bernard Bedford
Miss Julie Behan
Mrs Carol Behrens
Mr John Belfitt
Mr Rob Bell
Mr Richard Bell
Mr Gary Bell
Ms Vicky Bennison
Mr Philip Beniston
Miss Sheila E Bennett
Mrs Victoria Benning
Ms Joanne Benson
Mr Tim Bent
Mr Lloyd Bentley
Mrs Jiffy Benzie
Mr Mike Beresford
Mrs Jayshri Bhana
Miss Angi Bhole
Mr Mike Bigland
Ms Betty Birch
Mrs Rosemarie Bird
Mr Bob Bishop
Mr Alister Bisset
Mr Helge Bjordal
Miss Jazz Black
Miss Deborah Black
Miss Emma Blackburn
Mr Roger Blackburn
Mr Keith Blackwell
Mr Keith Blake
Mr Timothy Blake
Mrs Debra Blakeman-barratt
Mr John Blakey
Mrs Patricia Blamey
Prof R W Blamey
Ms Christine Blancher
Mrs Bronwen Blenkin
Mrs Mavis Blow
Mr Paul Blows
Mr Ralph Blumenau
Mr Kenneth Blyth
Mr John Bolgar
Mrs Julia Bolwell
Mr Saif Bonar
Miss Julia Bond
Mr Michael Bond
Mr Fred Bone
Mrs Muriel Bonner
Mr Steve Bonnet
Mr Graham Booth
Mrs Heather Booth
Ms Annabel Bosanquet
Mr David Botsford
Mr Philippe Boucheron
Miss Maeve Bourke
Mrs Judith Bourne
Mr Richard Bourne
Miss Dee Bowker
Mrs Valerie Bowman
Mr Roger Bowring
Miss Sharan Boyal
Mr David Boyd
Mr John Boyer
Miss Rachel Boys
Mr Ken Bracey
Mr Anthony Bradbury
Mr Julian Bradley
Mr Graham Bradshaw
Mr David Bradshaw
Miss Alison Braganza
Mr Tony Bramley
Mrs Mary Bramley
Mr Andrew Brammall
Mrs Jessica Braschi
Mrs Claire Brayne

Mr Sebastian Breaks
Miss Caitlin Breewood
Mr Blair Breton
Mrs Jonica Bridge
Mrs Silvana Briers
Mr David Briggs
Mr David Briggs
Mr David Briggs
Mr David Briggs
Mr RJ Briscoe
Ms Moyra Briston
Mrs Patricia Bristow
Mrs Allison Brittain
Mrs Christine Broadhurst
Ms Annie Bromwich-Alexandra
Mrs Susan Brookes
Mr T Brooks
Ms Celia Brooks Brown
Mrs Christine Brown
Mrs Julie Brown
Mr Adam Brown
Miss Amanda Brown
Mr Mik Brown
Mrs Nikki Brown
Mr Howard Brown
Mrs Kaye Brown
Mrs Kathleen Brown
Miss Catherine Brown
Mr Terry Brown
Mr Philip Brown
Mr Nelson Brown
Mr Richard Browne
Mr Nicky Brownell
Mr Christopher Browning
Mr Ronnie Bryant
Mr Colin Bryant
Ms Mary Bryden
Ms Katherine Bryden
Mr Douglas Bryden-Reid
Mrs Marie Brydon
Mrs Pam Buchanan
Mr Mike Buchanan
Mr Lewis Buckley
Mrs Janine Buckley-Hewing
Mr Peter Buckman
Mrs Ruth Bujack
Mr Antony Bull
Mr Steven Bullen
Mrs Nicola Buller
Miss Nicola Bullivant
Mr Chris Bulpitt
Mrs Veronica Bunyan
Miss Suzanne Burke
Mrs Julie Burkinshaw
Mr John W. Burley
Mr Ian Burnell
Mrs Sarah Burnett
Mr Terry Burns-Dyson
Mr Neil Burrows
Mr Dave Busson
Mr Jeffrey Butler
Mr John Butler
Mr Paul Butler
Mr Martin Butters
Mrs Joanne Buxton
Mr Brendan Byrne
Mrs Pauline Cade
Mrs Jane Caffrey
Mrs Emma Callery
Mr Harry Calthrop
Mr Roger Calverley
Mr Roger Calverley
Mr Martin Campbell
Mr Douglas Campbell
Mr Trevor Campbell
Mr Stuart Campbell
Mrs Philippa Camps
Mr Paul Canham
Mr Andrew Canning
Mrs Emma Canter
Ms Evelyne Canterranne
Mrs Nicola Capill
Mr Malcolm Carey
Mrs Joanne Carnell
Mrs Elinor Carr
Mrs Tina Carroll
Mrs Julie Carter

Mr John Carter
Ms Bernadette Carter
Mrs Judith Cartwright
Mrs Jacqui Cartwright
Mr Tony Caruana
Mr Paul Casella
Mr RH Cassen
Mr Dennis Casson
Mr Ian Caston
Miss Lynne Catterall
Mrs Rosie Cavies
Mr Alden Chadwick
Ms Joanne Chalcraft
Alex Chambers
Mr Steve Chambers
Mrs Samantha Chambers
Mr Vikran Chand
Mr Miles Chapman
Miss Rosalind Chapman
Mr Mark Chappels
Miss Kerri Chard
Miss Caron Chattwood
Mr Ken Cherry
Mr William Chesneau
Mr Stephen Chetrit
Mrs Marjorie Chilton
Mr David Chinery
Mr Stefan Chomka
Mr Tanni Chowdhury
Mr P chowdhury
Mr Steven Christie
Mr Richard Christopher
Ms Sarah Cielo
Mrs Eleanor Clamp
Ms Margaret Clancy
Mrs Pamela Clare
Mr Nigel Clark
Ms Caren Clarke
Mrs Leanne Clarke
Mrs Marilyn Clayton
Miss Cady Cleary
Mr Dave Clews
Mr Stephen Click
Ms Gilli Cliff
Mr Richard Clifford
Mr Robert Clifford
Mr J F Cobb
Mrs J F Cobb
Ms Sally Cockcroft
Mr Michaek Coe
Mr Nick Coffey
Miss Naomi Cohen
Mr Jason Colclough
Mr Andy Cole
Mrs C Cole
Mr Roger Colebrook
Mrs Deidre Coleman
Mr Martin Collier
Mr Neil Collins
Mrs Kate Collins
Mrs Fiona Collins
Mr Richard Colthurst
Mr R T Combe
Mr John Compte
Mr Flurin Condrau
Mr Dominic Conlon
Mr Pat Conneely
Ms Bridgett Cook
Mrs Karen Cook
Mr Nigel Cook
Mr Michael Cook
Mrs Anne-Marie Cook
Mr Danny Coope
Mr Andrew Cooper
Mr David Cooper
Mr Richard Cooper
Mrs Gainor Cooper
Ms Clare Corbett
Miss Alicia Corlett
Mr Jonathan Cornes
Mr Neil Cornick
Mr Paul Cottam
Mr Roger Cotterill
Mr Edward Coulson
Mrs Kate Cousins
Mrs Sarah Covey
Mr Kevin Cowan
Mr Nigel Cowdery

Ms Katharine Cowherd
Mr Ben Cox
Mrs Susan Cox
Mr Malcolm Cox
Mr Peter Craddock
Mr Carl Cramer
Mr Ronald Cramond
Mrs Helena Crawford
Mrs Vikki Crayden-Reed
Mr Colin Cregan
Mr Stephen Crick
Mr John Crisp
Ms Rosie Crook
Mr G. Crossley
Mr Les Crosthwaite
Mr William J Crouch
Mr Gary Crowe
Mr Joseph Crozier
Mr George Cruickshank
Mrs Karen Currie
Mr John Curtin
Mrs Lynne Curtis
Mrs Christine Cussans
Mr Stan Da Prato
Mr Bill Dacombe
Miss Leigh Danckert
Mr Nigel Daniels
Mrs Caroline Daniels
Ms Jacqueline Dare
Mr David Darrah
Ms Alison Davidson
Mr Keith Davidson
Mr Tom Davidson
Mr Eric Davidson
Ms Pam Davies
Ms Kirsty Davies
Mr Peter Davies
Mrs Molly Davies
Mr Jonathan Davies
Mr Barry Davis
Mrs Shakti Dawan
Mr William Dawson
Mr Peter Day
Mrs Chris Day
Mrs Katherine Dckie
Mr Gerrit de Bondt
Mr Guillaume de Brosses
Mrs Suzanne de Glanville
Mr Francis de Lima
Mr Wilf Deakin
Mrs Berenice Deakin
Mr Paul Dear
Miss Victoria Decmar
Mr Donald Decruz
Mrs Tsai Deere
Mr Alan Dell
Mr Geoffrey Dence
Ms Debbie Dennett
Mr Pete Desmond
Mr Eddie Deverill
Miss Rachael Dexter
Mr Phillip Dick
Mr J E Dickinson
Mrs Yvonne Dickinson
Mr Harry Dickinson
Mr Ian Dickson
Mrs Helen Difrancescomarino
Mr Shaun Dillon
Mr Chris Dinning
Mr William Dobbie
Mr Bill Dobson
Mr Martin Dodd
Mr Barry Dodd
Miss Marian Doherty
Mr Fergus Donachie
Mrs Janet Donbavand
Mrs Jennifer Donnison
Miss Christina Dore
Mr George Dorgan
Miss Katharine Douglas
Miss Faith Douglas
Mrs Kelly Dowding
Mrs Christine Downes
Mrs Helen Downing-Emms
Mr Dae Drew
Mr John Ducker
Mrs Adria Duckett

THANK YOUS

Mr John Duell
Mr George M Duffus
Mr Terence Duffy
Mrs Helen Dugdale Reed
Mr Alexander Duguid
Ms Angela Dunmall
Mr Malcolm Dunmore
Mrs Lynn Dunn
Mrs Heather Dunn
Mr Jon Dunne
Miss Emily Durbidge
Mr Roger Durrant
Mr Dominic Dwight
Mr Kevin Dyras
Mr W Dyson
Mrs Kirsty Dyson
Mrs Sheilagh Dyson
Mrs Sylvia Eades
Ms Emily Easter
Ms Sally Easton
Mrs Zoe Eastwell
Mrs Judith Eaton
Mr Michael Edwards
Mr Osian Edwards
Mrs Denise Edwards
Mr Marc Edwards
Miss Nabila Electricwala
Mr Gary Elflett
Mrs Jan Elford
Mrs Alexandra Ellis
Mr Peter Ellwood
Mr Robert Embleton
Mr Matthew Emery
Mr Robert Emsley
Mr Stephen Engel
Mrs Marilyn Escott
Mr Santiago Eslava
Mrs Lisa Esslemont
Mr Huw Evans
Mrs Margaret Evans
Mrs Sheridan Evans
Mr Mick Evans
Mrs Nichola Evans
Mrs Ann Eve
Mrs Janet Every
Mr Steve Falder
Mr Paul Falkingham
Mr Colin Fancourt
Miss Rebbecca Farquhar
Miss Lauren Fawkes
Ms Lorraine Fearn
Mr Stephen Fellows
Mr Ian Fenwick
Mr Sarah Fergusson
Mr Brendan Ferguson
Mr Nick Fermor
Ms Polly Fernandez
Mrs Marcela Fernandez Vilar
Mr Keith Ferris
Mr Fabrizio Fiabane
Mr Adrian Field
Mrs Laura Field
Mr Nigel Fielden
Miss Katy Finch
Mr Malcolm Fincken
Mr Ted Fineran
Ms Corey Finjer
Miss Veronica Finney
Mr Roger Firman
Miss Helen Firth
Mr F Fisher
Mrs Gillian Fitch
Mrs Amanda Fitzaden-Gray
Ms Jan Fitzgerald
Mr Simon Fitz-Hugh
Mr Ian Fitzpatrick
Mr Barry Fitzpatrick
Miss Lisa Flaherty
Mr Kieran Flatt
Ms Jenni Fleetwood
Mr Simon Fleming
Mrs Debra Fletcher
Mr Roy Flitcroft
Miss Helen Ford
Miss Carrie ford
Mr Ken Forman
Mr John Formston
Mrs Pamela Forrest
Mr Brian Forrester
Ms Beatrice Forster
Mr Philip Foster
Mr Gary Fothergill
Mr Laurence Fouweather

Mrs Sylvia Foxcroft
Mr Steve Frampton
Mr Colin Francis
Ms Liz Franklin
Mr Peter Franklin
Mr Felix Franks
Mr John Franks
Mrs Emily Fraser
Miss Tabitha Frazer
Mr Cliff Free
Ms Sue Freeman
Mrs Frances Frith
Mrs Wendy Froud
Mrs Julie Fuller
Miss Julia Furley
Mr Chris Galloway
Mr Kevin Galton
Mrs Christine Gardener
Mr Matthew Gardiner
Mr Geoff Gardiner
Miss Chantal Gardiner
Mr Matthew Gardiner
Mrs Christine Gardner
Ms Bridget Garner
Mr Mark Garnett
Mr Michael Garrison
Mrs Stephanie Garswood
Mrs Margaret Gash
Mrs Mary Gateley
Mr Gavin
Mrs Brenda Gayton
Mrs Julie Gearon
Mr Jeff Gee
Mr David Gee
Mr Tony Georgakis
Miss Lana George
Mrs Pamela Georgiades
Mrs Jane Geraghty
Mr Stevens Gerald
Mr Richard Gibson
Mr David Gibson
Mr John Gibson
Mr Richard Gigg
Mr Anthony Gilbert
Mrs Amanda Gilbert
Mrs Mary Ann Gilchrist
Mrs Julie Giles
Mr Michael Gilks
Mrs Gillian Gillam
Mr Paul Gillett
Mr James Gippesie
Mr Andrew Gittins
Ms Laura Gladwin
Mr Hugh Glaser
Mr John Glaze
Mr Don Glen
Mr Claire Glendenning
Mr Neil Glew
Mr Peter Gliddon
Mr Stephen Glover
Mr Christopher Godber
Mrs Maxine Godfrey
Mrs Debra Godrich
Ms Carol Godsmark
Mr J Gold
Mr Basil Golding
Mrs Pauline Goldsmith
Mr Des Goldsworthy
Mrs Chris Goldthorp
Mr Daniel Gonnm
Miss Victoria Gondzic
Mr David Goodchild
Mrs Lesley Goodchild
Mr Christopher Gooding
Mr Kenneth Goodwin
Mrs Elizabeth Gordon
Ms Anna Gordon
Mr Terry Gorman
Mr Ian Gorsuch
Mr Graham Gough
Mr David Gough
Mrs Jean Gould
Mrs Elizabeth Gould
Mr A Gower
Miss Caroline Graham
Mrs Amy Graham
Ms Doreen Grainger
Mr David Grant
Mrs Lisa Gratte
Mrs Doris Gravestock
Mr Lynton Gray
Mrs Christine Gray
Mr Iain Gray

Mr Alan Grayson
Mr James Greaves
Mrs Mavis Green
Mr Michael Green
Mrs Katherine Green
Ms Allison Greenberg
Mrs Linda Greenberg
Mr Neville Greener
Mr Chris Greenhalgh
Mr Mark Greenhalgh
Mr Duncan Greenwood
Mr Conal Gregory
Mrs Anneline Gregory
Miss Merlyn Gregory
Mr Dave Gregory
Mr Andrew Gresser
Mr George Grierson
Ms Fiona Griffiths
Mrs Linda Griffiths
Mr Peter Griffiths
Mr Graham Griffiths
Mr Clive Griffiths
Mr Ken Grimson
Mrs Gilly Groom
Mr Tom Grosvenor
Mr Howard Gudgeon
Mrs Rose Guild
Mr F Guinn
Mr Anthony Guylee
Mrs Clare Hagerup
Mr Erich Hahn
Mrs Julia Haines
Ms Yvette Hales
Mr Paul Halford
Mr Peter Hall
Mrs N J Hall
Mrs Brenda Hall
Mr Tony Hall
Mrs Mair Hall
Mr David Hall
Mrs M Hall
Mr Mark Hallam
Mr Sean Hamilton
Miss Jayne Hamilton
Mr Neil Hamilton
Mr Mike Hampson
Mrs June Hampson
Mr David Hancock
Mr Graham Handy
Mr Susan Hanley
Mr Jon Harber
Mr Mark Harding
Mr Richard Hardman
Hon Bernard Hargrove
Mrs Alison Harker
Mr Paul Harris
Mrs Iona Harris
Mr Neil Harris
Mr Mervyn Harris
Mr Paul Harrison
Mrs Diane Harrison
Mr Jonathan Harrison
Mr Daniel Harrison
Ms Lin Harrison
Ms Lindsay Harriss
Mr Phil Harriss
Mr Raymond Harm
Mr David Harrop
Mr Timothy Hart
Mr Tony Hartnell
Mr Ross Harvey
Mrs Adele Harvey
Mr Edward Harvey
Mr Alun Harvey
Ms Louise Harvey
Mrs Sharon Harwood
Mr John Hassall
Mr Joy Hatwood
Mrs Margaret Haughey
Mrs Kathy Havercroft
Mr David Haverty
Mr Richard Haycock
Mr Andy Hayler
Mr Ronald Hayman
Mrs Sam Hazell
Mrs Sandra Healey
Ms Debbie Hearn
Mrs Patricia Hedges
Mr Terence Hefford
Miss Natalie Heidaripour
Mr Hossein Heideripoor
Mrs Valerie Hemingway
Mr Philip Hendrick

Mrs Linda Hepworth
Mr John A Hepworth
Mrs Lynn Hewitt
Ms Kirsten Hey
Mrs Amanda Heydon
Mrs Helen Heyworth
Mr Tim Hickson
Mr Keith Hickson
Mrs Jane Higginbotham
Miss Nicola Higgins
Mr Graham Hill
Mr Patricia Hill
Mrs Nicola Hill
Ms Wendy Hillary
Mrs Jessica Hilton
Mr Angus Hinchliffe
Mr Roy Hincks
Miss Rebecca Hine
Mrs Ann Hirst-Smith
Mr Andrew Hoaen
Mr Dave Hoare
Miss Nicola Hobley
Mr Jean Hockings
Mr Michael Hockney
Ms Caroline Hoddinott
Mr Tim Hodges
Miss Philippa Hodgkins
Mr Dermot Hogan
Ms Angela Hoh
Mr D Holdsworth
Mr David Holes
Mr Clive Holland
Mr Peter Hollingsworth
Mr Steven Holmes
Mr Stephen Holt
Mrs Janet Holtby
Miss Beckie Holtham
Ms Leila Homans
Mr Keith Homewood
Mr Steve Hone
Mr Mark Hone
Mr Bernard Hood
Mr Scott Hood
Miss Julie Hooper
Mr Derek Hopes
Mr Stephen Hopkins
Miss Jenni Hopper
Mrs Carol Horn
Mr Colin Hornby
Mr Andrew Horsler
Mr Phil Horsley
Mr Roger Horton
Mr Robin Hosking
Miss Rachel Hotchkiss
Mr Mark Houghton
Mr Dave Houldsworth
Mrs Padi Howard
Mr John Howard
Mrs Julie Howard
Miss Jessica Howard
Mrs Donna Howarth
Mrs Sally Howe
Mr Adrian Howe
Ms Clare Hubbard
Mrs Rosamund Hubley
Mr David Hudson
Ms Natasha Hughes
Mr David Hughes
Mr Steve Hughes
Mr Robert Hughes
Mr Derek Hughes
Mr Jon Hughes
Mrs Julie Hulatt
Mrs Penny Hull
Mr Allan Hull
Ms Elizabeth Hulme
Mr Matt Hulse
Ms Carolyn Humphries
Mr Neil Hunter
Mr Christopher Hunter
Mr Stewart Hunter
Mr Ian Hurdley
Mrs Emma Hurst
Miss Natalie Hurst
Mrs Pauline Hurst
Mr Syed Huss
Mrs Mandy Hutchings
Mr Trevor Hutchinson
Mrs Claire Hutchinson
Mr Michael Hutchinson
Mr Stuart Huxtable
Mr David Hyde

Mr Jerry Ibberson
Mr Keith Ingram
Mrs Jessica Innocenti-Lampen
Mr Gordon Irvine
Mr Andrew Irwin
Mr Stuart Isaacs
Mr Yaasiin Islam
Mrs Iuhiu Iuh
Mr Leslie Ilversen
Mrs Madeleine Jackson
Ms Kate Jackson
Mr Ben Jackson
Mr Stephen Jackson
Mrs Susan Jackson
Mrs Sheila Jackson
Mr Paul Jacques
Mr Robert Jahnke
Miss Nicky James
Mr J James
Mr Stephen James
Ms Anita James
Miss Kathy James
Mrs Rosemary James
Mr John James
Mr Robert Jamieson
Mrs Sandra Janes
Mr Jonathan Jarratt
Mrs Adina Jarvis
Mrs Janet Jarvis
Mr Anthony Jay
Mrs Brenda Jeeves
Mr Martin Jeeves
Mr Syed Yasir Jehan
Miss Louise Jenkins
Mr Philip Jenkins
Mrs Diane Jennett
Mr Michael Jennings
Mr Steve Jepson
Mrs Heather Jervis
Mr David R W Jervois
Mr Simon Jewson
Mr Alec Jezewski
Ms Rachel Johnson
Mrs Karen Johnson
Miss Nicci Johnson
Mr Derek Johnson
Miss Ruth Johnson
Mr William Johnston
Mr Edward Johnston
Ms Doreen Johnston
Mr Iain Johnstone
Ms Brenda Jolley
Ms Pamela Jones
Mr Robert Jones
Mrs C Jones
Miss Caroline Jones
Miss Deborah Jones
Miss Sheila Jones
Mrs Penny Jones
Mrs Alison Jones
Miss Vivian Jones
Miss Anne Marie Jones
Ms Shirley Jones
Mr Andrew Jones
Mrs Jade Jones
Miss Sara Jones
Mrs Mary Jones
Mr Douglas Jones
Mr John Martin Jones
Mr Ian Jones
Miss Sarah Jowett
Mr Neil Joyce
Mr Rick Juckes
Miss Louise Judd
Mr Martin Jurasik
Mr Kevin Kane
Mrs Yasmin Karim
Ms Kawal Kaur
Mr John Kaye
Mr Kim Kaye
Mr Richard Kaye
Mrs Sandra Keane
Mrs Jac Keane
Mr Julian Keanie
Mr Barry Keates
Mr Robert Kelly
Mr Joseph Kelly
Mr Russell Kemp
Mr Robert Kendall
Mr Roger Kendall
Ms Vanessa Kendell
Mr Graham Kennedy
Mr Arthur Kennedy

Mr David Kenning
Ms Christine Kenny
Ms Sinead Kenny
Mrs June Kent
Mr John Kenward
Mr David Kenward
Ms Emily Kerrigan
Mr & Mrs Keys
Mr Sunil Khosla
Mr Vimal Khosla
Mr Roger Kidley
Mr Terence Kidson
Mr Sascha Kiess
Miss Bernadette Kilroy
Ms Sharon King
Mr Alex King
Mr Chris King
Mrs Mary Kingston-Ford
Mr Berwyn Kinsey
Mr Remmy Kinyanjui
Mr Terry Kirby
Mr Mark Kirkbride
Mr Steve Kirkwood
Mrs Suzanne Kirkwood
Mr Michael Kitcatt
Mrs Riki Kittel
Miss Sylvia Knapp
Miss Charlotte Knapp
Miss Jane Knight
Mr Keith Knights
Mrs Rosie Knowles
Mr Marios Koulias
Mr Jack Kouwenberg
Mrs Christine Kynoch
Mr Chris Lakin
Mrs Marian Laklia
Miss Vicky Lane
Mrs Sarah Lane
Mr Anthony Langan
Mr Richard Langley
Ms Christine Last
Miss Anna Lavel
Mrs Jane Law
Mr Ashley Lawrence
Ms Ayesha Lawrence
Mr Andrew Lawrence
Mr Brian Lawrence
Mrs Charmaine Lawrence
Mrs Ginny Lawson
Miss Rebecca Leach
Mr Kim Leary
Mr Chris Leather
Ms Beverley Le Blanc
Ms Deborah Lee
Mr Alex Lee
Mr Carl Lee
Mr Adam Lee
Ms Jo Leedham
Mr Marc Lees-low
Mrs Linda Lefevre
Mr Victor Legg
Mr John Legg
Ms Nikki Lehel
Mr Steve Leighton
Ms Sharon Lennon
Mrs Susan Leonard
Miss Susan Leslie
Mrs Kate Leslie
Mr David Lesser
Professor K M Letherman
Mrs R Letherman
Mr Malcolm Levitt
Mrs Lisa Lewis
Ms Janet Lewis
Mr Rich Lewis Jones
Mr Mike Leybourne
Mr Mark Leyland
Mrs Jenny Li
Mrs Brunhilde Liebchen
Mr Hans Liesner
Mrs Louise Lightfoot
Miss Linda Ligios
Mr Andrew Lindsay
Mrs Caroline Ling
Mr David Linnell
Mr Robert Lintonbon
Miss Alex Little
Mr William Lobo
Mrs Alex Lody
Ms Tina Lofthouse
Mr David Long
Mr Jonathan Longden
Mr Glynis Lord

Ms Jane Lorimer
Mrs Elspeth Lowe
Mrs Annabel Lowell
Mrs Avril Luke
Mr Kevin Lynch
Mr Chris Lyon
Mrs Audrey Lyon
Mrs Frances Lyons
Mr David Mabey
Mrs Fiona MacAulay-Rigby
Mr Colin Macaw
Miss Carleen Macdermid
Mr David MacDonald
Mrs Sonia Maceluch
Mr Bruce MacFarlane
Ms Catherine Mackay
Mr Jamie Mackay
Mrs E Mackintosh
Mr Hugh Mackintosh
Ms Lesley Mackley
Mrs Marcia Macleod
Mrs C Macrow
Mrs Ruth Madigan
Mr Eric Magnuson
Miss Sarah Mahoney
Miss Karine Maillard
Mr James Malcomson
Mrs Lynn Males
Mr Kaleem Malik
Ms Nicola Mallett
Mr Ian Malone
Mr Denis Maloney
Ms Wendy Maloney
Ms Beverley Mandair
Mr Paul Manley
Miss Rebecca Manning
Ms Emily Manson
Mrs Louise Markus
Mrs Louise Markus
Mr Bill Markwick
Mr Felipe Marquez
Mrs Christine Marris
Mr Chris Marsh
Mrs Linda Marshall
Mr Robert Marshall
Mr Paul Martin
Mr Gordon Martin
Mr Ian Martin
Mrs Maureen Martin
Ms Mary Martin
Ms Angela Martin
Mrs Sheila Martin
Mr Graham Martin
Mr Brian Ma Siy
Mrs Tracey Maskill
Mrs Sally Maslen
Mr Ken Mason
Mrs Jean Mason
Mrs Ilze Mason
Mr David Mason
Mr Nick Mason
Mr Don Massey
Mr Mark Massey
Mrs Diphna Mathew
Mr Stuart Mathews
Mr John Mathews
Mr David Mathewson
Mr Richard Matthews
Mr Simon Matthews
Ms Gill Maxwell
Mr Ian May
Mrs Joyce Mayhew
Miss Sharon Mayling
Miss Stephanie McAllister
Mr Peter McAndrew
Miss Helen McBay
Mr Derek McBride
Ms Andrea McCartney
Mr Neil McCole
Mr Ben McCormack
Mr Walter McCrindle
Mr Kenneth McDonald
Ms Cynthia McDowall
Mrs Anne McGilton
Mr Robert McGinty
Mrs Caroline McGoohan
Mrs Pamela McGowan
Mrs Cynthia McGowan
Miss Gemma McGowan
Ms S Y McGreavy
Mrs Susan McGrouther
Mr Patrick McGuigan
Mrs Christine McHenry

Miss Marie McHenry
Miss Sian McHenry
Mr Bill McHenry
Ms Fiona McInnes
Mr Robert McKay
Mrs Gayle McKay
Mr Craig McKay
Mrs Debra McKenna
Mr Charles McKenna
Mr Andy McKenzie
Mr William McKinlay
Mr Stuart McLaren
Mrs Karen McLaren
Mr John McLaughlin
Mr John McMillan
Miss Wendy McMillan
Miss Angela McNally
Mr Michael McNamara
Mrs Jo McNeish
Mr Richard McNulty
Mr Paul McPeake
Mr Pete McQueen
Mr Francis McSorley
Mr Deryk Mead
Mr Ranvir Mehta
Mr John Mercer
Mrs Doreen Mercer
Mr Lee Merrin
Mr Peter Messenger
Mrs Janet Messenger
Mr David Metcalf
Mr John Metcalfe
Mr Shane Metters
Mr Shahid Mian
Ms Jane Middleton
Mr John Middleton
Mr A G Milburn
Mr Douglas Miles
Mr Peter Miles
Mr Jonathan Miles
Mr James Millar
Mr Ged Millar
Miss Cara Neish Millar
Mrs Tina Millard
Miss Dahna Miller
Mr Ian Miller
Mr Luke Miller
Miss Mandy Miller
Mr Michael Miller
Mr Nic Miller
Mrs Helen Miller
Mr Roger Mills
Mr Richard Mills
Mrs C D Milne
Mr Nicoll Milne
Mrs Caroline Mitchell
Mr Mike Mitchell
Mrs Anne Mitchell
Mrs Carol Mitchell
Miss Lee Mitchell
Mr John Mitchellmore
Mr Stuart Mitchenall
Miss Tessa Mitchinson
Mr Sarang Mohinder
Ms Elizabeth Moles
Mrs Linda Montgomery
Mrs Alison Mooney
Mr David Moore
Mr Jon Moore
Mr Chris Moore
Mrs Jane Moore
Mr Francis Moran
Mr Corrado Morandi
Mr Jeremy Mordrick
Mrs Helen Morgan
Mr Brian Morgan
Mr Neil Morgan
Mr Manisha Morjaria
Ms Jacqueline Morley
Mr Peter Morris
Mr Bernard Morris
Mrs Sara Morris
Ms Shelley Morris
Miss Rachel Morrish
Mrs Eileen Morrison
Mrs Deborah Morrissey
Ms Valerie Morrow
Mrs Emma Moscrop
Mr Robert Moss
Mr John Mott
Mr John Moy
Mr Alastair Muir
Mrs Maureen Mullins

Mr Peter Munro
Mr Charles Murch
Mr David Murdoch
Mrs Eileen Murfitt
Mr Mike Murphy
Mr Paul Murphy
Ms Kimberley Murphy
Mrs Janis Murphy
Mr Gordon Murray
Mr Paul Murray
Mrs Morag Murray
Mrs Sue Muspratt
Mr Colin Mutch
Mrs Jill Naylor
Mrs Ragnhild Nee
Mr John Neilson
Mrs Sara Nelson
Mrs Carolyn Neri
Mr James Netting
Mr Mathew Newman
Mrs Norma Newman
Mrs Astrid Newman
Mr Peter Newton
Mr Jeffrey Ng
Mr Timothy Niall-harris
Mr Rodney Nichols
Mrs Anne Nicholson
Mr Nicolas Nicolaides
Ms Paula Nimmo
Mr David Noble
Mr Daniel Nolan
Mr Michael Nolan
Miss Vicki Norgan
Miss Yvonne Norman
Mrs Susan Norminton
Mr J G Norris
Mrs Alison Nottle
Mr Richard Noy
Mrs Marion OBrien
Mr Alan O'Brien
Ms Jane O'Brien
Mr Keith O'Brien
Mr Alan Oddie
Ms Caroline Ogden
Mr Timothy O'Keefe
Mr David Oldham
Ms Barbara Oldham
Mr Gayle Olsen
Mr Kevin O'Mahoney
Mrs Bree O'Neil
Ms Sian O'Neill
Mrs Lyndsey O'Neill
Mr John O'Reilly
Mr Geoffrey Ormrod
Mr Toby Orsborn
Mr Richard Osborne
Mr Martin Osborne
Mrs Lisa Osman
Mr John Oswald
Mrs Donna O'Toole
Ms Cathy Otty
Mrs Emma Oulton
Mr Graham Owen
Mr S Oxley
Mr Michael Page
Miss Rachel Page
Mrs Shelly Page
Mrs Susan Paice
Mrs Tracey Paine
Mr Vythianathan Palaniandy
Mr Richard Palframan
Mrs Clare Panton
Mr John Papadachi
Mrs Laura Park
Mr Mark Parkes
Mrs Anne Parkinson
Ms Chetna Parmar
Mr Sarah Parnaby
Mr Amol Parnaik
Mr Mike Parry
Mrs Diane Parslow
Mr Fraser Parsons
Mr Neil Partridge
Mrs Pat
Mr Michael Pater
Mr John Pattenden
Ms Caroline Pattison
Mr Michael Pawson
Mrs Janet Payne
Miss Mhairi Payne
Mr Chris Payne
Mr Nigel Peacock

Mr Brian Pearce
Mr Chris Pearson
Mr Edwin Peat
Mr Simon Peate
Mr Richard Peirce
Miss Anna Perez
Mr Anthony Perl
Miss Carlene Perris
Mr Tim Perry
Mr Brian Perryman
Ms Helen Peston
Mr Philip
Mrs Liz Phillips
Mrs Gaynor Phillips
Mr Chris Phillips
Miss Lynn Phillpots
Ms Amanda Philpott
Mrs Jennie Pickford
Mr Russell Pickup
Ms Veronica Piekosz
Mr Stuart Pierrepont
Sudi Pigott
Ms Catherine Pike
Mrs Noreen Pile
Mr David Pinchin
Miss Tia Pinnock-Hamilton
Mr John Pitt-Stanley
Mr James Pomeroy
Mrs Janine Ponsart
Mrs Lynda Pope
Ms Louise Porch
Ms Fiona Porter
Miss Lucy Powell
Mr David Powell
Mr Trevor Preston
Mr Simon Preston
Ms Victoria Prever
Ms Sandie Price
Mr David Price
Mrs Janet Price
Ms G Pritchard
Mrs Diane Proctor
Mr Ioannis Psomadakis
Mr Gavin Pugh
Mr Mike Pugh
Miss Miriam Pullar
Mrs Melanie Pullin
Miss Louise Purdie
Mr Terry Purkins
Mr Walter Purkis
Mr David Pybus
Mr Frederick Pyne
Mrs Siobhan Qadir
Miss Michelle Quance
Mr Doug Quelch
Mr John Quelch
Ms Rachel Quine
Mr John Radford
Mr Michael Raine
Miss Korina Ralph
Mrs Jane Ralston
Mr Iain Ramsay
Mr John Ramsay
Mrs Bridget Ramsay
Mr Euan Ramsay
Mr Jeremy Randalls
Mr Archibald Rankin
Miss Elizabeth Rattlidge
Mr John Rawlings
Mrs Jane Rawlinson-Cook
Miss Lorna Raynes
Mr Andrew Redfern
Mrs Victoria Redshaw
Mr John Reed
Mrs Anne Rees
Mrs Mary Reeve
Mrs Penny Reeves
Mr Martyn Reid
Mr Maurice Reid
Miss Jacqueline Reid
Mr Neil Renton
Mrs Caroline Repanos
Miss Lisa Reyburn
Mr A Reynolds
Ms Patricia Rhymer
Mr Peter Ribbins
Miss Kloe Rice
Mr Keith Richards
Mr Brian Richards
Miss Amy Richards
Mr David Richardson
Mr Alan Richardson
Mr Kenneth Richardson

Mr C John Richardson
Ms Sharon Richmond
Mr Mark Riddick
Mrs John Riddick
Mrs Ruth Ridge
Mr L C Ridgwell
Mrs Christine Ridley
Mr Trevor Rigby
Mrs Fiona Rigby
Mrs Anna Jo Righton
Mr Gordon Ringrose
Mr Geoff Roberts
Mr Gerald Roberts
Mr Mark Roberts
Ms Hannah Roberts
Mr Andrew Roberts
Mr Michael Roberts
Mr Keith Roberts
Ms Rebecca Robertshaw
Miss Rebecca Robertson
Ms Lynsey Robinson
Mr David Robinson
Mrs Ann Robinson
Mr Paul Robinson
Miss Cheryl Robinson
Mr Michael Robinson
Mr Alan Robinson
Mr John Robinson
Miss Jocelyn Robinson
Mr Samuel Robinson
Ms Carol Robson
Mr J Rochelle
Mrs Joanne Rockliff
Mr Will Rogers
Mr Peter Rogers
Mr Alan Roiter
Mr Andrew Root
Mrs Christine Roper
Miss Kelly Rose
Mr Phil Rose
Mrs Johann Rosser
Mrs Kay Rothwell
Mr Douglas Rounthwaite
Ms Jane Routh
Mr Christopher Row
Mr John Rowan
Mr Tony Rowed
Mr John Rowlands
Mr Richard Rowlands
Miss Mariel Roy
Miss Rebecca Royle
Mr Andy Rudd
Ms Lisa Rudrum
Mr Graham Ruff
Miss Jessica Ruiz
Mr Keith Rundle
Mrs Diana Runge
Mr Joseph Russell
Mr Hugo Russell
Mrs Bernadette Russell
Mr Peter Russell
Mr Fabrizio Russo
Mr Patrick Rutter
Mr Derek Ryder
Mr Ian Sabroe
Mr David Sainsbury
Mr Geoffrey Samuel
Ms Jayne Samuel-Walker
Mr Graham Sanderson
Mrs Ailis Sandilands
Miss Christine Sangster
Mr Gavino Sanna Smith
Miss Therese Sargent
Mr James Saunders
Ms Deborah Saw
Mr Derek K Sawyer
Mr Ian Scanlon
Mr Roger Scarlett
Mr Geoffrey Scarlett
Mrs Ruth Scarr
Mr Ronald Schwarz
Mrs Diane Scott
Mr William Searle
Mr Ken Seaton
Mr Graham Seddon
Mrs Jane Margaret Seddon
Mr Adam Sedgwick
Mr Gary Sedgwick
Ms Reshma Seeburrun
Ms Karan Sehgal
Mr Shajan Sehgal
Mr Dave Selby
Mrs Sylvie Sempala

Mr Ashim Sen
Mr Anthony Serre
Mrs Katharine Servant
Mr Andrew Shanahan
Mr John Sharp
Mrs Gill Sharpe
Mr George Shaw
Mrs Karen Shaw
Mrs Patricia Shaw
Mr Robert Shaw
Mr Matthew Shaw
Mr Peter Shearer
Mr Brian Shears
Mrs Jill Sheen
Mr Jerry Shelley
Ms Linda Shelmerdine
Mr Alan Shepherd
Mr Chris Shepherd
Mrs M L Sheppard-Bond
Miss Claire Sheridan
Mrs Emma Sherman
Mrs Sandra Sherriff
Mr Mark Sherrington
Miss Jennifer Shilliday
Miss Kirsty Shilling
Mr Trevor Shingles
Miss Becky Shipp
Mr Gilbert Short
Mr James Shotton
Mr Manoj Shrestha
Mr Peter Shrigley
Mr Chris Shrubsall
Mr Philip Sibley
Mr Peter Siddall
Mr Brian Siddall-Jones
Miss M Sidhu
Ms Mary ann Sieghart
Mrs Karen Sienkiewicz
Mr Rod Sigley
Ms Ros Simmons
Mrs Niamh Simms
Mr Matt Simpson
Mrs Thelma Simpson
Miss Katherine Simpson
Ms Sue Simpson
Mr Thomas Simpson
Mr Andrew Simpson
Mr Kenny Simpson
Mrs Barbara Sims
Mr Alan Sims
Mr Nav Singh
Mr Martin Sinnott
Miss Nicola Skeffington
Mr Greg Skinner
Mr Penny Slate
Mrs Hilda Slater
Mrs Andrea Slater
Mr David Sleight
Mrs Liz Sleith
Mr Johan Slotte
Ms Jo Small
Ms Judith Smallwood
Mr Adrian Smart
Ms Michelle Smith
Mrs Carolyn Smith
Mr Robert Smith
Mr David Smith
Mr Derek Smith
Mrs Fiona Smith
Mrs Jill Smith
Mr Jeff Smith
Mrs Joan Smith
Mr Ian Smith
Mrs Moyra Smith
Miss Anne Smith
Mr Andy Smith
Ms Julia Smith
Mr Tim Smith
Mr Juliet Smith
Mr Ivan Smith
Mr Antony Smithson
Mr Brian Smullen
Mr Alan Smythe
Ms Anita Soley
Mr Tim Soon
Mr Andy Soper
Mr Anne Soto
Mr Ben Southam
Mr Eric Southworth
Mrs Jacqueline Southworth
Mr Pat Spadi
Mrs Norma Speller
Mr Torin Spence

Mr Colin Spencer
Mr Harry Stadler
Mr Nick Staff
Ms Pauline Stafford
Mr John Stafford
Miss Jessica Stamford
Mr R J Stancomb
Ms Alex Standen
Mrs Mandi Stansfield
Mr Richard Stansfield
Miss Elizabeth Stanyer
Mr Jonathan Stapleton
Mr Neil Stein
Mrs Barbara Steiner
Miss Marcia Stephens
Mrs Kath Stepien
Mr Keith Stevens
Mrs Chrissy Stevens
Mr Paul Stevens
Mr John Stevenson
Mrs Lindsey Stewart
Mr Alan Stewart
Mr Ian Stewart
Mr Malcolm Stewart
Ms Ann Stewart
Mr Ian Stewart
Mr John Stewart
Mr Allan Stidwell
Mr D Stirk
Mrs Laura Stocker
Mrs Minou Stoddart
Mr Martin H Stone
Mrs Christine Stone
Mr Rodney Stone
Mrs Valerie Storm
Mrs Trudie Stott
Mr Robert Strain
Mr Matthew Streeter
Mr Jonathan Strong
Mr Gerd Strophff
Mr Mark Stuart
Mr Clive Stubbs
Mrs Rosemary Sturman
Mr Andrew Stylianou
Mr Sejal Sukhadwala
Mrs Diane Sumner
Mrs Lisa Sumpton
Miss Rachel Surcombe
Mr Ken Sutton
Mr John Sutton
Mr Christopher Syer
Mr Robert Sykes
Mr Steven Symonds
Mrs Rebecca Syson
Mrs Julie Taberner
Mr Douglas Talintyre
Mr Jim Tanfield
Mrs Kate Tanfield
Mr Anne Tate
Mr D W Tate
Mr Denis Tate
Mr Mark Taylor
Mrs Jean Taylor
Mr Andy Taylor
Mr John Taylor
Mr Matt Taylor
Mrs Glennis Taylor
Mrs Chrissie Taylor
Mrs Elizabeth Taylor
Mr Jack Taylor
Ms Lesley Taylor
Miss Lisa Taylor
Miss Hannah Taylor
Mr Simon Taylor
Mr Royston Tee
Mrs Karen Terkelsen
Mrs Tina Tester
Mr Richard Thomas
Mrs Maria Thomas
Mrs Sarah Thomas
Miss Karen Thomas
Miss Kim Thomas
Mr Kevin Thomas
Miss Janet Thomas
Ms Anita Thomas
Miss Sharon Thomas
Mrs Anne Thompson
Mr Paul Thompson
Mr Christopher Thompson
Mr Alun Thompson
Mrs Tina Thompson
Ms Claire Thomson
Mr Alistair Thomson

Mr Gordon Thomson
Miss Joanne Thomson
Mrs Kate Thorley
Mrs Barbara Thornton
Mr Alan Thorpe
Mr Graeme Tickle
Mr Philip Tindal-Carill-Worsley
Mr John Titley
Mrs Susan Tomlin
Mr Roger Tomlinson
Mr Richard Tomlinson
Mr David Tonge
Mrs Jayne Towgli
Miss Katie Townsend
Mr Martin Townsend
Mrs Hylary Trayer
Ms Karen Trekelsen
Mr Matt Trott
Mr Christopher Trotter
Mrs Sally Trusselle
Mr Christopher Tuck
Mrs Susan Turley
Ms Jacquie Turner
Mrs Sandra Turner
Mrs Susan Turner
Mr Pamela Turner
Mr Dominic turner
Mr John G. Turner
Mr Gordon Turner-Tymm
Ms Jill Turton
Mrs Lesley Tweddle
Mr Naseen Ul-Alam
Miss Ashley Underwood
Mr Peter Urquhart
Mr John Urry
Mr Paul Valentine
Ms Barbara van Amerongen
Miss Caroline van Kampen
Mr Phil Varney
Mr Anthony Vaughan
Mr Stephen Vernon
Mr Hernan Vilar
Mrs Alta Viljoen
Mr Tom Vincent
Mr Martin Vowell
Mr Jeremy Wagg
Mr Benno Wagtenveld
Mr Christopher Waite
Mr Daniels Walker
Mrs Sara Walker
Mr Matthew Walker
Miss Joan Walker
Mr Kenneth Wall
Miss Fiona Lauren Wallace
Mrs Kerrie Wallis
Ms Cathy Walsh
Ms Lorraine Walsh
Mr Mark Waltham
Mr Stuart Walton
Mrs Susanne Wang
Mr Peter Wang
Mr William Warburton
Miss Sara Ward
Mr David Ward
Mr Philip Ward
Mrs Jayme Wardell-Appleton
Mr Andrew Wardrop
Mr Stuart J.H. Waring
Mr Sanjaya Warnatilake
Mr Glynn Warner
Mr Maurice Warwick
Miss Emma Wasden
Mr Waters
Mr William Watson
Mrs Maria Watson
Mr William Watt
Mr John Watts
Mr Robert Weatherburn
Ms Jan Webb
Mrs Penny Webber
Mr Neil Webber
Mrs Deborah Webster
Mrs Caroline Welch
Mr Roger Weldhen
Mr Robertson Wellen
Ms Margaret West
Mr J F M West
Ms Helen West
Mr J West
Mr Graham Westgarth
Mrs Jill Weston

Mrs Carole Weston
Miss Tania Whale
Mr Peter Wheeler
Mrs Jacqueline Wheeler
Ms Hannah Whibley
Ms Jenny White
Mr Bob White
Mrs Sally White
Mr Peter White
Mr Pam White
Mr Andrew White
Miss Romney Whitehead
Mr Peter Whitehead
Mrs Ellen Whitehouse
Mrs Di Whiteley
Ms Marion Whitfield
Mrs C C Whitlock
Mr Paul Whittaker
Miss Teresa Whittaker
Mr Stephen Whittle
Ms Becky Wicks
Mr Andy Widdowson
Mrs Gemma Wiggins
Mr John Wilkinson
Mrs Sandra Wilkinson
Mr Glyn Williams
Mr Steven Williams
Mr Desmond Williams
Mr Huw Williams
Mr Harold E. Williams
Mr Robert Williams
Miss Amy Williams
Miss Michelle Williams
Mrs Julie Williams
Mr Chris Williams
Mrs Kirsten Williams
Mrs Catherine Williamson
Mr Brian Williamson
Mr Phil Wills
Ms Sue Wilshere
Mrs Trish Wilson
Mr David Wilson
Mrs Carole Wilson
Mr Rob Wilson
Miss Fiona Wilson
Mrs Doreen Wilson
Mr Ralph Wilson
Mr Colin Wimble
Mr Ross Wincott
Mr John Window
Mr Terry Windsor
Ms Michelle Winslow
Mr Colin Winspear
Mrs Carol Winter
Mrs Barbara Withers
Ms Lucie Wood
Mr Christopher Wood
Mr Michael Wood
Mr Chris Woodland
Miss Cheryl Woods
Mr Graham Woodward
Mr N Woodward
Miss Penny Woolford
Mrs Janet Woolliscroft
Mrs Janet Wormald
Mr John Worth
Ms Mandy Wragg
Mrs Meg Wraight
Mr Ros Wright
Mr William Wright
Mr Fay Wright
Miss Jayne Wright
Mr Richard Wright
Mrs Martina Wyatt
Mr R A Wyld
Mr Alex Wynter
Mrs Alison Yates
Mr John Yelland
Miss Joyce Yeung
Ms Flora York Skinner
Ms Juliette Young
Mrs Micheala Young
Mr Steven Young
Mr Morris Zwi
Mr Daniel Zylbersztajn

Special thank yous

We'd like to extend special thanks to the following people:

Luke Block, Elizabeth Bowden, Martin Chapman, Claudia Dyer,
Michael Edwards, Sarah Fergusson, Nicola Frame, Alan Grimwade,
Ros Mari Grindheim, Alex Hall and Ben Kay at Charterhouse,
Andy Hayler, Alan Jessop at Compass, Simone Johnson,
Deborah Jones, Rebecca Leach, Michelle Lyttle, David Mabey,
Simon Mather at AMA, Alison Morrison, Angela Newton,
Jeffrey Ng, John Pinkney, Louise Shepherd, Kelly Smith,
Oliver Smith, Emily Taylor, Judi Turner, The Vegetarian Society,
Stuart Walton, Chris White, Blanche Williams and Emma Wilmot.

Picture credits

Mateusz Atroszko, Linda B, Anna Byckling, Sue Campbell,
Romina Chamorro, Michel Collot, Guy Drayton, Erik Dungan, Damir
Fabijanic, Rachel Gilmore, Neil Gould, Steve Gould, Tanja Grbic,
Lucy Hayward, Herry Lawford, Pawel Libera Fabrizio Lonzini,Victor
Machado, Anthony Mahieu, Jacob Metzelder, Paul Raeside, Ingrid
Rasmussen, Karen Rennie, Mr Sasvari, Stephanie Schleicher, Manjari
Sharma, Karen Sparrow, Chris Steer, Marcin Szczepanski, Michal
Szydlowski, Candase Trawford, Manuel Trejo, John Trenholm, Steve
Woods, visitlondonimages/britainonview, Kristy Zerna

Map credits

Maps designed and produced by Cosmographics,
www.cosmographics.co.uk. UK digital database © Cosmographics
2007, Greater London map © Cosmographics 2006, North and
South London Maps © Collins Bartholomew 2007, West, Central
and East London maps © BTA (trading as VisitBritain) 2007
produced by Cosmographics and used with the kind
permission of VisitBritain.

Please send updates, queries, menus and wine lists to: goodfoodguide@which.co.uk
or to: The Good Food Guide, 2 Marylebone Road, London, NW1 4DF.

Coming soon...

The Good Food Guide 2009

Full nationwide edition publishing September 2008

THE GOOD
FOOD GUIDE
LONDON

WINE VOUCHER

THE GOOD
FOOD GUIDE
LONDON

WINE VOUCHER

THE GOOD
FOOD GUIDE
LONDON

WINE VOUCHER

THE GOOD
FOOD GUIDE
LONDON

WINE VOUCHER

THE GOOD
FOOD GUIDE
LONDON

WINE VOUCHER

THE GOOD
FOOD GUIDE
LONDON

WINE VOUCHER

THE GOOD
FOOD GUIDE
LONDON

WINE VOUCHER

THE GOOD
FOOD GUIDE
LONDON

WINE VOUCHER

THE GOOD
FOOD GUIDE
LONDON

WINE VOUCHER

THE GOOD
FOOD GUIDE
LONDON

WINE VOUCHER

THE GOOD FOOD GUIDE LONDON
WINE VOUCHERS

TERMS & CONDITIONS

This voucher can only be used in participating restaurants, highlighted by the ♉ symbol. It is redeemable against a pre-booked meal for a minimum of two people, provided the customer highlights the intention to use the voucher at the time of booking. Only one voucher may be used per table booked. This voucher may not be used in conjunction with any other scheme.

Offer valid from 01/03/08 to 28/02/09.

For additional terms and conditions, see below.

TERMS & CONDITIONS

This voucher can only be used in participating restaura highlighted by the ♉ symbol. It is redeemable against a pre-booked meal for a minimum of two people, provid the customer highlights the intention to use the vouch at the time of booking. Only one voucher may be use per table booked. This voucher may not be used in conjunction with any other scheme.

Offer valid from 01/03/08 to 28/02/09.

For additional terms and conditions, see below.

TERMS & CONDITIONS

This voucher can only be used in participating restaurants, highlighted by the ♉ symbol. It is redeemable against a pre-booked meal for a minimum of two people, provided the customer highlights the intention to use the voucher at the time of booking. Only one voucher may be used per table booked. This voucher may not be used in conjunction with any other scheme.

Offer valid from 01/03/08 to 28/02/09.

For additional terms and conditions, see below.

TERMS & CONDITIONS

This voucher can only be used in participating restaur highlighted by the ♉ symbol. It is redeemable against a pre-booked meal for a minimum of two people, provi the customer highlights the intention to use the vouc at the time of booking. Only one voucher may be use per table booked. This voucher may not be used in conjunction with any other scheme.

Offer valid from 01/03/08 to 28/02/09.

For additional terms and conditions, see below.

TERMS & CONDITIONS

This voucher can only be used in participating restaurants, highlighted by the ♉ symbol. It is redeemable against a pre-booked meal for a minimum of two people, provided the customer highlights the intention to use the voucher at the time of booking. Only one voucher may be used per table booked. This voucher may not be used in conjunction with any other scheme.

Offer valid from 01/03/08 to 28/02/09.

For additional terms and conditions, see below.

TERMS & CONDITIONS

This voucher can only be used in participating restau highlighted by the ♉ symbol. It is redeemable against pre-booked meal for a minimum of two people, prov the customer highlights the intention to use the vouc at the time of booking. Only one voucher may be us per table booked. This voucher may not be used in conjunction with any other scheme.

Offer valid from 01/03/08 to 28/02/09.

For additional terms and conditions, see below.

TERMS & CONDITIONS

This voucher can only be used in participating restaurants, highlighted by the ♉ symbol. It is redeemable against a pre-booked meal for a minimum of two people, provided the customer highlights the intention to use the voucher at the time of booking. Only one voucher may be used per table booked. This voucher may not be used in conjunction with any other scheme.

Offer valid from 01/03/08 to 28/02/09.

For additional terms and conditions, see below.

TERMS & CONDITIONS

This voucher can only be used in participating restau highlighted by the ♉ symbol. It is redeemable against pre-booked meal for a minimum of two people, prov the customer highlights the intention to use the vouc at the time of booking. Only one voucher may be us per table booked. This voucher may not be used in conjunction with any other scheme.

Offer valid from 01/03/08 to 28/02/09.

For additional terms and conditions, see below.

TERMS & CONDITIONS

This voucher can only be used in participating restaurants, highlighted by the ♉ symbol. It is redeemable against a pre-booked meal for a minimum of two people, provided the customer highlights the intention to use the voucher at the time of booking. Only one voucher may be used per table booked. This voucher may not be used in conjunction with any other scheme.

Offer valid from 01/03/08 to 28/02/09.

For additional terms and conditions, see below.

TERMS & CONDITIONS

This voucher can only be used in participating resta highlighted by the ♉ symbol. It is redeemable agains pre-booked meal for a minimum of two people, pro the customer highlights the intention to use the vou at the time of booking. Only one voucher may be u per table booked. This voucher may not be used in conjunction with any other scheme.

Offer valid from 01/03/08 to 28/02/09.

For additional terms and conditions, see below.

Vouchers are valid from 1st March 2008 to 28th February 2009. Only one glass of wine voucher can be used per table booked (for a minimum of 2 people). No photocopies or any other kind of reproduction of vouchers will be accepted. Some participating establishments may exclude certain times, days or menus from the scheme so long as they a) advise customers of the restrictions at time of booking and b) accept the vouchers at a minimum of 70% of sessions when the restaurant is open. Please note that the nu of participating restaurants may vary from time to time.